BY MICHAEL B. OREN

Ally: My Journey Across the American-Israeli Divide

Power, Faith, and Fantasy: America in the Middle East, 1776 to the Present

Six Days of War: June 1967 and the Making of the Modern Middle East

Origins of the Second Arab-Israel War: Egypt, Israel and the Great Powers, 1952–56

Sand Devil: A Negev Trilogy

Reunion: A Novel

ALLY

RANDOM HOUSE

NEW YORK

ALLY

My Journey Across
the American-Israeli Divide

MICHAEL B. OREN

Published in the United States by Random House, an imprint and division
of Penguin Random House LLC, New York.

RANDOM HOUSE and the HOUSE colophon are
registered trademarks of Penguin Random House LLC.

ISBN 978-0-8129-9641-8
eBook ISBN 978-0-8129-9642-5

Grateful acknowledgment is made to *Foreign Policy* for permission to
reprint excerpts from " 'A' Jewish State vs. 'The' Jewish State" by Michael Oren
and David Rothkopf, *Foreign Policy,* May 15, 2014. Reprinted
by permission of *Foreign Policy.*

All photographs, unless otherwise indicated,
are from the author's collection.

Printed in the United States of America on acid-free paper

randomhousebooks.com

4689753

Maps by Stephen Reich
Book design by Carole Lowenstein

To Ariel and Romi,
my first two Israeli grandchildren

CONTENTS

FOREWORD

Crowded into the basement of a low-budget hotel, we stared at the double doors and counted the seconds. Even now, more than four decades later, I can still feel the anticipation. Along with some fifty other fifteen-year-olds in our Zionist youth movement, I bused from New Jersey to Washington, D.C.—my first-ever visit to our nation's capital. I suppose we toured the Capitol, the White House, and the sites along the National Mall. My only memory, though, is of that basement glazed in fluorescence and the moment those doors swung open.

He marched in with curt, single-minded strides, ahead of his security guards, who struggled to keep up. A shorter man than the giant I imagined, he climbed onto the foot-high riser that served as a stage. "On behalf of the State of Israel," he said, "I want to thank you for your commitment and support." Or at least that is what I think he said, for his voice was also surprisingly small, almost bashful, and our cheers drowned him out.

We sang at the top of our teenage voices, "Heveinu Shalom Aleichem"—we welcome you in peace—and clapped until our hands grew numb. I could scarcely believe that I was seeing him. Here, only yards in front of me, stood the hero of the 1967 Six-Day War, the former commander of the Israeli forces who rescued Jewish dignity from the pall of the Holocaust, who enabled us—so American Jews claimed—to stand with our backs straight. And now he addressed us as Israel's ambassador to the United States, the representative of the reborn Jewish State to the world's greatest power.

He spoke only for a few minutes and concluded with a reticent smile. He then stepped off the improvised dais so that the guards could hurry him back through the doors. As he passed me, I managed to extend my hand. He accepted it—shyly, eyes looking down—and gave me a perfunctory shake. But that was enough. Silently, I vowed, "That is what I'll be someday—Israel's ambassador to America."

His name was Yitzhak Rabin. And his life remained a model for mine. Following his example, I would devote myself to Israel, fight in its wars, and defend it from critics. I shared his vision of peace in spite of disappointments and bloodshed. Years later, together with countless candle-holding mourners, I filed past Rabin's casket. Though I never had the opportunity to tell him about the impact he had on me, I never forgot that encounter in the basement. Or the pledge I made to myself.

Forty years would pass before the day arrived that I—however improbably—moved into Rabin's Washington residence. With Israeli flags fluttering from its hood, a limousine pulled up and bore me along Pennsylvania Avenue. Through the wrought-iron gates, the limo glided onto the crescent-shaped driveway of the White House. I entered, nodding at the Marine guards stiffening to attention, and proceeded to the Oval Office. There, presenting my credentials to the president, I fulfilled that vow I made at age fifteen. I had become Israel's ambassador to America.

If only a few miles, my journey from that Washington hotel to the White House was scarcely effortless and marked by at least as much tragedy as triumph. It took me from baseball fields to battlefields, from work in kibbutz fields to interrogations by the KGB. Burnt-out buses and peace-signing ceremonies, "dumb" classes and Ivy League halls, orthopedic braces and athletic medals, the scars of racism and lustrous family mementos—all lined that path. But the journey did not end in the Oval Office. Exiting that illustrious place, I embarked on the most tortuous and exalting passage yet.

This is the story of that journey. It crosses two countries and spans their extraordinary relationship. The United States and Israel are bound by ideas far older than both, by values they commonly cherish, and interests they have come to share. Theirs is the deepest bilateral friendship that either has sustained since Israel's founding in 1948. And the reasons are many-sided and profound.

In addition to a spiritual affinity unrivaled by that between any modern nations, Israel and the United States are akin in their commitment to democracy. Listeners to Israel's Declaration of Independence can easily hear the echoes of 1776. In America, Israel has an immensely generous source of diplomatic support and annual defense aid. In Israel, the United States has a stable, loyal, and militarily proficient asset—a scientific and technological powerhouse—and a pro-American island in an often toxic sea. Surveys regularly show that Americans and Israelis lead the world in patriotism and in their willingness to fight for their country. They are ideologically, strategically, and naturally allied.

Ally is a simple, beautiful word. It evokes warmth—indeed, fraternity—and its meaning is invariably positive. One may be a partner, but never an ally, in crime. *Ally*'s Hebrew counterpart is even simpler and more stirring. *Ben brit,* literally the son of the covenant, recalls the circumcision rite and, beyond that, the Jewish people's special relationship with God. Fittingly, a "special relationship" is said to exist between Israel and the United States. And like its biblical precedent, that *brit* is both physical and eternal.

Or, at least, in theory. For the reality is that, alongside their immemorial ties, the U.S.-Israel relationship includes bitter differences. The United States does not recognize Israel's capital or its claim to large parts of the ancestral Jewish homeland. Israel frequently disagrees with America's approach to peacemaking with the Palestinians and its friendship with Middle Eastern rulers who are technically or actively at war with the Jewish State. Vocal segments of the American Jewish community—a vital component in the alliance—are critical of Israeli actions, while Israel, in turn, does not validate the ways in which many of those Jews practice their religion. Israel is a contentious issue in the American press and on many American campuses. In recent years, public disagreements between the two countries' leaders have become commonplace. America and Israel are allies in the most meaningful sense, yet their alliance is scored with divides.

This is the story of that alliance and also its divides, as experienced by one who treasures his American identity while proudly serving the State of Israel. My personal journey intertwines with that story and never more intimately than during the more than four years—from mid-2009 to late 2013—that I represented Israel in Washington.

This was a transformative period for America and a time of violent revolutions throughout the Middle East. Hundreds of thousands of the region's people were killed, and the lives of millions more threatened. Israel and America grappled not only with the peace process and other complex bilateral issues, but with the terrorism and

Iranian nuclearization that imperiled the world. The alliance would be subjected to enormous strains and its future questioned by commentators in both countries. On more than one occasion, the friendship's very fabric seemed close to unraveling. At all times, though, it was my task—and my privilege—to hold it together.

The job of ambassador is widely misunderstood in today's world, in which presidents and prime ministers can chat or shout at each other by videophone, without any need for go-betweens. But ambassadors not only represent leaders, they link peoples, and none more closely than Americans and Israelis. As Jerusalem's envoy to Washington, I enjoyed a strategic viewpoint and a depth of access unattainable by even the most senior Israeli officials. That unique perspective is also part of the story.

It is a story for those who care about Israel and America and the challenges they face in the Middle East. It is a quintessentially American story of a young person who refused to relinquish a dream irrespective of the obstacles, and an inherently Israeli story about assuming onerous responsibilities. It is both a chronicle and a confession. Never before have I written in the first person, as a participant in history rather than a dispassionate observer of it. Instead of distant figures from the past, I have described my contemporaries, among them many colleagues, family members, and friends. More than a memoir, this is a testament. It is my tribute to the enduring bonds between the United States and Israel. This is the story of an alliance that was and, I unreservedly believe, will remain vital for both Americans and Israelis, and beneficial to the stability of the world.

Michael B. Oren
Tel Aviv, 2015

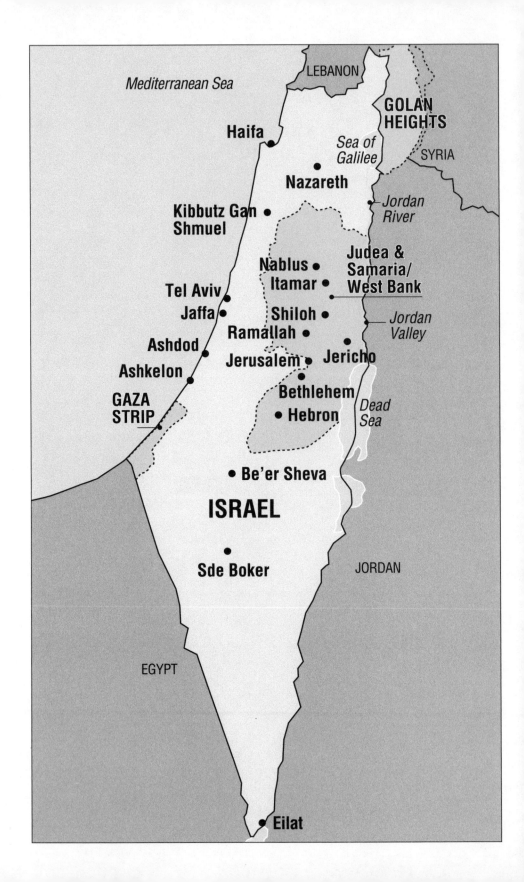

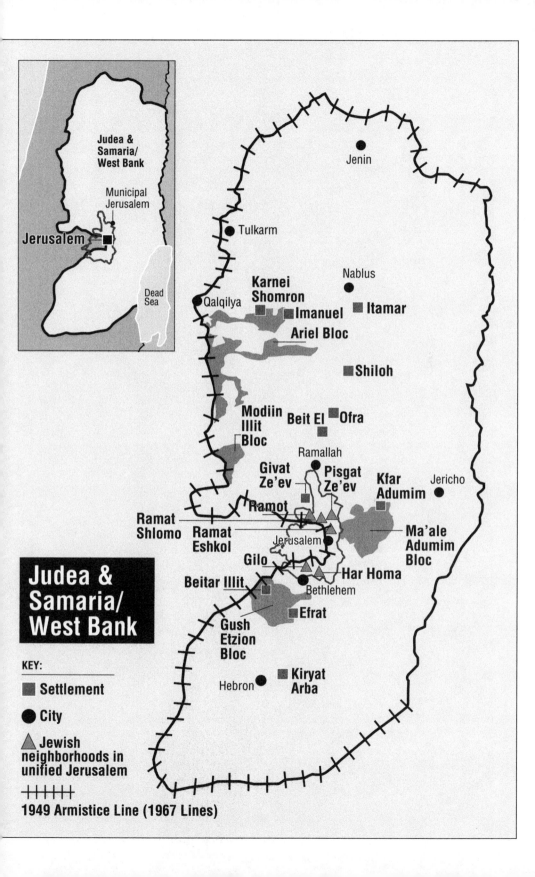

Judea &
Samaria/
West Bank

KEY:

■ Settlement

● City

▲ Jewish neighborhoods in unified Jerusalem

+++++ 1949 Armistice Line (1967 Lines)

ALLY

THE PERFORATED PASSPORT

THE EMBASSY OF THE UNITED STATES TO THE STATE OF ISRAEL should be a majestic structure. After all, it is the hub of America's most special relationship with any foreign nation. And yet the building—squat and colorless—looks like a bunker. Perhaps the purpose is to discourage the hundreds of Israelis who daily line the sidewalk outside to apply for tourist visas, or to confound any terrorist who managed to skirt the concrete obstacles girding the grounds. Whatever its purpose, the bleak exterior reflected my mood as I entered the compound in early June 2009 and presented my passport.

That Yankee-blue document announced that I had been born Michael Bornstein, in Upstate New York and had been a U.S. citizen for more than half a century. With a faded cover and pages tattooed by customs, it had accompanied me on innumerable transoceanic flights. Presenting that passport at Newark's Liberty International Airport, a twenty-minute drive from where my parents raised my two sisters and me, I beamed each time the inspectors wished me, "Welcome home."

I believed in that passport—in the history it symbolized, the values it proclaimed. Awareness of the nation's darker legacies, such as slavery, did not make me less sentimental about America. My eyes still misted during the national anthem, brightened at the sight of Manhattan's skyline, and marveled at the Rockies from thirty-five thousand feet. Once, when reading aloud the inscription on the Lincoln Memorial and already choking at "four score and seven years ago," my children rolled their eyes and sighed, "There he goes again. . . ."

My affection for America sprang naturally. Growing up in the northern New Jersey town of West Orange, I played Little League baseball, attended pep rallies, and danced—in a lamentable banana tux—at my senior prom. My father, who fought in World War II and afterward served in the army reserves, took me to his unit's reunions and to summer maneuvers to watch the color guards parade. I, too, marched, albeit across halftime gridirons puffing into a baritone horn. At Boys State, the American Legion's semimilitary seminar, Vietnam vets put me and other selected seventeen-year-olds through a basic training in American democracy. The following year, I starred as Don Quixote in our high school's production of *Man of La Mancha,* the musical based on Cervantes's classic. Arrayed in rusted armor, I tilted at windmills and strained for the high notes while enjoining the audience to "Dream the Impossible Dream."

Yet there were handicaps. Like many in our working-class neighborhood, my parents struggled financially. They could not afford to send me to the pricey Jewish summer camps, and instead packed me off to a rustic YMCA program with mandatory church services and grace before meals. Overweight and so pigeon-toed that I had to wear an excruciating leg brace at night, I was hopeless at sports. And severe learning disabilities consigned me to the "dumb" classes at school, where I failed to grasp elementary math and learn to write legibly.

Yet, fervently determined, I managed to overcome these obstacles. At fourteen I went on a draconian diet and slimmed down, forced myself to run long distances while keeping my feet straight, and forged myself into an athlete. Meanwhile, my mother lovingly showed me how to type on an old Fleetwood on which I began to peck out poetry. After publishing my verse in several national magazines, I was transferred into a "smart" class, taught myself grammar and spelling, and ultimately attended Ivy League schools. All the hallmarks of an American success became mine, I acknowledged, thanks in part to uniquely American opportunities.

If sentimental about the United States, I also felt indebted. From the time that all four of my grandparents arrived in Ellis Island, through the Great Depression in which they raised my parents, and the farm-bound community in which I grew up, America held out the chance to excel. True, prejudice was prevalent, but so, too, was our ability to fight it. Unreservedly, I referred to Americans as "we."

Now I was about to forfeit that first-person plural. The Marine behind the glass booth at the U.S. embassy in Tel Aviv examined my passport and wordlessly slipped it through the window. The coolness of his reception would soon become routine. Landing at Liberty Airport, I would never again be greeted with "welcome home."

Americans, I would often remind Israelis, are painstakingly nice—until they are not. "Have a nice day" can become "screw you" in an instant. That morning, officials at the U.S. embassy were in courteous mode, expediting the security check, escorting me between the cubicles of the consular section. There passports are extended and new ones issued. Mine would be neither.

My knees felt rubbery and my shirt, already dabbled by the humidity outside, stuck to my flanks. Relief came in the teddy-bearish form of Luis Moreno, the deputy chief of mission, an old acquaintance. Luis brought me into the office of U.S. Consul General Andrew Parker, who sat behind his desk surrounded by mementos from his previous postings and fronted by a gold-trimmed Stars and Stripes. We exchanged pleasantries, griped about the *khamsin*—the gritty desert wind plaguing Tel Aviv—but could not ignore the reason for my visit.

Bespectacled, neatly goateed, Parker could be mistaken for a kindly professor if not for his undertaker's tone. Raising my right hand, he asked me to repeat after him: "I absolutely and entirely renounce my United States nationality together with all rights and privileges and all duties and allegiance and fidelity thereunto pertaining." I repeated those words while gazing at the flag to which I had pledged allegiance every school day from kindergarten through high school. Then, across his desk, Parker arrayed several copies of an affidavit. This reaffirmed "the extremely serious and irrevocable nature of the act of renunciation," acknowledging that, henceforth, "I will become an alien with respect to the United States."

I signed each copy, swearing that I knew precisely what I was doing and that I was acting of my own free will. I must have appeared shattered because Luis Moreno leaned over and gave me a hug. But the ordeal was not yet complete, Consul General Parker indicated. Officiously, almost mechanically, the consul general inserted my American passport into an industrial-sized hole puncher and squeezed. The heart of the federal eagle emblazoned on the cover of the document was pierced.

Growing Up American

How did I reach this unnerving moment? Back in the sixties, young radicals burned their passports and cursed their fascist country,

"Amerika." But my reverence for the United States had always been deep—deeper than any hole puncher could bore. No, renouncing my American citizenship was not an act of protest. It reflected, rather, a love for another land—not that of my father, but of my forefathers.

That love could not be presented in a passport, nor could it be renounced. When did it begin? There was the distant cousin who arrived one day from a far-flung place and gave me, an eight-year-old numismatist, a shiny coin inscribed with letters I recognized from Hebrew school. Somewhere, I intuited, people actually spoke that language. There were the nerve-fraying weeks of May 1967, when the enemies of those people amassed and my parents murmured about witnessing a second Holocaust. Then, the miracle. A mere six days transformed those victims into victors. Draped in belts of .50-caliber bullets instead of prayer shawls, paratroopers danced before the Western Wall in Jerusalem. They were *our* paratroopers, suddenly, *our* people.

Because Israel was young and righteous and heroic, I fell in love with it. The country appeared to be everything to which I—at age twelve still incapable of learning the multiplication tables or of running around the bases without tripping over my own pigeon-toed feet—aspired. Even then, I had a keen sense of history, an awareness that I was not just a lone Jew living in late 1960s America, but part of a global Jewish collective stretching back millennia. Already I considered myself lucky to be alive at this juncture, when my existence coincided with that of a sovereign Jewish State. I fell in love with Israel because I was grateful, but also because I was angry.

The only Jewish kid on the block, I rarely made it off the school bus without being ambushed by Jew-baiting bullies. Those fistfights left my knuckles lined with scars. One morning, my family awoke to find our front door smeared with racist slogans; one night our car's windshield was smashed. Then, when I was a high school freshman, the phone rang with horrendous news: a bomb had blown up our synagogue. I ran to the scene and saw firemen leaping into the flames to rescue the Torah scrolls. The next day, our rabbi stood with Christian clergymen and led us in singing "We Shall Overcome." But no display of brotherhood could salve the pain.

In the post–World War II, WASP-dominated America in which I grew up, anti-Semitism was a constant. Hardly confined to my blue-collar neighborhood, it festered in the elite universities with their quotas on Jewish admissions, and pervaded the restricted communities and clubs. Superficially, at least, we American Jews ranked among the nation's most successful minorities. We took pride in the Dodgers' ace pitcher Sandy Koufax, in folksinger Bob Dylan, and actors Tony Curtis and Kirk Douglas. It tickled us that Jewish humor became, in large measure, America's humor, and the bagel grew as popular as pizza. Jewish artists wrote five of America's most beloved Christmas songs and practically invented Hollywood. One could hardly imagine a community more integrated, and yet we remained different. Alone among the hyphenated ethnic identities—Italian-American, African-American—ours placed "American" first. And only ours was based on religion. No one ever referred to Buddhist or Methodist Americans. As Jews and as Americans we were sui generis, as difficult for us to define as for others. A graffito on the wall of my bathroom at school asked, "Are Jews white?" A different hand scrawled beneath it, "Yes, but . . ."

Anti-Semitism completed that sentence. Whether being beaten up for my identity or denied certain opportunities because of it, I often encountered hatred. And after each incident, my father took me down to our basement. There, in a cubbyhole behind the stairwell, he secreted a musty album that his brother, another veteran, had brought home from World War II. Inside were yellowing photographs of concentration camps, piles of incinerated corpses, and snickering Nazis. "This is why we must be strong," my father reminded me. "This is why we need Israel."

Those photographs needed no captioning, as the Holocaust haunted our lives. The ovens of Auschwitz, I often felt in high school, still smoldered. Yet American Jews hesitated to talk openly about the murder of six million of their people, as if it were a source of shame. Then, in my sophomore year, survivor and world-acclaimed author Elie Wiesel visited our community. He spoke of his ordeals in Romania's Sighet ghetto and the Buchenwald concentration camp. In a voice at once frail and unbroken, he challenged us to face the Final Solution publicly, not only in our basements. We did, but confronting the horrors of Jewish helplessness also forced us to face the harrowing truth that America did nothing to save the Jews. Worse, America sent thousands back to be murdered and closed its doors to millions.

That knowledge alone would have sufficed to make me a Zionist. This meant, simply, that I believed in the Jews' right to independence in our ancient homeland. But there was more. Zionism was not merely a reaction to discrimination, but an affirmation of what I felt from an early age to be my fundamental identity. For deep-rooted reasons, Zionism defined my being.

Though I was not raised religious—I read my Bar Mitzvah in transliteration—the Jewish story of the Exodus from Egypt to the exodus from Europe resounded with meaning. Our story was the vehicle for our values: family, universal morality, social justice, and loyalty to our land. Half of humanity believed in the one God we introduced to the world nearly four thousand years ago and refused to relinquish, even under unspeakable tortures. God owed us an explanation for the Holocaust, I insisted. But Zionism offered a way of saying "we're finished with you, God" and "thank you, God," simultaneously. It allowed us to assert our self-sufficiency, even independence from formal religion, but in the one place that our forebears cherished as divinely given. Zionism enabled us to return to history as active authors of our own story. And the story I considered the most riveting of all time was that of the Jewish people.

I belonged to that people and needed to be part of its narrative. Being Jewish in America, while culturally and materially comfortable, felt to me like living in the margins. The major chapter was being written right now, I thought, and not in New Jersey. History, rather, was happening in a state thriving against all odds, thousands of miles away. How could I miss it?

That is why I joined the Zionist youth movement that brought me to Washington in May 1970, when I shook Yitzhak Rabin's hand. That is why, throughout that year, I mowed lawns and shoveled snow from neighbors' driveways to raise the airfare. And why I made repeated trips into New York City, alone, to browbeat kibbutz movement representatives into accepting me as a volunteer despite being two years short of the minimum age. The representatives relented and, in the summer of my pivotal fifteenth year, I finally purchased my ticket. I acquired my first U.S. passport and boarded a plane for Israel.

Rising to Israel

Descending the ramp, the Israeli heat hit me, hammering-hot. But even more fazing was my encounter with the country I had only imagined: smelling the citrus-scented air, seeing trees alien to New Jersey and all the signs in Hebrew. This was Israel of 1970, before serious talk of peace or the Palestinian issue, when fighting still raged on the Egyptian and Jordanian fronts. The hourly news, announced with a series of beeps, had passersby running ear-first for the nearest radio.

Behind the tension, though, lay a raffish élan and self-confidence. Toughened old-timers could still recount how they drained the swamps, battled malaria and British occupation troops, and struggled bitterly for independence against invading Arab armies. Along with its valorous past, Israel's present was scintillating. The streets thrummed with shoppers, beggars, policemen, workers, stunning young women and men in olive army uniforms, almost all of them, inconceivably to me, Jewish.

A few days after my arrival, a wobbly Israeli bus dropped me into the dust of Kibbutz Gan Shmuel. Invented by Zionist pioneers at the turn of the twentieth century, the *kibbutz*—in the Hebrew plural *kibbutzim*—was an utterly revolutionary concept. Members of these hardworking agricultural communities shared all their worldly possessions, ate every meal in a common dining room, and raised their children in separate "houses" managed by nursemaids. Ideologically utopian, the kibbutzim fulfilled the practical goal of settling the land and absorbing Jewish immigrants. In wartime, the farms served as fortified redoubts. Though representing only a fraction of Israel's populace, "kibbutzniks" served in the toughest combat units, accounted for as much as half of all officers, and fell in disproportionate numbers. Well after the founding of the state, the kibbutz remained the apex of the Zionist ideal—selfless, grounded, caring, and, throughout successive battles, courageous.

Some of that patina had nevertheless worn off by the summer of 1970. But Gan Shmuel clung to its radical roots. After outgrowing the children's houses, teenagers moved into the *mossad*—the institution—and took responsibility for maintaining their own quarters, preparing their food, and reporting for work in the fields. Once assigned to the mossad, I received dark blue work clothes, sturdy boots, and a brim-down sailor's cap called a *kova tembel*—"the idiot's hat," Israel's signature headwear. Each sunrise, a tractor hauled me out to the alfalfa pastures where I lugged irrigation pipes through calf-high muck. And each evening we danced to Israeli folk tunes or huddled around a gas stove eating boiled corn. Back in America, the youth culture convulsed with protests and drugs, but Israel was my rebellion, my stimulant. Israel was cool.

"When I walk around Gan Shmuel at night I'm in such ecstasy, for I know who I am and what I am doing here," I wrote my parents. I described the rigorous work but also the kibbutz bomb shelter decorated, paradoxically, with a poster of Picasso's *Guernica*. Though surrounded by war, I concluded, Israelis never ceased craving peace. "There is God in all of them."

Did I fail to face the bloodshed out of which Israel had been born and the improbability of a Jewish state serenely integrated into the Middle East? Could I see the conflicting Israeli identities of secular and religious, right and left, Arab and Jew, and the mess that sovereignty invariably entails? In time I would, certainly. The fantasy of Israel would eventually dissipate, but never the dream.

On the contrary, I would cherish the contradictions, for they were ours alone. Throughout most of our history, Jews rarely had the right to wrestle with sovereign problems and, for our statelessness, we paid an unspeakable price. But sovereignty also came at a cost. Theodor Herzl, Zionism's founder, famously said, "If you will it, it is no dream," to which I always appended a quote from Irish laureate William Butler Yeats, "In dreams begin responsibility." Zionism, for me, meant Jews taking responsibility for themselves—for their dreams as well as for their mess.

As a teenager, though, my Zionism was still simple, a passion for an Israel that furnished muscular answers to anti-Semitism and a dignified response to the Holocaust. Someday I would live there, I knew. Until then, I would return to America and prepare myself politically and spiritually. Back in New Jersey, I marched in protests demanding freedom for the millions of Jews suffering under Soviet rule and prevented from immigrating to Israel. A Chabad rabbi, Shalom Gordon— cherubic face, copious beard—volunteered to teach me Talmud. Rejoining the Zionist youth movement, I began to learn about Israel's historic alliance with America.

During the movement's meetings, I often heard the words of Louis Brandeis, the first Jewish U.S. Supreme Court justice, who said, "Every American Jew who supported Zionism was a better American for doing so." The United States and Israel, I came to value, were both democracies, both freedom-loving, and similarly determined to defend their independence. One could be—in fact, should be—a Zionist as well as a patriotic American, because the two countries stood for identical ideals. Quite naturally, I stood and sang "The Star-Spangled Banner" and, in the next breath, Israel's national anthem, "Hatik-vah," the Hope.

Meanwhile, I mowed more lawns, shoveled and raked, to save enough to work each summer in Israel for free. At eighteen I was on horseback rounding up cattle on the Golan Heights. The job had risks—cows occasionally set off old Syrian antitank mines—but it further transformed me. Once wan and tender-looking, I became leathery and fit. No longer a stranger in my own land, I blended with my ancestors' topography and conversed in their language. I longed to become Israeli. The last stanza of America's national anthem still left me cheering, but the conclusion of Israel's, "to be a free people in our land, the Land of Zion," made me yearn.

Yet, still I did not move to Israel, telling myself I could contribute more to it with an undergraduate education. My assumptions were that Israel would remain invincible and largely above reproach, but then these proved wrong. Suddenly attacked by Egypt and Syria on the afternoon of Yom Kippur, 1973, Israel was nearly overwhelmed. Though it eventually drove back and encircled the invaders, in a mere three weeks the Israeli army lost a staggering 2,500 soldiers—the equivalent of 230,000 Americans today.

The Yom Kippur War signaled the beginning of other onslaughts. On the diplomatic front, a holster-packing Yasser Arafat, founder of the militantly anti-Israel Fatah movement and chairman of the Palestine Liberation Organization (PLO), received a standing ovation at the United Nations General Assembly. A year later, that same assembly equated Zionism with racism. Palestinian terrorists infiltrated the Israeli towns of Ma'alot and Qiryat Shmona, machine-gunning women and children.

I covered these travesties for Columbia College radio and, in the numbing cold, stood on street corners handing out Zionist leaflets. I felt useless and absurd. While jointly completing BA and master's degrees in Middle East studies at Columbia, the questions still hounded me: Why was I a student instead of a soldier? Pulling fraternity pranks and not guarding Israel's frontiers?

My life bifurcated. Outwardly, I was all-American: the recipient of a State Department–affiliated scholarship, the author of novels, plays, and film scripts, one of which won first prize in the PBS Young

Filmmakers' Festival. Such proclivities led me westward, to Hollywood, where I spent a summer nervously holding cue cards for a splenetic Orson Welles. At the same time, I studied Hebrew literature and Arabic, rowed varsity crew, and ran marathons to prepare for the paratroopers. And I worked—as a security guard, bartender, even a football scoreboard operator—to save enough money to move east, to Israel.

But then, after graduation, I again delayed my departure in order to serve as an "advisor"—so my ID defined me—to Israel's delegation to the United Nations. My responsibilities included explaining Israeli policies to American Jews, many of them senior citizens whose first question was, invariably, "Are you married?" I also observed special UN sessions where Arab diplomats in tailored suits accused Israel of poisoning Palestinian wells and rendering Palestinian women infertile. Saudi ambassador Jamil al-Baroudi wondered aloud whether Jews were in fact human.

In addition to listening to diplomats in three-piece suits spouting anti-Semitism, I had to sit among some of Israel's fiercest foes. The Jewish State's name in English begins with the letter *I*, awkwardly placing its delegates next to those of Jordan, Kuwait, Lebanon, and Libya, as well as the Iraqis and Iranians. The only respite came from Ireland, whose jaunty young diplomats comforted me with Guinness. They also arranged a family-hospitality tour of their homeland that left me hooked on Irish music and soul.

Fortunately, my last experience at the UN proved to be the most memorable—Foreign Minister Moshe Dayan came to address the General Assembly. Standing before me with his trademark eye patch was one of the mythic figures of my youth, the storied warrior. He came to the UN not to talk about war, though, but about the groundbreaking peace agreement between Israel and Egypt. I helped him write his speech, aware of his frailty—he died two years later—and the failing sight in his remaining eye. In those pre-computer days, I had to scour all of New York for a printer with letters large enough for Dayan to read.

Dayan's speech was an inspiring respite from the revolting hatred of Israel I encountered almost daily at the UN. With immense relief, I concluded my service in New York and at last embarked on that life-altering journey. In Zionist parlance, one does not merely immigrate to Israel but rather goes up—makes *aliya*—and in 1979, finally, I rose.

3335335

The ascent was less than exalted. I arrived alone, in the middle of a driz-zly night, with only a backpack. No one greeted me at the airport or offered me a ride to the Jerusalem absorption center, where no one was awake to open the door. Yet the mop, the foam rubber mattress, and mini-refrigerator I received as a newcomer to the state seemed like trea-sures to me. I stared at the meager contents of that refrigerator, all pur-chased at an Israeli store, and thought, "Wow, that's mine. I'm home."

Under Israel's Law of Return, any Jew making *aliya* can almost immediately become a citizen. From then on, I would carry two pass-ports, both of them blue, one American and the other Israeli. I also Hebraicized my name to Oren, meaning pine tree, which recalled my American roots but also my regeneration in our ancestral land. Those two identities finally felt melded in me. I could not have been luckier.

The next few months were spent working for a social service agency, visiting the "other" Israel of poor development towns and remote Arab villages. The poverty often shocked me, as did the sometimes vast cultural gaps between Israel and the United States. Unmindful of the personal space so precious to Americans, for example, Israelis would cut into lines, leer at adjacent drivers at stoplights, and lecture total strangers on the best way to raise their kids. Unlike the Ameri-cans, who were swift to hit and slow to shout, Israelis would yell at each other for hours without ever coming to blows, and occasionally end up having coffee. And whereas Americans always wished me "Have a nice day" but did not always mean it, Israelis sometimes said, "Shalom"—peace—and always did.

Still, in spite of the privations I witnessed and the social chasms that needed to be crossed, I felt privileged to be part of Israel. My great-grandparents fleeing pogroms would have been envious of my opportunity to assist the inhabitants of a free Jewish state and to learn their ways, however different. My forebears would have thought them-selves blessed to be able to protect that state from harm. I know I did, opening the plain brown envelope inscribed with a sword sheathed in olive leaves. This was the symbol of the Israel Defense Forces—the IDF—and inside the letter were orders summoning me to the Bakum, the central induction base.

Most recruits no doubt feel jittery while first putting on a uniform. Buttoning the epauletted shirt with *Tzahal*—the Hebrew acronym for the IDF—stitched on the breast pocket, I, too, felt nervous. Yet, along with anxiety was the pride of becoming part of the first Jewish army in two thousand years. This was the answer to exile, to the Holocaust. The fact that here, too, Jews were given numbers only underscored the contrast—and the justice. Excitedly, I became Personal Number 3335335.

That elation ended when I tried to fulfill my goal of joining the paratroopers. I never forgot the image of those airborne troops dancing in Jerusalem during the Six-Day War and was determined to be one of them. No other unit would do. Unfortunately, the army had other ideas and assigned me to the artillery corps. I refused to board the bus to basic training, even under threat of court-martial. "Go ahead, arrest me," I dared the officers, who promptly confined me to my tent. Days passed before they relented. Perhaps they understood what I never imagined, that the tryouts would prove so grueling that they hospitalized me for a week. But in the end, I made it into the paratroopers.

Or at least into the paratrooper course. No amount of rowing and marathon running could have prepared me for the next seventeen months. There were nightlong marches that flayed our feet, and daylong drills crawling through brambles or laying our bodies across barbed wire while others used our backs as springboards. The drinking water was rationed, sleep denied, and showers virtually unavailable—I once went six weeks without one. Less than a third of the unit finished the course, and often I questioned whether I could. Such as the wintry night we finished maneuvers at 5 A.M. with reveille set for forty-five minutes later, and a twenty-minute guard duty in between. While lacing up my boots, my eyes involuntarily welled with tears. I forced myself to remember the Jews of 1948, who held off Arab armies with handguns, the pioneers who gave their youth, and often their lives, to cultivate a patch of our homeland. It worked. I sleeve-dried my eyes and knotted my laces.

All that was agonizing enough, yet not all of the army's challenges were physical. My knowledge of Hebrew, while sufficient to order falafels, fell short of understanding rapid-fire orders or instructions for dissembling a gun. I was a "lone soldier," without a family to feed me and clean my fatigues when I came home famished and filthy. The

IDF of the seventies was poor and I was poorer still, unable to afford the expensive woolen socks the army did not furnish. But my Hebrew improved and I grew accustomed to caring for myself. Each time our bivouac moved, I collected the socks that invariably remained behind, brought them home, and boiled them until I amassed some forty pairs. Lacking sufficient hot water to take a bath and wash my uniforms, I did both, simultaneously.

Despite the exhaustion and the loneliness, I still felt indebted—for the camaraderie, the maturity, and the chance to protect my country. Never would I light the Hanukkah candles without remembering the soldiers who huddled with me over a tin military-issue menorah and shielded its flames from the rain. Never would I come in from the biting cold and not recall the cup of oversweet tea that my sergeant handed me after completing an eight-hour, open-jeep patrol. No one could take away the silver wings and the paratroopers' red beret and boots I won. By the same token, I never got over my fear of jumping out of an airplane, at night, while lugging my 7.62 mm machine gun, five hundred rounds of ammo, and C-rations. Rather, two hefty men, positioned on either side of the open hatch, *pushed* me out.

The day I completed my compulsory service, March 16, 1981, Sally Edelstein arrived in Israel. A native San Franciscan, she had hung out with Janis Joplin and Jefferson Airplane in the sixties, traveled through Europe at age seventeen, studied at Berkeley, and performed modern dance in New York. Like Israel, she was cool, and bewilderingly alluring. I could hardly bear to glance at her. She was also worldly, crisp-witted, effortlessly warm, and real. And, like me, she felt secure in her American and Israeli identities, a harmonious amalgam of the two.

After chancing to meet Sally on Jerusalem's Street of the Prophets, I rushed to call my parents and inform them that I had just met my future wife. That was obvious from our first date. We rendezvoused on a rocky field that separated our neighborhoods, in front of a Jordanian tank knocked out in the 1948 war, and climbed up to my moonlit roof. There we sang every moon song we knew.

Indifferent to material goods and willing to haul jerry cans of kerosene to fuel the stoves that heated our spartanly furnished apartments, Sally was the resilient partner I needed as I pursued this often rugged Israeli path. Here was a person who shared my dreams and commitments. That bond, welded with love, would enable us to weather any trials, I thought—perhaps too heedlessly. A few months later, I was underground in a hostile country, subjected to gruff interrogations, and wondering if I would ever see Sally again.

A Free People in Our Land

Though difficult to fathom today, the empire then known as the Soviet Bloc denied the right of three million Jews to freely practice their religion, learn Hebrew, or make *aliya*. For committing such "crimes," the refuseniks, as they called themselves, were fired from their jobs and relentlessly hounded. Others labored in the infamous Siberian camps known as gulags, or, like the math and chess master Natan Sharansky, languished in solitary confinement. The Soviets also backed Israel's Arab enemies and spurned all relations with the Jewish State.

Israel took responsibility for the Jews behind the Iron Curtain. It dispatched teams to make contact with members of the Zionist underground, to smuggle in Jewish books as well as the blue jeans that could be traded for food. Most crucially, Israel assured them they were never forgotten. Israelis who served in combat units and who held two passports were especially sought after for these missions. Meeting those criteria and having demonstrated throughout my youth to free Soviet Jewry, how could I decline? The training was cursory, the warning blunt: if you get caught, you're on your own. You could be sent to a gulag or simply disappear.

Before departing, I proposed to Sally. I got down on one knee, a position too traditional for this former flower child, which only made her chuckle. Still, she accepted, but then suggested that my motives might be mixed. "I know what you're thinking," she said as she helped me to my feet. "You're thinking, 'If I get arrested, I want a wife like Avital Sharansky who'll send me food packages and campaign to get me out.'"

Sally had a point, I admitted to myself after landing in Moscow. Except for my partner, Yitzhak Sokoloff, a spirited Columbia College friend and fellow IDF veteran, I was utterly alone in a dangerous land thousands of miles from home. Our cover story as American photojournalists was thin. Stiffly, we approached the border guards, who eyed us coldly before stamping our U.S. passports. Then we entered the city.

The Soviet Union in the late winter of 1982 was in its death throes and looked it. Behind mounds of garbage and open ditches of sludge sagged immense gray buildings that appeared on the verge of collapse. Food lines stretched endlessly. Everywhere, we assumed, lurked agents of the secret police—the ruthless KGB—and their local informers.

Fearing they might fall into the KGB's hands, we carried none of the refuseniks' names, phone numbers, or addresses. Rather, we had spent weeks memorizing them. The easiest for me to recall was Yuli Edelstein, who shared Sally's last name. He answered the phone immediately and, within minutes, met us on a darkened subway platform. The handsome and self-confident twenty-three-year-old had been arrested for his Zionist activities and expelled from the university. Now he was cleaning streets and would soon be sent to Siberia. Yet Yuli was anything but broken. Instead, he intrepidly introduced us to other activists and sneered at our KGB tails.

Several days later, we boarded a train that bore us over the snow-packed Trans-Carpathian Mountains and into the Soviet Ukraine. There we linked up with underground cells composed of people from incongruous backgrounds—scientists, factory workers, teenagers, retirees—whose only tie was their insistence on being Jews and living in Israel. Secretly listening to radio broadcasts from Jerusalem, these Prisoners of Zion taught themselves fluent Hebrew and followed the Israeli news as closely as if they were living there. They sang Israeli commercials as if they were prayers. All of them knew that the authorities would eventually arrest them, set them before a kangaroo Soviet court, and sentence them to years in the gulag. They were ordinary people of superhuman courage.

Such was Yehudit Nepunyache, the leader of the Odessa underground, sixteen years old and barely five feet tall. Once, while crossing a courtyard for a meeting with her cell, I was accosted by several club-wielding KGB thugs. Knowing that I was about to be beaten, she threw herself into the arms of the largest brute and began shouting "Rape! Rape!"—so loudly that all the windows in the courtyard flew open. The agent dropped his bat, clutched her throat, and lifted her off the ground, but Yehudit did not flinch. Instead she looked him in the eye and said, "So, you're going to hit me, too?" The goon released his grip, cursed, and led his gang out of the courtyard.

Yehudit saved me, but only for a while. My partner Yitzhak Soko-loff and I were repeatedly arrested and interrogated at length. Sometimes the KGB subjected us to full-body searches, other times to endless harangues about the "hoodlums" we contacted. They implied that we could face beatings and imprisonment. Our response was to insist that we were merely American photojournalists. We waved our blue passports and demanded to see the U.S. ambassador.

Released, we went right back to work. This often meant rising before dawn and going out for a jog in the arctic air because, we discovered, the KGB kept regular hours. Before daybreak, we could reach the refuseniks unimpeded. But one time, in a grim industrial town, we failed to shake the agents trailing us and, in frustration, finally jumped into a cab. Our destination was a workers' dormitory and the Zionist activist Isaac Skolnik. His wife and daughter had been allowed to leave for Israel years before—the communists delighted in separating families—and he had not seen them since. Our mission: to send Skolnik their love.

In the cab's rearview mirror, I saw five government cars following us and felt sick to my stomach. As we headed into the bleak countryside, the convoy doubled, including military vehicles. We arrived just ahead of the KGB and dashed across frozen mud to the prisonlike dormitory. But the babushka at the desk told us that Skolnik was not there. Devastated, we turned around to face a throng of angry KGB goons. "If you get out of this alive," I muttered to Yitzhak, "tell Sally I loved her." In the lobby, they set up a blinding lamp and two chairs and ordered us to sit.

Hours of furious interrogation passed before the KGB brutes brought in another suspect, a young man, slight, dark, balding—and beaten, with huge welts across his face. They sat him next to us and continued to pummel us with questions.

"Who sent you here? What is your real identity?"

"We're American journalists photographing the scenic Ukraine," we responded as innocently as possible. "We demand to see the U.S. ambassador."

The interrogators ignored our story and began shouting at us. I began to wonder whether my face would soon resemble that of the young man seated next to me. Just then, he leaned over and whispered to me in English, "Keep it up. You're doing very well."

"Are you sure?" I asked him. "You don't look so good."

"I'm fine. Don't worry about me."

I shrugged. "And just who are you?"

"Don't you know?" He smiled. "I'm Skolnik."

Eventually, they let us go, but then Yitzhak refused to leave the dormitory without giving Skolnik a box of Passover *matzah*. The thugs started screaming at us again, and I hissed at Yitzhak, "Enough, let's get out of here." But he would not concede and finally the KGB gave in. Yitzhak handed Skolnik the *matzah*. We hugged him and said, "Shalom, we'll all be reunited soon in Israel." Our interrogators laughed.

Passover came early that year and we celebrated it like Spanish Jews during the Inquisition—in a locked room with the shades drawn. Despite the risks, our hosts, ranging in age from fifteen to sixty, were determined to celebrate the festival of freedom. Then the pounding started, nearly unhinging the door. Jackbooted KGB agents burst in, apprehended Yitzhak and me, and hustled us down the stairs toward yet another interrogation. I trembled uncontrollably, but then suddenly I heard the refuseniks gathering on the landing above us. Together they sang "Hatikvah," Israel's anthem: "To be a free people in our land, the Land of Zion."

Our mission completed, Yitzhak and I prepared to depart for London. Waiting for our plane to take off, I feared the KGB would come on board and arrest us. The relief, seeing Moscow fading below, was overwhelming. I returned to Israel gaunt and pallid. Sally met me at the airport, where I asked her to drive me directly to the Western Wall. There I conveyed the prayers of all those who were denied that sacred right.

I was free in my own land, but that "Hatikvah" sung in captivity kept reverberating in my mind. Walking the streets in Jerusalem, working as a night editor on Israel Radio, I could not escape that sound. Nor had I recovered from the clash of the courage and the cruelty I witnessed when, three weeks later—on June 6, 1982—Israel again went to war.

Peace for the Galilee?

Earlier that week, Shlomo Argov, Israel's venerable ambassador to Great Britain, walked out of a reception at London's Dorchester hotel and into the sights of three Arab gunmen. They shot him in the head, leaving him crippled for life. The attack followed years in which Palestinian terrorists loyal to Yasser Arafat fired rockets from South Lebanon into the Galilee. Life in dozens of Israeli villages and farms became intolerable. Though perpetrated by Arabs opposed to Arafat, Argov's shooting served as a pretext for eliminating those PLO strongholds. Three days later, the Israeli government of Prime Minister Menachem Begin and his defense minister, Ariel Sharon, ordered an invasion of Lebanon.

Suddenly the sidewalks teemed with husbands and sons, fathers and brothers, toting olive green duffle bags and going off to war. And I would shortly join them. Like most former IDF soldiers, I now served in the reserves for as many as sixty days a year, and my unit, a forward recon team, was swiftly mobilized. Sally drove me to the base only to learn that the last of our jeeps had already been helicoptered to the front. But instead of returning home with my fiancée, I signed out on combat gear and hitchhiked across the Lebanese border. From there I joined various outfits battling up the coast.

Together with my adopted battalions, I made my way through the Lebanese cities of Tyre and Sidon, often fighting house-to-house, occasionally stumbling into enemy ambushes. I eventually caught up with my unit, only to discover that my direct commander, the cupid-faced Aryeh Zukerman, the father of a newborn baby girl, had been killed. Everybody else in the vehicle—the one I had just missed—was wounded.

While listening to my father's war stories growing up, I often wondered how I would conduct myself under fire. Now I knew. My Zionist bravado shrank before the reality of whizzing scraps of white-hot metal. But the courage of others astonished me. There was the officer who calmly directed our column while bullets smacked near his feet. Yitzhak Sokoloff, my college friend who accompanied me to the Soviet Union, volunteered for combat duty and fearlessly evacuated wounded under fire. Much time in warfare would pass before I grew indifferent to the hiss of projectiles overhead or the sight of scattered body parts. Once, while being strafed by a Syrian jet, I eyed a beetle creeping in the dirt in front of my face and thought, "How I envy your obliviousness."

The war, originally named Operation Peace for the Galilee, ostensibly aimed at driving the terrorists beyond rocket range of Israel. But then orders arrived to press northward. The new objective was to liberate Lebanon from its Syrian occupiers as well as Palestinian terrorists, replacing them with a pro-Western government. These were laudable goals in theory, but in practice they were unattainable—and increasingly controversial overseas and even back in Israel.

While antiwar protests mounted in Jerusalem, my column fought fiercely through the Shouf Mountains. Later remembered as Israel's Vietnam, the Lebanon War had a brutally surreal quality rare in Israel's earlier conflicts. There was the Druze family, who invited my squad to join them for lunch on a veranda stacked with food and bullet-ridden bodies. And there was the enemy officer—a blue-eyed man with a trimmed mustache—who kept me company in the drainage ditch where I cowered from sniper fire and with whom I kept up a one-way conversation because he was dead. There were the Syrian troops who waved a white flag to our assistant battalion commander and then shot him in the face, and the Israel Radio announcement of a cease-fire that sent us all laughing because we just then were under intense fire. Especially bizarre was the time when, clearing out a hostile village, I ran smack into a hard-baked U.S. Marine colonel.

"'Day to you, son," he said in a gritty Texas accent as he picked his way through the rubble.

"'Day to you, too, Colonel. What are you doing here?"

He pointed to the blue UN patch on his shoulder. "Observin'."

"See anything around?"

"Nah. You're good to go."

I shook his hand, hoisted my rifle, and pressed on.

Yet no sight seemed stranger than the one that sprawled below me, suddenly, as my jeep turned a hairpin bend. Sooty-brown, half-shrouded in smoke: Beirut. Cheering Lebanese showered us with rice and hailed us as liberators. But such receptions are common in Middle Eastern wars, I knew, and fleeting. "We'll never get out of here," I thought. Little did I imagine that Israel would remain stuck in Lebanon's mire for the next eighteen years.

But that summer I did manage to extract myself for a few days' leave in order to get married. In the age before cellphones, Sally had not heard from me for weeks and wept when I returned, blackened and feverish, from the front. We wed under a canopy composed of four broomsticks and my prayer shawl, on a Jerusalem hillside overlooking a sunset-gilded Old City. And then we danced *debkas* to the single-stringed fiddle of a Bedouin friend. But the next morning, while opening gifts, Sally broke out crying again when my leave was abruptly canceled.

Hours later, an ammunition-laden jeep picked me up outside our apartment and drove eight hours straight to Beirut. The boom of artillery fire—like oil drums thumping down stairs—hit me in the gut. We arrived at our headquarters, set up inside a church made of concrete so thick no shell could penetrate it. From the sandbagged portico, I watched, as if hallucinating, entire neighborhoods flaming with phosphorous and the night sky ablaze with tracers.

I wondered when I would ever see Sally or be able to attend Princeton University, where I had been accepted into the doctoral program in Near Eastern Studies. The semester was set to begin in just a few weeks, but soldiers could not go home for overnight leave, much less travel abroad. Fortuitously, the IDF determined that my unit had sustained too many casualties and demobilized the few of us still unscathed. Scampering onto the back of a canvas-covered truck—a welcoming target for the snipers bristling along the serpentine road—I left Beirut behind me.

But I could not leave war, not while living in Israel. The following summer, when our first child, Yoav, was born, I turned to the obstetrician and vowed, "That kid will never wear a helmet." He did, though, and so would his younger sister, Lia, and their younger brother, Noam. Already during the Persian Gulf War, in 1991, when they were still children, all three donned gas masks and took shelter in sealed rooms as Iraqi Scud missiles battered the country. Later, they lost a beloved relative as well as young people they knew to terror—so many that the thirteen-year-old Yoav cried to me, "Abba, I've been to more of my friends' funerals than Bar Mitzvahs."

Six years later, Yoav, now strikingly handsome and strong, completed his training in a special IDF recon unit, a *sayeret*. During my paratrooping days, I took part in a handful of operations, but Yoav's outfit undertook one almost every night. Knowing that, I wandered our neighborhood until dawn, worrying. Then, in 2004, a terrorist holed up in a house in Hebron began firing from behind his own children. While trying to extricate the kids, Yoav was shot.

Rushing into Hadassah Hospital's emergency room, I froze at the sight of my son's bloody, shredded uniform on the floor. Thankfully, the doctors assured me that his wounds, while below the belt, were neither life-threatening nor incapacitating. Yoav's friends needled him about having balls of steel, but that night I was more relieved than humored. For the first time in years, I slept soundly.

Such successive traumas led Sally and me to wonder if we had indeed decided fairly. We decided consciously to fulfill our Zionist dream but, by doing so, denied that free choice to our children. "Did we make a mistake?" we asked them one Shabbat morning after breakfast. To our astonishment, they instantly replied, "Raising us in Israel was the single best thing you could have done for us as parents."

I would always cherish that response. It reminded me that having an Israeli family represented my proudest accomplishment, exceeding my youthful dreams. It justified all the slogging through the alfalfa and battlefields, the grappling with situations that any normal family would find nightmarishly abnormal. Yet we had prevailed. The backpack I shouldered that drizzly night I made *aliya* had blossomed into a furniture-filled home alight with laughter. And this was our home, rooted, in Israel.

Wars of Words

All of that—both the darkness and luminance—still lay years in the future. For the time, in September 1982, I left the hell of Lebanon and landed with Sally in idyllic Princeton. The program of Islamic philosophy, medieval and modern history, and Arabic, was rigorous, and my professors—including the preeminent Middle East scholar Bernard Lewis—superb. While studying, I also taught outstanding undergraduates and honed my political thinking. I came to respect Islam as a potent force in the Middle East, not just an expression of grievances but a deeply imbued worldview and catalyst for action. At the same time, I started doubting the staying power of those Arab states established by Europeans after World War I to satisfy long-defunct European interests. Weaken the kings and dictators at their helms, I concluded, and those states would fall apart.

My thesis, on the origins of the Suez Crisis, also led me to some basic conclusions about America's role in the region. In 1956, Egyptian ruler Gamal Abdul Nasser, backed by the Soviet Union, nationalized the Suez Canal and threatened Israel's existence. Yet when Britain, France, and Israel—America's friends—tried to stop Nasser, U.S. president Dwight Eisenhower turned against them. The invaders, Eisenhower concluded, represented imperialism while the Egyptian dictator somehow stood for liberation. Through America's intervention, Nasser was saved, yet he remained ungrateful. Two years later, he tried to overthrow virtually all the pro-American Arab governments. A chastened Eisenhower appealed to Britain, France, and Israel for help. The lesson: when dealing with the shifting loyalties of Middle Eastern autocrats, stick with your stable, democratic allies.

This was the first time in my life that I lived in America as an Israeli. That dual perspective enabled me to see the multidimensional ties between my two countries. Along with the common ideals and cultural affinities, I gained a clearer view of the long-term strategic interests binding them. The Middle East was becoming increasingly perilous—and not only for Israelis. The 1983 killing of 241 U.S. servicemen by a suicide bomber in Beirut, the subsequent kidnapping and murder of Americans by jihadist agents, and Libyan and Iraqi terror against American targets all underscored the fact that we faced identical enemies. Defeating them required the closest U.S.-Israeli cooperation. And that partnership proved vital not only to the security of the United States and Israel, but to the stability of the Middle East and regions beyond. Our alliance was beneficial to the world.

That view certainty was scarcely popular at Princeton, though. The mood on many American campuses had turned against Israel and even against America. This was the legacy of the sixties revolutionaries who briefly occupied those quads, denounced the West, and embraced those they considered downtrodden. But, having failed to export their concepts much beyond the universities, the radicals locked the gates behind them and became educators.

Their ideas found fullest expression in *Orientalism,* a book published in 1978 by Edward Said, a Columbia literary critic and spokesman for the Palestinian cause. Said denounced Middle East experts—the Orientalists—as "racist, imperialist, and almost totally ethnocentric," and accused them of abetting the region's conquest by the West. Only by identifying "wholeheartedly with the Arabs" and becoming "genuinely engaged and sympathetic . . . to the Islamic world" could these scholars redeem themselves. They had to shun traditional Middle East professors such as Bernard Lewis and reject Israel, which Said maligned as the ultimate Orientalist project.

Said's book became canonical in many Middle East Studies departments, pressuring students and professors to prove they were *not* Orientalists. Israel's history was subjected to withering revisionism.

Among Israel's most serious crimes, a self-styled school of new historians argued, was the "original sin"—a curiously Christian term—of expelling Palestinians during the 1948 War of Independence.

Still, the transformation of Israel's image was more than the product of just one generation of professors or even a single book. From the plucky David of the Six-Day War, Israel after the Lebanon War seemed to resemble a Goliath-like bully. Further challenging Israel's reputation was its construction in areas captured in 1967—in East Jerusalem and in the "territories" of the West Bank and Gaza. Much of the world denounced these new neighborhoods and settlements as illegitimate if not illegal, and blamed them for precipitating the Arab-Israeli conflict.

Such trends compelled me to stand my ground. I worked to expose Said's Orientalism screed, noting that the first experts on the Middle East came from Germany and Hungary, neither of which ever colonized the region. "By condemning [the West's] laudable curiosity about other cultures as imperialism," I wrote, "Said planted a sequoia of self-doubt in the innermost courtyard of academic inquiry."

Defending Israel's past, I acknowledged that the IDF indeed ordered many Palestinians to leave their homes in 1948, but reminded readers that the vast majority fled after failing to destroy the Jewish State. This was a war of national survival in which Israelis could not surrender, because most of those who did were butchered. In those areas of Palestine conquered by Arab forces, not a single Jew remained. By contrast, all of the Arabs who stayed in Israel—nearly 160,000—became citizens. They and their descendants now constituted 20 percent of Israel's population.

Similarly, I recognized that the Lebanon War had tarnished Israel's image but had not changed the reality of a Jewish state surrounded by vastly larger forces determined to destroy it. Some settlements, I admitted, were of questionable strategic and diplomatic value, but they were not the cause of the conflict. The Arabs fought Zionism for fifty years before the first Israeli settlers even broke ground. Hatred of Israel held the Arab states together between the 1948 and 1967 wars, both of which they launched to annihilate Israel. The terrorists, together with their Arab and Iranian state supporters, would still try to massacre us even if every settlement were removed.

I held firm but the academic atmosphere regarding Israel remained toxic. Once, during a visit by the ambassador of Syria's totalitarian regime, my department head, a retired State Department Arabist, exhorted me to refrain from posing difficult questions. Yet, when a spokesman for Israel's government came to campus, that same professor publicly excoriated him, "Sir, I pity you!" This paternalist treatment of the Arabs, denying them agency and responsibility as adults, disgusted me. So, too, did the tendency to single out Israel. Any liberal, democratic state could be criticized, of course, but never more so than its monarchical and tyrannical neighbors.

Still, Israel continued to draw fire, and not only from faculty members. The darling of the press after the Six-Day War, Israel by the 1980s was the focus of escalating media critiques. In addition to the Lebanon and settlement issues, news outlets faulted Israel for frustrating Palestinian aspirations. Subtly, the once-prevalent question "Why should terrorists target the Jewish State?" was supplanted by "What has Israel done to the Palestinians to drive them to such desperation?" And, propelled by the nightly news and the front page, this change in attitude penetrated one of the final bastions of unquestioning love for Israel. For the first time, prominent American Jews publicly disassociated themselves from the democratically approved policies of the Israeli government. A delegate of American Jewish intellectuals—one of my professors among them—met with a remorseless Yasser Arafat and branded him a man of peace.

The downturn in Israel's stature meant that I could no longer confine my counterarguments to Princeton. These had to be made on other campuses and before Jewish communities across the United States. I had to teach myself to speak passionately yet persuasively. Faltering at first, failing at moments that would still sting me years later, I learned that the most convincing speech emanated from the heart, avoided propaganda, and touched even the most flammable topics. "I want Israel to be the 'good guy,'" I told one audience, "but when I put on a uniform, I will do everything to protect us no matter how it looks in the press." American Jews, I said, had a duty to warn Israel "when a truck is bearing down on us," but added that "I'd think a hundred times before making the recommendations for Israel's future advanced by some of them." I spoke about the challenges facing the Jewish people as a whole. "In America, the problem is a scarcity of Jewish identity, while in Israel, the problem is a superabundance. I, for one, would rather deal with a superabundance."

Over time, the names and locations of these lectures became

blurred. Decades later, people would approach and flash a yellowed photograph of me attending some rally I embarrassingly no longer recalled. One occasion, though, stuck with me. On a frozen, wind-whipped football field in Yardley, Pennsylvania, under snapping Israeli flags, I waited for hours before alighting the bleachers and greeting a crowd of ten. My hands were too numb to hold my notes, so I spoke off the cuff about an Israel that remained worth fighting for and America's irreplaceable friend. I would remember that speech in future years while appearing in comfortably heated halls and addressing thousands. The memory kept me centered, reminding me of my journey's purpose.

Receiving postdoctoral fellowships from Tel Aviv University and Hebrew University, I returned to Israel in the mid-1980s. Later, I spent five years in the Negev desert, writing Israeli history at the Ben-Gurion Research Center at Sde Boker. Sally and I now had three children, all packed into a single bedroom at night, but during the day free to ride their bikes limitlessly in any direction. As a hobby, I rebuilt an old Willys jeep that ferried my family through the wadis and dunes, occasionally without breaking down.

The Lebanon War ground on and the economy staggered under 450 percent inflation. But this was also a time of miracles. Israel airlifted tens of thousands of Ethiopian Jews, and, following the collapse of Soviet communism, absorbed nearly one million Russian and Eastern European Jews. Freed from the gulag, Yehudit Nepunyache and the underground activists who so inspired me achieved their dream. Occasionally, I would encounter one of them in the middle of some Jerusalem street and we would just stand there, two Israelis, staring at each other wordlessly. Yuli "Yoel" Edelstein, the former street cleaner, eventually became Speaker of Israel's Knesset. After nine years of forced labor and solitary confinement, Prisoner of Zion Natan Sharansky became a free man in the Land of Zion and a minister in several Israeli governments.

These wonders went unnoticed by Israel's critics. On campuses they continue to accuse Israel of colonialism and ethnic cleansing, even genocide. Confronted with this onslaught, I could easily have stepped aside. Instead, I stood up for the state, both on the page and in the classroom. The objective was not to justify everything Israel did but to judge it fairly by rational standards. Yet pursuing even that modest goal left me isolated, often a lone voice in an increasingly one-sided harangue.

Perhaps I had never fully escaped my high school role of Don Quixote, the protector of outmoded causes. But Zionism, for me, was far from passé and Israel's enemies were no mere windmills. Unlike the Don, driven to an early death by his futile struggles, my quixotic efforts for Israel were enlivening. And the only cost I paid was professional. Publisher after publisher rejected my books, precluding an academic career. Though Sally never gave up on me as a writer, my closest friends urged me to show mercy on myself and find some other profession.

Dark Decade

Stymied in academia, I tried my hand at managing a major software company and ghostwriting for the legendary Israeli statesman Abba Eban. But the high-tech bubble burst and Eban tragically passed away. To pass the time while unemployed, I wrote several novels and a screenplay about Orde Wingate, the storied British general who pioneered modern guerrilla tactics during World War II and taught Israel's founders how to fight. The novels came painfully close to being published, and the screenplay, though twice optioned, never reached production. Barely able to support my family, for the first time I wondered if I could afford to remain in Israel.

Then, in 1992, Yitzhak Rabin was elected prime minister. The man who had motivated me as a teenager to follow in his ambassadorial footsteps now inspired me with his leadership and his principled vision of peace.

That vision appeared near realization a year later, when President Bill Clinton embraced Rabin and Yasser Arafat on the White House lawn. The Oslo peace process, named after the city where it was secretly negotiated, called for staged Israeli withdrawals from the territories and the creation of an autonomous Palestinian Authority. Though not spelled out in the accords, the process would presumably culminate in the emergence of a Palestinian state living side by side with Israel. A century of bitter conflict would end.

The Oslo process sparked both optimism and fear in Israel. On the night of the signing ceremony, I stood atop an office building in downtown Jerusalem. From there, I could see the city's Arab areas sparkling with holiday lights while the Jewish neighborhoods remained darkened. I, too, was skeptical of a rapidly reached peace, and not only because of Arafat's bloody past. Lacking stable institutions and farsighted leaders, the Palestinians seemed unlikely to maintain a cohesive state or a long-term peace with Israel. Their identity was heavily dependent on rejecting ours. True reconciliation, rather, would take many years, perhaps generations, to achieve—much as it did among Germany, Great Britain, and France.

Yet, still, I supported the process. Even if we could not immediately achieve peace, we were morally bound to lay its foundations. We had to convince the world and, more importantly, our own children, that Israel had done its utmost to avoid confrontation. Hundreds of thousands of Russian and Ethiopian Jews were arriving in Israel, and absorbing them required beating some swords into plowshares. So, too, did transforming our economy, long girded for war, into a global, high-tech contender. And while the Land of Israel—including the West Bank—remained our birthright, sustaining it came at a rising international price.

Moreover, I believed in Rabin. Having obtained an invitation to the signing of the Israel-Jordan peace treaty in Israel's Aravah desert in October 1994, I watched as the prime minister and King Hussein warmly clasped hands. Hundreds of white doves and thousands of balloons in the signatories' national colors were released over the rugged, tawny terrain. Upward they soared toward clouds pierced by a rainbow that, just at that moment, bridged both sides of the border.

The realization of Israeli-Jordanian peace coincided with the fulfillment of my dream of working for Rabin. I secured a job in the Prime Minister's Office, as Advisor on Inter-Religious Affairs. I did not report directly to Rabin, though I often encountered him in meetings and passed him in the halls. Sometimes I would shake his hand, amazed that this was the same lax grip that so seized me thirty years before and fixed my life's direction.

Back then, when still in high school, my interest in ancient Israel led me to ask a local Baptist minister—Pastor Miller—for lessons in the New Testament. The one condition was that he teach me the Gospel solely as Jewish history and not try to proselytize me. The sessions with the young pastor were enlightening, but none of them prepared me for the labyrinthine task of liaising with Israel's Christian communities. Dozens of churches competed over holy spaces, even over procession time during holidays. The Catholic and Orthodox clergy often shunned their Protestant counterparts, but also jostled with one another. In one macabre case, a Russian Orthodox priest murdered a nun from a competing order. Israel, though, afforded Christians freedom and security rarely enjoyed by their coreligionists elsewhere in the region. And they had access to a neutral intermediary—ironically, a Jew raised in New Jersey.

In addition to churches, my job description also included mosque affairs and brought me into contact with many Muslims. Sensitized to their views, I became more convinced of the need to take small but concrete steps toward reconciliation. One such step took place on August 21, 1995, when I supervised the first-ever pilgrimage of Israeli Muslims to Mecca. As the buses trundled over the Allenby Bridge to Jordan, news arrived of another first. A Palestinian bomber had blown himself up inside a Jerusalem bus, killing several people. Next came an anxious call from Sally. Her sister, Joanie, was missing.

Unlike her parents and three sisters, Joanie did not make *aliya*. She remained a dedicated teacher at a Jewish school near New Haven, Connecticut. Receiving a one-year scholarship to Hebrew University in 1995, she moved to Jerusalem and commuted each morning to the Mount Scopus campus. But that day her bus never completed its route. After frenetic hours of combing emergency rooms, Sally's family and I were taken to the national morgue. Having seen so much death in Lebanon, I insisted on making the identification. She had died instantly, I saw with some solace, and then went out to inform my wife and in-laws of the excruciating news. Israel granted a state funeral for Joanie and a pension to her daughter, Maya. Each year, when gathering around the grave site in Jerusalem, we still find thank-you notes from the students whose lives Joanie enriched.

The suicide bombings multiplied, stoking opposition to the Oslo process. Rabin's twin platforms of peace and security grew violently incompatible. Outside the Prime Minister's Office, protesters bombarded us with tomatoes. Posters depicting Israeli leaders in Arab kaffiyehs, even SS uniforms, proliferated. "They're going to assassinate someone," I told Sally, suggesting Foreign Minister Shimon Peres as a likely target. I could not conceive of anybody harming Rabin.

On the evening of November 4, Rabin penned a condolence letter—his second—to Sally's parents. It remained on the prime minister's desk, though, unsigned, as he left to attend a peace rally in Tel Aviv. After leading the crowd in a classic Hebrew peace song, he descended the rostrum and was shot to death by a radical right-wing opponent of the peace process.

The next night, I joined with hundreds of thousands of mourners filing before Rabin's casket, displayed outside the Knesset. Countless memorial candles fought back the darkness, but my dream of Israel dimmed. We had survived wars and surmounted towering challenges, I knew, but could we overcome the prime minister's murder by an Israeli Jew? More than any other national trauma, Rabin's assassination cast doubts over the state's raison d'être. The life that embodied Israel's luminous story had been extinguished.

Two thousand years before, while a Roman legion besieged Jerusalem, the Jews inside the city fought one another. That hatred, the Talmud taught us, rather than the Romans' torches, destroyed the Second Temple. Rabin's assassination threatened to ignite yet another internecine inferno, I feared, and consume our modern state.

Six Days Re-created

The need I felt to regain a sense of Israeli unity brought me back to June 1967—the Six-Day War—the moment Israelis stood most indivisibly together. The declassification of formerly secret diplomatic files from the period afforded fresh and unprecedentedly detailed insights into the war and its origins. And the need for such a perspective was urgent. The same revisionist historians who previously condemned Israel's "original sin" of 1948 now claimed that Israel precipitated the 1967 war in order to expand territorially. I set out to preempt that assault and received the backing of the Shalem Center, a dynamic research institute founded in Jerusalem by several Princeton graduates. "Great wars in history invariably become great wars of history," I wrote, and launched a four-year research campaign across four continents.

In libraries in Washington, London, Paris, and Moscow, I pored over official cables never before viewed by historians. I interviewed major players from the period, among them U.S. defense secretary Robert McNamara and White House advisors Eugene and Walter Rostow, senior Israeli and Arab commanders, even the former head of the KGB's Middle East desk. I secured access to private archives in

Cairo and Amman, and, with the help of Arab middlemen, discreetly purchased Syria's war records.

The sources showed me that, in 1967, Nasser again threatened America's friends in the Middle East and clamored for Israel's destruction. Most of his attacks were merely rhetorical, though, and not intended to trigger war. But they created a combustible atmosphere in which mere border flare-ups eventually ignited a regional conflagration.

Shorn of allies, short on basic commodities and ammunition, Israel did not anticipate the war, much less provoke it. Levi Eshkol, Israel's owlish prime minister at the time, did everything he could to prevent hostilities and stood up to the generals who insisted on attacking immediately. No, Eshkol responded, Israel must first exhaust all possible diplomatic options. By proving beyond a doubt that the Arabs could not be mollified, he succeeded in convincing Israelis—and the world—that Israel had no choice but to fight.

Beginning on June 5, Israel fought for six days and gained one of the greatest triumphs in military history, expanding territorially nearly fourfold. The victory eventually brought peace with Egypt and Jordan but also unending conflict with the Palestinians. And the war had another, fateful, outcome. American leaders who previously balked at aiding the Jewish State suddenly saw it as a crucial Cold War asset in a region vital to America's security. So arose the U.S.-Israel strategic alliance. Six years later, during the Yom Kippur War, President Richard Nixon—whose private tapes were riddled with anti-Semitic slurs—ordered the airlift of game-changing armaments to Israel. Later, America fortified Israel with billions of dollars' worth of military aid, enhanced its tactical and intelligence capabilities, and defended it diplomatically.

One has to work hard to dull the drama of the Six-Day War, which ranks among history's most spellbinding epics. Taking the advice of Roger Hertog, head of the Shalem Center board, that "people love to read about heroes," I focused on the roles of Eshkol, Dayan, Abba Eban, and even Nasser. I wrote furiously, reliving from the inside the saga that, as a kid, I could only watch on TV. The concluding chapter was nearly complete when the ultimate thunderbolt struck.

Major Steve White, a U.S. Marine friend at the American embassy, called to inform me that a civilian airliner had just struck one of the World Trade Center towers in New York and that it looked like a terrorist attack. Less than a half hour later, Steve called back and said that the second tower had just been hit in the same way and certainly by terrorists. I was, of course, shocked, but then even more horrified when I remembered that our eighteen-year-old son, Yoav, was on a pre-army trip to lower Manhattan. That very day, he and several Israeli friends had agreed to meet on the center's roof. The international phone lines collapsed and it took hours to reach him—safe but severely shaken. His rendezvous was set for 11:30 A.M., by which time both towers had collapsed. Instead, he photographed the massacre from a Brooklyn rooftop. I told him to go down into the basement—who knew how and when the terrorists would strike next—and not come out until the confusion cleared.

The trauma of that September 11 day would remain with me always. The twin skyscrapers that as a youth I glimpsed from a ridge in my hometown, and later wandered awestruck as a New York student, had vanished. So had the lives of nearly three thousand innocent civilians and the sense that America—unlike Israel—was beyond the terrorists' reach.

The viscous cloud raised by the towers' destruction might have obscured the events that occurred in the Middle East in 1967, but in fact it highlighted their relevance. About to embark on Middle Eastern wars, Americans were ravenous for background. After decades of receiving only rejection notices, I could scarcely believe that the prestigious Oxford University Press agreed to publish my manuscript. Never in my dreams did I imagine that *Six Days of War: June 1967 and the Making of the Modern Middle East,* as I titled it, would sell out in a week.

The book was a life-changer. For the first time, Sally and I were able to buy a car that was not thirdhand and to give our three children rooms of their own. Overnight, I became a commentator on news programs, a frequent op-ed contributor, and a guest on *The Daily Show* and *Charlie Rose.* The lecturer once snubbed by academia was now a visiting professor at Yale and Harvard. And the editors who once rejected me with form letters now published two of my novels—*Sand Devil* and *Reunion*—and inquired about my next work of history.

Throughout this period, the trials and the successes, I remained an Israeli. I thrilled at the mass *aliya* from Ethiopia and the former Soviet Union, and watched as the once-agrarian state astonishingly evolved into a science and high-tech hub. I followed the strengthening of our alliance with the United States. Through successive presidents, in spite of continuing differences over the settlement and Jerusalem issues, the ties further burgeoned, advancing seamlessly from Cold War challenges to the war on terror. I remained the proud holder of two passports, but only one uniform. I wrote largely for an American audience, but fought for Israel's people.

Firing Line

My life was indeed double, divided not only between Israel and the United States but also between the literary and the military. Serving in the reserves in the 1980s and '90s meant protracted stints patrolling the wind-lashed hills of South Lebanon and trading fire with the Iranian-backed terrorists of Hezbollah. I saw fine Israeli soldiers, veterans of elite units, break from the physical and psychological strain. There was one phone per firebase, placed atop a sandbagged trench from where I could see incoming rockets. "Hold on," I would say to Sally, "I need to duck." Returning home, I experienced the sense of disconnect that affects so many combat veterans. How can people sit in cafés—I'd ask myself—shop for shoes, argue over parking spaces, when there's a war going on? How could I be one moment playing with my children in the living room and then drive only a few hours to a bunker where total strangers tried to shoot me?

The Lebanon war dragged on, but for me and many Israeli reservists the terrain changed in 1987 when the Palestinians in the territories rose in revolt. The Intifada—Arabic for "shaking off"—saw crowds of Palestinian youths hurling rocks and Molotov cocktails at Israeli troops. Leading squads down fetid Gaza alleyways or through the lightless casbah of Nablus, I became a target for concrete blocks dropped from rooftops, slingshotted steel balls, and, once, even a grenade. These assaults only steeled my conviction that the status quo in the territories had to change.

By the summer of 1990, the Intifada was sputtering out when, suddenly, Iraqi forces under Saddam Hussein occupied Kuwait. A U.S.-led coalition expelled the invaders, spurring Saddam to fire Scud missiles—some rumored to have chemical warheads—at Israel. The IDF prepared to fight back, but, at America's request, held its fire in order to appease the coalition's Arab members. Instead, the U.S. and

Israeli militaries joined in an unprecedented effort to defend the Jewish State. My role was to sit with U.S. Navy pilots in a bunker beneath the Kiriyah—Israel's Pentagon—and monitor the search for Scud launchers in the Iraqi desert. When the sirens whined, we all put on our gas masks and waited for the impact. Serving shoulder-to-shoulder with these airmen gave me a deep sense of fulfillment. We were fighting the same enemy, upholding identical ideals. There, in the bunker while the sirens outside wailed, I saw the alliance at work. And I saw it later, too, when I helped bring in U.S. Patriot missile batteries to shield Israel against the Scuds. In their first encounter with American soldiers, Israelis nearly buried those Patriot crews beneath mounds of flowers and cakes.

Despite its perils, army service still offered the opportunity to live a soldier's life, protect the country, and escape my writer's solitude. With the new century, though, I reached mandatory retirement age from the reserves. By that time I had become active in media and the IDF suggested that I sign on as a spokesman. "Why not," I figured, picking up the pen I thought would replace the sword. Who could have guessed that the post would prove no less hazardous?

The dangers became apparent in September 2000 as a Black Hawk helicopter transported me and my combat gear across the West Bank. The previous night, I looked out from our Jerusalem balcony and saw crimson fireworks bursting over the West Bank. Arafat had recently met with President Clinton and Israeli prime minister Ehud Barak at Camp David and turned down their offer of Palestinian statehood in Gaza, virtually all of the West Bank, and half of Jerusalem. The Palestinians were now celebrating the failure of peace. "Sally," I called from the balcony, "I think we're in trouble."

The depth of that trouble, though, was as yet unimaginable. After opposition leader Ariel Sharon visited Jerusalem's Temple Mount, holy to both Jews and Muslims, the Palestinians rioted. Rather than curbing the disturbances, though, Arafat and other Palestinian leaders exploited them to mount a Second Intifada. Ambushes and suicide bombers eventually killed a thousand Israelis, eight of them in the restaurant right under my office. And I was called up to serve as a spokesman for the Israeli brigade fighting in the northern West Bank.

The Black Hawk landed in the middle of a vicious firefight, soldiers scrambling in all directions. The brigade commander—unfazed by the enemy bullet lodged in his helmet—ran toward me, shouting above the din, "You're supposed to be dead!" Two other reservists who reported to my base had made a wrong turn into a Palestinian crowd that beat them to death and mutilated their bodies. The army assumed I was one of them.

That evening, the brigade commander took me to a ramshackle settlement—a trailer park—perched on a desolate hilltop. Suddenly, a pregnant Jewish woman came running toward our jeep, arms flailing. The IDF guards had disappeared, she screamed, and the settlers, including her husband, had gone looking for them. Hundreds of women and children from other settlements awaited us back at the base, protesting the army's alleged failure to defend them.

I ended the night hunched with the brigade commander in a sandbagged mountain position as an IDF gunship fired bursts into terrorist positions below. Palestinian gunmen shot back—not at the helicopter but at us. Tracer bullets, like some angry code, pulsed over our heads.

If the First Intifada was not sufficiently convincing, the Second thoroughly persuaded me that Israel had to change the status quo in the territories. Yes, these were our tribal lands. The Bible speaks of the West Bank cities Bethlehem, Shiloh, and Hebron, not of Tel Aviv or Haifa. And many of the settlements helped thicken our pre-1967 lines, which were as narrow as nine miles across. But Israel had to weigh its historic rights and security needs against the moral and political costs of dominating another people. It had to reconcile its real fears of the West Bank becoming a terrorist haven similar to South Lebanon, with its need to preserve its right to defend itself and its international legitimacy as a sovereign Jewish state.

That same calculation apparently preoccupied Prime Minister Ariel Sharon. Shortly after Israel prevailed over the Intifada's terror, in August 2005, Sharon ordered that Israel would uproot all its military bases and civilian settlements in Gaza. The operation, Israel's largest since the Yom Kippur War, involved fifty-five thousand troops, an elite corps of which was assigned to evacuate some nine thousand settlers. Accompanying that corps, I filed through blazing barricades only to be met by children dressed as concentration camp prisoners and denouncing us as Nazis. Women cursed and spat at us. Men bolted themselves into synagogues from which they had to be hauled, wailing. From such a synagogue, I carried a Torah-bearing rabbi, Menachem Froman, famous for his attempts to forge peace with Palestinian imams. Caught by cameras, the image of my face—as white as the rabbi's skullcap—flashed globally.

More than any war, the Disengagement from Gaza scarred me. While recoiling from the extremism displayed by some of the settlers, I mourned the memory of Jews dragging Jews from their homes. Israel should not return to Gaza, I felt, but neither could it ignore the hundreds of rockets that Hamas—the Palestinian branch of the Muslim Brotherhood—and other terrorist groups proceeded to fire at southern Israeli towns. Israel's reluctance to retaliate for those atrocities emboldened the terrorists. Exploiting a truce to tunnel under the border, Hamas gunmen killed two Israeli soldiers and kidnapped a third, Corporal Gilad Shalit.

Israel's failure to deter Hamas also bolstered Hezbollah in Lebanon. There, too, a hasty Israeli withdrawal—in May 2000—encouraged the terrorists to seize control of the area and launch attacks against northern Galilee. On July 12, 2006, Hezbollah gunmen ambushed an Israeli border patrol and then battered northern Israel with missiles. Thousands of Israelis fled south, among them close Arab friends of ours who took shelter in our Jerusalem home. Meanwhile, the IDF reacted massively, with ground operations and air strikes, in what Israelis later dubbed the Second Lebanon War.

Years of conducting SWAT-like arrests in the West Bank had rendered the IDF unprepared for large-scale fighting in Lebanon. I received a rifle that fell apart in my hands and had to pilfer a helmet and flak jacket. No instructions arrived from headquarters, leaving our small group of officers to work throughout the night devising press messages on our own. Luckily, we were joined by Dan Gordon, an IDF veteran and screenwriter of blockbusters such as *The Hurricane*. At the first report of war, Dan abandoned cozy Hollywood, got on a plane, and again risked his life for Israel. In a dinky rental car, Dan and I crisscrossed the front, briefing journalists and dodging Katyusha rockets. One of the missiles hit just up the road from our base and killed twelve reservists. Another struck on the far side of a tree where Dan had stopped to relieve himself. Shrapnel peppered the trunk but left Dan unscathed and relieved indeed.

Between assignments, I dashed off to Haifa's Rambam Hospital, where my daughter, Lia, was serving as a medical social worker with the Golani Brigade, which took the brunt of the IDF's casualties. Almost a replica of her mother—freckled, hazel-eyed, whimsically self-effacing—Lia was overwhelmed by the influx of wounded. She cried in my arms but then, just as another ambulance arrived, she pulled away and ran, utterly composed, to meet the stretchers.

Finally, international pressure produced a cease-fire, but before it could go into effect, Israel mounted an offensive. The objective was to enhance the IDF's ground position, but the operation only brought us additional censure from abroad and more than thirty military funerals. Just before dawn, on a crater-pocked Lebanese road with flares streaming tearlike down the sky, Dan Gordon and I encountered a squad of Israeli commandos. Weighed down by their weapons and their faces grimy with fatigue, they nevertheless advanced unfalteringly, still determined to fight. Gazing at them, I thought, "You deserve better." Israel could never again be unprepared.

At the conclusion of thirty-four days of combat and 165 Israeli fatalities, with Hezbollah unbowed and world opinion deploring us for displacing thousands of Lebanese, the Second Lebanon War seemed even more ill-conceived than the first. Returning dejected to our base after the cease-fire, I ran into Natan Sharansky. Short but pugnacious, he had quit the Israeli government in protest over the Gaza withdrawal and joined the Shalem Center. There we endlessly debated the Disengagement. The former Prisoner of Zion insisted that Israel's departure from Gaza strengthened the terrorists, while I countered that it also strengthened our case against them. Now, looking up at my bedraggled uniform, Sharansky grinned and asked, "Do you still think the Disengagement was a good idea?"

The answer was both yes and no. Israel could settle those parts of the territories vital to its defense but not those containing large numbers of Palestinians. Yet Israel could not abandon areas from which terrorists could shell our biggest cities and industrial centers. While uncomfortable with the word *occupation*—a people cannot occupy its own homeland—Israel, I believed, needed to preserve its democratic and Jewish character. Consequently, Israel needed to establish a reality in which the maximum number of Jews would live within Israel and the Palestinians would not be under our rule. We needed to define borders Israel could defend.

Speaking for the IDF sharpened not only my political thinking but also my media skills. Reserve service prepared me to handle hostile questions and enabled me to log hundreds of interview hours under the most stressful conditions. I worked with some of the world's foremost correspondents. Among them was John Roberts, then of CNN and later with Fox, oblivious to fire as he reported from the Lebanese front, and Anderson Cooper calmly broadcasting as 155 mm cannons blasted around his ears. Ann Curry of the *Today* show once came to our house to film a segment on "The Oren Family at War." Jeffrey Goldberg, a good friend and fellow IDF veteran who reported for *The New Yorker*, never tired of reminding me of the Israeli commander who jokingly asked whether the journalists I escorted were anti-Semites. "No," I replied matter-of-factly. "They're NBC."

An American Legacy

At the conclusion of each crisis, I came home, exchanged my fatigues for office clothes, and returned to writing. Success, I discovered, could be as harrowing as rejection, as people wondered whether my next book would rival *Six Days of War* or if I was merely a "one-trick pony." My friends suggested I write a slim volume on a narrow topic—a single battle, say. Instead, I decided on a sweeping survey of more than two hundred years of history.

The idea first occurred to me in graduate school, when I heard about a troop of Civil War veterans who served in the Egyptian army and introduced Arab officers to American notions of patriotism and democracy. Their story surprised me since I subscribed to the widespread notion that America's interest in the Middle East began after World War II, when the United States became dependent on Arab oil. But the presence of Rebs and Yanks on the Nile in the late 1860s suggested that American involvement in the region began much earlier, and was far more nuanced.

Now, with the United States so critically engaged in the area, I felt that Americans needed a sense of this legacy. So when an editor friend of mine, Bob Weil, asked me at dinner, "What is the one book about the Middle East that needs to be written but hasn't?" I answered unhesitatingly, and scribbled a table of contents on my napkin.

That serviette signaled the beginning of another four-year period of negligible sleep and limitless fascination. I read about how the United States waged its first foreign war against the Barbary Pirates of Libya, Tunisia, and Morocco, and built its first overseas universities in Istanbul, Cairo, and Beirut. I learned that the Arabs were once dependent on *American* oil. The Middle East, for its part, influenced the making of the Constitution, fired the imaginations of authors such as Mark Twain and Herman Melville, and inspired freedom fighters from Frederick Douglass to John F. Kennedy. I recorded the single best American insight into the Middle East—by former Union Army General-in-Chief George McClellan, who in 1874 warned that the United States would never understand its peoples "so long as we judge them by the rules we are accustomed to apply to ourselves."

The most startling revelation of all, though, was the essential tie between the idea of America and the concept of a Jewish state. Indeed, in the minds of many early Americans, the two were indivisible. Regarding themselves as the "New Israel" in a new promised land, the Founders' generation—Christians all—felt a powerful responsibility for restoring the Old Israel to the original Promised Land. "I really wish the Jews in Judea an independent nation," John Adams, America's second president, professed. Discovery of this "restorationist" strand in mainstream American thinking came as a shock to me, and a deep source of gratification. I felt as if Adams was validating a belief that quietly guided my life. Beyond their common strategic interests, Israel and the United States were spiritually and morally bound. That conviction could be traced back to many American leaders, not only Adams. At the height of the Civil War, Abraham Lincoln pledged that he, too, would work to restore the Jews to their homeland once America was reunited.

These findings were compressed into six hundred pages—and another hundred of notes—in a volume I titled, *Power, Faith, and Fantasy: America in the Middle East from 1776 to the Present*. Like *Six Days of War* before it, I strove to make the text accessible to all readers. They could learn about the Middle Eastern roots of "The Star-Spangled Banner" and the American roots of Arab nationalism. They could trace Hollywood's romance with desert sheikhs to Washington's occasional—and almost always unfortunate—fascination with Arab rulers. They could see images of America's oldest war memorial, to the U.S. sailors killed by Libyan pirates in 1805, and the original Statue of Liberty, commissioned by Egypt, which featured a veiled Arab woman holding a torch. The gallery concluded with a horrific view of the twin towers' collapse, with credit given to the photographer, Yoav Oren, the author's son.

Despite its heft, *Power, Faith, and Fantasy* became an instant bestseller. The year was 2006 and Americans were still embroiled in two painful Middle Eastern wars, with no end in sight for either of them.

The book gave some meaning to this dolor by placing it in an historical context. Starting with George Washington, American leaders were always torn between their need to preserve economic and strategic interests in the Middle East and their urge to seed it with American ideas. And while the United States saw its task as enlightening Middle Easterners, the peoples of the area considered Americans infidels and interlopers. Negotiating with a representative of the Libyan pirates in 1786, Thomas Jefferson was told that the Quran commanded the destruction of all nonbelievers, Americans included. And yet, when President Thomas Jefferson later made war on Libya, he dreamed of transforming it into a democracy.

Because it determined that America had done more good than harm in the Middle East, *Power, Faith, and Fantasy* was sometimes portrayed as a conservative book. In truth, my politics were difficult to pigeonhole. Early in the Iraq War, I told a congressional subcommittee that the American invasion would speed the spread of Iranian influence westward to Jordan and the West Bank. I further predicted that Americans could not employ the savagery needed to keep Iraq together and, like the British before them, would soon lose their stomach for it and leave. "Strike back at terror," I told the legislators, "but do not get involved in Middle East state-making."

My opposition to the Iraq War should have alienated me from the Bush administration. Instead, Secretary of State Condoleezza Rice was reportedly "curling up" with my book at night and urging the press corps to read it. Vice President Dick Cheney invited me to discuss Middle East matters at the White House and to brief the president's staff. Then, in May 2008, George W. Bush selected me to be the only Israeli-American delegate on his first official visit to Israel.

At all-time depths in the American polls, Bush's popularity soared in Israel. "Israel's population may be just 7 million," the president told a cheering Knesset on the eve of Israel's sixtieth anniversary. "But when you confront terror and evil, you are 307 million strong, because the United States of America stands with you."

As part of the delegation, I was invited to give a lecture aboard the aircraft carrier *Truman,* cruising somewhere in the Eastern Mediterranean. Two hours after taking off from Ben-Gurion Airport, the U.S. Navy transporter landed on the flight deck with an eyeball-catapulting jolt. But, as the cargo door lowered, the scene that unfolded was dazzling. Here, in the middle of the sea, with seventy warplanes and a crew of more than five thousand, rose an island of American might. Emblazed on the bridge, a quote associated with the thirty-third president said it all: GIVE 'EM HELL.

That night, I dined with Captain Herm Shelanski, the Truman's Jewish skipper. Herm showed me the ship's chapel, containing one of the Torah scrolls confiscated by the Nazis for their "extinct Jewish people" museum. Nearby, an exhibit about Harry Truman recalled how the president ignored the advice of all his counselors who opposed Zionism. Eleven minutes after Israel's creation on May 14, 1948, Truman made America the first nation on earth to recognize the nascent Jewish State.

As during the 1991 Gulf War, I felt the pride of liaising with U.S. forces, of sharing a common purpose. Though separated by seven thousand miles of sea, the United States and Israel were intrinsically linked. Defending the same values, we confronted similar threats, from Soviet communism to Saddam Hussein and jihadist terror. Of course, the interests of no two countries can ever be entirely confluent, especially not those of a superpower and a tiny Middle Eastern state. But then again, no two countries had more in common spiritually, ideologically, and strategically. And the fact that Americans and Israelis were willing to fight for their ideals placed us in a slimmer category yet, even among Western nations.

I saw the uniqueness of the relationship aboard the USS *Truman*. I saw it in the sailors from rural towns and inner cities who gathered for a Holocaust memorial ceremony belowdecks, and heard it in the earnest questions they asked me about life in Israel. They listened raptly to my lecture about the history of America in the Middle East, and about the legacy of American support for Jewish statehood.

Anti-Semitism indeed plagued my youth and anti-Israel agitation later confronted me on American campuses. I forgot none of that. But neither could I undervalue the warmth and admiration that the overwhelming majority of Americans, including the *Truman*'s crew, held for Israel. When we looked at one another, those sailors and I, we saw a familiar reflection. I thought to myself, *brit*—covenant. They thought: ally.

Hope, Change, War

Never linear for me, life after Bush's 2008 Israel visit zigzagged. I went on a speaking tour in the United States just as the presidential race got under way and met the Republican front-runner, John McCain. He approached me after one of my speeches, offered me a ride to the train station, and, rather than doze, regaled me with war stories. In Congress, a brash and bantam representative named Rahm Emanuel invited me to update him on Middle East issues. Rahm—a Hebrew name meaning "lofty"—the son of a veteran of Israel's independence war, was passionate about the Jewish State but censorious of its settlement policy. Basically, Rahm briefed *me*, but we established an enduring friendship.

Nationally, Hillary Clinton was leading the Democratic pack. Closing in behind her, though, was a young Illinois senator as renowned for his eloquence as for the singularity of his name. Moreover, Barack Obama's campaign was infused with a spiritual zeal. The first time I saw a bumper sticker with his image haloed and adorned with the word *Hope,* I immediately called Sally and told her, "It's messianic."

The longing for that hope as well as for change lured millions to hear Obama's speeches, at once earthy and soaring. The possibility of electing the first black president captivated a great many Americans, but some Israelis looked on confused. Accustomed to leaders like McCain, crusty old soldiers and seasoned pols, they could not understand why Americans would choose a candidate lacking in any military, administrative, or foreign policy experience. Overweight, short, bald, or bespectacled candidates stand little chance in a U.S. presidential election, but Israelis readily voted for portly Ariel Sharon, diminutive Ehud Barak, and Menachem Begin, who was both follically and visually challenged. Americans prefer their presidents to be eloquent, attractive, and preferably strong-jawed. Such qualities, in the life-and-death stakes of Israel, are irrelevant.

But Israeli political preferences were alien to most Americans, even to American Jews, nearly 80 percent of whom supported Obama. My own family members back in the States bedecked themselves with Obama pins and even slept in Obama pajamas. Some Jews, though, were troubled. They pointed to Obama's twenty-year association with Jeremiah Wright, the Chicago minister who accused Israel of ethnically cleansing the Palestinians and of provoking the 9/11 attacks. After taking the title of his career-making book, *The Audacity of Hope,* from one of Wright's sermons, Obama disassociated himself from the pastor and eventually quit Wright's church.

Still, some of the uneasiness lingered and raised questions in my own mind as well. Curious about this cipherlike candidate, I accepted an assignment from a security affairs journal to write about Obama's views on Israel and the Middle East. I culled all of his statements on the subject, his interviews and speeches. My findings, though I could not foresee it at the time, helped ensure that the future president would rarely surprise me.

With remarkable candor, Obama revealed his opposition to Israeli settlement building and his support for Palestinian rights. "Obama might be expected to show deeper sympathy for the Palestinian demand for a capital in Jerusalem," I surmised, "and greater flexibility in including Hamas in negotiations." The Democratic candidate seemed to regard the Arab-Israeli conflict as a root of Middle Eastern disputes and Arab-Israel peace as the key to regional stability. Calling for "less saber-rattling and more direct diplomacy," he pledged to engage with Syria and Iran. At the same time, Obama consistently stressed his admiration for Israel and his commitment to its security. But he never masked his discomfort with the Israeli right wing as epitomized by the Likud party, which, though at the time in opposition, had long dominated Israeli politics. "There is a strain within the pro-Israel community that says unless you adopt an unwavering pro-Likud approach to Israel, then you're anti-Israel," Obama said, indicating his preference for Israeli parties to the left of Likud.

Prophecy was not required to foresee that an Obama presidency might strain the U.S.-Israel alliance, "especially," I wrote, "if Netanyahu and the Likud return to power." Even then, I urged pro-Israel voters to focus less on the candidates' policies than on their capacity for leadership. Political upheaval in the Middle East, civil strife, and Iran's accelerating nuclear program—these challenges, and not Israel, would determine the course of American decision making. "Israel is best served by a president capable of grappling with rapid and often turbulent change."

• • •

But most Americans were not focused on the Middle East. They were writhing under the worst economic depression since the 1930s, with millions out of work and left penniless. They wrestled through a brutal presidential contest rife with race issues and conspiracy theories. This was the America, glum and polarized, I encountered that fall as I began a sabbatical year at Georgetown University in Washington.

Despite my frequent visits, I had not lived in the United States for nearly two decades and found the country significantly altered. The mostly middle-class, white, and Protestant-dominated society I remembered had been largely replaced by a more financially strapped, multiracial, and religiously diverse population. Once right of center, America now leaned leftward. I felt like Rip Van Winkle of the old Dutch American folk tale, who wakes up from a twenty-year nap and can barely recognize his own village.

Obama personified these changes and cloaked them in virtuous mystique. To the unemployed crowding the corners of gentrified Georgetown, to the students facing uncertain futures, and the families of soldiers serially deployed overseas, he offered more transformations still. His declarations of "Yes we can!" belied the out-of-business signs I saw in the store windows near campus. On the rainy evening of November 2, I ducked into a Washington bar to hear the newly elected president address a quarter of a million euphoric supporters in Chicago. "Change has come to America," Obama proclaimed. "America, I have never been more hopeful." I watched as all the customers in that bar stood at attention, tears streaming down their cheeks.

That radiant moment was soon eclipsed by plumes of white phosphorous. While planning our winter break on some silken Caribbean beach, Sally reflexively said, "No, let's go home and visit the kids." That was how, in the last week of 2008, I found myself back in Israel and once again at war.

The fighting broke out in Gaza, though its origins could be traced to Ramallah in the West Bank, the seat of the Palestinian Authority. Since Arafat's death four years earlier, Mahmoud Abbas had presided over both the Authority and the PLO. In contrast to his predecessor, he opposed violence and declared his support for negotiations. Yet, despite his credibility as one of Fatah's earliest members and the international legitimacy he gained as a man of peace, the seventy-three-year-old Abbas—familiarly known as Abu Mazen—was unpopular among his own people. They tired of Fatah's corruption and despaired of a diplomatic breakthrough. When, in 2006, the Palestinians went to the polls, a majority voted for Hamas, the terrorist group that the Bush administration insisted on including on the ballot. Abbas, though, refused to accept the outcome, prompting a Hamas uprising. He managed to hold on to the West Bank, but in Gaza, Hamas gunmen hurled Fatah loyalists from rooftops and shot them in the streets. Israel, in response, blockaded Gaza, and Hamas intensified its rocket fire.

Israel paid an immense price for supporting Abbas, but he responded by turning his back on peace. In September 2008, Prime Minister Ehud Olmert offered to create a Palestinian state in Gaza, almost all of the West Bank, and half of Jerusalem. The plan gained the support of the Quartet, the consortium created by President Bush and composed of the United States, Russia, the European Union, and the United Nations. But Abbas never bothered to respond.

By December, with Hamas rockets pummeling the country's southern half, a million Israelis were dashing for bomb shelters. Among them was our daughter, Lia, an undergraduate at Ben-Gurion University in Beersheba. Olmert and his foreign minister, Tzipi Livni, practically begged for a truce. Yet the missiles and mortars kept striking—eighty-seven of them on the twenty-fourth, alone, the day our plane landed in Israel. Seventy-two hours later, Israel launched a counteroffensive against Gaza and I again reverted from Professor Oren to Major Oren, IDF spokesman.

Code-named Cast Lead—a reference to a hymn sung that Hanukkah week—the operation aimed at restoring peace to southern Israel. But bringing quiet meant silencing the Hamas positions embedded among Palestinian civilians. As in the Second Lebanon War, when Hezbollah pulled bodies from old graves and inflated the number of civilian casualties, Hamas accused Israel of committing numerous atrocities, including the killing of fifty children at a UN school. The media reported these fictions, often uncritically, generating international pressure on Israel to submit to a Security Council cease-fire.

The spokesman's role was to bustle between journalists confined to a hillside overlooking the battles. Armed and helmeted, I interviewed throughout the night, with machine-gun fire for background. Once, while producers from an Arab news agency pinned a microphone to my ceramic vest, the rocket-alert siren sounded, meaning we had exactly fourteen seconds to take cover. I shouted at the producers, "Leave it, run!" and dragging sound equipment behind me, sprinted after them into a building site. We huddled together in the dust until the rocket exploded nearby and then, in a moment of coexistence, wished one another "mabruk" and "mazal tov."

Far less heartwarming was the chronic trauma suffered by the residents of Sderot, the Israeli border town pounded for years by many thousands of missiles. A young woman standing next to me in the shelter as the siren howled pulled at her hair and screamed uncontrollably. She kept on screaming, even after the blast.

I left Gaza for Georgetown in the first week of 2009, arriving in the same disoriented state as when I departed Beirut for Princeton more than a quarter century before. The campus atmosphere was similarly poisonous and, entering my building, I had to step over supine protesters with signs saying "Dead Gazan." Once again I had to snap out of it in order to defend Israel in public. Audiences had to be reminded of the myriad leaflets the IDF had dispersed warning Palestinian civilians to leave combat areas and about the operation's unprecedentedly low ratio of civilian-to-combatant casualties. I had to relate the story of the West Bank Palestinian reporter who grilled me while on the air but, once off camera, whispered, "Whatever you do, don't stop until you crush Hamas." In spite of the uproar unleashed by Cast Lead, I expressed continued hope for a two-state solution, even though I still doubted whether any Palestinian leader was willing or able to sign on to one. In the absence of a negotiated agreement, I still believed, Israel should take measures that guaranteed our Jewish and democratic future.

The operation inconclusively dragged on, but its end was predetermined. Even if the IDF reconquered Gaza, no one—not the Palestinian Authority, no Arab government—would accept its keys. Most pressing was the need to conclude the fighting by January 20. Though rockets continued to smash into the south, Israel could not steal the spotlight from the inauguration of America's forty-fourth president.

Unclenched Fist

Well before dawn we awoke and joined the silent procession to the Mall. The mood was solemn as Sally and I ascended through the cold roseate light to the Washington Monument. There, shivering shoulder-to-shoulder with more than a million Americans, we witnessed Barack Obama take the oath of office.

Whatever transpired later, that moment would remain for me resplendent. That sense of oneness—most of those crowding that hill were African-Americans—of hallowedness, and, yes, of hope. I still cherish the hand-warmers that well-wishers distributed for free, and the memory of a glimpse I caught of Obama as his motorcade passed. I would remember that day wistfully in the tempestuous times ahead. Yet, even at that uplifting moment, my thoughts vacillated between optimism and dread.

Throughout the campaign, Obama proudly recalled his Muslim family members and his childhood time in Indonesia, an Islamic state. He promised to close the Guantánamo detention camp for accused Islamist terrorists and replaced the Bush-era term "war on terror" with "the war on violent extremism," because, the president said, America cannot make war against a tactic. Polls showed that significant segments of the American public believed that Obama, a self-described devout Christian, was in fact a Muslim.

Unfazed, Obama used his inaugural address to call for "a new way forward" with Muslims "based on mutual interest and mutual respect." This appealed to those Democrats who believed—unfairly, I felt—that Bush had warred against Islam, and who shared Obama's vision of renewal. I had no difficulty with Obama's ties with Muslims or his offer to "extend a hand if you are willing to unclench your fist." And as someone who thought of himself as a natural link between two countries, I could hardly criticize anybody who offered to bridge two cultures. Still, I thought it unusual for a president to address the adherents of a faith as if their views were monolithic. I wondered about the ramifications of reconciling with a Muslim world widely opposed to Israel's existence, and whether Obama's desire to dissolve "the lines of the tribe" included my tribe, the Jews.

My concerns were heightened by a conversation held that January with one of Washington's most incisive minds. David Rothkopf, my former Columbia roommate who had served as undersecretary of commerce and director of Kissinger Associates, met me at a Thai restaurant. "The first thing Obama will do in office is pick a fight with Israel," he told me, and I nearly spilled my curry. I knew there would be difficulties between Israel and the new administration, but did not think the clash would be so head-on and so immediate. "The previous administration was perceived as too pro-Israel," he elaborated, "and Obama's policy will be ABB." The initials stood for "Anything But Bush."

This prediction went a long way in explaining the president's initial actions. He reportedly made his first foreign phone call to Palestinian president Mahmoud Abbas—before Prime Minister Ehud Olmert—assuring him of America's commitment to rebuild war-struck Gaza and pursue peace. The following day, Obama appointed former Senate majority leader George Mitchell as his Special Envoy for Middle East Peace.

Of Lebanese descent, Mitchell had tweaked Israeli sensibilities during the Second Intifada by exonerating Arafat of any involvement in the violence and calling for a total settlement freeze. Soon after his appointment, the new emissary announced that his mediation efforts would "incorporate" the Arab Peace Initiative. This Saudi plan, floated in the aftermath of 9/11 and later endorsed by the Arab League, called for normalizing relations with Israel in return for its withdrawal to the 1967 lines, including East Jerusalem, and a "just settlement" of the refugee issue. Though I thought Israel could have been more welcoming of the plan, focusing on the normalization and overlooking the provisions for borders and refugees, the government all but dismissed the initiative. But the Palestinians embraced the Arab League plan, and so did George Mitchell.

If less than enthused by Mitchell's appointment, some Israeli officials looked askance at Obama's choice for national security advisor. The post, which exerts immense influence on America's strategic policy toward the Middle East, is crucial for Israel. And the president's nominee, General James (Jim) Jones, had extensive Israel experience. Back in 2007, while serving as a special State Department envoy, Jones filed a sharply critical report on Israeli actions in the territories.

Further highlighting his new approach, Obama gave his first presidential interview to the Al Arabiya television station in Dubai. "I am absolutely certain that we can make significant progress," he said of the peace talks he promised to resume. He also reemphasized his Muslim family connections and expressed his desire to restore America's relations with the Middle East to what they were "twenty or thirty years ago." The aspiration puzzled me. Twenty years earlier, I calculated, America bombed Libya and blew up Iranian ships in the Gulf. Thirty years ago, Iranian students overran the U.S. embassy in Tehran.

Such signs troubled several Israeli commentators, yet I still believed that a domestically and internationally popular president best served Israel's interest. Rahm Emanuel's appointment as White House chief of staff heartened me, as did Hillary Clinton's as secretary of state. Especially encouraging was the return of my friend Dennis Ross, America's most experienced practitioner of Middle East diplomacy, to the State Department as Clinton's special advisor. To the interviewer in Dubai—and to listeners throughout the Arab world—Obama stated, "Israel is a strong ally of the United States [and] will not stop being a strong ally. And I will continue to believe that Israel's security is paramount." There would be friction, I assumed, but the alliance would ultimately hold.

That proposition would be tested three weeks after the inauguration when Israelis went to the polls and returned Benjamin Netanyahu to office. Voted out as prime minister in 1999 after only three years in office, Netanyahu had subsequently served as foreign and finance minister and leader of the Likud. Now less beset by the coalition crises that burdened his first term, Netanyahu prepared to meet some of Israel's steepest challenges. Along with renewing the peace process and meeting the Iranian nuclear threat, he faced the imposing phenomenon of Barack Obama.

The two men had first met in the summer of 2008, during Obama's campaign stopover in Israel, when Netanyahu led the opposition. Their conversation, from what I could glean from the press, appeared friendly. Obama justified his support for negotiations with Iran. "Serious direct diplomacy is not because I'm naïve," he explained. "[It] puts us in a stronger position to mobilize the international community." He nevertheless upheld Israel's right to defend itself, whether against Iran or Hamas. "No democracy can tolerate such danger to its people." Now, half a year later, President Obama called Netanyahu to congratulate him and to reaffirm his commitment to Israel's defense.

And Israel needed defending. Just then, a coalition of radical leftists, Islamic extremists, international forums, and European courts accused Israel of committing atrocities in Gaza. Israel's longtime friend Turkey joined the attack. Furious that the recent fighting in Gaza stymied his attempts to mediate between Israel and Syria, and ideologically close to Hamas, Turkish prime minister Recep Tayyip

Erdoğan became flagrantly anti-Israel. On January 29, 2009, in the middle of a talk in Switzerland with Israeli president Shimon Peres, the burly Turkish leader stomped off the stage shouting, "When it comes to killing, you know well how to kill!"

Abbas, meanwhile, launched a legal attack against Israel. The same Palestinian president who quietly supported the blockade of Hamas-controlled Gaza now called publicly for reconciliation with Hamas and an investigation into Israeli "war crimes." More outrageously, this inquiry into Israel's alleged atrocities would be carried out by the UN Human Rights Council.

Unique even by the UN's anti-Israel standards, the UNHRC condemned Israel more than all other countries combined. Article 7 of its charter mandated an automatic annual censure of the Jewish State, and its special rapporteur on Palestine, Richard Falk, regularly compared Israelis to Nazis. Disgusted by its anti-Israel bias, President Bush withdrew America's representative to the council. But that did not stop the UNHRC—with Abbas's blessing—from charging Israel with crimes against humanity.

Into this diplomatic thicket rushed the new Obama administration. The president's first trip abroad brought him, in early April, to Turkey. Describing himself as a bridge between the Western and Muslim worlds, Obama declared, "The United States is not, and will never be, at war with Islam." He also expressed admiration for Turkey's democracy and his personal regard for Erdoğan. "I'm not naïve," Obama once again claimed, but many Israelis grew skeptical. They recalled that Erdoğan's Turkey jailed more journalists than either China or Iran. They saw how, when asked by Turkish students to comment on the prime minister's recent outburst against Israel, Obama simply replied, "I wasn't there."

Then, just as the UN Human Rights Council prepared to send its fact-finding mission "to investigate all violations of international humanitarian law by Israel," the United States renewed its seat in the UNHRC. Susan Rice, America's UN ambassador, asserted that "we believe that working from within, we can make the Council a more effective forum to . . . protect human rights." But all of the Israelis I spoke with believed that America's membership in the UNHRC would do nothing to improve the council's anti-Israel record. Rather, they added, the presence of a U.S. representative in the organization would merely legitimize its bias.

No less perplexing for Israelis was the administration's policy on Iran. The International Atomic Energy Agency—the UN's nuclear watchdog, the IAEA—reported that the Iranians for the first time had produced enough low-enriched uranium for one bomb. Near the western city of Arak, they roofed a heavy-water plant, preventing satellites from observing work on what the IAEA assumed was a plutonium bomb. All of these activities, from Israel's perspective, had a single purpose: to obliterate the Jewish State. Iranian president Mahmoud Ahmadinejad made no effort to dissemble his desire for Israel's disappearance. He repeatedly denied the Holocaust, while simultaneously asserting that "the illegitimate Zionist regime is an outcome of the Holocaust." This was the Iran with which President Obama now pledged to reconcile.

In a videotaped message on March 20, the Persian New Year, the president invited Iranian leaders to "honest" talks "grounded in mutual respect" in order to restore Iran to "its rightful place in the community of nations." That goal, Obama cautioned, could not be attained by Iranian terror, but neither would it require coercion. I watched the video, stunned, as the president negated the possibility of levying sanctions much less using military force against Iran. "This process [of U.S.-Iranian peacemaking] will not be advanced by threats," he said. In the same vein, Obama reportedly initiated a correspondence with Ali Khamenei, the supreme leader and unopposed ruler of the Islamic Republic. The administration regarded Khamenei's reply, which chronicled America's sins against Iran, as encouraging.

Perhaps not surprisingly, the main target of American displeasure at this point appeared to be Israel. The crux was the question of peace with the Palestinians. If President Bush demanded that the Palestinians renounce terror and embrace democracy before receiving peace, the new administration expected Israel to make the first move. Israel, Obama insisted, must suspend all settlement construction and endorse the two-state solution. But such concessions were too much to ask of the head of the newly elected leader of Likud, especially so soon after Abbas had turned down Ehud Olmert's offer of Palestinian statehood. Netanyahu also suspected that Abbas would merely pocket any Israeli concessions and still refuse to negotiate. And Abbas did not trust Netanyahu to give him more than Olmert proposed. "I will wait for Israel to freeze settlements," he told *The Washington Post.*

"Until then, in the West Bank we have a good reality . . . the people are living a normal life."

Nevertheless, the new administration continued to lean on Netanyahu. In his repeated visits to Jerusalem, Senator Mitchell pressed the prime minister to announce a settlement freeze and commit to creating a Palestinian state. "A comprehensive peace in this region is in the national interest of the United States . . . and of the entire region," the special envoy declared. "A two-state solution is the only solution." But Netanyahu resisted this pressure, insisting instead on Palestinian recognition of Israel as the Jewish State, and stoked the president's ire.

At loggerheads over Gaza, Turkey, the UN, Iran, and the peace process, the United States and Israel were likely headed for a showdown. The contest would, of course, be lopsided, pitting a minuscule state against a superpower. Beyond that, though, it also set an adored and immensely powerful leader against a widely disdained and domestically hobbled one. The media adored Obama—*The New York Times* published a coffee-table book about him—and most of the world revered him. Netanyahu, by contrast, was pilloried by the press and scorned by much of international opinion. While Netanyahu presided over an unwieldy coalition of ministers who often espoused irreconcilable policies, Obama's Democratic Party controlled both houses of Congress. Netanyahu governed by hard-wrought consensus and Obama, seemingly, by fiat.

Yet not only in their popularity and clout were the president and prime minister unevenly matched. Netanyahu refused to be politically correct, while Obama was PC incarnate. One promised hope and change and the other defense and stability. Previous U.S. presidents bonded with Israeli prime ministers of similar ideological outlooks— Clinton and Rabin, Bush and Sharon—but America's leadership was now left of center and Israel's center-right. Portentously, one of Obama's first acts on entering the White House was to replace a bust of Winston Churchill, America's unflagging World War II ally, with that of Abraham Lincoln. Netanyahu reentered the Prime Minister's Office and promptly hung Churchill's photograph on the wall behind his desk.

Such were the rifts—diplomatic, political, and personal—scoring the U.S.-Israel alliance in the first months of 2009. From the sidelines of Georgetown, I watched those fissures widen. I was watching them still on March 6, when I learned that Israel's ambassador to Washington had resigned.

Hat in the Ring

"Should I put my hat in the ring?" I asked Sally as I paced our par-queted Georgetown floor. The expression came from the early days of boxing, when a man who wanted to fight tossed his stovepipe at the reigning champion's feet. The image was apt. By declaring my interest in the ambassador's job, I was liable to be laughed at or drubbed.

The post of Israel's ambassador to the United States is exception-ally senior, similar to that of many government ministers. America is vital to Israel's security, arguably even its survival. It provides the tiny Jewish State with strategic and diplomatic depth and lifesaving mili-tary assistance. Understandably, then, the ambassador is almost always handpicked by the prime minister from among his most trusted friends. When Netanyahu won the elections, it was only natural that his prede-cessor's chosen envoy to Washington, Sallai Meridor, step down.

But how well did I know Netanyahu? We met in 1983, when he served as Israel's deputy chief of mission in Washington and came to lecture at Princeton. When heading the opposition, he asked me to brief him on the mood in Congress and the White House. I sometimes encountered him at the annual memorial service for Levi Eshkol, the Labor prime minister whom Netanyahu and I both admired. While discomfited by the memory of Netanyahu's criticism of Rabin before his assassination, I nevertheless respected the prime minister's mili-tary and policy-making experience, his resilience in rebounding from political defeat. Our families were both bereaved—his by the death of his older brother, Yoni, during the 1976 Entebbe rescue, and ours by Joanie's murder.

Even so, I was never a close associate of Netanyahu or even a member of his party. Realistically, then, what were the chances that he would select me for Israel's most sensitive overseas job? And should I get the job, what were my chances of surviving? Netanyahu opposed the Gaza withdrawal; he rejected limits on settlement building and opposed the two-state solution. "Could you really work with him?" Sally wondered. And then there was Netanyahu himself, a figure por-trayed by Israeli journalists as alternately spineless and tyrannical, easily swayed and hard-nosed, irrationally loyal to some people but exploitative of others. Anybody identified with him would instantly be targeted by Israel's vehemently anti-Netanyahu press. My wife worried and asked, "Do you want to expose yourself to all that?"

Her questions definitely merited thought. Yes, I disagreed with some of Netanyahu's positions on the peace process, but I knew from history that right-wing Likudniks—rather than left-leaning Laborites—possessed the legitimacy to make peace. I believed that Netanyahu, like Begin and Sharon before him, could adapt to changing political realities. After all, Netanyahu was the last Israeli leader to sign an agreement with the Palestinians—at the Wye River Plantation in 1998.

Moreover, I agreed with Netanyahu that sustainable peace could only be based on the mutual acceptance of the Jewish and Palestinian peoples' rights to self-determination in their homeland. I supported his insistence that any peace agreement provide Israel with a mechanism for defending itself if the treaty broke down. Like Eshkol, Netanyahu appeared to understand the need for Israeli leaders to exhaust all reasonable diplomatic options.

But, also like Eshkol, Netanyahu recognized a threat to Israel's existence. Iran's fanatical rulers swore to "wipe Israel off the map" and were likely building the nuclear bombs to accomplish that. "Humanity stands at a hinge of history," Netanyahu told Jeffrey Goldberg, now of *The Atlantic*. "A messianic apocalyptic cult wants to get hold of the weapons of mass death." Preventing that catastrophe was the purpose for which the prime minister believed the Israeli public—and Jewish history—had chosen him.

Iranian nuclearization, for me as well, was our generation's paramount challenge. The differences I had with Netanyahu on the peace process and other issues paled beside our common conviction on Iran. Absent some extreme ethical dilemma, I could proudly represent his government in Washington.

And I would not only be Netanyahu's envoy, but the State of Israel's. In effect, becoming ambassador was like reenlisting in the IDF. Once I put on those fatigues, I forfeited the right of self-expression for the privilege of defending our democratically decided policies. Though pinstripe gray rather than army green, a diplomat's garb was a uniform just the same. The terms of service were similar.

My suits, I imagined, would also be of rusted armor, for I remained quixotic, in quest of improbable dreams. I never abandoned them, never stopped preparing myself with writing, interviewing, speaking publicly about Israel and its synergetic relationship with America. But the two countries had changed markedly and were in danger of drifting apart. I believed I could help prevent that by representing Jerusalem to Washington as well as Israel to the United States. And my sense of purpose, as much as real armor, would help steel me against any drubbing I might take. "We can weather it," I said to Sally. "Both of us can."

Dialing our family friends, Jerome and Ellen Stern, I asked if they would put in a word with an attorney I once met at their house, Yitzhak "Yitzik" Molcho, Netanyahu's diplomatic advisor. But the Sterns advised me to phone him myself. "If you don't," they said, "you'll always regret not calling." So I did. In the gruff but jaunty tone I would come to expect and appreciate, Yitzik replied, "I've got nothing to do with those matters. You're asking the wrong man." And, yet, hanging up the receiver, I sensed my message would be delivered.

A week later, while walking to a Washington lunch, my cellphone rang. The temperature had slipped below zero and my insensate fingers could barely tap the answer key. On the other end, in Jerusalem, was Ron Dermer. The son and brother of Miami Beach mayors, Ron was the prime minister's closest advisor—so close that he was popularly known as "Bibi's Brain." "Would you be interested in being considered for the post of ambass—" Ron started inquiring, but never finished the question. My answer cut him off.

In spite of our world-revered intelligence services, Israelis can seem incapable of keeping secrets. Sometimes we act as if we are still living in a shtetl—a village in the old Russian Pale—crowded together and gossiping. Shortly after my conversation with Ron, rumors about my candidacy began floating. Suddenly, the press was scrutinizing my past and questioning my suitability. Right-wing bloggers dug up my teen years in the Marxist kibbutz movement and my more recent call on Israel to take its own initiatives in the West Bank. But most of Israel's media leans leftward, and several pundits recalled my inclusion in Bush's first delegation to Israel. My 2008 article about Senator Obama's Middle East policies was adduced as evidence of my pro-Republican bent. An Israeli television commentator even claimed that Sheldon Adelson, the conservative casino magnate, had personally backed my nomination.

Adelson and I indeed worked together on Jewish and Israeli issues, but when it came to naming the ambassador, he endorsed a different contender. I never revealed that, though. Neither did I follow
some of the other aspirants' example by leaking my candidacy to the
press. Ron had asked me to keep our contacts secret and I did. Others,
though, emerged in my favor, among them Rahm Emanuel and those
heroes of my youth, Elie Wiesel and Natan Sharansky. Some even
complimented Netanyahu for his unconventional choice, a person capable of connecting with both left and right. Dan Gordon, the Hollywood screenwriter who served with me in the Second Lebanon War,
blogged about an episode I had tried to forget. One night, the army
asked for several officers to go into the battle area and help escort the
bodies of Israeli soldiers killed in action across the border. "Michael
was the first to volunteer. . . . [I]t was too dangerous for helicopters to
land," Dan recalled. "Flares were going off above us. . . . We served as
the covering force while the fallen were evacuated."

Less dramatic, perhaps, but equally exacting, were the three trips
I made from Washington to Israel in under twelve days that April. In
lengthy sessions, the prime minister probed my personality and political backbone. "I know you can say 'Yes,'" he plied me, "but can you
say 'No'?" In response, I cited several Israeli ambassadors whom I had
studied and who, believing themselves smarter than their governments, ignored express orders. "An ambassador can never see the
whole picture the way a prime minister does," I said. "Ambassadors
must convey the truth as they see it. They can't be afraid to raise questions. But in the end, they must carry out instructions."

Netanyahu, it turned out, had read my book *Power, Faith, and
Fantasy* and was impressed by my knowledge of America's history in
the Middle East. He regarded understanding the past as the key to
interpreting the present. That was perhaps the main reason I even
merited an interview. And yet I also felt that Netanyahu intuited the
need for someone with a wide perspective on the United States—not
only its conservative wing, but also its liberals and progressives, its
minorities as well as its establishment—and someone with significant
media experience. We indeed discussed history but, above all, the
prime minister wanted to hear my analysis of contemporary America
and its future relations with Israel.

"We have to gauge which direction the tides are flowing and navigate them as best as we can," I responded. America was changing, I

said, economically, socially, and demographically, and Obama was
both the cause and symptom of those changes. More than just the first
African-American president, he aimed to be transformational, altering the country's priorities both domestically and overseas. "It's not
the America you remember," I told the prime minister, a member
of the Massachusetts Institute of Technology's Class of 1975. That
was the year that the U.S. forces evacuated Vietnam, dumping military
helicopters into the sea. Now, still bogged down in Iraq and Afghanistan, Americans were once again war-weary. "They're tired of our
region," I concluded. "They want to go home."

Between interviews, I trekked the nature trails outside Jerusalem
and pondered my unmarked future. In the worst case, I consoled myself, I would return to a fulfilling life of lecturing and history writing.
No more attacks on me in the Israeli press, no need to bridge a potentially yawning American-Israeli divide. Suddenly, several of my close
friends came hiking directly toward me. My presence in Israel was still
a secret and, thieflike, I ducked behind a tree. Only then, cowering as
they passed, did I admit that not becoming ambassador would mean
failing to fulfill the vow I made to myself at age fifteen.

I returned to America at the end of the month and resumed my
academic routine. Days passed and I began to realize that the criticism
of me in the press had probably voided my appointment. Visiting
Miami for a speaking engagement, Sally and I gazed wistfully at the
ocean and sighed, "Well, it was a good try. . . ."

Resigned, we flew back to Washington on the first day of May to
attend the annual convention of the American Israel Public Affairs
Committee—AIPAC. The Policy Conference, as it was called, represented the country's largest and most influential pro-Israel gathering.
Many members of Congress, governors, and federal officials past and
present attend. Vice President Joe Biden had just told the organization, "You're not going to like my saying this, but do not build more
settlements," chafing some of his listeners. Caught in the corridor outside the main hall, jostled by seven thousand AIPAC supporters, I
could not hear the speech or stay close beside Sally. But I did catch
sight of her frantically waving our cellphone.

For a frozen moment, the four yards separating us felt as long as
the nearly forty years I had waited for this moment. Perhaps from the
flushed expression on Sally's face or my own sense of premonition, I
knew that our pessimism had been misplaced. The hat I had thrown in

the ring was about to land on my head. I clasped the phone and cupped it around my ear to make out the muffled but unmistakable voice on the receiver. In his unaccented American English, Prime Minister Netanyahu congratulated me: "Good luck, Mr. Ambassador."

Boot Camp

Instantly, the whirlwind began. Flying back to Israel, I spent entire days answering questions posed by an intelligence interviewer, documenting every stage of my life, every job held and country visited, and many of my acquaintances. I endured extensive medical and security examinations that torment any nominee—Israeli or American—for office. I described my Zionist path from New Jersey to Jerusalem, the wars, the losses, the hopes. I spoke at length about my time in the Soviet Union, about the head of the Kiev underground who, with the KGB lurking outside, raised a glass of homemade, industrial-strength vodka and toasted us "Yiddin"—Jews—with "l'chaim." Even the interviewer looked teary-eyed.

Between vettings, I sought out the Israelis who best understood our relationship with America. I sat and listened to the heads of Mossad and Shin Bet, Israel's internal security service, seasoned Knesset members and IDF generals. Especially instructive—and sobering—were my meetings with the former Israeli ambassadors to the United States.

Maintaining relations between Obama and Netanyahu might be the least of my challenges, I heard. Responsible for the entire embassy and nine consulates nationwide, the ambassador had virtually no authority to hire or fire any of their hundreds of employees. The professional diplomats on the staff, moreover, tended to resent the appointment of an outsider to their most coveted post and often took their frustrations to the press. Answerable to both a prime minister and a foreign minister who were often from different parties, the ambassador could receive contradictory instructions. And while an ambassador who was not especially close to his prime minister might enjoy greater latitude in expressing his own opinions and easing bilateral tensions, he might also be dismissed as irrelevant by Washington's elite.

Most dauntingly, the ambassador's desk served as the intersection between the White House and the State Department, 535 members of

Congress, the Pentagon, the U.S. intelligence and business communities, American Jews, church and ethnic groups, the international press—all that and some 25 Israeli government ministers, 120 members of the Knesset, the IDF and the intelligence services, the commercial sector, and the Israeli press. "Is it winnable?" I asked each of my predecessors. Not all of them said yes.

One concern, at least, was allayed by my meeting with Foreign Minister Avigdor—"Evet"—Liberman. The Tel Aviv address I was given led to a locked restaurant. I stood in the 10 P.M. rain and pounded on the door until, as if in some vintage movie, an aperture slid open and a raspy voice asked what I wanted. "I came for the minister." Inside, brawny activists in Liberman's mostly Russian-backed Yisrael Beitenu (Israel Is Our Home) Party hunkered around a long table clouded in cigarette smoke. They glared at me as I passed and entered a private booth where Liberman waited, puffing a stout cigar.

Having quit previous governments in protest over the Gaza Disengagement and the peace process—"Negotiations on the basis of land for peace will destroy us," he warned—the foreign minister now headed the third-largest party in the Knesset. Some of his politics, including demands for displays of loyalty by Israeli Arabs, were surely not mine. But I respected him as an immigrant who had landed in Israel with nothing and worked his way up, and agreed with him on the hazards of Iran's nuclear program. Round-faced with a clipped beard, Liberman asked about my background and my views about Obama, but then abruptly cut me off. "You're Bibi's appointment, I get that," he interjected. "You'll have no problem with me."

A more immediate obstacle arose on my return trips to Washington, where, as ambassador-designate, I resided in the same city as the serving ambassador, Sallai Meridor. This troubled the American protocol officials and might have created confusion. Fortunately, Sallai Meridor was Israel's equivalent of a Kennedy, a man of quiet refinement and service. Over the course of several hours, he graciously shared with me his views on Washington, on whom I could rely, and on whom less so. And he furnished me with the one piece of advice that would always guide me. "You are the ambassador of Israel. Not of Belgium, not even of Britain and France. No other country has Israel's special relationship with America," he said, suddenly animated. "And no other ambassador has your stature."

While I solicited Sallai's counsel, others proffered their own. One octogenarian American Jewish leader pulled me aside and whispered, "Obama has no real principles. Stick to your positions and he'll cave." Several Washington pundits characterized the administration's attitude as a combination of arrogance and ignorance. Congress members Howard Berman and Ileana Ros-Lehtinen, the first a Democrat and the second a Republican, both of them friends from the past, called to offer me partisan advice. The awkwardness of some of these conversations was compounded by my newfound circumspection in conducting them. Others were likely listening in, our security people warned me, and not all of them allies.

Much of that period would stay blurred in my memory, a mélange of twelve-hour flights during which I graded my students' term papers and dodged questions from curious passengers. The most distinct recollection remains a mid-May trip to Israel in which I landed only to take off the next day as a "special advisor" to the prime minister's entourage. Our destination was only a few miles from our Georgetown apartment.

A visiting Israeli prime minister, requiring maximum security, merits the third-largest motorcade in America. If the president's is the longest, whose then is number two? I later posed this trivia question to several people who gave varying answers—the vice president, Chinese leaders, even rock stars—but never the right one. The pope. The morning of May 18, though, my only question was the one I put to myself. Was I really speeding through stoplights with sirens wailing in the elongated cavalcade of sedans conveying Netanyahu to his first visit to Obama's White House?

The drill that later became routine was thrillingly new that day. The swoop of our cars into the crescent driveway, the Marine guards stiffening to attention, the surprisingly modest foyer in the world's most powerful home. Around a lunch table near the Lincoln Room, we waited, shifting our weight, until the door swung open and he entered.

Successive years of controversy and disappointment would invariably dull its sheen, but Obama's image then was near blinding. Here was the leader who, like a deus ex machina, had just allocated $787 billion to stimulate the American economy while pledging to reduce his nation's deficit by one-half. He announced the withdrawal of all

U.S. troops from Iraq by 2011, revealed his ideas for far-reaching health-care, educational, and energy reforms, and unveiled his plan for worldwide nuclear disarmament—all in his first one hundred days. But this was also the president who, according to press reports, was gearing up to tell Netanyahu that the era of unconditional U.S. support for Israel had ended. And here was the Israeli prime minister who—perhaps insensitively—presented him with a mint edition of Mark Twain's *Innocents Abroad,* about naïve Americans blundering across the Middle East.

Introduced as the incoming ambassador, I shook Obama's hand and noticed his long and elegant fingers, fit for an El Greco painting. Rather than the distant man I expected, he seemed gracious, blessed with impeccable comic timing even when joking—surprisingly—at his own expense. His movements were effortless. This is a man, I later told my ex-dancer wife, at ease in his body.

The conversation was relaxed as well. Over lunch and a dessert that Obama never touched, we discussed the major regional issues. The president's team included the taciturn national security advisor Jim Jones and the far less reserved Rahm Emanuel, along with Dan Shapiro, the NSC's Israel and Middle East expert, whom I first met during Obama's campaign stop in Israel. Netanyahu was bracketed by his advisors, among them Yitzik Molcho and Uzi Arad, General Jones's Israeli counterpart.

Both sides seemed eager to avoid disagreements, until they reached the subject of Gaza. Obama had already come out against Israel's blockade and allocated $300 million for restoring Gaza's war damages. Now the president reiterated Israel's need to end the embargo on civilian goods and alleviate the Palestinians' suffering. Previously silent, I interjected and related how, during the Gaza operation, we learned that Hamas had ten times more smuggling tunnels than estimated. These served as conduits for arms as well as food. "There is no way to separate the rockets from the flour," I explained, "and no way to ensure that construction materials won't be used to make bunkers." Obama nodded intently as I spoke and yet he remained, I sensed, unpersuaded.

After lunch, Obama and Netanyahu adjourned to the Oval Office for their one-on-one talk, while the teams chatted in the adjacent Roosevelt Room. I stood alone under the portraits of an avuncular FDR and a bullish Teddy charging up San Juan Hill, and was all but ignored. I was too new to the relationship for most of either the Americans or Israelis to take notice. "Slowly, slowly," I told myself, "this will take time," while the advisors interacted around me. Thankfully, after an interminable ninety minutes—thirty more than scheduled—a protocol officer invited us to join the principals.

Like much of the White House, the Oval Office is understated, appointed with comfortable rather than magisterial furniture, washed in soothing colors and the South Lawn's satiny light. Obama and Netanyahu sat on armchairs angled to enable them to address both each other and the press. Their remarks again seemed designed to defray any hint of friction. Israel, Obama opened, was a "stalwart ally of the United States, the only true democracy in the Middle East," and "a source of inspiration and admiration for the American people." Maintaining Israel's security as a Jewish state was a "U.S. national security interest," he continued, and reaffirmed his determination to prevent Iran from threatening Israel with nuclear weapons. Netanyahu extolled his host as a "great leader of the United States, a great leader of the world, a great friend of Israel," and affirmed that America and Israel faced the same terrorist threats and sought the same goal: peace.

The bonhomie continued that evening at an intimate meal with Hillary Clinton. During his term as prime minister in the late 1990s, Netanyahu had a famously strained relationship with President Clinton, who greeted Netanyahu's electoral defeat to Ehud Barak by trumpeting, "I'm as excited as a kid awaiting a new toy." The Clinton-Netanyahu connection, I would later learn, was much more complicated, but still I anticipated some friction at dinner.

To my relief, the prime minister and secretary of state spent the night bantering like old pals. In the State Department, a stunningly bland building with upper floors refashioned in Early American motif, we dined by candlelight, on colonial china and cut crystal, and reminisced. I first met Hillary in 1995 when I worked as the inter-religious affairs advisor for the Rabin government. Back then, the keenness of her mind astonished me, as did the cobalt-blue color of her eyes. Now, at sixty-one—"it's the new thirty," she said laughing—she had lost none of that acuity. Hillary emphasized the need for Arab gestures for peace, and applauded my idea for holding a summit of Israeli and Arab leaders in Riyadh. When told that the worst word one could call an Israeli was *freier*—Hebrew slang for a sucker—and that Israelis could never be seen as the *freiers* of any peace deal, the secretary practically roared. "I'll have to remember that!"

By all outward appearances, and to me at least, Netanyahu's first meeting with Obama went smoothly. But the press was quick to emphasize the tenseness of the two leaders' body language and their presumed disagreements. Obama insisted on the cessation of all settlement activity, opening Gaza's borders, and creating a Palestinian state, but Netanyahu said only that the Palestinians should govern themselves. Obama reaffirmed his intention to reach out to Iran and put no time limit on the negotiations, while Netanyahu merely thanked him for keeping "all options on the table." Face-to-face, I later heard, Obama had demanded that Netanyahu cease all building not only in the territories but also in the disputed areas of Jerusalem. "Not a single brick," the president purportedly said. "I know how to deal with people who oppose me."

An outsider still, I was not yet privy to that kind of information. Yet the visit introduced me to that world in which a cordial discussion between allies could be interpreted by the press—or be spun to the press—as a train wreck. "There wasn't a single blister that Obama didn't step on," one leading Israeli columnist wrote, "and Netanyahu didn't seem to care."

Only a few weeks had passed since Netanyahu's phone call congratulating me on my appointment, but it felt as if I had endured another yearlong basic training. Now, emerging from that boot camp, I knew at least what was required to survive in this complex and potentially hazardous diplomatic world. I would have to master its nuances, its pitfalls and twists. I would have to learn the full meaning—and the limits—of that deceptively straightforward word, *ally*.

Metamorphic Month

Once approved by the Israeli government, my appointment as ambassador was submitted for acceptance by the United States. Though rarely withheld, this *agrèment* took several weeks, during which I was forbidden to fly back to Washington. This gave me the opportunity to pack up our Jerusalem apartment and to witness the three events that, in a single month, shook the Middle East.

The first occurred on June 4, when Obama met another group of Middle Eastern students, this time in Cairo. More passionately than ever, he described his personal connections with Muslims and his conviction that "Islam is part of America." He reiterated his vision of a new era of understanding between the United States and Muslims based on "mutual interests and respect" and the shared American and Quranic values of "justice and progress, tolerance and the dignity of all human beings." Then, with unprecedented detail, Obama spelled out his Middle Eastern policies.

"No system of government can or should be imposed on one nation by any other," he said, eschewing Bush's democracy agenda. "No single nation should pick and choose which nation holds nuclear weapons," he said, and envisioned a world in which all countries, Iran included, could enjoy peaceful atomic energy. Yet the lion's share of the speech dealt with the Israeli-Palestinian conflict. Describing American-Israel bonds as "unbreakable," he also demanded a halt to the building of "illegitimate" Israeli settlements. The Palestinians, for their part, should never resort to violence, but neither should they "endure the pain of dislocation [and] the daily humiliations . . . that come with occupation." Americans, Obama vowed, "will not turn our backs on the legitimate Palestinian aspirations for dignity, opportunity, and a state of their own."

Since his first day in office—presidential advisor David Axelrod later wrote—Obama had contemplated making a statement that transformed America's relations with Islam. The Cairo speech was indeed revolutionary. As in his inaugural address, Obama spoke to a body of believers, only now not from the Capitol steps but from a venerable Muslim capital. He spoke to a Muslim world without borders while at the same time signaling an end to American pressure on repressive Islamic regimes. To an unrivaled extent, Obama identified American interests with the Palestinians. And, for the first time, America recognized Iran's right to peaceful nuclear power.

Despite this unprecedented outreach, reactions in the region were mixed. Most tepid were the Arabs, who, while praising Obama's tone and Quranic quotes, preferred concrete acts to rhetoric. Iran's Supreme Leader Ali Khamenei reminded Obama that "the nations of this part of the world . . . deeply hate America." Surprisingly more welcoming were Israeli leaders, from Shimon Peres's "a brave speech, full of vision," to Netanyahu's "We share President Obama's hope . . . to end the conflict and . . . [achieve] Arab recognition of Israel as the homeland of the Jewish people."

I listened to the speech in the Kiriyah, the IDF's headquarters, along with several senior commanders. Their reactions typified that of a great many Israelis. They scoffed at what they regarded as Obama's inexperience with the Middle East, where magnanimity is often seen as weakness. They cringed at his tendency to equate America's moral foibles with the honor killings, human trafficking, and the suppression of women, foreign workers, and indigenous minorities rampant in many Muslim societies. Yet none of the officers downplayed the seriousness of Obama's embrace of the Palestinian cause and his demand for a settlement freeze. True, the president introduced Israel's validity into the heart of the Arab world, but he then linked that legitimacy to the Jews' "tragic history" in the Holocaust.

That linkage seemed to me to be the most damaging part of his speech. The Arabs had long complained that they were forced to pay the price of the Jews' near eradication by Europe, which dumped the survivors in Palestine. That narrative denied three thousand years of unbroken Jewish connection to our land. It overlooked the fact that Jews had always lived in the country and that millions of Israelis hailed not from Europe but from Africa and the Middle East. Yet that Arab narrative was now America's. And why should the Arabs make peace with a country that even its ally, the United States, seemed to label alien? As if to fortify that impression, Obama's Middle East tour skipped over Israel. Instead, the president flew with Elie Wiesel to visit the Buchenwald concentration camp.

No sooner had Obama returned to Washington than, on June 13, large-scale protests racked Tehran. Tens of thousands of students and unemployed workers took to the streets challenging Ahmadinejad's fraudulent reelection and demanding democratic reforms. This "Green Revolution"—the color of the defeated opposition—for the first time raised hopes of toppling one of the world's most extremist regimes. Aptly, that regime responded with beatings by its thuggish Basij henchmen and gunfire that killed as many as 150. A young woman named Neda Agha-Soltan bled to death in front of the cameras.

The inspiring scenes of young Iranians risking their lives for freedom was greeted standoffishly by Obama. "It is up to the Iranians to decide who Iran's leader will be," the president explained to the press. "We respect Iranian sovereignty." True to his Cairo speech and other public remarks, the president remained committed to engaging the Iranian regime, not replacing it. "We are not meddling," he said.

Obama appeared to be referring to the 1953 overthrow of Iran's nationalist prime minister, Mohammad Mosaddegh, by a CIA-engineered coup. That putsch remained an open wound in U.S.-Iranian relations and was often listed as one of the Islamic Republic's grievances against America. Consequently, I could understand Obama's reluctance to interfere in internal Iranian politics. He feared tainting the Green Revolution with red, white, and blue. Yet, following his warm interaction with students in Turkey and Egypt, the president's indifference toward the murder of Iranian youths was chilling. Israelis were especially distraught by America's support for a violent regime that clamored for their destruction. Unlike Obama, Netanyahu extolled the Iranian people who faced bullets in defense of democracy. "Something very fundamental is going on," he observed, "an expression of a deep desire for freedom."

The Green Revolution, though ruthlessly repressed, presaged the great uprisings that would soon grip the entire region. And Obama's reaction to the revolt, like his Cairo speech, signaled the thrust of his policies. America would reconcile with Islam, reach out to Middle Eastern adversaries, and rigorously pursue a two-state solution.

This new direction in America's relations with the Middle East raised fateful questions for Israel. Could we find a common path with Obama and still preserve our vital interests? Conversely, in the face of rising regional threats, could we afford to alienate a globally celebrated president? Such questions preoccupied Netanyahu in those first ten days of June as he prepared to make a groundbreaking statement on peace.

The location for the speech—Bar-Ilan University, the bastion of Israel's religious Zionists—was deliberately chosen. Known by their knitted *kippas,* these Israelis regarded the entire Land of Israel, including the territories, as the Jews' biblical patrimony, and the settlements as the vehicle for redeeming it. Though they made up only a small percentage of all the settlers, most of whom moved to Judea and Samaria in search of affordable housing, the religious Zionists represented an ideological vanguard and a core constituency for Likud. Speaking at Bar-Ilan, the prime minister could address these supporters, reassuring them that he would continue to demand Palestinian recognition of the Jewish State and oppose the redivision of Jerusalem. He could reassert his commitment to preserve Israel's security in the aftermath of any peace accord. He could, in short, reaffirm his long-held positions before adopting what was, for him, a radically new one.

With a sense of anticipation, I joined Netanyahu's motorcade to the Bar-Ilan campus on the night of June 14. Although the tension in the hall was palpable, the prime minister appeared at ease. He took pains to rebuke the Cairo speech, rejecting the connection between the Holocaust and Israel's founding. "Had Israel been established earlier," he said, "the Holocaust would not have occurred." Only then, after taking issue with several of Obama's statements, did Netanyahu unveil the vision Obama urged him to embrace. Israel would seek peace with the Arab states, including a Palestinian state. "In this small land of ours, two peoples will live freely, side by side, in amity and mutual respect," he declared. "Each will have its own flag, its own national anthem, its own government."

So Netanyahu became the first Likud leader to come out publicly for the two-state solution. The left predictably lauded him and the extreme right denounced him, but the Israeli center—the solid majority—approved. The press, by contrast, assailed the prime minister for alternatively buckling to Obama's pressure on the Palestinian state and for rebuffing the president's demands for a settlement freeze. "If I walked on the Sea of Galilee," Netanyahu told me, half in jest, "the Israeli papers would write, 'Bibi Can't Swim.'"

The most critical question, for me at least, was, How would the White House react? Obama acknowledged that Netanyahu had taken "a big step forward" and credited him with making "an overall positive development." But there was no outpouring of support, no appreciation of the fact that Netanyahu had broken with many decades of right-wing opposition to recognizing any Palestinian rights in the Land of Israel, much less to statehood. Rather, Washington's reaction was tepid, at best, suggesting that the prime minister had merely performed a long-overdue duty.

Netanyahu's endorsement of the two-state formula indeed placed him within the American mainstream and removed one of the principal progressive complaints against Israel. This would make my job easier, though I harbored no illusions about the travails awaiting me in America. Obama's Cairo speech and his coolness toward the Green Revolution reflected deep metamorphoses in U.S. policy that would inevitably impact Israel. My task was to identify and analyze these transformations and recommend changes in long-standing Israeli policy. But first I had to alter myself, fundamentally, at America's Tel Aviv embassy.

• • •

It was an American, rather than an Israeli, requirement. Reflecting, perhaps, centuries of Jewish wandering, the Jewish State did not care how many passports its ambassadors held. But not the United States. By federal law, any American who officially served a foreign country had to renounce her or his U.S. citizenship. "It's no fun, but you'll live—I did," Ron Dermer, a former American who acted as Israel's economic attaché in Washington, consoled me. Netanyahu, who lived for years in the United States, also pooh-poohed the process, assuring me that he had undergone it twice—the first time as a commando in the IDF, and then, in America, as deputy chief of mission.

Sacrificing for Israel had become second nature, and yet pulling up this deep-seated root of my identity made me wince. No one could cure my addiction to football, my Civil War mania, or, especially, my chronic sentimentality about America. But the thought that I would be the only non-American in my family—Sally and our children remained citizens—was tough to internalize. Trying to cheer me up, my friends said that I could someday apply for a green card.

But no solace could stay the procedure's execution. At the appointed time, I arrived at the U.S. embassy and reported, sweating, to the consul general's office. I watched wordlessly as my passport was perforated. Then, in the manner of a condemned man, I had the opportunity to make some last remarks.

"The values I acquired as an American—the love of liberty, a dedication to equal rights, religious freedom, and democracy—were integral to my decision to move to Israel," I began. "My loyalties to the United States and the Jewish State are mutually validating." The renunciation of my citizenship, though painful, "did not render me less American in my culture, principles, and spirit," and I remained supremely grateful for the opportunities afforded me by the United States. Indeed, there could be no honor more rewarding for me than working to reinforce the bonds between the two countries I most revered by "representing my homeland to the home of my birth."

Somewhat dazed, I headed for the embassy's exit, but paused before the twin glossy photographs of America's leaders. These were nothing like the official portraits of Israeli presidents and prime ministers. Determined to project strength, Israeli officials confront the camera with a mixture of intelligence and grit. Their lips never smile, never even part. The U.S. president and his vice president, by contrast, virtually beamed from their frames with twinkling eyes and a flash of teeth. They appeared beneficent, charismatic, and nice. "That is," I thought, "until they're not."

Emerging into Tel Aviv, that bustling landmark in Israel's saga, I thought about my own journey to this moment and the unchartered terrain ahead. The peace process, the Iranian nuclear threat, the Middle East spiked with incalculable dangers—all that and two leaders, Barack Obama and Benjamin Netanyahu, divided by worldviews and dispositions. The sheer uncertainty of it all was enough to make me reel. Yet one constant remained and strengthened me. Irrespective of the tensions and the personality differences, I believed that the alliance was solid. The United States and Israel would stay bound by ideas and interests. For all the asymmetries, we needed each other. And the world—especially Israel's calamity-prone corner of it—needed us, too.

While remaining committed to two countries, I exited the embassy possessing only one passport. Star-of-David blue and branded with a silver menorah, the document had been freshly printed by the Foreign Ministry and rushed to me in time for my departure to Washington. It identified me as Extraordinary and Plenipotentiary, meaning, in diplomacy, that I was authorized to speak in my government's name. A month of metamorphoses had culminated in my own transformation. I was, the passport stated, His Excellency, the Ambassador of Israel to the United States.

UNBREAKABLE,
UNSHAKABLE

IN CONTRAST TO AMERICA'S FORTRESSLIKE EMBASSY IN TEL AVIV, Israel's counterpart in Northwest Washington at least makes an aesthetic effort. Situated at the terminus of an "embassy row" near the legations of Ethiopia, Bahrain, Bangladesh, and Jordan, and across the street from China's gleaming postmodern compound, the Israel Embassy to the United States once conveyed pluckiness. With beige brick siding suggestive of Jerusalem stone and archways evoking the Old City, the structure no doubt looked trendy when it was built in the early 1980s. After thirty years, though, the bricks had faded and the archways seemed to sag. Plucky gave way to shabby, trendy to seedy. When entering the compound once, Netanyahu kicked a water-stained wall and instructed me, "Michael. Replace it."

Still, my chief priority was not renovating the embassy's exterior, but learning its inner workings. New American ambassadors—all told, Obama appointed more than one hundred—undergo an intensive course in diplomacy and embassy-running. They learn the titles and roles of their subordinates, the principles of protocol, and the proper way to file a report. I, on the other hand, received zero instruction. No one briefed me on Israel's positions on crucial issues such as bilateral trade and nuclear nonproliferation. Except for the cable-craft picked up from years of researching diplomatic correspondence, I knew little about how an embassy functioned.

Nor did everyone at the embassy know about me. Entering the building on June 21, my first day on the job, I was promptly stopped by a security guard. A strapping graduate of an elite IDF unit, he pressed me in frenetic English: "Who are you? What is your purpose here?" His commander fortunately ran to the rescue. "Gaon"—genius—he chided the guard in Hebrew. "He's the ambassador."

I took the elevator to the second floor. Rising, I remembered being back in the paratroopers, clutching the static line in the C-130 plane. I remembered the vicious hiss as the hatch swung open, the alarm sounding as the green light flashed, signaling me to jump. Just then, the elevator's bell rang and the door slid open.

I crossed into the glass-encased executive suite colloquially known as the Aquarium and entered my office. This was as run-down as the rest of the embassy, with fatigued furniture from the 1980s and a profusion of Judaica—shofars, silver menorahs, leather-bound Bibles—crowding its shelves. I had scarcely lowered myself into the Reagan-era swivel chair when a rangy, easygoing man in his middle thirties sauntered into the office and introduced himself as Lior Weintraub, my chief of staff. "You can trust me entirely," he said, and my first instinct was not to.

Many of my predecessors had described the embassy as a "hornets' nest" in which diplomats conspire against one another and align against the ambassador. The challenge was especially acute for politically appointed ambassadors, who would leave the Foreign Ministry after their terms expired and could not advance the professionals' careers. Lior's position was the least likely to breed loyalty. With an office positioned just outside the Aquarium, the chief of staff must fend off, often physically, the 150 embassy employees—including attachés, congressional liaisons, spokespeople—whose need to speak to the ambassador was always urgent. Allegiance to me would make Lior permanently unpopular. Why, I asked myself, would he jeopardize a promising foreign service future for a political appointee?

I had the same doubts about the newly named deputy chief of mission (DCM), Dan Arbell. In charge of the embassy's day-to-day administration, controlling the content and flow of cables and supervising senior staff, the DCM in Washington often carries ambassadorial rank and the promise of significant promotion. Though exceedingly affable, the middle-aged Dan would surely place his long-term aspirations before those of any one-time envoy.

Every one of my doubts proved groundless. Guided by a supreme sense of duty, Lior and Dan became indispensable, trustworthy, and available to me around the clock. Whatever resentments seethed beyond those glass walls, regardless of crises roiling outside the embassy, each day began with Lior ambling into my office followed by Dan, thickset and balding, with his congenial limp. Together we sat and dissected the issues, weighed options, and played *iphah mi'stabra*—devil's advocate, in Aramaic—to my decisions. And we laughed. The belly-deep guffaws that my children like to imitate mixed with Lior's cynical chortle and Dan's horsey wheeze. Passersby in the hallway would pause and wonder what, with the Middle East and much of the world unraveling, could be so comical.

The answer, in truth, was: not much. Innumerable obstacles loomed, not the least of which was establishing my authority as ambassador. Unlike Americans who salute the rank—a policeman is always "officer," and a former president is still "Mr. President"—Israelis salute the person. The commander of the IDF is not called "General" and the chief justice of the Supreme Court is not "Your Honor." Rather, they are addressed by their first names and, more frequently, their nicknames—Moti (for Mordechai) or Rikki (Rebecca). This informality, a vestige perhaps of the biblical contempt for kings or the time when Israel's population was minuscule, removes interpersonal barriers. But it also erases private space. Inbred by my father's U.S. Army experience, my own respect for rank could not be renounced like my U.S. citizenship. Israelis universally refer to Netanyahu as Bibi (for Benjamin), but for me he was always "Mr. Prime Minister."

Unfortunately, I could not expect such deference from others. Everywhere in Washington I was "Your Excellency" or, most colloquially, "Mr. Ambassador," except in the Israeli embassy. There, the Hebrew word for ambassador, *shagrir,* went virtually unuttered. And in spite of dogged efforts to establish myself as Meekha'el—my Hebrew name—I remained My-kel, my American moniker.

And while I was no longer legally bound to the United States, I remained in Israeli eyes an *Amerikai*. This, too, was an impediment. Growing up, I remember how, on American television, naïve characters often had a southern drawl—think L'il Abner and Gomer Pyle—but naïfs on Israeli TV frequently sound like Americans. That accent still tinged my Hebrew. Americans who make *aliya,* moreover, can be disdained by those Israelis who, though die-hard Zionists, question why anyone sane would exchange cushy America for the hardscrabble Middle East. Surely, if you gave up living in a big Long Island house with a lawn and a two-car garage for squeezing into a similarly priced three-room apartment lacking a space for your thirdhand car but fully equipped with a bomb shelter, you had to be strange, some Israelis reasoned. The inflections in my speech and my decision to move to Israel remained impediments—however subliminal—to earning the embassy's respect.

That passage would take time, I understood, combining firmness, hard work, and demonstrable success. But it also required risk. Another principle inherited from my father, who left the military to head an inner-city hospital, is that all people, neurosurgeons and janitors alike, deserve dignity. I would esteem my staff. But beyond appreciation, I quickly discovered, Israeli diplomats value information. They yearn to be privy to secrets. Satisfying that longing without violating the government's trust represented yet another delicate challenge.

Leaks are the bane of any political system, above all those with free presses. Headline-hungry journalists are often sated by officials who, for personal or policy-driven reasons, feed them classified morsels. Such scoops were especially prevalent in the U.S.-Israel relationship with its countless "gov-to-gov" communications and intimate security contacts. Fairly or not, Israel's foreign service was reputed to be particularly porous. Once, after a quiet lunch, an ambassador from a Middle Eastern country not known for its fondness toward Israel urged me not to write a cable about our conversation. "Your foreign ministry is like one of those pots, you know"—his hands traced the shape of a bowl—"with holes in the bottom."

The goal, then, was to determine which information could be responsibly shared and which had to remain confidential. That balance had to be struck each week when I gathered senior diplomats and department heads to discuss politically delicate issues. The meetings were conducted in a special room in the embassy that reminded me of the "Cone of Silence" from the sixties comedy *Get Smart,* and which I dubbed the Cohen of Silence. No one understood the joke, of course, but all grasped the need for secrecy. For more than four years, throughout periods of acute sensitivity in Israel's relations with America, the Cohen of Silence stayed leakproof.

The same, unfortunately, could not be said of quarters outside the embassy. A cable authored by Consul General Nadav Tamir in Boston, a sensitive and intelligent man, accused Netanyahu of inflicting "strategic damage" to Israel's ties with the United States and likening his conduct to that of Iranian and North Korean leaders. Our equally capable consul in Los Angeles, Yaki Dayan, cabled the contents of a confidential talk in which Rahm Emanuel purportedly told him that Americans were fed up with missed Israeli opportunities to make peace and were liable to disengage from the process entirely. Leaked to the press, both cables made headlines—and headaches for me, Israel's ambassador.

Yet I made a similar mistake by briefing the foreign ministry's ultrasecure intelligence department. I surveyed the "tectonic shifts" in American foreign policy under Obama and stressed Israel's need to calibrate those changes and adapt ourselves accordingly. The next day's papers barked "Oren Cites Tectonic Rift in U.S.-Israel Relations." I learned a neologism—*disleaktion,* combining *leak* and *distortion*—and a lesson never to brief that department again.

No wonder Dan Arbell, Lior Weintraub, and I laughed each morning. Not because of the difficulties of establishing my authority among querulous diplomats or reconciling their demands for secrets with the state's insistence on stealth. We laughed, rather, because those challenges seemed so risible compared to the more than one hundred thousand rockets now in the hands of Hamas and Hezbollah, the refusal of the Palestinians to negotiate with us, and Iran's race for the bomb.

We laughed, too, because the annoyances of press leaks and the embassy's internal politics seemed so picayune compared to the grand sweep of Israel's most crucial alliance. Along with the more than $3 billion in annual defense assistance, the United States provided Israel with diplomatic support in often-hostile international bodies, such as the UN. America was the guarantor of Israel's essential peace accords with Egypt and Jordan, its protector against overwhelming threats, and the mediator of the all-too-frequent disputes with its neighbors. Israel, in turn, shared its expertly gained intelligence with the United States, its weapons development know-how, and its experience combating terror. Israel furnished airstrips and ports to American forces, and warehouses for prepositioning nearly a billion dollars in U.S. military gear. The staffs of most Israeli embassies included a military attaché, but only Washington had a defense attaché, signifying the unique breadth of Israel's security relations with America.

Beyond the strategic and tactical bonds, Israelis and Americans were conjoined by history. Only in the United States could streets be named for David Ben-Gurion and Golda Meir. And Israel was the only

Middle Eastern country to erect memorials to John F. Kennedy, Dr. Martin Luther King, Jr., and the victims of 9/11. Only Israel would have not one but two exact replicas of the Liberty Bell, each inscribed with the words from Leviticus, "Proclaim liberty throughout the Land."

We laughed—Dan, Lior, and I—because we understood that Israel's ability to weather the gathering turbulence in the Middle East hung in part on our American lifeline. We understood that any alliance, no matter how deep and multifaceted, could fray and even snap. We laughed bitterly, knowing that the three of us, sometimes alone, would have to hold together U.S.-Israel ties that were already taut.

New Realities

The strain was palpable from my initial days on the job. The leftist *Haaretz* newspaper claimed that Netanyahu had been heard describing Rahm Emanuel and senior White House advisor David Axelrod as "self-hating Jews." Attributed to no one in particular, the quote became the butt of Washington humor—"Rahm is many things," one jokester put it, "but self-hating isn't one of them." Netanyahu was not entertained. "Call them, tell them I never said it," he urged me. Contacting the White House Situation Room for the first time, I reached Rahm and David. Their response was polite but incredulous. "People say all sorts of things when they're upset. . . ." They clearly did not believe Netanyahu's denials, nor did they sound disturbed by the report. Tension was becoming a permanent feature of the relationship and, some seemed to think, a useful one.

The purpose was to pressure Israel into accepting a settlement freeze. The administration was adamant in demanding that Israel cease all construction in the areas it captured from Jordan in the Six-Day War. More than half a million Jews now lived beyond what was commonly called the 1967 borders, but which were in fact the armistice lines delineated in 1949 after Israel's War of Independence. The freeze, according to the White House, must be total, with no exceptions made for the "natural growth" building of children's bedrooms, clinics, and nursery schools. In addition, the administration demanded that Israel dismantle unauthorized settlement "outposts" while refraining from demolishing illegally built Arab structures. The policy applied not only to the West Bank but equally to Jerusalem.

• • •

Of all the issues in the peace process, none was more complex and combustible than Jerusalem. The holiest city in Judaism—the third most sacred to Muslims, and revered by Christians as the place of Jesus's passion—the city is studded with shrines. But it is also a metropolis of more than eight hundred thousand people, some 65 percent of them Jewish. The rest are mostly Palestinian Arabs who, even if not Israeli citizens, receive Israeli social, medical, and educational benefits. When secretly polled, more of these Arabs prefer life under Israeli, rather than Palestinian Authority, jurisdiction. Yet tensions can still flare behind the ancient walls of the Old City as well as in the New City, with its Jewish and Arab neighborhoods, some of them increasingly mixed. Alongside the modern buildings stand Roman, Arab, Crusader, Turkish, and British structures—monuments to the city's successive conquerors—scarred by the two twentieth-century wars that in many ways never ended.

The first was Israel's War of Independence, sometimes called the 1948 War but which actually began in November 1947, when the UN partitioned Palestine into Arab and Jewish states. Jerusalem belonged to neither, remaining in theory an international city. In reality, Jewish and Arab forces battled over every street.

The conclusion of an armistice in 1949 saw the city divided. The Arab half was centered in the east, with flanges curving around the north and southwest. This was a Jordanian city, a distant second to the capital of Amman, and never considered Palestinian. Jewish Jerusalem, located in the west, contrastingly became Israel's capital. Access to the holy places of all faiths was guaranteed on the Israeli side, while the Jordanians prohibited Jews from praying at the Western Wall and other consecrated sites.

The second war—in 1967—began when Jordanian forces attacked the Israeli side of Jerusalem and IDF troops, in response, captured the Jordanian half and reunited the city. A month later, Israel formally annexed the Jordanian areas—unlike the newly conquered West Bank, which remained "administered"—and declared all of Jerusalem its capital. Israel subsequently launched robust construction projects beyond the 1949 armistice line, many of them designed to ensure that Jerusalem would never again be divided.

None of this was acceptable to the United States. For the first

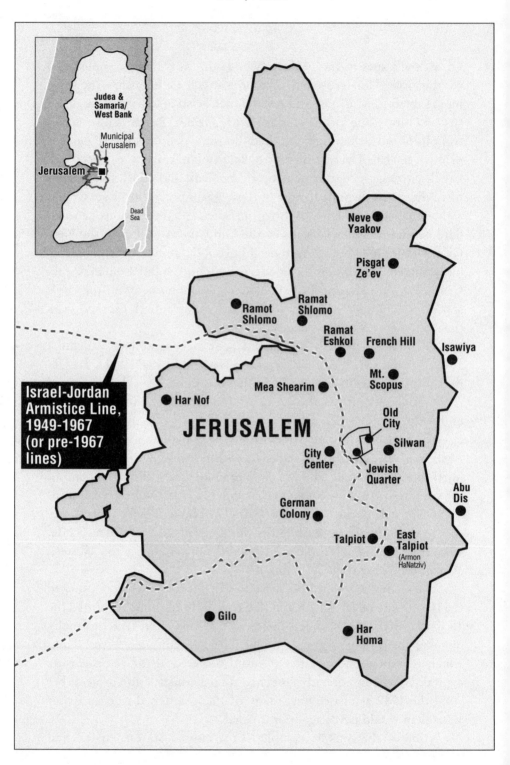

IDF chief of staff during the 1967 Six-Day War and two-time prime minister of Israel
Yitzhak Rabin also served as Israel's ambassador to Washington. There,
as a fifteen-year-old member of a Zionist youth movement, I met him.
That handshake changed my life.

Reuters

On kibbutz as a teenager, working as a cowboy on
the Golan Heights. "I'm in such ecstasy," I wrote my parents,
"for I know who I am and what I am doing here."

As an advisor to Israel's delegation to the UN "listening to diplomats
in three-piece suits spouting anti-Semitism."

In the Israeli paratroopers. In spite of the exhaustion and the loneliness,
I still felt indebted to the camaraderie, the maturity,
the chance to protect my country.

Beirut, 1982.
On a captured PLO jeep
with the city of Beirut
in the background.
At night, "I watched,
as if hallucinating, entire
neighborhoods flaming
with phosphorus and
the night sky ablaze
with tracers."

Next to an incapacitated Israeli tank
during the Second Lebanon War, 2006.

The Soviet Union was in its death throes and looked it.
Sagging gray buildings encrusted in garbage, endless food lines,
and the thinly disguised secret police—the ruthless KGB.

With Yitzhak Sokoloff (second from left) and members of the Zionist underground. Scientists, factory workers, teenagers, retirees—their only bond was their insistence on being Jews and their right to live in Israel. Soon to be sentenced to hard labor in the gulags, they were ordinary people of superhuman courage.

At Babi Yar, outside Kiev.
Here, in two days in 1941, the Nazis shot some 34,000 Jews. Forty years later, the Jews of the Soviet Ukraine were still yearning to be "a free people in our land."

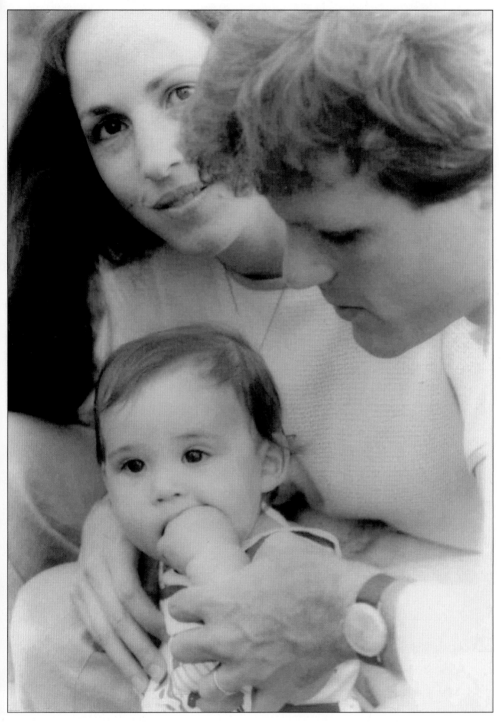

When our first child, Yoav, was born, I vowed, "That kid will never wear a helmet."
But he did. Twenty-one years later, while apprehending a Hamas terrorist,
Yoav was shot and wounded. His sister and brother would also wear helmets—
the price of Israel's defense.

Family photo with our first Israeli grandchild, Ariel, and his parents, Ayala and Yoav (to my left), and (to Sally's right) Lia and Noam. In response to our question whether we, by fulfilling our Zionist dream, had endangered them, our kids told us, "Raising us in Israel was the single best thing you could have done for us as parents."

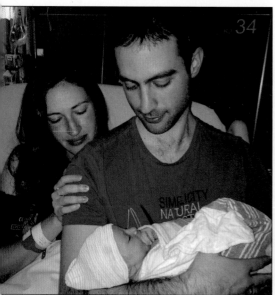

Lia and Yair with their newborn daughter, Romi. Having Israeli grandchildren is, for Sally and me, a crowning life achievement.

Grappling with situations that any normal family would find nightmarishly abnormal, we ultimately prevailed. The backpack with which I arrived in Israel blossomed into a furniture-filled home alight with laughter.

nineteen years of Israel's existence, Washington clung to the UN's plan for internationalizing Jerusalem. Consequently, the United States located its embassy in Tel Aviv, and even prohibited its personnel from meeting Israeli leaders in their Jerusalem offices. America gradually lifted this ban after 1967, but still treated Tel Aviv as Israel's capital. This policy generated numerous absurdities. The State Department maintained one consulate in West Jerusalem, serving mostly Jews, while an eastern consulate acted as a de facto legation to the Palestinians. Visitors to the East Jerusalem consulate's website, available in English and Arabic, would not know that a single Jew lived in the city. The passports of U.S. citizens born in Jerusalem—our daughter, Lia, for one—could not list their "place of birth" as "Jerusalem, Israel" but simply, anomalously, as Jerusalem.

Why, if the U.S.-Israel alliance was so sound, would one party in that union not respect the hallowed capital of the other? The reason was peace. Parallel to strengthening its ties with Israel, the United States after 1967 assumed the leadership of what came to be known as the peace process. The goal was a comprehensive treaty between Israel and the warring Arab states. At first this meant American mediation between Israel and Jordan to resolve all the outstanding issues between them, including Jerusalem's status. But then, after the 1993 Oslo Accords, Washington began viewing East Jerusalem as the potential capital of a future Palestinian state. Though Congress voted to move the embassy to Jerusalem, Republican and Democratic presidents alike overrode those bills in the interests of diplomacy. They also opposed Israeli building in Jerusalem's "Palestinian" areas, asserting that such construction "altered the character of the city" and erased the 1949 armistice line—or, as it was now called, the pre-1967 lines.

Few Israelis, though, remembered those lines. Growing up in southern Jerusalem, my three children would be astounded to learn that the two neighborhoods adjacent to their own—Armon HaNatziv and Gilo—arose on land beyond the pre-1967 lines. Such communities accounted for more than half of the city's Jewish population and were, by law, inseparable from the Jewish State. Contrary to widespread assumption, a prime minister has no more authority to freeze building in Jerusalem than a U.S. president has to stop construction in Chicago.

Acknowledging this and the fact that nearly a half century of Israeli development had permanently changed the demography of the

West Bank and Jerusalem, George W. Bush wrote to Ariel Sharon. Dated April 14, 2004, the letter affirmed:

> As part of a final peace settlement, Israel must have secure and recognized borders, which should emerge through negotiations between the parties. . . . In light of the new realities on the ground, including already existing major Israeli population centers, it would be unrealistic to expect that the outcome of the final status negotiations will be a full . . . return to the armistice lines of 1949.

Those "new realities," both Bush and Sharon understood, referred to the cluster of West Bank Jewish towns built to thicken out Israel's perilously narrow pre-1967 lines. Roughly 80 percent of the settlers lived in these "blocs," which, Bush indicated, would remain Israeli even after the creation of a Palestinian state. But "new realities" also referred to the Jewish neighborhoods in formerly Jordanian Jerusalem. While the exclusively Arab areas of the city could, conceivably, form the nucleus of a Palestinian capital, Israel could count on retaining those districts it had long considered sovereign.

The letter was a masterpiece of diplomacy. Endorsed by both houses of Congress—by then-senator Hillary Clinton and then-congressman Rahm Emanuel—it persuaded the Israeli public that ceding territory could yield concrete commitments from the United States. It safeguarded secure borders for the Jewish State. And it created diplomatic space for Israelis and Palestinians alike. The letter enabled Israeli governments to ease pressure from right-wing groups by building in those "major population centers" without precluding the establishment of a viable Palestinian state. Though they officially opposed any Israeli presence beyond the 1967 lines, Palestinian leaders understood that the areas suggested by the Bush-Sharon letter were nonnegotiable.

Shockingly, then, shortly after taking office, the Obama administration disavowed the letter. Denying the existence of any "informal or oral agreement" on Israeli construction in Jerusalem and the settlement blocs, the State Department further asserted that the letter "did not become part of the official position of the United States."

The announcement, reflecting Obama's need to distance himself from Bush and the president's deep aversion to settlements, profoundly impacted the peace process. Israel's center-right coalition no longer had a safety valve for palliating its settler constituency. And no Israeli government—right or left—could lawfully halt building in the country's capital. My children, who would have been surprised to learn that Armon HaNatziv and Gilo were once part of Jordan, were now shocked to hear that Washington considered them settlements.

Yet refuting the Bush-Sharon letter also boxed in the Palestinians. Mahmoud Abbas could not be less Palestinian than Obama. Far more than achieving an historic peace, possibly winning the Nobel Prize, and guaranteeing his place in diplomatic history, Abbas wanted to remain in power and stay alive. To achieve this, the Palestinian leader could not fall afoul of West Bank popular opinion. Already impressed with Hamas and fed up with Fatah corruption, that public might react violently to a Palestinian Authority that agreed to negotiate while Israel continued building in the territories. If the president of the United States demanded a freeze in all of the West Bank and Jerusalem, so, too, must Abbas.

America's new policies set conditions for talks that Israel could never meet and that Palestinians could not ignore. For the first time in the history of the U.S.-Israel alliance, the White House denied the validity of a previous presidential commitment. The dearth of trust that already plagued relations between Netanyahu and Abbas was compounded by both leaders' lack of confidence in Washington. And Jerusalem, that most intractable and flammable of issues, was once again pushed to the fore.

Daylight on Pennsylvania Avenue

The Jerusalem controversy and other flashpoints in U.S.-Israel relations could not, of course, be contained in the Aquarium or addressed from behind my desk. Leaving the timeworn yet secure confines of the Israeli embassy, I met with the architects of American foreign policy on my first excursions up Pennsylvania Avenue.

The initial stop was just south of the avenue, in Foggy Bottom, the formerly swampy district that was synonymous with the State Department. This, more than any other federal institution, had long had a reputation for opposing Zionism and Israel. My master's thesis, "The State Department and the Jewish State," profiled on the American diplomats who strenuously opposed any attempt to rescue European Jews from the Holocaust and labored to prevent Israel's creation. These were "the striped pants boys," as President Truman called them, the Ivy League dandies who he believed were anti-Semitic. My subsequent research chronicled the department's resistance to any pro-Israel gesture by the United States prior to the 1967 war. Not until Henry Kissinger—the first Jewish secretary of state—took over the department in the early 1970s did it fully come to terms with the legitimacy of Israel and its alliance with America. Because of Kissinger or, perhaps, the changing times, the once WASPs-only club of the State Department now welcomed minorities, women, and Jews.

These changes did not necessarily render the building entirely amenable to Israel, though. Lining its long, dull halls were the offices of the many diplomats who had served in Arab and Islamic countries, spoke their languages, and often internalized their attitudes toward Israel. Other officials interfaced with international organizations— the United Nations and the European Union—that were routinely critical of Israel. The fact that there was only one Jewish State and one people who spoke the Hebrew language meant the few careerists who specialized in Israel and understood us would always be massively outnumbered.

For those reasons, the State Department remained somberly associated in my mind with the name Foggy Bottom. There, even the most civil conversations could quickly become bogged down in disagreements.

Discord indeed mired my initial meeting with Deputy Secretary of State Jim Steinberg. A Harvard-and-Yale-educated statesman, he was also a dedicated angler renowned for tying flies in his spare time. Fittingly, Steinberg's attitude toward the Jewish State called to mind the old Israeli adage, "He loves us like a fisherman loves fish."

After accepting my *agrément* on June 26, Steinberg invited me back to his faux-colonial seventh-floor office to complain about Israeli policies. The first of these was our failure to live up to previous commitments to the United States and dismantle unauthorized outposts in the territories. I admitted that Israel had indeed not fulfilled its pledges, but noted that removing each outpost meant permanently stationing a battalion of troops on the site to prevent the settlers from coming back. The outpost problem could only be solved within an overall peace agreement, I explained, which the Palestinians unfortunately refused to discuss. Steinberg next protested Israel's demolition of two Arab "houses" near Jerusalem. In response, I produced the list of legal rulings that authorized the demolitions as well as aerial photographs proving that both structures were, in fact, stables.

Boyish despite his salt-and-pepper hair and wire-rimmed glasses, Steinberg could be imperious. He regarded me unflappably as I termed the department's Jerusalem policy as "non-implementable and prejudicial." Under the administration's policy, a Jew could only build his home in certain Jerusalem neighborhoods but an Arab could build anywhere—even illegally—without limit. "In America," I said, "that's called discrimination."

From Foggy Bottom, I continued up Pennsylvania to the neoclassical White House and its gray Victorian neighbor, the Eisenhower Executive Office Building (EOB). Both contained the offices of the National Security Council, with its experts on Israel and the Middle East. My most frequent NSC host was Dan Shapiro, senior director for the Middle East and North Africa. He occupied a cubicle with a curiously sloped ceiling that required us both to stoop. The room's contours served as a metaphor for a region that afforded limited maneuverability to Americans and Israelis, and forced us to keep our heads down.

When I first met Dan in Israel during the summer of 2008, I suggested that the Oslo formula, still a failure after fifteen years, might be reconsidered in favor of creative interim steps. But the administration fervidly embraced Oslo, as did Dan, an early Obama acolyte. My response was to wager that the demand for a settlement freeze would not bring the Palestinians back to the negotiating table but rather drive them further away. "Why should they enter talks in which they'll have to pay for concessions when they can get them for free without talking?" Such logic failed to impress Dan, who, the bookishness of his clipped Vandyke beard and pea-shaped glasses notwithstanding, could react temperamentally. "The dignity and credibility of the president—and his relationship with the prime minister—hinges on the freeze," he retorted. We concurred to disagree and toasted each other with cans of Diet Mountain Dew, the soft drink reputed to have the highest legal level of caffeine.

Elsewhere in the EOB, in an office endowed with more physical and political space, sat Dennis Ross. Having languished for several ineffectual months in the State Department, Dennis at the end of June transferred to the NSC, where he served as Special Assistant to the President on Middle East and South Asian Affairs. This put him in charge of virtually every major American conflict as well as the Israeli-Palestinian and Iranian nuclear issues.

As was the case with Dan Shapiro, I had met Dennis before my appointment. We taught together at Georgetown and Sally knew his family from San Francisco. But in contrast to Dan, a former congressional staffer for Democrats, Dennis had more than thirty years' experience in what he called statecraft—the title of his most recent book—and had worked for presidents of both parties. A person of process, he had helped mediate the Oslo talks and believed in a negotiated solution to Iran. He loyally followed the president's lead in opposing all Israeli building in the West Bank and East Jerusalem.

This approach should have generated some tension between us, but it never did. Perhaps because of the tenderhearted smiles he attached to even his bleakest critiques of Israeli policy, my meetings with Dennis were invariably rewarding. He understood the fears that underlie much of Israeli policy and the fact that Netanyahu, more than any of Israel's current leaders, had the authority to make peace. Moreover, Dennis had the guts to make that case to his colleagues.

From No. 1600, Pennsylvania Avenue ascends to Capitol Hill. "The White House" is a metonym for the administration and its policy implementers throughout the Pentagon, the State Department, and numerous federal agencies. So, too, "the Hill" refers to the bicameral legislature, the Capitol, and the adjoining complex of office buildings serving its members and their staffs. But unlike the White House, which is accessible to a range of Israeli officials, the Hill is the ambassador's exclusive domain. It is also the bastion of pro-Israel sentiment, reflecting the affection of a sizable American majority for the allied Jewish State.

Climbing to the Hill once a week was, from the start, an extravaganza. Displayed before me was a kaleidoscope of personalities and viewpoints, of humor and tragedy, profanity and eloquence. Here I could reunite with John McCain, who told me that after losing the 2008 presidential election, he slept like a baby. "I dozed for two hours and woke up and cried," he said. "Dozed for two hours, and woke up and cried." I listened to Republican senator Lindsey Graham deconstruct Obama in lilting South Carolina tones. The soft-spoken majority leader, Harry Reid, came to our first meeting with a list of questions about my books, all of which he had read. I could discuss Lincoln's war strategy with Congressman Steve Israel, a fellow Civil War buff, or talk football with massive Jon Runyan, who once played tackle for the Houston Oilers and Philadelphia Eagles. I could confer with long-standing friends Steny Hoyer and Kevin McCarthy, House whips from either side of the aisle, and establish unconventional friendships with the House Armed Services Committee chairman Howard "Buck" McKeon, a devout Mormon in cowboy boots, and progressive Democrat Keith Ellison, Congress's first Muslim member.

Beyond initial schmoozing, though, conversations on the Hill dealt with the often-brutal business of the Middle East and the occasionally divergent ways Israel and the United States conducted it. Here, too, the challenge was to preserve across-the-board support for Israel in the face of paralyzing congressional partisanship. And then there were the issues that cut across party lines and blindsided me.

In our first conversation, Senator Bill Nelson of Florida caught me off guard with a letter from a constituent alleging "Israeli economic apartheid" in the territories. I quickly refuted the charge, citing Israel's removal of dozens of Intifada-era roadblocks, the reopening of Jordan River bridges, and the consequent growth of the Palestinian economy by a record 8 percent. Introducing herself, Senator Dianne Feinstein offered me a glass of select California wine and said, "I am a peacemaker but you are a fighter." She criticized reports of an Israeli plan to replace the Arabic name for Jerusalem, *al-Quds,* with the Hebrew *Yerushalayim* on Israeli road signs. I admitted that place-names could sometimes be controversial—southerners never refer to the Battle of Manassas as northerners prefer to, Bull Run—but assured her that even if such a plan existed, Israel's Supreme Court would overrule it. "And," I added, "sometimes you have to fight before making peace, like Yitzhak Rabin." More surprising still, Senator Mitch McConnell—unlike Nelson and Feinstein, a Republican—also raised a complaint in our initial talk, about Israeli tariffs on Kentucky bourbon. I wondered, do Israelis even *drink* bourbon?

But more than the Palestinian economy, Jerusalem road signs, and taxes on whiskey, the major issue on the Hill remained the settlement freeze. It dominated my first encounter with the Jewish members of Congress. There were thirty of them, all but one of them—Eric Cantor, absent that day—Democrats. They had impressive voting records on Israel and, after a summer of coolness toward the Jewish State, I was looking forward to a warmhearted embrace. Instead, I stumbled into a blizzard.

"President Obama has asked Israel to freeze settlements," Florida's burly representative Robert Wexler began, "and Netanyahu ignores him." I reminded the members that a construction halt had never before been a condition for talks. Netanyahu had nevertheless pledged to refrain from building new settlements, I explained, and to confine construction to existing ones, thereby preserving the "peace map." Yet my remarks generated little sympathy. Others accused Netanyahu of showing ingratitude toward the United States and of fanning anti-Obama sentiment in Israel. Clearly, the congressmen were upset about a recent *Jerusalem Post* poll that showed that, after his Cairo speech, the president's popularity among Israelis had plunged to an unprecedented 4 percent. Israelis were less disappointed with Obama than they were frightened by his revolutionary outreach to the Muslim world. That anxiety was communicated to some American Jews who subsequently complained to Jewish legislators. They, in turn, dealt me what would remain my most troubling experience on the Hill.

In time, my odysseys up and down Pennsylvania Avenue became an almost daily routine, and frequently concluded back at the embassy. There, resubmerged in the Aquarium, I analyzed the day's discussions. One of the overriding challenges of Israel's ambassador is to cull information from multitudinous sources—not just the State Department, the White House, and the Hill, but press commentators, public intellectuals, foreign diplomats—and identify coherent themes. Those conclusions are then conveyed to Jerusalem, along with recommendations on how Israel should best proceed. That process requires time and clear-sightedness and a gravitas born of the realization that the ambassador's words might impact the lives of millions. Quiet is also essential to thinking cogently. But silence, I learned, was the rarest ambassadorial luxury. Invariably, while I sifted mentally through the chaff of data for vital kernels of truth, my phone started ringing. It rang—shrilly, I imagined—on July 13, with the news of Obama's first meeting with the leaders of American Jewry.

Such meetings had become standard in formulating U.S. policy toward the Israeli-Palestinian conflict. The assumption was that American

Jewish leaders, though often divided on domestic and ritual issues, were united in their support for Israel and served as a natural bridge between the White House and Jerusalem. For Obama, though, the briefings were less a means of garnering support than of muting opposition. Indeed, what many American Jewish leaders saw as the placing of undue pressure on Israel, the president regarded as displays of restraint. "He felt he had pulled his punches with Netanyahu," David Axelrod later wrote, "to avoid antagonizing elements of the American Jewish community."

Crowding into the Roosevelt Room, representatives of fourteen Jewish organizations heard Obama reaffirm his "unbreakable" and "unshakable" commitment to Israel and its security. He promised to be more evenhanded in asking all parties, not just Israelis, to make sacrifices for peace. Yet the meeting would be remembered as a turning point in the administration's approach toward the Jewish State.

The shift was apparent from the guest list. Included for the first time with the mainstream Jewish leaders were the heads of Americans for Peace Now and the newly founded J Street, both organizations stridently critical of Israel and its traditional American supporters. Their presence rattled the other participants, many of whom had been personally slighted by these parvenus.

More jarring was Obama's exchange with Malcolm Hoenlein, the perennial executive of the Conference of Presidents of Major American Jewish Organizations. Hoenlein insisted that Israelis took risks only when they were convinced that the United States stood with them. Obama, though, disagreed, recalling the eight years when Bush backed Israel unequivocally but never produced peace. The president's response disappointed many of those present. Bush's support for Israel had, in fact, emboldened Olmert to propose establishing a viable Palestinian state—an offer ignored by Mahmoud Abbas. Nevertheless, the president concluded, "When there is no daylight, Israel just sits on the sidelines and that erodes our credibility with the Arabs."

Commenting on the discussion, J Street founder Jeremy Ben Ami cited Obama's ability to connect with the Muslim world and his immense standing in America and abroad. "He was very clear that this is a moment that has to be seized and he intends to seize it." By contrast, the other American Jewish leaders emerged from the meeting concerned about Obama's departure from the long-standing principle of "no daylight" in U.S.-Israel relations.

Historically, that principle applied to the alliance as a whole, without differentiating between its diplomatic and defense aspects. Counterintuitive as it sounded, daylight was bad and darkness—that is, the absence of open disagreements on policy—optimal. Obama, though, clearly drew a distinction. The dimmer the light separating the United States and Israel on security issues, the administration held, the brighter it could be on peace.

From its outset in office, the administration adopted the mantra "security ties between the United States and Israel have never been closer." This was true, and I had no difficulty reaffirming it. Every Israeli general and intelligence chief I spoke with attested to the intimacy of relations with their American counterparts under Obama. In areas as diverse as weapons development, joint training, intelligence sharing, and educational exchanges, the cooperation was superb. When Obama said, "Israel is the most powerful country in this region," he could justifiably claim part of the credit.

Obama's commitment to Israel's security was genuine and fulfilled a fundamental American interest, but it also helped realize his vision. By highlighting its contributions to Israel's defense, the administration could justify pressuring Israeli leaders on peace. This dual approach eased the anxieties of the president's pro-Israel supporters while presumably placing our enemies on notice that, diplomatic differences notwithstanding, the allies remained militarily bound. On Iran, too, the White House sought to distinguish between security closeness and political distance. American contributions to the IDF's missile defense, for example, diminished Israel's case for striking Iranian nuclear plants preemptively, and generated more time for talks. Israelis referred to this approach sardonically as a "hug"—in Hebrew, *chibbuk*—intended to keep us close.

The problem with the "no daylight on security but daylight on diplomacy" tactic was that, in the Middle East, it did not work. Unlike in the West, where security is measured in tanks, jets, and guns, security in this part of the world is largely a product of impressions. A friend who stands by his friends on some issues but not on others is, in Middle Eastern eyes, not really a friend. In a region infamous for its unforgiving sun, any daylight is searing.

By illuminating the gaps in their political positions, the administration cast shadows over Israel's deterrence power. Foes such as Hamas and Syria were liable to perceive policy differences as indicating a lack of unity on defense. Iran could conclude that the *chibbuk* was a bear hug that tied Israel's hands while the ayatollahs raced forward on their nuclear program and transferred advanced missiles to Hezbollah. In the Middle East, when the White House pressured Israel on peace, the enemies of peace could conclude that America might not stand beside Israel in war.

Other actions of the Obama administration, especially arms sales to the Arabs, impacted Israel's ability to defend itself, but few as substantively as its insistence on daylight on issues unrelated to security. For that reason, I felt compelled to deny that distance in all my media interviews, op-ed articles, and public speeches. As ambassador, the only responsible message had to be: "Yes, we may sometimes disagree on tactics, but our goals remain the same." And, "Friends always tell one another the truth as they see it, even when it's hard. That is the definition of ally."

After a career of striving to write the truth about history, bending it in the interests of security did not come easily to me. The seventeenth-century English author Henry Wotton observed, "An ambassador is a man of virtue sent abroad to lie for his country." But Wotton underestimated the dilemma. An ambassador sometimes lies for two countries.

This, more than any other aspect of my new role, took a toll on me emotionally and even physically. Two months after starting the job, I emerged from my first medical checkup to be told by the doctor that my body was deficient in vitamin D. "You need to get out more into the sun," he recommended. I was grateful for his prescription, but nevertheless demurred. "No thanks," I replied. "I've already seen enough daylight."

At Home and on the Water

Evenings, I left the office for the seven minutes' drive to the Residence, the home of every Israeli ambassador since 1962. If the embassy looked run-down, much of the Residence appeared dilapidated. Appropriate for the poor socialist country of fifty years ago, the building had become a mite-infested museum of aging art and ruptured plumbing. Any attempt to convince the Foreign Ministry to refurbish what was, in effect, Israel's face in Washington, or to drag visiting ministers into the misery of its kitchen, proved useless. None of them wanted to wake up to headlines accusing them of funding diplomatic frills when working-class Israelis could barely buy groceries. The decision became clear: either devote my time to a dubious campaign for home renovation or concentrate on safeguarding an alliance. The Residence remained an eyesore.

More propitiously, I prepared to present my credentials to the president. After receiving *agrèment*, ambassadors must personally convey a letter naming them as their country's exclusive envoy. Only then can they formally do business in the White House. For convenience's sake, numerous new ambassadors present their credentials on the same day, yet the ceremony remains festive and tradition-rich. Our three children flew in for the occasion, as did my mother and father, which ruffled some procedural feathers. The spouses and offspring of ambassadors were welcomed, the protocol officers said, but not the ambassadors' parents. To which I replied, "But those other ambassadors are not from a *Jewish* state." After the heartache I caused them by raising my family in far-off Israel, after all their worrying while I fought in wars, my parents *deserved* to be at the White House.

We waited outside the Residence until the black sedan arrived, American and Israeli flags flickering from its hood, and bore us behind motorcycle escorts up Pennsylvania Avenue. This was the ultimate pinch-me moment. Sally, our children, all hugging one another and expectantly giggling, my parents silent and proud, and me glancing at the cloudless sky overhead and saying to myself in Hebrew, *Todah rabah*. Thank you. For just that moment—and I knew it would be the last for some time—there were no disagreements over the peace process and Iran, no friction over Turkey or quarrels in the UN. There was only the South Lawn, as dazzlingly green as the day Thomas Jefferson planted it. There were only the Marine sergeants who greeted the limousine and came to attention as I emerged.

Entering the West Wing, the protocol officers led me into the Cabinet Room and waited, annoyed, while I took too long signing the guest book. My inscription recalled the support of previous presidents—Adams, Lincoln, Wilson, Theodore Roosevelt, Truman—for Jewish statehood, and pledged "my paramount efforts" to join Obama "in upholding the historic America-Israel alliance." Rahm Emanuel came in to congratulate me and thump me on the chest with a hearty "Mazel tov, buddy." We stayed schmoozing while my family was ushered into the Roosevelt Room and from there into the Oval Office, where I caught up with them chatting with Obama.

The protocol people asked me to prepare an "elevator speech," a four-minute statement such as I might make on the unlikely chance that the president and I were ever stuck in an elevator. I planned to talk about our common goals of making peace and preventing Iran from nuclearizing. But Obama was deep in conversation with my parents. This lasted the entire four minutes, leaving me just enough time to shake the president's hand, pass him my credentials, and pose with him for a celebratory photo.

That evening at the Residence, Sally and I received hundreds of guests—childhood friends, college buddies, community and congressional leaders. Their expressions of support both moved and invigorated me, but none more tenderly than those from our three children. Each was a page-turner of a book about overcoming social and educational handicaps, about unquestioning national service, roller-coaster romances, internal searches, athletic excellence, intellectual curiosity, and laughter. Especially laughter. To spend an evening with Lia, Noam, and Yoav was to risk bodily injury from kid-induced paroxysms of glee. That night was no exception, as they presented me with a fake American passport listing my sex as "uncertain" and an "ambassadorial first aid kit" containing Rescue Remedy, Vaseline, and vodka.

Later, looking over the reception's detritus, I asked Noam, our youngest, how he thought it went. Muscle-bound yet gentle, beautiful but shy, Noam had a preternatural ability to pick up on cues. "Fine, Abba," he answered, "but there was something in your expression, in your jaw, that seemed to say, 'Can I really do this?'"

Noam was right. And it concerned me that my fears might be showing. An Israeli ambassador, especially one serving in such supercharged circumstances, cannot afford even a semblance of self-doubt. Yet the possibility that the job was unwinnable, as some of my predecessors deemed, harried me. And if insurmountable to them, serving in far calmer times, could I prevail?

Fortunately, summer came and Washington emptied out, much of it to shorelines farther north. The media was fixated on the tragic death of singer Michael Jackson and the arrest of Henry Louis Gates, Jr., an African-American Harvard professor, outside his own Cambridge, Massachusetts, door. Obama denounced this as a "stupid act," but then convened a "beer summit" between Gates and the arresting police officer at the White House.

This momentary focus on domestic, rather than Middle East, affairs, left me time for that rarest of causes—myself. Though chronically unphotogenic, I managed to take an official ambassadorial portrait thanks to the patience and persistence of my photographer friend, Anne Mandelbaum. The photo eschewed the cheery American fashion of big smile and many teeth in favor of Israel's tight-lipped, don't-mess-with-me mode.

I also acquired an ambassadorial wardrobe. "You can't dress like that," Ellen Stern—the same Ellen who originally urged me to apply for the ambassadorship—scolded, pointing to my rumpled professorial garb. She sent me all the way to Brooklyn, to the four-story workshop of Martin Greenfield, the dapper and undiminished Holocaust survivor who served as tailor to Bill Clinton and Colin Powell. The journey was arduous and the refittings many, but I understood the need. Israelis can be indifferent to clothing. Collar stays—for which there is no Hebrew translation—are unknown to them, and some will even wear combat boots to Congress. But Americans take their apparel seriously, and a Greenfield suit, its lapel adorned with crossed U.S. and Israeli flags, would help them to take Israel more seriously.

Those clothes fit better when, after months with no opportunity to exercise, I joined the Potomac Boat Club. I had not rowed competitively since representing the United States in the 1977 Maccabiah Games in Israel. Long unpracticed, my sculling was at first wobbly, but eventually I regained my balance and my stroke. My security detail fretted on the banks as I found peace. While sliding across the reflection of the Washington Monument or, upstream, plying through a pristine nature reserve, I could contemplate vexing issues. My relationship with God, always personal if amorphous, also crystallized on the water, an ideal place for prayer. Each time, I returned to the Residence physically and spiritually replenished. Only then was I ready do what any newly accredited ambassador should, namely, his homework.

Obama 101

Ambassadors are principally communicators, the conveyors of official messages to the media and privileged information to senior officials.

A typical ambassadorial day includes interviews on television and radio, YouTube greetings, and as many as three speeches. But while their primary function may be talking, a legate's most crucial task is, in fact, to listen. And whenever I could that summer—and throughout the years ahead—I sought out individuals worth hearing.

The quest took me to Vernon Jordan, the African-American lawyer, civil rights activist, and advisor to Democratic presidents whose outsize reputation more than matched his monumental physique. In his office paneled with honorary doctorates, Vernon told me that Obama was not Israel's chief problem. Rather it was America's economic crisis, which showed scant sign of abating, and its retreat from global leadership. "The old mare ain't what she used to be," Vernon lamented.

A similar sentiment was voiced by James Carville, former campaign advisor to the Clintons and the architect of Ehud Barak's victory over Netanyahu in 1999. In a Louisiana twang I had heard only in movies about the antebellum South, the garrulous and glabrous Carville explained that Israel's biggest problem was not Obama's inexperience but America's inability to pay its bills. "You all in Israel got to wake up," he warned me. "That till is *empty*."

Every lunch, every coffee break, produced some illuminating viewpoints. They came from the contrarian *Wall Street Journal* columnist and future Pulitzer Prize laureate Bret Stephens, whom I first met when he was the twenty-eight-year-old editor in chief of *The Jerusalem Post*. Others were supplied by the endlessly engaging Donna Brazile of the Democratic National Committee and CNN, and by Elliott Abrams, the Scoop Jackson Democrat turned Republican presidential advisor, an outspoken Israel supporter, and the brains behind the Bush-Sharon letter. Though each struck distinctive chords in describing the state of U.S.-Israel relations, they sounded a common refrain: transformation. The tectonic shifts I described at the Foreign Ministry were proving to be deeper and more seismic than I had originally gauged. They threatened to become the "tectonic rifts" disleaked to the press.

No one confirmed that assessment more authoritatively than Henry Kissinger. Arguably the twentieth century's towering diplomatic figure, the mastermind of Cold War strategies and architect of the Pax Americana in the Middle East, he had previously invited me to his New York office to discuss history and his place in it. But in my new position, the topic was no longer the past but rather the current diplomatic situation and the state of U.S.-Israel relations.

Sympathizing with Netanyahu's predicament, Dr. Kissinger urged him to navigate cautiously between the shoals of the peace process and the Iranian nuclear issue. He seemed skeptical about Obama's ability to effectively mediate the Israeli-Palestinian conflict and pessimistic about his eagerness to reconcile with Iran. "But surely the White House understands that Iran with nuclear capabilities means the end of American hegemony in the Middle East," I protested. In his legendary Bavarian accent, deepened and graveled by age, he asked, "And what makes you think anybody in the White House still cares about American hegemony in the Middle East?"

In between listening and absorbing, I read and took notes. Among the most enlightening sources I consulted was a 2008 paper titled "Strategic Leadership: Framework for a 21st Century National Security Strategy," published by Jim Steinberg and other international relations professors soon to occupy senior administration posts.

The authors began by rejecting the notion that "America must always be in charge." Rather, they held, the United States should adopt a collegial approach to world affairs, working with other nations and international bodies to resolve disputes. Among these was the Iranian nuclear threat, "which should not be underestimated nor overhyped," and that could be addressed through a dual-track policy of deterrence and engagement. They also advocated a new approach to the Muslim world based on economic development and democratization, but also on "improved relations with more moderate elements of political Islam" and a "narrative of pride in the achievements of Islam." While keen to preserve Israel's security and Jewish identity, the authors do not list it among America's strategic partners. Rather, they describe the Jewish State as a party to the peace process that America must—in contrast to other global issues—lead.

The paper served as a primer on the administration's foreign policy. "Our destiny is shared," Obama told the UN General Assembly in 2009. "No balance of power among nations will hold." Similar sentiments informed Obama's Cairo speech, his high regard for the UN, and his policy toward Iranian nuclearization. They resounded in the administration's respect for the "international community," a grouping that included North Korea, Pakistan, and Sudan, and which many Israelis considered an oxymoron.

As someone who had spent several years on American campuses, all of these ideas rang familiar to me. They echoed the sixties' revulsion to military strength, the romance with developing societies, and the questioning of American primacy. Regarding the Middle East, in particular, one could discern the reverberations of Edward Said's *Orientalism,* which had become the single most influential book in the humanities. Teaching at Harvard in 2006, I was stunned to hear students tell me that they had read *Orientalism* several times in courses as diverse as French colonial literature and Italian-African history.

Also while at Harvard, several students urged me to look at the website of the university's John F. Kennedy School of Government, which had posted a new paper by reputable scholars Stephen Walt and John Mearsheimer. The article lumped American Jewish organizations together with *The New York Times, The Wall Street Journal,* evangelist Jerry Falwell, and the progressive Howard Dean, labeling them collectively as "The Israel Lobby." This nebulous cabal made support for Israel, portrayed as a militantly theocratic and colonialist state, the centerpiece of America's postwar Middle East policy and the primary source of Muslim rage against the United States.

Devoid of archival sources and tainted with inaccuracies—oil, of course, and not Israel, was America's Middle East priority—"The Israel Lobby and U.S. Foreign Policy" was even less academically sound than *Orientalism.* Utterly ignored were the vast advantages that Israel afforded the United States in intelligence sharing, weapons development, and high tech. Israel's indispensable role as America's sole democratic and unreservedly pro-American ally in the Middle East also went unmentioned. Instead, Walt and Mearsheimer—disciples of the so-called Realist School, which sought a foreign policy detached from values and domestic opinion—advanced a conspiracy thesis of undue Jewish influence on Congress and the media. Even Christopher Hitchens, a frequent Israel critic, dismissed the article as "smelly."

Nevertheless, the assertion that U.S. support for Israel had precipitated 9/11 and other jihadist attacks against Americans, and that, far from an asset, Israel represented a strategic liability for the United States, tapped into strong campus currents. Graduates of those universities naturally gravitated toward the press and government service. So "The Israel Lobby," refined into a bestselling book, penetrated the Beltway.

This did not mean that Obama had internalized the views contained in either *Orientalism* or "The Israel Lobby." Still, there was no gainsaying the books' impact on the academic and policy-making worlds from which his administration's attitudes sprung. The notion of the need to revise America's global role, to palliate Islam, and achieve diplomatic distance from Israel had become conventional by the time I arrived in Washington. Even the term "Israel Lobby," once confined to racists such as Ku Klux Klan leader David Duke, entered the mainstream media. Israel's own policies no doubt accelerated these trends and endowed them with a moral pretext. As David Rothkopf often reminded me, Obama's first memory of Israel would not be the heroic Six-Day War, but rather its 1982 invasion of Lebanon.

My goal, though, was not merely to understand the origins of Obama's policies but to anticipate how they would shape the course of U.S.-Israel relations. My goal was to never be surprised. Achieving that objective, though, required deeper research into the president's personal outlook. I needed to dig beneath the layers of articles for and against him, below the rumors of his friendships with sixties radical Bill Ayers and Palestinian professor Rashid Khalidi, a protégé of Edward Said. I needed to reach the bedrock Barack Obama.

The excavation took me to the two most authentic sources, the books he had written about himself. Alas, *The Audacity of Hope,* composed when Obama was already a presidential candidate, served more as a grandstand than as an intimate window into his thinking. A far more penetrating glimpse was accorded by Obama's stirring and remarkably candid memoir, *Dreams from My Father,* published nearly fifteen years before.

Frankness, for me, was the book's principal asset, for it traced a young man's search for self from laid-back Hawaii to religiously stringent Indonesia and then on to the Kenyan villages where he seemed to feel most at home. En route, he cultivated the aversion to tribalism later cited in his inaugural speech as well as his empathy for Islam. Yet it was only in the cauldron of inner-city America that Obama's identity was finally forged. There he became, for the first time, conscientiously African-American and adopted the internationalist and social justice ideas long popular at the urban universities where he studied and taught—Columbia, Chicago, and Harvard. His pervasive belief in the power of words, instilled by his legal studies, reminded me of the ancient Aramaic incantation "Abracadabra," meaning "I speak therefore I create."

Most people form their identities in childhood, but Obama learned who he was and what he stood for relatively late, in his twenties. His early years were plagued by instability; he was raised by a twice-divorced mother and a grandmother Obama later described—dispassionately—as "a typical white person." That same sangfroid characterized a chilling chapter in the book in which the nine-year-old Obama sees his Indonesian stepfather decapitating a chicken:

> Blood shot out in a long, crimson ribbon. [The chicken] landed with a thud, then struggled to its feet, its head lolling grotesquely against its side, its legs pumping wildly in a wide, wobbly circle. I watched as the circle grew smaller, the blood trickling down to a gurgle, until finally the bird collapsed, lifeless on the grass. [We] ate quietly under a dim yellow bulb—chicken stew and rice. . . . Later . . . I listened to the crickets chirp under the moonlight and remembered the last twitch of life that I'd witnessed a few hours before. I could barely believe my good fortune.

The fact that the young Obama was dazzled by this grisly sight revealed a remarkable degree of emotional detachment. At a similar age, I went fishing with my father and watched as he caught a carp and mangled it. But instead of being fascinated, the experience traumatized me. Years passed before I could even look at seafood.

More alarming for me still were Obama's attitudes toward America. Vainly, I scoured *Dreams from My Father* for some expression of reverence, even respect, for the country its author would someday lead. Instead, the book criticizes Americans for their capitalism and consumer culture, for despoiling their environment and maintaining antiquated power structures. Traveling abroad, they exhibited "ignorance and arrogance"—the very shortcomings the president's critics assigned to him.

From Obama's autobiographical works arose the image of an individual who had overcome adversity early in life, who displayed resilience and contempt for weakness but also a cold-blooded need for control. Projecting that need, not surprisingly, made his administration the most centralized since World War II, with many key decisions made in the Oval Office. At the risk of armchair psychoanalyzing, I wondered whether Obama had replicated his rearing by his dominant mother and grandmother by surrounding himself with powerful women advisors, including his formidable wife, Michelle. Perhaps, too, his rejection by not one but two Muslim father figures informed his outreach to Islam.

Passionate about his community, Obama was less enthused about other aspects of America, especially the bankers and businessmen he was compelled to bail out or those in the working class whom he later said "cling to guns and religion." And while sincere in his commitment to cooperate with international actors—some pundits labelled him "the first post-American president"—Obama's personal detachment inhibited him from forming close friendships with foreign leaders. In spite of his declared sympathies for the downtrodden, Obama became the first president in twenty years to refuse to receive the Dalai Lama for fear of alienating China.

But what did any of this mean for Israel? Instinctively, human beings seek order in the universe and, in politics, a clear formula for decision making. In reality, though, randomness—whims, quirks, gaffes—determines much of the relations between individuals, just as it does among nations. This observation, born of a career trying to make sense of historical processes, did not absolve me of the need to get inside Obama's mind and try to see the world as he did. Accordingly, I culled his memoirs, extrapolated from all that I had heard and read, and formulated several basic assumptions.

The first was that Obama was not anti-Israel. He cared for Israel certainly as much as he cared about most other foreign countries and understood the deep affection for Israel felt by his many American Jewish supporters as well as by the large majority of Americans generally. Contrary to his detractors' claims, I believed that he would stand by Israel if ever we were attacked. But Obama admired an idealized Israel—not the Israel of the settlers and their right-wing backers, a state that was part of the solution, not the problem. Repulsed by the colonialist legacy he encountered in Kenya, he may also have shared the sense of identification felt by some African-Americans—among them Condoleezza Rice—with the Palestinians. "For centuries, black people in America suffered the lash of the whip as slaves and the humiliation of segregation," he said in his Cairo speech, and then segued to the plight of the Palestinians. By contrast, the Zionist narrative of an indigenous people returning to our homeland did not as yet resonate with the president.

Though of relatively recent provenance, Obama's outlook nevertheless contained what I called his *kishke*—Yiddish for gut—causes. These included creating a Palestinian state, reconciling with Islam, and preventing nuclear proliferation. All three intersected with Israel's interests, and in potentially abrasive ways. The president's cold-bloodedness, while perhaps a plus in fighting terrorism, could also lead to browbeating us. Overseas, I saw an Obama who sought to depart from America's century-long reliance on Western alliances and the projection of military power. Rather, he gave preference to soft power and peaceful cooperation with international bodies. The fact that Israel was a traditional ally, heavily dependent on American might, and at odds with many of those international organizations, compounded my concerns.

More than policy, I concluded, Barack Obama was about ideology and a worldview often at variance with Israel's. Yet he was the president with whom our leaders would have to interact for the next four years and, I already believed in the summer of 2009, for another four after that. Millions of Americans read the same books and heard the same opinions I had but rather than recoiling from them, raved in approval. Israel remained the essential ally of the United States—of that I was certain—its only stable and unconditional Middle Eastern friend. But Israel would have to remind some Americans of that reality. And the president would have to be convinced.

No less vitally, I had to persuade Israelis of the need to make their case to America. Many Israeli leaders were American-educated and remembered the much different country of decades past. For them, the Obama phenomenon could seem like a momentary detour from an otherwise unbroken path of American preeminence and exceptionalism. As I saw it, a crucial part of my job was unearthing American truths and conveying them to Israeli power. The homework I began in August 2009 never really ended. The time I could devote to it dwindled, however, as the U.S.-Israeli alliance was sorely tested by—who could have guessed?—a deluded Jewish judge.

Blood Libel

On paper, at least, Richard Goldstone was the paragon of righteousness. A Johannesburg-born magistrate who rose to the bench during the harshest years of South African apartheid, he wielded his gavel to break that racist system and presided over the reconciliation between blacks and whites. He subsequently prosecuted those accused of committing war crimes in the former Yugoslavia and Rwanda. In return, he won the friendship of Nelson Mandela and academic appointments to Harvard, Cambridge, and the Hebrew University. But Goldstone's nondescript and seemingly guileless mien masked strata of self-righteousness. The UN Human Rights Council played to that egotism when it invited him to head its fact-finding mission on "grave human rights violations" by Israel during the 2008 Gaza operation. Flattered, Goldstone readily accepted. The possibility that the UNHRC chose him because he was a Jew who could shill for the biased inquiry apparently eluded him.

The Israelis, by contrast, viewed the mission as a travesty and Goldstone as its dupe. The UNHRC never condemned even one of the thousands of Hamas rocket strikes on Israel, but rather blamed Israel for provoking those attacks and for perpetrating war crimes. The three other judges accompanying Goldstone previously denounced alleged Israeli atrocities; one claimed that Israel had been struck by "something like two rockets, likely fired by dissident groups," and compared Israel's actions in Gaza to the fascist bombing of Guernica, Spain, during the Spanish Civil War. In his defense, Goldstone implored both sides, Israeli as well as Palestinian, to investigate all human rights violations, but the UNHRC ignored that symmetry and deplored only Israel.

Israelis, meanwhile, wondered whether their government should cooperate with Goldstone. Netanyahu held—and I strongly agreed—that the mission's findings were foregone and that any Israeli input would serve only to legitimize them. Those charges would contribute immensely to the international campaign to deny Israel the right to defend itself and, eventually, the right to exist.

The administration's thinking, though, was less categorical. No American official pressured us to receive Goldstone but, then again, no one backed our decision not to. Less opaquely, Deputy Secretary of State Jack Lew urged me to spur Israeli leaders to expedite our own investigation of purported war crimes. I lashed back—"That's like telling medieval Jews to investigate charges of blood libel"—unfairly, since Jack, a devout Jew who cared avidly about Israel, was merely trying to help. He knew what we all feared: that Goldstone was no mere PR disaster, but potentially the basis for international sanctions against Israel.

Most egregiously from our perspective, Goldstone's mission equated Israel, a democratic state with an independent judiciary, and Hamas, a terrorist organization with a covenant calling for Israel's destruction and the annihilation of every Jew worldwide. Hamas, moreover, would handpick the Gazans who appeared before the mission and carefully vet their testimony. "Israel is being summoned to a court in which its guilt was already presumed, in which the jurors have already declared Israel guilty, and in which the witnesses for the prosecution are the murderers," I told Gwen Ifill on *PBS NewsHour*. "No country in the world would participate in such a farce."

Goldstone published his 452-page report on September 15, between the holiest Jewish holidays of Rosh Hashanah and Yom Kippur. On these Days of Awe, a Jewish judge condemned the Jewish State. As predicted, the fact-finding mission faulted Israel for triggering the clash with Gaza through its blockade of the Strip and—outlandishly— its occupation of the West Bank. The findings also accused Israeli soldiers of shooting civilians who waved white flags, of shelling a crowded mosque, and of bombing family homes and a UN school. "Unprecedented in their severity," Israel's Gaza operations, the report concluded, deliberately and disproportionately sought to "humiliate and terrorize a civilian population, radically diminish its local economic capacity both to work and to provide for itself, and to force upon it an ever increasing sense of dependency and vulnerability."

These verdicts evoked an onslaught of criticism from Israel. President Peres castigated Goldstone for failing to distinguish between brutal aggression and legitimate self-defense, for sanctifying terror and tying democracy's hands. "Members of the Goldstone Mission would have never compiled such a report if their children resided in Sderot and suffered daily rocket fire," Peres wrote. Moshe Halbertal, a brilliant Israeli jurist associated with the left, derided the report as "false and slanderous . . . biased and unfair." Both he and the ever-articulate Harvard professor Alan Dershowitz took Goldstone to task for applying separate methodologies for Israel and Hamas, ignoring evidence of Israel's innocence while explaining away or even ignoring proof of Hamas's guilt. Said Dershowitz, "the conclusions reached in the Goldstone Report are not worthy of consideration by people of goodwill."

Halbertal and Dershowitz were both respected friends and I admired their courageous responses to Goldstone. The report, nevertheless, remained a threat to Israel's standing in the world and even in

Washington. Though J Street refrained from formally endorsing the report, activists in the organization escorted Goldstone to Congress for meetings with progressive members. Assistant Secretary of State Michael Posner told the UNHRC of America's disappointment with the document's double standards. But he also cited Goldstone's "distinguished record of public service," and called on the Palestinians to investigate Hamas abuses. This, for Israelis, was tantamount to asking al-Qaeda to investigate 9/11.

Like Jack Lew, Mike Posner cared earnestly about Israel, yet to Israel's detriment, his remarks in the council fell short of distinguishing between racist thugs who hid behind Palestinian civilians while striving to kill ours and a democratic state trying to defend itself in a morally ambiguous environment. "This unjust report is a clear-cut test for all governments," Netanyahu declared. "Will you stand with Israel or will you stand with the terrorists?" Privately, on the phone, his voice took on greater urgency: "The council wants to create a situation where our fighter planes can't take off. It wants Israel's hands tied while our cities are destroyed." His tone conveyed his cabinet's opinion, formulated in a series of emergency meetings, that Goldstone constituted a strategic threat.

There was little I could say to assuage him. The administration's response to Goldstone had actually *exceeded* my expectations, much reduced by my research into Obama's worldview. But then, more in line with my assumptions, the White House intimated to me that Israel could not expect a more rigorous American stand against the report until we made more concessions in the peace process. Under the circumstances, I could do little more than second Jack Lew's request that Israel refute Goldstone's accusations as swiftly and exhaustively as possible.

Israel eventually launched an internal probe, examining 150 instances of alleged misconduct by IDF soldiers—many more cases than those cited by Goldstone—and bringing thirty-six of them to trial. Interestingly, the report also refuted the bulk of Goldstone's conclusions. A Palestinian flour mill that, according to Goldstone, Israel targeted in order to starve civilians turned out to have been a Hamas firing position. A sewage treatment plant that he claimed had been destroyed to poison Palestinian fields had, in fact, been sabotaged by Hamas to impede IDF movement. The inquest mounted by Israel's attorney general and its military advocate general surpassed the highest international standards. Yet this did not prevent the UN General Assembly from endorsing Goldstone's charges of war crimes.

More than a year later, Richard Goldstone publicly recanted. In an op-ed article published in *The Washington Post*—and rejected by *The New York Times* editors who welcomed his original findings—the judge admitted that subsequent revelations exonerated Israel of deliberately targeting civilians. While he repeated the preposterous regret that "there has been no effort by Hamas to investigate the allegations of . . . possible crimes against humanity," he upbraided the UNHRC for its anti-Israel slant and upheld Israel's "right and obligation to defend itself against attacks from abroad and within."

This mea culpa was extracted by Shmully Hecht, an enterprising Chabad rabbi who once hosted me at Yale and who later ushered Goldstone toward atonement. Shmully asked me to meet Goldstone and accept his penitence but, rather coldly, I refused. I had seen too many Israeli soldiers risk and even lose their lives in an attempt to avert civilian casualties. I remembered my son Yoav, wounded by a Hamas leader shooting from behind his own family. Not only my conscience but duty too prevented me from acceding to Shmully's request. Richard Goldstone endangered the safety of the Jewish State, and its ambassador held no authority to forgive him.

Autumn of Malcontents

Goldstone represented my introduction to knotty Middle East diplomacy. That initiation proved timely as I entered my first autumn in office. The issues swiftly grew more combustible, as I learned from the first of several predawn phone calls from Rahm Emanuel.

"I don't like this fucking shit," he began, not untypically. While slicing lunch meat as a teenager, Rahm had lost half of his right middle finger. The accident, Obama once joked, also cost him half of his vocabulary. I heard the other half. Groggily, I croaked, "Well, I don't like this fucking shit, either." The White House chief of staff went on to stress the need for the settlement freeze, which, he believed, would unthaw the gelid peace process. "And it's time for the Arabs to step up to the fucking plate as well." Rahm reiterated his deep concern for Israel's fate and his readiness to work seriously with Netanyahu. "Tell your boss he's going to get a victory," he assured me. "It's a win-win."

Rahm, I knew, was not enamored of my boss or of the American

Jewish leaders whom he faulted for backing Netanyahu unconditionally. That Yom Kippur, he buttonholed one of those leaders at synagogue and told him—notwithstanding the fast—just what he should eat. Their rabbi, the wise and saintly Jack Moline, learned of the incident and demanded that Rahm apologize. *Now.* And he did. Rahm could be both a misanthrope and a mensch, but I never doubted his commitment to Israel.

Rahm, though, would have been surprised to learn the lengths Netanyahu was ready to traverse in order to renew negotiations. Over the coming years, much debate would surround the depth of the prime minister's seriousness about peace. A conventional wisdom held that Abbas was willing but unable to end the conflict while Netanyahu was able but unwilling. Some commentators believed that Netanyahu was torn between his desire to achieve an historic accord and his opposition to territorial concessions. Others, though, remained convinced that he at best paid lip service to the two-state solution. They cited his consistent demand for Palestinian recognition of Israel as the Jewish State, accusing him of placing an artificial obstacle to compromise.

I disagreed. Palestinian acceptance of Israel's Jewishness was essential for peace. Speaking on campuses, I often compared the Israeli-Palestinian conflict to an argument between two families over a single house. The only answer was to divide the house. But what would happen, I asked, if one family accepted the other's legitimate claim to its half, while the second family still demanded ownership over the entire dwelling? The result would be an unending dispute. Israel recognized the existence of a Palestinian people endowed with the right to self-determination in its homeland—its side of the house. Genuine peace can only be attained, I concluded, once this recognition was mutual.

In addition to the Jewish State issue, Netanyahu was adamant about security. "We have to preserve the peace if the peace treaty unravels," he frequently said, referring to the need for a prolonged IDF presence in sensitive parts of the West Bank even after the creation of a Palestinian state. Here, too, I concurred with the prime minister. Our problem with Lebanon was not Israel's border with the country, but Syria's border with Lebanon, and our problem with Gaza was not our border with the Strip, but Egypt's. Tens of thousands of rockets had been smuggled across those porous Arab borders—despite the presence of international peacekeepers. Similarly, Israel could not afford to sit idly while a West Bank Palestinian state became a launching pad for countless missiles aimed at our heartland. Only Israeli forces could prevent the flow of missiles from Iran and Syria across the Jordan River. Should peace ever be achieved, I knew, Israeli troops would need to preserve it.

Yet, along with his commitment to Israel's security, Netanyahu was also concerned about Israel's future as a Jewish and democratic state. Both were threatened by continued Israeli rule over more than two million West Bank Palestinians. Some Palestinians and anti-Israel activists abroad were already calling for the creation of a binational state incorporating all people living in Israel, Gaza, and the West Bank. The country would soon have a Palestinian majority, compelling Israelis to choose between maintaining a minority-rule government and relinquishing their dream of a Jewish state. Netanyahu understood that the "one-state solution" meant Israel's dissolution, and that we somehow had to detach ourselves from the Palestinians.

Either way, by creating a Palestinian state or maintaining the status quo, Israel faced existential risks. That was Netanyahu's—and Israel's—dilemma, not between peace and occupation but between two potentially lethal options. That was why the prime minister insisted on obtaining Palestinian recognition of Israel as the Jewish State and guarantees for its security. In exchange, he was willing to make far-reaching concessions.

At the same time, the prime minister was aware of the need to mollify Obama. To this end, he delivered the Bar-Ilan speech. The president's demand for a settlement freeze proved tougher to meet, though, given Likud's settler constituents. "We will simultaneously advance the diplomatic process while allowing you to lead normal lives," Netanyahu reassured them, signaling his willingness to consider a time-limited "moratorium" on Israeli construction in the territories.

While fully behind any effort to shore up the alliance, I was ambivalent about the moratorium. It created a precedent of paying for the peace talks Israel should have received gratis and prevented Mahmoud Abbas from ever negotiating *without* a moratorium. Preferably, I thought, Israel should have unilaterally applied the Bush-Sharon letter, building only within those areas we could keep in any peace deal—Jewish Jerusalem and the settlement blocs—and signaling our seriousness about creating a viable West Bank Palestinian state. We could have shown more openness toward the Arab Peace Initiative, ignoring its demands for a withdrawal to the 1967 lines and for the return of Palestinian refugees to Israel, and embracing its call for normalization with the Jewish State. We could have done more, but Netanyahu was constrained by a right wing that opposed both Bush-Sharon and the Arab Initiative, and Obama was fixated on the freeze. Facing up to Israel's political realities and eager to ease tensions with Obama, I put my reservations aside and supported the moratorium.

And, as feared, Abbas called for a building freeze not only in the West Bank but also in East Jerusalem. This accorded with Obama's position but posed a precondition that no Israeli prime minister could meet. Further damaging to peace prospects, Abbas called on the International Criminal Court to try Israeli leaders for war crimes in Gaza. Pressing such charges might have satisfied Palestinian opinion, but it incensed Israelis. The Goldstone Report, launched by the United Nations, now received a tailwind from the Palestinian Authority.

The diplomatic gulf separating Israel and the Palestinians was no deeper than the political abyss between Republicans and Democrats. This, too, became one of the thornier challenges confronting me that fall. For the first time, angry Americans took to the streets and called themselves the Tea Party.

All societies have their fault lines. Israel's runs through Jews and Arabs, religious and secular, Jews from Western backgrounds and Jews originating from the East. In the United States, the fissures divide black and white, church and state, and what I often referred to as "San Francisco and Boston"—the sexually-free frontier versus the pilgrim tradition that makes America at once one of the world's most prurient and puritan nations. Perhaps the widest gulf, though, separates centralized government and individual freedoms. Israelis, very few of whom own firearms, frequently asked me why Americans needed so many guns when they had such a powerful army. "They need guns to *protect* them from the army," I explained.

That same impulse to defend liberty from big government gave rise to the Tea Party, named after the revolutionary-era protest against British tyranny. Aware of these historical roots, I instructed my congressional liaisons to undertake a thorough analysis of the group. They sniggered at the request—"the ambassador's wasting our time," carped one email that accidentally crossed my desk—but I stuck by it. The Tea Party, I concluded, was yet another symptom of the deadlock gripping the nation.

More shocking evidence of the impasse appeared on September 9, when the president unveiled his health-care plan. Together with other ambassadors, I filed into the Capitol, where both houses of Congress sat in seemingly respectful civility. If America is a Roman-style republic, Israel is an Athenian democracy. Compared to Israel's raucous Knesset, Congress is prim. But no sooner did Obama start speaking than Republican members began heckling him and one of them, Joe Wilson of South Carolina, shouted out, "You lie!" It was a troubled moment for American politics and a potentially problematic one for me. I was seated only a few feet from Wilson and feared the cameras would couple us.

My concerns were not groundless, I discovered, as the season progressed. After addressing a Rosh Hashanah reception at the Residence, a Democratic congresswoman called and rebuked me for merely praising the administration and not the Obama administration. "You couldn't bring yourself to say the word 'Obama,' could you?"

Also irksome was the embassy's continued imbroglio with J Street. Unlike my predecessor, Sallai Meridor, who had shunned the lobby, I initially engaged it in a dialogue. I had no illusions about the group, which received funds from anti-Israel contributors, supported every legislator critical of Israel, and stridently attacked mainstream American Jewish leaders. Though J Street defined itself as "pro-Israel" and "pro-peace," its logo bore no connection to Israel whatsoever, not even the color blue, and portrayed other pro-Israel organizations as anti-peace. Before becoming ambassador, I chanced to meet one J Street board member and asked him why he had joined. "I'm uncomfortable with the special relationship," he told me. "I want to normalize U.S.-Israel ties." Yet I knew that other J Street members, particularly students, genuinely cared about Israel. Reaching out to them, I believed, was in Israel's interest.

But then, outrageously, J Street members hosted Goldstone in Congress and began lobbying against sanctions on Iran. These actions were deeply deleterious to Israel's security—"they endangered seven million Israelis," I said—and made interacting with J Street virtually impossible. Both the prime minister and the foreign minister vetoed any official participation in its annual conference.

Jewish groups critical of Israeli policies periodically appear in the United States, I knew, and just as frequently disappear. J Street differed only in contributing to its preferred candidates' campaigns and in fashioning itself as the administration's wing in the American Jewish community. Obama acknowledged that fact by sending his National Security Advisor Jim Jones, one of Washington's most powerful officials, to greet the organization. "I'm honored to represent President Obama at the first national J Street conference," Jones ebulliently declared. "And you can be sure that this administration will be represented at all other future J Street conferences." The media, meanwhile, criticized my absence from the gathering. Obama's newly appointed advisor on anti-Semitism, Hannah Rosenthal, an early J Street supporter, issued her first denunciation not of anti-Semites, but rather of me for boycotting the summit. Hannah eventually became a friend and I never took her comment personally. Nor did I believe that she acted on her own, since I later learned that some of the criticism emanated directly from the White House.

Such scuffles did not discourage me from trying to keep open channels with the administration. I reached out to Hillary Clinton, asking for a private meeting, only to be rebuffed. The secretary, I was told, did not receive ambassadors. Nevertheless, remembering Sallai's frequent meetings with Secretary of State Rice and his axiom that "No other country has Israel's relationship with America," I renewed my requests. In a testament to her humor, Hillary once approached me and socked me in the arm, laughing, "Michael Oren! I've been calling you and calling you but you never return my messages!" But still no meeting took place.

Less entertaining but even more estranged were the conversations held with General Jones. Beginning as a platoon and company commander in Vietnam, he rose to the four-star command of the Marine Corps and of NATO. This dour former officer was of a type well known to Israelis, the majority of whom serve in the IDF. In America, though, where less than half of a percent of the population volunteers for the armed forces, the gap between the military and civilian cultures can be glaring. And the Obama White House had the lowest proportion of veterans of any administration in history. Jones, then, acted as a one-man bridge across the Potomac, between Pennsylvania Avenue and the Pentagon. Similarly, he could traverse any fissure between Washington and Jerusalem—or so one might expect.

In reality, Jones often seemed ill-disposed toward Israel. Though he had trained with the IDF as a young Marine and, as Supreme Allied Commander in Europe, oversaw the U.S.-Israel military alliance, the State Department mission he headed to the West Bank in 2007 left him questioning Israel's commitment to peace. He returned convinced that resolving the Israeli-Palestinian conflict would end all other Middle East disputes. "Of all the problems the administration faces globally," he told the J Street conference, "I would recommend to the president . . . to solve this one. This is the epicenter." The notion of "linkage"—all Middle Eastern disputes are tied to that between Israel and Palestinians—became doctrine in the Obama administration and Jones's belief in it bordered on the religious. As he once confessed to an Israeli audience, "If God had appeared in front of the president and said he could do one thing on the planet it would be the two-state solution."

The Israelis were flummoxed. Did the national security advisor really give precedence to solving the Israeli-Palestinian conflict before ending the massacres in Sudan, relieving hunger, or curing AIDS? Did he truly hold that reconciling Jews and Arabs could cease the centuries-long strife between Shiites and Sunnis or even the more modern split between Islamists and secularizers? No less puzzling for many Israelis was the administration's tendency to view settlements as the heart of the Israeli-Palestinian conflict. Reminding White House officials that the removal of all twenty-one settlements in Gaza had brought not peace to Israel but thousands of Hamas rockets proved futile.

But on settlements, no less than on linkage, Jones remained adamant. The national security advisor is the natural point of contact for many senior Israeli officials, including our own national security advisor, Uzi Arad, and the Mossad's illustrious chief, Meir Dagan. Both short and stocky—Arad called to mind an intellectual George Costanza and Dagan a swarthy Buddha—their physiques contrasted starkly with Jones's, towering and fit. But the physical differences were the least conspicuous in his West Wing office. In his deceptively impassive monotone, the general informed his guests that their country's willingness to implement a settlement freeze would determine the future of U.S.-Israel relations. "You ask and you ask," he said. "Now we're doing the asking."

Arad came away from these meetings muttering, "They have no real Middle East experience—it's all an experiment for them," while Dagan wore an inscrutable, rueful smile. I left the White House with a bitter pit in my gut and the conviction that Israel had to do the utmost—short of compromising its security—to avoid a public spat with Obama. Though I saw many of the administration's assumptions as off-base, at best, we had no choice but to address them.

George Mitchell, meanwhile, continued to shuttle between Jerusalem and Ramallah. With his quaint New England inflections, his quiet but compassionate demeanor, and kindly eyes, Mitchell was fiercely likable. That high-minded charisma helped elevate him to the Senate majority leadership, to the chairmanship of the Walt Disney Company, and to diplomatic success as President Clinton's special envoy for Northern Ireland.

Yet Mitchell's insistence that the same trust-building strategy that enabled him to mediate between Irish Protestants and Catholics would work with Jews and Palestinians mystified his Israeli hosts. Yitzik Molcho, the wiry scion of an old Jerusalem family and a wily Levantine bargainer, was always reminding him, "This is the Middle East, George, where one-sided concessions don't build trust. They build the demand for the next concessions." The settlement freeze, Molcho warned, would mislead Abbas into thinking he could gain more by not negotiating and weaken Netanyahu at the outset of a process for which he would later need immense political strength. "He has to climb a high hill, George. Don't shoot him in the knee at the bottom."

Meanwhile, as Mitchell traversed the Middle East, Ehud Barak became a monthly guest in Washington. Leading his Labor Party into an anomalous coalition with Likud, Barak shifted the cabinet from the right to the center-right and secured his own place as defense minister. This made my job somewhat easier, enabling me to present the government as one of the most broadly based in Israel's history. It also pleased the Americans, who believed that Barak was more compliant than Netanyahu on peace issues.

The Americans may have been misled and, if so, were hardly the first. Barak was a skein of incongruities. Impish with a pronounced lisp, he scarcely fit the image of Israel's most decorated soldier, the former head of the IDF's Sayeret Matkal commando unit, and, later, chief of staff. A Stanford-educated economist, concert pianist, and obsessive dismantler of clocks and locks, he once graphed out the peace process in terms of axes and quadrants.

Barak was the sort of wunderkind that only Israel could have produced—and which only Israelis could quickly reject, voting him out of office after less than two years as prime minister. Nevertheless, Obama remembered that, as prime minister in 2000, Barak had offered statehood to the Palestinians in Gaza and almost all of the West Bank, including half of Jerusalem. The president consequently put considerable stock in the defense minister and welcomed him—sometimes personally—in his frequent visits to the White House.

Those visits were enjoyable and anxious occasions for me. Enjoyable because, in spite of the enmity he aroused in some Israelis, I could not resist liking Barak. Israelis are not accustomed to complimenting others and refer to flattery with the Yiddish word *firgun*. I've often thought that the exit from Ben-Gurion Airport should be graced with a sign warning, "You are now entering a *firgun*-free zone." But Barak was unfailingly generous in his *firgun* to me and genuinely interested in my interpretations of America. I tried explaining to him that in the United States, one requests a "one-on-one" conversation and not, as in Hebrew, a "four-eyed" meeting, since "four-eyed" could be a slur for someone who wore glasses. I even jokingly wondered whether Moshe Dayan's conversations had been "three-eyed." He laughed and was laughing still when, entering the White House, he requested a "four-eyed" talk with General Jones.

The contents of those "four-eyed" discussions was the source of my anxiety. For all his geniality, Barak, I knew, was a cunning politician who could reach understandings that might or might not be supported by the rest of the government. As such, I was always careful to report my assessments—to the degree I could validate them—of Barak's conversations in Washington. Here was another ambassadorial balancing act between fulfilling my duties to the prime minister and maintaining the defense minister's confidence and friendship.

I also had to clean up the messes often left after Barak's departure. He quietly cut aid deals with the Pentagon without consulting members of the House and Senate appropriations and armed services committees, whom I then had to conciliate. The administration similarly needed calming when Barak, who as defense minister had that power, authorized the building of 455 houses in the territories. "The United

States does not accept the legitimacy of continued settlement expansion and we urge that it stop," insisted White House spokesman Robert Gibbs. My next job, I told my chief of staff Lior Weintraub, would be custodial, so adept had I become with a broom.

And the cleaning up continued. Absent a freeze, the settlements remained the administration's anathema. Labeling them "illegitimate" was the White House's way of ratcheting up pressure on Israel. Previous presidents had referred to these communities as "unhelpful" and "obstacles to peace" but refrained from questioning their legality. Foreign Minister Liberman fired back that the demand for a settlement halt merely enabled the Palestinians to boycott peace talks and to sanction Israel under the Goldstone Report. The administration urged Abbas to rescind his endorsement of Goldstone, and the Palestinian president agreed, but only in return for intensified American demands for the freeze.

The stage seemed set for an all-out confrontation in late September at the opening of the UN General Assembly. But Barack Obama remained the world's most revered leader—he would soon win the Nobel Prize in anticipation of his contributions to peace—and rebuffing him could still be risky. He declared that "it is past time to talk about starting negotiations," which "must begin and begin soon." However reluctantly, Abbas acceded to the president's request to join him and Netanyahu for a trilateral meet at UN headquarters.

The September 22 session was derided by the press as a mere photo op, but the three remained closeted for well over an hour. I spent the time in an adjacent room with several White House staffers—Palestinian diplomats waited separately—eager to hear of any possible resumption of talks. Photographs were indeed taken, but the question of whether Abbas would return to the table remained unanswered. Netanyahu, I felt, sincerely wanted to engage in negotiations, but other officials remained doubtful of the Palestinian leader's sincerity and the chances for a durable peace.

The meeting, in fact, made headlines, but little else, and the focus quickly shifted to Netanyahu's and Obama's speeches before the UN plenum. In preparation for the former, I was admitted—tentatively, at first—into the room where Ron Dermer and Gary Ginsberg, the shrewd yet good-natured Time Warner executive who volunteered his talents and time, fine-tuned Netanyahu's address. This, I learned, abounded in Churchillian references and touched on monumental themes: the Bible, the Holocaust, Israel's right to self-defense. Iran denied all three, the speech next emphasized, and threatened Israel with nuclear extinction. A section on peace with the Palestinians was also de rigueur, with Gary assigned to add "music" to Netanyahu's hang-tough tone. But there was nothing controversial in the text, nothing to arouse American concerns the way the prospect of Obama's speech unnerved the Israelis.

Along with "no daylight," another time-honored principle in the U.S.-Israel alliance was "no surprises." In previous years, Israeli leaders would receive advance drafts of any American announcement that touched on their interests and were welcomed to submit their comments. That practice, too, was now jettisoned, partially because Obama kept editing his words right up to the minute of their delivery. Netanyahu, meanwhile, sat petulantly in his suite. "What's he going to say?" he rasped at me. I tried texting Dan Shapiro, the NSC's Middle East and North Africa advisor, whose terse reply arrived only minutes before the president spoke. "You won't be disappointed," it read.

Netanyahu was not, at least not entirely. Obama devoted a large portion of his remarks to Israeli-Palestinian issues. There was poetry in his evoking "the Israeli girl in Sderot who closes her eyes in fear that a rocket will take her life in the middle of the night," and "the Palestinian boy in Gaza who has no clean water and no country to call his own." There was muscle in denouncing those who "fail to couple an unwavering commitment to [Israel's] security with an insistence that Israel respect the legitimate . . . rights of the Palestinians." And he called for the unconditional renewal of talks, which, within one year, would achieve peace between the "Jewish state of Israel" and a "contiguous" Palestinian state. "I'm not naïve," he concluded, "but all of us must decide whether we are serious about peace or whether we will only lend it lip service."

A collective phew resounded in the prime minister's suite. Though the president had made no distinction between the Palestinians and America's staunchest Middle East ally, he had upheld Israel's need for security and legitimacy and referred to it as "the Jewish state." This, we all understood, walked back the Cairo speech in which the Holocaust—rather than the Jews' ancient connection to their homeland—justified Israel's existence. He had sided with Israel in rejecting any preconditions for restarting talks. And Israel could live with Obama's reference to contiguity, meaning that the Palestinian populations of the West Bank would be joined territorially and linked to Gaza by a road. As long as no mention was made of the 1967 lines, which Israel regarded as indefensible, Netanyahu seemed pleased.

I certainly was, and relieved. As in his reaction to the Goldstone report, Obama's remarks surpassed my expectations. While the president's media critics confronted me with his moral equivalency—likening the rockets fired at Sderot with Gaza's lack of clean water—I listed the positive points of the speech. Yet the suspicion that Obama's appearance at the UN represented a passing respite, and that the pressure on Israel would resume, nagged me. Much like the autumn leaves on Washington's cherry trees, the ties of trust between the United States and Israel might soon be wilting.

The word *withering* indeed described the October 31 meeting at Ben-Gurion Airport between Foreign Minister Liberman and the secretary of state. According to protocol, the ambassador accompanies all administration officials of cabinet rank, including, of course, the secretary of state. The plane returning me to Israel landed just minutes before Secretary Clinton's. I dashed across the tarmac to greet Clinton and escort her to a dimly lit room where the foreign minister waited. "I do not understand why the U.S. would want to create another failed state in the Middle East that will not only harm Israel's interests but yours," he started in his grim, Russian-accented English. "Anybody who believes that a peace deal is possible soon is delusional." Though momentarily taken aback, the secretary swiftly retorted that the two-state solution was and would remain the administration's goal—"a vital interest for the United States and, we believe, for Israel." Opposing that objective, she made clear, could lead to serious friction with the White House. Such tensions were already conspicuous between Liberman and Clinton, who would rarely meet over the next few years.

The rapport, fortunately, was better between Clinton and Netanyahu. As during their last tête-à-tête at the State Department, this was a meeting of well-attuned minds, if not kindred hearts. "Bibi would fight if he felt he was being cornered," she later remembered, "but if you connected with him as a friend, there was a chance you could get something done together." In that spirit, Clinton urged Netanyahu to help build up Abbas and Palestinian prime minister Salam Fayyad, a moderate committed to institution building. But the prime minister resisted, saying that "Abbas can best build himself up by joining peace talks." Yet Netanyahu did agree to withhold approval for new housing projects in the settlements—a gesture that Clinton, if not entirely pleased, nevertheless described as "unprecedented."

Clinton's visit completed my entrée into serious Middle East diplomacy. The American and Israeli teams together thrashed out the Terms of Reference—TOR—for the possibly renewed talks. The TOR had to square contradictory Israeli and Palestinian policies and place the United States in a viable mediating position. Each phrase, each word, was subjected to microscopic scrutiny. The result represented a mastery of statecraft—and double-speak—in which settlement blocs became "subsequent developments" and "the 1967 lines" were set as Palestinian, rather than American, parameters. The final text was virtually inscribed on my soul:

> We believe that through good-faith negotiations the parties can mutually agree on an outcome which ends the conflict and reconciles the Palestinian goal of an independent and viable state based on the 1967 lines, with agreed swaps, and the Israeli goal of a Jewish state with secure and recognized borders that reflect subsequent developments and meet Israeli security requirements.

Gaping disagreements remained—on Jerusalem, especially—but some progress had been achieved in the U.S.-Israel talks and Netanyahu wanted to maintain the momentum. The General Assembly of the Jewish Federations of North America, the largest gathering of the community's most important philanthropic and educational organization, was scheduled to be held in Washington in early November. It offered an ideal opportunity for Netanyahu to address a genial crowd and a convenient excuse to meet with Obama. Only the White House claimed it knew nothing of the prime minister's request, prompting headlines about a possible presidential snub. Once again, I went into my public "there's no crisis" mode, all the while working furiously to arrange the summit.

At the last moment the meeting was set and, just before dawn on November 8, Netanyahu landed at Andrews Air Force Base. Every prime ministerial visit to the United States begins with a sleep deficit for the ambassador, who must leave the Residence in the middle of the night to stand on the tarmac on time. Poor Sally had to join me for these nocturnal slogs and shiver beside me on the red carpet until the prime minister's aircraft arrived. Israel has no Air Force One, just rented El Al planes. Each of these bears the name of an Israeli town— this one, I noticed proudly, was Dalyiat al-Carmel, a Druze village near Haifa. Netanyahu descended the ramp, embraced Sally, and laughed, saying, "I bet you didn't know what you were getting yourself into?"

All thought of exhaustion and the cold departed, suddenly, when the prime minister invited me to brief him in his limousine. I suggested ways of improving the relationship with Obama, of moving forward with the moratorium and restoring the principle of "no surprises." I emphasized the power of the president's intellect and his global stature. Netanyahu agreed, "It's not easy to get that job." To help frame the coming discussion, I quizzed him, "Who was the only U.S. president with less managerial, military, financial, and foreign policy experience than the current one?" Netanyahu, though a proficient historian, looked stumped by the answer: "Abraham Lincoln."

Later, we arrived at the White House and, without pomp or pleasantries, Netanyahu entered the Oval Office. The rest of the prime minister's entourage—including Ehud Barak and Yitzik Molcho— adjourned to Rahm Emanuel's office.

Unlike the "me walls" of Washington, which are festooned with photographs of the famous, Rahm's room was adorned with family portraits. He duly made us feel at home, made coffee for us, and brought Barak a beer. Somehow we got onto the subject of eulogies, and I mentioned the one given by Moshe Dayan for his friend Ro'i Rotberg, killed by terrorists in 1956, that surprisingly acknowledged the Palestinians' suffering. This brought us back to the peace process and the conversation turned prickly.

Barak began by criticizing the administration for opposing possible interim agreements with the Palestinians and even for interfering in internal Israeli politics. Rahm snapped back, "If you're accusing us of something, say so. We're being frank here." Frankly, I said, the administration had never said a positive word about the democratically elected government of Israel. Jim Jones, who was also present, tried to interject, but Rahm stopped him: "General, you should know better than to try interrupting Jews having a debate."

Just then, Obama and Netanyahu emerged beaming. They had

reached an agreement on the settlement moratorium. Though only partial—excluded from its terms were schools and synagogues, 2,500 units already under construction, and all of Jerusalem—the freeze was the first ever for Israel and a serious inducement for the Palestinians. The restrictions would last for ten months—"a long enough airstrip," Rahm commented, "to get the talks in the air."

Back at the hotel, Netanyahu sat with Molcho calculating the millions of shekels the moratorium would cost the government in lawsuits from builders and homeowners whose contracts were frozen. "You should have heard your ambassador," Molcho informed the prime minister. "He really stood up for you with Rahm." I should have savored this rare display of *firgun* and the sense that the U.S.-Israel alliance was once again on track. "I suppose I should take a victory lap," I told my friend Yossi Klein Halevi in a call from the Andrews base after Netanyahu's plane took off. "But the victory won't last."

It certainly did not. I had asked Rahm to say something positive about Netanyahu's decision before the Jewish Federations, but he merely acknowledged the prime minister's understanding of the importance of peace. In Israel, I noted in *The Wall Street Journal,* "Mr. Netanyahu's decision has been fiercely criticized. The Knesset has considered a vote of no-confidence in his leadership. And the most recent poll shows that more Israelis oppose the freeze than support it." The Palestinians, for their part, rejected the moratorium. "Israel has to make peace with us, not the Americans," remarked Palestinian Authority negotiator Saeb Erekat.

The American public, too, took little notice of the freeze, which went into effect on Thanksgiving. Attention then focused on the massacre of U.S. soldiers by an army psychiatrist—an Islamic radical—at Fort Hood, Texas. Finally, the moratorium was overshadowed by a routine announcement from the Jerusalem municipality.

The city declared its intention to construct nine hundred housing units in Gilo, the large Jewish neighborhood built over the 1967 lines in the city's southeast. In the administration's eyes, the forty-year-old suburb and its more than forty thousand residents was no different than a remote hilltop settlement. Visibly furious, Obama paused in the middle of his China tour to condemn the announcement. Building in Gilo, he declared, "embitters the Palestinians in a way that could end up being very dangerous."

Netanyahu, already paying a hefty political price from his constituents opposed to the freeze, was nonplussed. The president had furnished the Palestinians with an excuse to keep rejecting talks and even to initiate a Third Intifada. "Your policy puts a pistol in the hand of anybody—Israeli or Palestinian—who wants to stop the peace process," I complained to Dennis Ross, who seemed to agree. But the policy would not change.

The branches were now bare in Washington, and the city braced for some of the worst blizzards in its history. Americans turned on their news to hear of Obama's decision to send an additional thirty thousand troops to Afghanistan but then to withdraw all U.S. forces from the country in nineteen months. Al-Qaeda chief Osama bin Laden took credit for the so-called Christmas Day Bomber—the failed attempt to blow up a Detroit-bound airliner with explosives sewn into a terrorist's underwear. But another suicide bomber succeeded, killing seven CIA agents in Afghanistan.

Most Americans turned on their Christmas lights and Rahm lit the White House menorah. Obama told invitees to his Hanukkah party how honored he was by my presence, but I did not actually hear him. I was deep in conversation with David Axelrod, the president's senior advisor, listening to his complaints about our policies while trying to remind him that Israelis respond more to embraces than to abrasiveness. "Try love," I said.

The longest autumn I could recall had ended, and with it, any belief that the schisms I encountered—in the Jewish community, in Congress, and between Obama and Netanyahu—could easily be spanned. True, I had learned a great deal, but my educational curve as ambassador continued. With an innocence I would later abjure, I carped to administration officials about the "lack of effective intimacy" between Washington and Jerusalem. "Lack of effective intimacy?" David Rothkopf snickered. "That usually means someone's not getting screwed enough."

Chrysalis

The Hanukkah lamp at the Residence, though more modest than the White House's, burned as radiantly, and while not lit by the chief of staff, was kindled by no less a luminary than Ben Affleck. The acclaimed actor, director, and screenwriter had come at the invitation of Rich Klein, a producer who hailed from New Jersey—we attended rival high schools—and an unflagging friend of Israel. My staffers kept pressing Ben to pose with them and nearly prevented him from touching match to candles, but that seemed the least of my concerns. The main challenge was Ben's guest, New York congressman Anthony Weiner, later to gain notoriety for sexting, but then renowned for his outspokenness on virtually every issue, including U.S.-Israel relations.

"Admit it, the president screwed up by focusing on the settlements," the high-strung congressman verbally lunged into me as soon as we reached the table.

The remark would have been sufficiently awkward in a private setting, but seated with us were a number of Washington personages, including, directly to my right, Susan Sher, the first lady's chief of staff.

"No one has a monopoly on making mistakes, Congressman," I replied. "But the important thing is to move on and get the peace talks restarted without preconditions."

Not becalmed, Weiner, though a Democrat, kept criticizing Obama and compelling me to defend him. Susan looked shocked. An alumna of yet another rival high school, Susan's physician father had long known mine, and I felt a special warmth toward this smart, engaging woman. She leaned leftward to whisper, "Who is this asshole?" But I was too busy fending off assaults on the president's policies to answer. Happily, Ben Affleck stepped in with questions of his own.

Bearded for his role in the Academy Award–winning *Argo*, he displayed a statesman's knowledge of the Middle East, which he had studied in college. I could not imagine a more enjoyable conversation or a more welcomed one.

The Hanukkah dinner came in response to a series of difficult questions I had to ask myself. Given the tensions in the relationship, how could I shore up the existing bonds and build new ones? In view of the centralized nature of the Obama White House, how could I gain access to top decision makers? How could I avoid the pitfalls of polarization and gain trust on both sides of the aisle? Most pressing, how could an ambassador not known for his closeness to the prime minister—the usual key to diplomatic success—establish an authoritative presence in Washington?

One way was to reach out. Washington is famous for its opulent diplomatic residences—Britain's looks like Buckingham Palace and Italy's like a Tuscan villa. By comparison, the Israeli Residence may resemble a kibbutz but, because of the special relationship, VIPs still want to be seen in it. And those who "give good table" in Washington "get good table" in return. Achieving that status required forethought and work. On his whiteboard, chief of staff Lior Weintraub mapped out the "influentials" in the city and the social networks linking them. Every invitation, then, represented a strategic decision. Even the seating arrangements—to say nothing of the menu—were deliberated.

Fortunately, as Jews, we were never short of excuses for entertaining. Most Jewish holidays, an old joke goes, can be reduced to nine words: "They tried to kill us. We survived. Let's eat." Not only Hanukkah, but Passover, Purim, even the more obscure Tu B'Shvat—the Holiday of Trees, ideal for hosting environmentalists—provided occasions for scrumptious Israeli fare. Most suitable, though, was the seven-day harvest holiday celebrated in a temporary outdoor booth, the Succah.

Having always set up a Succah in our home in Israel, I decided to become the first ambassador to erect one at the Residence and invite prominent figures to our festival. A local rabbi lent us a booth that Jewish elementary school children, among them Rahm Emanuel's daughter, decorated. That night—October 4, 2009—our thirty guests included Dianne Feinstein, Dennis and Debbie Ross, and the ambassadors from Russia and Egypt. Before they arrived, though, it rained, ruining the decorations and collapsing half of the Succah. The staff managed to salvage the table and drag it out into the courtyard as the sky seemed to clear. Senator Feinstein was just reproaching my Egyptian colleague on his government's policies when the rain, almost biblically, resumed.

"Reaching out" not only meant establishing rapports with Washington notables but generating understanding with the broader public. Roughly 60 percent of Americans characterized themselves as pro-Israel—an extraordinary proportion compared to the Europeans who regularly rated Israel among the world's most despicable countries. Yet I could not afford to be cavalier and ignore crucial American communities largely unfamiliar with the Jewish State. So I prepared a list of dream dinners with Hispanic leaders, well-known Irish- and African-Americans, and the heads of the Greek, Arab, and even Iranian communities. The nexus would be music. Israel has a dizzying diversity of bands—flamenco, Celtic, Laïkó, Middle Eastern, Persian—which I envisioned bringing to the Residence to perform for community leaders. Hearing this idea, Noam Katz, the embassy's dedicated secretary of public diplomacy, together with my tireless social secretary, Jennifer Sutton, both looked at me blankly. But their gazes turned to gapes when I presented them with my next idea.

The concept occurred to me at the White House, where Obama, continuing a tradition begun by President Bush, held an Iftar—the dinner breaking the fast each day of Islam's month-long Ramadan holiday. Though seated at the "Jewish table" together with Susan Sher, Dan Shapiro, David Axelrod, and Rahm, I was impressed by the evening's healing message. I thought: since nearly 20 percent of Israel's population is Muslim, why not host an Israeli Iftar for American Muslims? This time, not only Noam's and Jennifer's jaws dropped, but also those of my security people.

Bogged down in the Foreign Ministry's bureaucracy, these events would take months to arrange. In the interim, there was Washington's own social calendar featuring dozens of dinners, balls, galas, concerts, and fund-raisers. These, too, had to be selected strategically according to the criterion, "the U.S.-Israel relationship is special and the Israeli ambassador goes only to premier events." Yet that could still leave as many as three affairs each night, three stages on which I had to be alert, in character, and "on."

At any given function, I could find myself mixing with senior administration officials, Supreme Court justices, members of Congress, and the Joint Chiefs of Staff—all essential for networking and much of it genuine fun. But despite my convivial veneer, I could never let down my guard, never forget that I was not merely me but the emissary of the Jewish State. This, too, was part of the job and a physically exacting one. When the staff went home at 7 P.M., the ambassador, adjusting his shirt studs and bow tie, began another day.

Though I was gregarious by nature, my transformation from private person to national personification did not come easily. Later, recalling some of the things I said during my first months in office could still make me wince. It took time to master the small talk that sounded spontaneous instead of calculated, to appear carefree even when trailed by security guards. I had to comport myself as though every word, every action, could be the subject of the next day's headlines. "You have no choice," Yossi Klein Halevi broke it to me; "you're going to have to become Ambassador Oren." I understood what he meant. No longer an individual with feelings and fears, but a symbol, a brand.

The challenge of changing myself socially, however arduous, nevertheless paled beside that of conceding my individuality as a writer and commentator on current affairs. Ambassadors are frequently dismissed as holdovers from the past, their jobs rendered obsolete by the media. But just the opposite is true. The modern press means that the ambassador is no longer confined to court and to whispering in royal ears, but can broadcast to entire realms—as it were—publicly. "I have three words of advice for you," Netanyahu told me in one of our first meetings. "Media. Media. Media."

But my first forays into that media proved lackluster. I did not quite know who I was, a commentator or an ambassador, and the sheer mass of issues—Goldstone, settlements, Iran—induced a kind of writer's block. Netanyahu, his impatience oozing from the phone, upbraided me: "Suck it up and get writing."

I wrote, but my opening article, a *New Republic* piece on the prime minister's UN speech, contained such cerebral phrases as "Reasserting the factuality of the Holocaust is a prerequisite for peace," and "Millions of Muslims subscribe to the syllogism: If Israel was created by Europeans and the Holocaust never occurred, then Israel's existence is unjust." Similarly, my first speech posited that the physics genius Albert Einstein became a Zionist because he realized that only God could have created universal laws such as the speed of light. Accordingly, the father of modern physics concluded that Jewish history—and the rebirth of Israel—had meaning. "Einstein understood that and so can we," I concluded, "with all the alacrity, and the clarity, of light."

Professors can revel in such flourishes, but not ambassadors. The Israeli press lambasted my highbrow attempt to link the Holocaust with Goldstone and the threat of Iranian nukes. After the Einstein speech, *Haaretz* headlined "Israeli ambassador believes God played a role in Israel's creation"—a scandal.

I admitted, then, that I had to find my diplomatic voice and fashion it into prose. It took weeks, but my next opinion piece straightforwardly stated that the Goldstone Report "bestows virtual immunity on terrorists and ties the hands of any nation to protect itself" and "must be rebuffed by all who care about peace." My speeches homed in on the issues—the peace process, Iran, relations between American and Israeli Jews. I felt at first like a slam poet forced to pen rhymed haiku, but the rule-bound genre grew on me. Together with a trusted press assistant, Aaron Kaplowitz, who typed while I paced and dictated, I published more than forty op-eds and full-length articles, an Israeli diplomatic record. And not all of it was straightlaced. My audiences also heard how Israel exported wine to France, caviar to Russia, and gluten-free pasta to Italy. They heard that Israelis had won more Nobel Prizes than Olympic medals, "and only a Jewish state would be proud of that."

A similar switch was needed for my television appearances. In America, a strong TV presence means power. This especially held true for the Obama administration, staffed in no small measure by former journalists. I took note of how the evening news reported that an African-American federal employee, Shirley Sherrod, had made racist comments. The administration instantly fired Sherrod but then, after the news revealed that the charges were groundless, begged to reinstate her.

The administration's sensitivity to the news cycle lent me a certain advantage. An ambassador not known in Washington to be a longtime associate of his prime minister, and a virtual stranger to his foreign minister, can easily be dismissed. But an ambassador who establishes a strong media presence simply cannot be ignored. So I set out to create that presence, interviewing on radio and television and briefing journalists whenever possible.

By being proactive in the press, I gradually gained the administration's ear, but often at the risk of losing its heart. Rarely did I appear on any news program without being asked whether Obama was good or bad for Israel. "Tell the truth, Mr. Ambassador," the interviewer typically opened. "For Israeli-American relations, isn't this the worst crisis ever?"

As an historian, I knew what a real crisis between the countries looked like—Suez, 1956, for example, when President Eisenhower threatened to levy sanctions on Israel—and nothing so earth-shattering had yet occurred. Compressing historical comparisons into seven-second sound bites was difficult, though, and I had to remind myself of the need to deny daylight between the two governments. Even the semblance of disagreements could encourage Israel's enemies and be seized by critics of Obama, turning Israel into a wedge issue. So I smiled back at the broadcaster and begged to disagree. "Even the best of friends can sometimes differ," I said. "Relations between the United States and Israel are, to quote the president, 'unbreakable and unshakable.'"

In spite of these best efforts, Netanyahu judged my initial television appearances as "bloodless." He was right. Once again I found myself in identity no-man's-land, aware of where I needed to be persona-wise yet unsure of how to get there. Fortunately, the persona came to me, unexpectedly, in a Q&A with CNN's Fareed Zakaria.

Incisive and genteel, Fareed had sharp policy differences with Israel and no reticence about expressing them. In my previous academic life, I always enjoyed sparring with him. But now, confined to a list of "messages" formulated by the Prime Minister's Office, I felt hobbled entering his studio. That is, until, out of the blue, Fareed asked me, "Why should the Iranian nuclear program threaten you when Israel has two hundred nuclear bombs?" Without thinking, I fell back on Israel's traditional opacity: "Israel will not be the first country to introduce nuclear weapons into the Middle East." Undeterred, Fareed asked me the same question again and again and each time I gave the identical response. Finally, I smiled at him and said, "It's your interview, Fareed. If you want to spend it all like this, be my guest."

Almost accidentally, I had slipped into my ambassadorial TV character. And I slipped into it again a few weeks later when journalists asked me to comment on the assassination in a Dubai hotel of Hamas agent Mahmoud al-Mabhouh, allegedly by the Mossad. "I know nothing about this incident," I said with a shrug, then added: "Though it's curious how the press seems more interested in speculating about what Israel might have done than asking why an internationally wanted terrorist was openly operating in Dubai."

In time, I could appear on programs as diverse as *The View* and *Meet the Press, The Colbert Report,* and *Morning Joe,* and maintain my diplomatic character. "My father was Jewish, can I be, too?" the irreverent Bill Maher asked me during one of our interviews. "You want to be in," I factually responded, "you're in."

After a few months in Washington, my transition period was at last concluding, but Sally's had just begun. This former flower child, kibbutznik, and modern dancer was compelled overnight to become a Washington socialite, a hostess of attentiveness and grace. Accustomed to jeans and sandals, she was suddenly shoved into glimmering evening gowns—God forbid someone should be seen wearing the same one twice—and the high heels that felt, to her, like medieval torture devices. She had to be manicured, made up, presentably coiffed and accessorized—to be metamorphosed into what one of her friends called "ambassadorable."

Such a radical makeover was daunting for Sally, who was also grappling with our family's challenges back home. In Jerusalem, her mother was agonizingly dying from cancer. Our youngest son, Noam, had entered the army—a "lone soldier," without parents in the country, just as I had been—while Lia and Yoav, both at college, wrestled with the learning disabilities they had inherited from their dad. Beyond deciding the floral arrangements for our next dinner or managing the Residence's bickering staff—"Israel's highest-ranking unpaid diplomat," I called her—Sally had weightier concerns.

Yet she fulfilled her duties nobly, lovingly, and by all accounts, sensationally. She volunteered to teach Israeli songs and folk dances at an elementary school in one of the most impoverished parts of Washington. When bus drivers refused to enter the crime-ridden neighborhood at night to take the pupils to a Nationals' baseball game, she sponsored a special afternoon at the stadium. Star players gave the kids batting and fielding tips while Sally served them kosher hot dogs—Hebrew Nationals Day, she called it.

When not working with inner-city children, Sally mixed with Washington's elite. The Israeli ambassador's wife is invited to join International Club Number One, founded in 1952, which brought together the spouses of prominent diplomats, congressmen, Supreme Court justices, journalists, and senior administration figures including Michelle Obama. Nothing could be further from San Francisco's Fillmore Auditorium, where Sally first danced to Creedence Clearwater Revival and the Doors. But she drew on her family's century-deep roots in the United States, her commitment to Israel, and our shared devotion to the two countries' alliance. By 2010, I could walk into a State Department reception and not know a soul while Sally ran up and hugged half the dignitaries. And the International Club, which never before had a single Israeli officer, eventually named Sally its president.

But Sally's success arose not only from soirees and luncheons but from the pages of *The Atlantic*. Learning that the sixties' band Jefferson Airplane composed two songs about her, Jeffrey Goldberg proposed writing a profile of Sally for the magazine. Seemingly unobjectionable, Jeff's request nevertheless raised some strategic questions:

should Israel be associated with the sixties drug culture, which Sally—a mere fifteen-year-old at the time—generally shunned? We thought about it and concluded that Israel, always in the news for some war or crisis, should for once be considered cool.

The article featured a garlanded caricature of her dancing with Jimi Hendrix and Bibi Netanyahu and opened with the question: "How many degrees of separation exist between [the] Israeli Prime Minister and . . . Jerry Garcia?" The answer, Jeff replied, was one:

> The person who connects . . . Shimon Peres to Jim Morrison, and, for that matter, Palestinian Authority President Mahmoud Abbas to Janis Joplin—is Sally Oren . . . who plays the role of diplomat's spouse with distinction and grace. She hosts embassy functions . . . wears elegant gowns and attends White House parties. Forty-five years ago, however, she played Frisbee with the Grateful Dead and served as Jefferson Airplane's muse.

The profile went viral. In addition to deferring to her presidency role, the International Club women now referred to her as the Queen of Cool. Once, while at Ben-Gurion Airport to greet the secretary of defense, I was flabbergasted—and flattered—when his young staffers ran off the air force plane and rushed to shake my hand. "You're Sally Oren's husband!" they shouted above the din. "We're honored!"

Gradually, by dint of our outreach, our hospitality, and our willingness to engage unconventionally, Sally and I accessed those "good tables," an important tool for diplomatic networking. I, too, became the subject of profiles, all thankfully favorable, two of them in *The New York Times*. But though occasionally introduced as Israel's ambassador to Washington, I was, in fact, my country's envoy to the United States. Beyond the Beltway, between the coasts, were fifty states that also fell under my purview, and more than three hundred million Americans with whom I was privileged to interact.

Escaping Washington, with its critical congressional debates and visiting Israeli delegations, was never easy. Each opportunity I snatched. With security team in tow, I set off for Atlanta, to lay a wreath at the grave site of the Reverend Dr. Martin Luther King, or to San Antonio, to meet with Mayor Julian Castro and the city's Hispanic leadership. Chicago's National Museum of Mexican Art and the DuSable Museum of African American History hosted me, as did the Chinese Historical Society in San Francisco. There were many visits to synagogues, of course, but at least as many to churches. Whether by the ten thousand evangelicals in the Bel Air Presbyterian Church in Los Angeles or by the gospel-rocking African-Americans in Cincinnati's New Jerusalem Church, I was exuberantly received by the congregants. Such uplifting moments reminded me that America is not just Pennsylvania Avenue or the press, and that the nation is fundamentally, instinctively, pro-Israel.

Yet, even as I crisscrossed the country, Washington was never far from my mind. Throughout my travels, I sought individuals who could help me understand the mood in Congress and the White House and gain a sense of the directions in which America was heading. And in no city were such individuals more densely concentrated than in Chicago, the hometown of Obama and so much of his senior staff, including Rahm Emanuel, David Axelrod, and the president's closest advisor, Valerie Jarrett. Washington, I used to jest, had become a settlement of Chicago.

I visited the Windy City repeatedly to glean insights from those who knew Obama earlier in his public career and had supported his ascent to power. Among these were his early Jewish backers—Lester Crown, Alan Solow, Lee Rosenberg—exceptional individuals all, and Rabbi Capers C. Funnye, a man even more extraordinary than his name. The first African-American member of the Chicago Board of Rabbis, Capers was also a cousin to Michelle Obama. But that White House connection became incidental for me as I grew to admire this inspirited community leader and passionate advocate for Israel.

Most meaningful, though, were my pilgrimages to the New York office of Elie Wiesel. Sitting together among his myriad books and multiple literary awards, we discussed the challenges confronting the Jewish people, from assimilation to radicalism and Holocaust denial. I consulted with him about Obama, appreciative of his personal rapport with the president and his advice on how to enhance his relations with Israel. We spoke about contemporary issues, but I could never forget the impact Elie had had on my youth. I listened, all the while looking at this debonairly disheveled eighty-year-old, the survivor, the laureate, and marveling that I now called him friend.

In addition to these rewarding relationships, there were—admittedly—some perks. In Sacramento, the California State Assembly presented me with a bobblehead of the Kings' star scorer, Omri

Casspi, the first Israeli to play for the NBA. And the U.S. Naval Academy gave me a hat stitched with the logo "Go Navy Beat Army"—in Hebrew. My love of football, which I also never renounced, led me to New England Patriots owner Robert Kraft. The builder of Israel's only football stadium, where Jewish and Arab linebackers bashed each other fraternally, Robert hosted me at several Patriots games and afterward took me to the locker room, where he held hands with his players and prayed. I attended the 2011 Super Bowl, sat between the dazzling Teresa Scanlan—also known as Miss America—and football immortal Roger Staubach, whom I surprised by recalling his Heisman-winning record at Navy but who delighted me more by revealing his lifelong admiration for Israel. At halftime, someone tapped me on the shoulder. "Great to see you, Michael," President George W. Bush said with a smile. "Or should I say Mr. Ambassador?"

And the ambassador gets to meet celebrities, an astonishing number of them connected to Israel. Among these were Michael Douglas, whose father, Kirk, donated the Jerusalem park where our kids used to play, and Jason Isaacs, star of *Awake* and Harry Potter, most of whose family lives north of Tel Aviv, and Scarlett Johansson, as brave as she is beautiful, a defender of Israel against boycotts. The still-stunning Richard Gere, a veteran peace activist, lectured Jeffrey Goldberg and me about Israel's need to reconcile with Hamas. "Just invite Hamas parents over for coffee and talk about your kids," he repeatedly explained while Jeffrey and I nodded numbly and our wives both gawked. At Quentin Tarantino's reception for his alternative history film, *Inglourious Basterds,* producer Lawrence Bender introduced me to the Jewish actors, one of whom boasted, "We shot Hitler! We made our parents so proud!" At another Hollywood party, a tall, gangly young man chatted with me in fluent Hebrew until, embarrassed, I asked his name. It was Sacha Baron Cohen, the ingenious comedian, whom I had never seen out of costume. In time, though, even the flashiest glitter wears off. Once, at the Louis XVI–style French Residence, Sally declined to join me in a conversation with Oscar-winning actor George Clooney because her feet, all night in heels, were killing her.

Along with the privileges and the perks, traversing the country involved barely survivable schedules, controversy, and even danger. Most tempestuous were the university lectures that I insisted on delivering at least once per month. America is home to nearly seven thousand college campuses, some of which are effusively pro-Israel, but others accommodate—and in some cases encourage—against us. These were the campuses that I intentionally targeted, hoping to interact with those students most opposed to Israel and open their minds to a different understanding of us. This made for some tough encounters.

At Harvard, several students rose to read from pre-prepared questions, one of which accused me of defaming the Palestinians in *The National Review,* a conservative publication. I denied writing such libels or ever publishing in *The National Review.* Still, a student insisted, "But it says here that the article appeared in TNR.com." Calmly I explained that TNR.com stood for *The New Republic,* the liberal magazine where I had been a contributing editor.

Whether reading from leaflets or speaking from the heart, all students deserved to be treated respectfully, I determined, and answered. Despite the heroic efforts of pro-Israel advocacy groups such as StandWithUs and AIPAC, many of these young people had been exposed to anti-Zionist hype within and outside the classroom. Consequently, I reserved the right to call on those raising their hands and made a point of choosing those who—telling by their dress or demeanor—were likely to be the most contentious. And the questions could be tough.

"Why can Jews from New York move to Israel and immediately receive citizenship," I was frequently asked, "while a Palestinian-American cannot?" The answer was to explain that Israel is a nation-state like the vast majority of countries in the world, and that, like Israel, many of those countries have laws enabling members of that nationality to come home. "Israel's Law of Return is affirmative action for two thousand years of Jewish statelessness that resulted in unspeakable suffering for my people," I replied. "And someday I hope the Palestinians will have a nation-state to which their nationals can return as well." Whenever possible, I would talk about the painful sacrifices that not only Israelis would have to make for peace but also the Palestinians—eschewing their claims to Jaffa and Haifa, acknowledging the Jewish State's legitimacy—and the need for each side to coexist with the other's narratives.

All questions remained kosher but two. The first was, "Isn't Israel an apartheid state just like South Africa was?" And the second, "How can Israel treat the Palestinians the way the Nazis once treated Jews?" Both of these received curt questions in return. "How does Israel, where Arabs serve in the Knesset, on the Supreme Court, and in the army, remotely resemble an apartheid state?" and "Has Israel put six million Palestinians in gas chambers?" In each case, I concluded, "Shame on you."

My campus challenges were not, unfortunately, always verbal. Demonstrators outside the halls in which I spoke occasionally tried to intimidate interested students from entering. Protesters at the University of Texas held up posters accusing me of war crimes and climbed onto the stage. My greatest fear, though, was not for my safety but for theirs. The security detail—Americans and Israelis—were trained to disable any protester who got too close me. Fortunately, none of them did.

But no campus experience proved more shocking and, as it turned out, more pivotal, than my February 8, 2010, appearance at the University of California, Irvine. Having lectured at the campus before becoming ambassador, I knew of its pronounced anti-Israel atmosphere, but even then was struck by the sight of dozens of Muslim students praying at the entrance to the hall. Inside were hundreds of anti- and pro-Israel activists, prepared for an on-camera showdown. As usual before a difficult public appearance, I prayed that I would be given the strength and the wisdom to handle this one honorably, to do my country proud. That prayer proved timely, as I learned seconds after beginning my talk.

One of the protesters, strategically placed mid-row to prevent his rapid removal, stood and shouted, "Michael Oren, murderer of children!" The attendees roared, for and against the heckler. I resumed my speech only to be interrupted by another screaming student. "This is not London or Jerusalem, but it's also not Tehran," I said. But the disruptions continued. To their credit, the university heads condemned what they immediately deplored as a violation of my freedom of expression as well as the audience's right to listen. I reminded the demonstrators of the Middle Eastern custom of showing hospitality to any guest, even an ostensible enemy. "I've come into your home and I'm asking you for hospitality."

For years afterward, people would approach me asking how, in the face of that chaos, I managed to keep my cool. Usually, I would just shrug and cite my thirty years' experience of coping with hostile crowds. In reality, vivid memories were coursing through my mind. I recalled being back in high school, still suffering from learning dis-abilities but writing the poetry that caught my teachers' attention and convinced them to transfer me out of the "dumb" class. I remembered pausing, terrified, in the hall before entering Honors English. "I've been through worse than this," I thought.

The howling in the Irvine auditorium became too loud to con-tinue and I left the stage, but only for a few minutes. I used this time to confer with the local police chief, who agreed to arrest the hecklers for public disturbance. Then, turning to Lior Weintraub, I said, "We're going back out."

Stepping up to the lectern, I restarted my speech and, predictably, another student rose up and yelled. And was promptly taken into cus-tody. All told, the police detained eleven students who were brought to court and found guilty of two misdemeanors. The Irvine Eleven, as they tried to fashion themselves, appealed this sentence and failed. Israelis won a landmark victory for their right to speak and be heard on campuses.

The YouTube clip of my Irvine lecture attracted close to a million viewers. Some of them might have seen a Quixote-like figure standing up to a churning mob, but, in truth, I no longer relished that role. "I wish they had stayed," I told the audience after the last of the protest-ers was ejected. "They were precisely the students I came to engage." I even wrote those students an open letter offering to return to campus and dialogue with them. They never responded.

In *firgun*-free Israel, the Irvine incident earned me a headline— I considered framing it—in which an unnamed foreign ministry offi-cial accused me of deliberately stirring up anti-Israel sentiment on American campuses. But news of the episode reverberated positively through Washington and further strengthened my ability to convey Israel's message. It helped address those burning questions that I ini-tially posed—how to gain access, maintain bipartisan respect, and establish a compelling presence? Those answers proved critical early in 2010, as the White House and the Prime Minister's Office pitched to-ward collision.

Tremors

The clash, ironically, was preceded by a real disaster—and a moving display of U.S.-Israel harmony. It began on January 14, forty-eight hours after a massive earthquake devastated Haiti. Vast swaths of the impoverished Caribbean country lay in ruins, with at least 150,000 dead. With its war-born experience in dealing with casualties, its expert medical teams, and its biblical traditions of caring for the weak, Israel responded. More than two hundred Israelis, many of them volunteers from the IsraAID relief organization, immediately took off for Haiti and set up the first completely equipped hospital unit. Yet the operation could not have been mounted without the logistical assistance of the United States. Some of the Israelis even slept in chairs at the U.S. embassy. Throughout, I was on the phone around the clock with the State Department, coordinating our joint efforts. Aftershocks further ravaged that tragic island, but the cooperation between the United States and Israel remained firm.

But other tremors were indeed rattling the relationship, and their epicenter—to use Jim Jones's word—was once again the peace process. Abbas rejected the moratorium on Israeli building in the West Bank because it did not include Jerusalem and criticized Obama for no longer demanding a total freeze. Nevertheless, he was willing to enter into "proximity talks." This meant that Israeli and Palestinian leaders would not meet face-to-face but only pass messages through an intermediary, Special Envoy George Mitchell. But while the Palestinians insisted on discussing substantive issues—borders, especially— via proxy, Netanyahu would only address them in direct talks with Abbas. The Palestinians wanted to talk about territory first and the Israelis about the security measures that would enable us to safely give up land. Mitchell wanted to tackle territory and security simultaneously and seemed to fault Israel for the impasse. In an interview with Charlie Rose that I suspect he later regretted, the U.S. special envoy suggested that the United States could use a "stick" on Israel by withholding financial aid.

The Arab states, meanwhile, refused to make even a single gesture toward peace. A request for allowing Israeli airliners to cross Arabian Peninsula airspace, saving hours of flying time to India and China, was denied. Yet the onus for the lack of progress in the peace talks remained permanently on Israel. "The ball is not in our court," I told the prime minister, "because it's not a ball. It's a stake."

My sense of foreboding only deepened on January 15, when Obama issued an official statement on Haiti. "Help continues to flow in, not just from the United States but from Brazil, Mexico, Canada,

France, Colombia, and the Dominican Republic," the president declared. Omitted from the list was Israel, the first state to arrive in Haiti and the first to reach the disaster fully prepared. I heard the president's words and felt like I had been kicked in the chest.

And still I believed Israel should make every reasonable effort to avoid confronting Obama. "Israel is a strong U.S. ally and I will never waiver from keeping its people safe," he told students at the University of Tampa on January 28, persuading me that the situation was not hopeless. Yet, for every reaffirmation of the alliance, the administration took steps that disconcerted or even imperiled Israel.

On February 16, for example, the United States aroused Israeli ire by naming a new ambassador, Robert Ford, to Syria. This ended a five-year suspension of ties in response to the assassination of Lebanon's pro-Western prime minister by elements close to Syrian ruler Bashar al-Assad. The son of an air force officer who seized power in Damascus in 1971 and retained it brutally, Assad was proving to be his father's savage equal. Starting in 2007, he collaborated with North Korea in trying to build a secret military nuclear facility and helped Iran supply tens of thousands of rockets to Hezbollah. Three years later, he smuggled long-range Scud missiles into Lebanon, bringing every Israeli city within range.

Yet the administration remained reluctant to confirm reports of Syria's arming of Hezbollah. Instead of a reckless dictator, the White House saw Assad as a pragmatist and potential partner for peace. Ford's appointment, it claimed, represented another attempt to engage and moderate America's antagonists in the Middle East. Israel, on the contrary, viewed the move as a reward for abominable behavior and an incentive to all those in the region who emulated it. In diplomacy we say that "no-comment is also a comment," and when the press asked for a reaction to the renewal of U.S.-Syrian relations, the embassy's response was: no comment.

But such silence could not be easily maintained on the subject of Jerusalem. The administration continued to regard any Israeli construction in the city's formerly Jordanian sectors as a provocation and an obstacle to peace. And Israel kept insisting that Jerusalem was sovereign Israeli territory and the Jewish capital for three thousand years. "Is America's policy that Israel should stop building in Arab areas?" Netanyahu rhetorically asked me. "But should Arabs stop building in Jewish areas? And what about mixed neighborhoods?" The dissonance intensified and then, at the end of February, threatened to erupt as Jerusalem mayor Nir Barkat prepared to unveil a historic renovation project.

The plan called for transforming a Jerusalem slum into a tourist mall, complete with parks, galleries, and a community center. Overlooking the Old City and arising—according to legend—on the ruins of royal Israelite orchards, the new arcade was anointed the "King's Garden." But the slum belonged to an East Jerusalem Arab village where, in order to make room for the overhaul, Israeli bulldozers would have to demolish a number of illegally built structures. The administration would surely explode.

I first met Nir Barkat when he was a sprightly paratrooper commander in Lebanon in 1982. Thirty years later, he was still Dorian Gray–like in his youthful energy, a successful high-tech entrepreneur who sought to apply proven business models to the religiously riven Holy City. I enthusiastically endorsed his candidacy for mayor and we remained in close touch. But his right-of-center politics put him at loggerheads with the White House, which viewed him as a loose—and loaded—cannon.

The administration was already livid over a building project in Sheikh Jarrah, in East Jerusalem, where Jews reclaimed the deeds to land captured by Jordan in 1948 and then liberated by Israel in 1967. The site became a flashpoint for weekly confrontations between Israeli police and pro-Palestinian demonstrators, and a magnet for international condemnations. Now the State Department learned of Barkat's plans to proceed with the King's Garden. "Hillary nearly blew her top," one senior American official informed me. "We practically had to scrape her off the ceiling."

I tried to explain the delicacy of the situation to Barkat, but he remained obdurate. Israel could rightfully build anywhere in Jerusalem, he said, and praised the King's Garden as a win-win proposition for both Arabs and Jews. Knowing that Obama did not recognize that right and that a lose-lose situation loomed for U.S.-Israel relations did not deter Barkat. The groundbreaking ceremony was set for March 1, a few days away.

Fortunately, Uzi Arad, our national security advisor, was in Washington, and I took the occasion to inform national security advisor Jim Jones of the unveiling. In his office, together with a distraught Dennis Ross and a nail-biting Dan Shapiro, Jones told Arad that inaugurating the King's Garden project would doom the indirect "proximity talks" between Israel and the Palestinians. Arad, aware suddenly of the danger, called Molcho, who in turn updated the prime minister. I never learned what transpired next, only that Barkat delayed the ceremony. The State Department noted appreciatively "that the mayor is going to continue his discussions with [Palestinian] residents before proceeding with the plan." The Americans thanked me, but I felt no sense of accomplishment. What may have been a diplomatic victory for us was undoubtedly a cultural and economic loss for the people of Jerusalem.

And the proximity talks went nowhere. George Mitchell continued to shuttle the five-mile stretch between Jerusalem and Ramallah, and Ehud Barak made his almost-monthly stops in Washington, but zero progress ensued. The focus, rather, switched to the impending tour of Israel by Joseph Biden, America's irrepressibly upbeat vice president.

Blood and Treasure

Concerted effort is required not to be charmed by Joe Biden, the rare politician who truly adores politics, who enters a roomful of eight hundred people and seems to say to himself, "Wow, eight hundred people, I'm going to meet them all!" He always greeted me warmly—after hugging Sally—and reiterated his love for Israel. That affection arose from Biden's firm religious faith as well as the backing he had long received from Israel's American supporters. He first visited Israel in 1973 and met Prime Minister Golda Meir. "We Jews have a secret weapon," she told the then-freshman senator. "We have nowhere else to go." I would hear that Golda story many times.

Biden similarly retold his aphorisms, most of which began with "as my father always said . . ." Unusually, perhaps, for a Jew, I especially liked "As my father always said, never crucify yourself on a small cross." But the administration expected precisely that of Netanyahu. Freezing settlements and stopping construction in Jerusalem were small crosses that could cost him an election well before he faced the biggest cross of all, creating a Palestinian state.

Biden again waxed aphoristic during an intimate conversation on the eve of his Israel visit. Inviting me into his White House office and seating me before a roaring fire, Biden stressed the president's seriousness on the peace and Iranian issues and the depth of Obama's commitment to Israel. That dedication would not be weakened, even by differences over settlements. "Israel could get into a fistfight with this country and we'd still defend you," he said. Yet he urged Netanyahu to accommodate Obama, whatever their differences—"One comes with baggage and the other without bags," he said—and assured me that the president would win a second term. I responded by urging the administration to restore the traditional U.S.-Israeli intimacy. The vice president nodded and said, "We must have no daylight between us." This reaffirmation of our alliance's central pillar heartened me, and I asked if his coming trip signaled a larger role for him in the peace process. No, Biden responded, that would remain the State Department's bailiwick. "As my father always said, never mow another man's lawn."

A week later, I stood between the paired American and Israeli flags on Ben-Gurion Airport's runway as Air Force Two taxied to a halt. Biden once referred to Israel as his second home and when he descended the stairs, a beacon of silver hair and gleaming teeth, I gripped his hand and wished him, "Welcome home, Mr. Vice President."

The tour began festively. Sally escorted Dr. Jill Biden and Sara Netanyahu on a tour of the Jerusalem YMCA, while I drove in the motorcade to the Prime Minister's Residence for talks between the Israeli and American teams. Following a two-hour private discussion in his study, Netanyahu and Biden emerged arm in arm and went out to the courtyard for a press conference. The decades-long friendship between them was evident as they piled praise on each other and on the alliance. "Bibi," Biden colloquially began and proceeded to contradict Obama's position on the peace talks, "progress occurs in the Middle East when everyone knows there is simply no space between the United States and Israel." A clearly pleased Netanyahu presented Biden with a certificate attesting to the trees Israel planted in his mother's memory. But the frame dropped and its glass smashed on the prime minister's lectern—the first sign, perhaps, that the visit might go awry.

A second omen occurred at our next stop, Yad Vashem, Israel's national Holocaust memorial. The lights went out in the middle of Biden's speech, seemingly for effect but in reality due to a power outage. Squinting in the harsh sunlight outside, I glanced at my cellphone and noticed the publication of Interior Ministry plans to build 1,600 apartments in Ramat Shlomo.

This was a Jewish area in Northwest, not East, Jerusalem, that Israelis regarded as an integral part of their state. Nevertheless, the neighborhood had been built on former Jordanian land that the Obama administration considered Palestinian. Perhaps some right-wing officials were trying to spoil the vice president's visit, or some left-wing journalists were trying to embarrass Netanyahu—I would never know. Still, I hoped the Americans would not notice, but, of course, they did. "What the hell is this!" Dan Shapiro practically lunged at me back at the hotel, pushing his BlackBerry toward my face. Dennis Ross would not even look at me.

The Biden crisis, as the press called it, commenced. All of our explanations—that the announcement had emanated from a midlevel bureaucrat, the prime minister knew nothing about it, and that the apartments would take years to build—failed to dispel the impression that Biden had been deliberately face-slapped. At once, the vice president delayed his dinner with the Netanyahus and his staff canceled their meal with me. Sally and I wandered the dark Jerusalem streets, half in shock, half despondent. Passing a tony Italian restaurant, we considered going inside but then saw former ambassador Sallai Meridor and his wife, Noa, cheerily raising their wine glasses. We did not want to spoil their moment, so we went to eat hummus instead.

After midnight, I joined the prime minister and his advisors in an attempt to work out a compromise text that Biden could incorporate in his forthcoming speech at Tel Aviv University. The consensus was that Israel could not apologize for building in a Jewish neighborhood in the sovereign capital of the Jewish State. But we could express regret for the announcement's timing and pledge to prevent similarly embarrassing situations in the future. In an effort to learn the Americans' expectations, I phoned Dennis Ross, who indicated that Israel should refrain from beginning construction on the homes for several years. This required the cooperation of the interior minister, Eli Yishai, of the Ultra-Orthodox Shas party. He, too, sauntered into the prime minister's study, seemingly unperturbed. Other officials ran in and out before, finally, close to 2 A.M., Ron Dermer and I ran with a handwritten draft to the hotel lobby where Dan Shapiro waited peevishly. He visibly brightened, though, when he read our assurances. We typed them up in the business center and went upstairs for a few hours' sleep.

The air itself felt supercharged the following day as the vice president rose to the Tel Aviv University podium. He spoke about feeling at home in the Jewish State, about the "unbreakable bond . . . impervious to any shifts," between it and the United States, which "has no better friend than Israel." He quoted his father and Golda Meir, and referred to the prime minister as "Bibi." He called for the release of Gilad Shalit, the IDF corporal held hostage by Hamas, and for peace with the Palestinians—all to exuberant applause. But then he turned to the Ramat Shlomo plan, which, he said, undermined the trust required for productive negotiations. "At the request of President Obama, I condemn it immediately and unequivocally."

Some left-wing students clapped at this as well, but other Israelis seethed. Diplomacy provides a word-scale for expressing levels of displeasure, beginning with *regret* and *disapprove* and escalating to *denounce* and *deplore*. But the harshest of all is *condemn*. "The administration never condemned Iran for killing its own people," Ron muttered, "but Israel gets condemned for building homes in a Jewish neighborhood in our capital city." That sentiment reflected mine as well and yet I still felt a surge of relief. One word seemed a sufferable price to pay to put a damaging crisis behind us.

Following the speech, Biden and his party drove to Ramallah for a meeting with Abbas. On Dennis Ross's suggestion, the vice president asked the Palestinian president to look him in the eye and promise that he could make peace with Israel. Abbas refused. The experience left a durable impression on Biden, as did his next item on his itinerary: a helicopter tour of Israel. This revealed the country's tiny contours, with Greater Tel Aviv only a few minutes' flight from the West Bank. Biden landed at Ben-Gurion ever more zealous for Israel's defense. He praised Israel repeatedly as I escorted him across the tarmac, through a hot, sandy wind, to the stairs of Air Force Two.

We managed to end the trip on a favorable note and, I thought, avert a major collision. My sole regret was that the prime minister had not taken my advice and parted from Biden personally at the airport. "A photo of the two of you shaking hands would have made it hard for anyone to claim that he went away mad," I suggested. Instead, the vice president shook my hand, after he hugged Sally.

Air Force Two took off and I turned to tell Israel's *Meet the Press* that there was no crisis, that the Ramat Shlomo incident proved yet again how two allies could swiftly overcome their differences. Then I, too, boarded a plane and arrived in the United States at five o'clock Friday morning to learn that Secretary of State Clinton had excoriated Netanyahu for forty-five minutes over the phone, rebuking him for humiliating the president and undermining America's ability to deal with pressing Middle East issues. "I didn't enjoy playing the bad cop," she later recalled, "but it was part of the job." And then I heard that the State Department, protesting "the deeply negative signal about Israel's approach to the bilateral relationship," had summoned me to an immediate meeting.

As in the case of the word *condemn,* diplomacy provides a calibrated lexicon to describe requests for high-level meetings. The scale descends from the amicable "respectfully invited" to the more neutral "asked to come." The lowest, by far, is "summoned."

Before reporting to State, though, I conferred with Lior Weintraub and DCM Dan Arbell at the Residence. I informed them that, while I would continue to adhere publicly to the "all's well" pose, behind the scenes I would forcibly resist this attempt to fabricate a crisis. "I will give as good as I get," I said, and feeling rather feisty, departed for Foggy Bottom.

There, waiting in his not-nice American mode, was Deputy Secretary Jim Steinberg, who proceeded to read me the text of Hillary's conversation with Netanyahu. This contained a list of demands, including a total building freeze in East Jerusalem as well as the West Bank, most of which would be unacceptable to any Israeli prime minister, much less a Likudnik. Steinberg added his own furious comments—department staffers, I later heard, listened in on our conversation and cheered—about Israel's insult to the president and the pride of the United States. Then came my turn to respond.

"Let me get this straight," I began. "We inadvertently slight the vice president and apologize, and I become the first foreign ambassador summoned by this administration to the State Department. Bashar al-Assad hosts Iranian president Ahmadinejad, who calls for murdering seven million Israelis, but do you summon Syria's ambassador? No, you send your ambassador back to Damascus. Israelis, then, will see this as nothing but a pretext to arm-twist us and beat up on us." Steinberg wanted to know if that was Israel's official response. No, I said, that was my personal observation. Officially, Israel took note of the State Department's position and assured the deputy of its highest consideration.

Returning to the embassy, I spent hours on the phone with Netanyahu. He seemed startled and hurt by the administration's conduct. The calls continued late into that evening—3 A.M., Israel time—and repeatedly interrupted my talk at the Potomac synagogue of my great friend Rabbi Stuart Weinblatt. Rahm Emanuel telephoned as well. "America is Israel's thin blue line," he warned; "don't cross it." Israel asked for America's help on Iran, on Goldstone, and all the United States was asking of Israel was a "zoning issue," he said. I countered by protesting what Israelis saw as a fabricated crisis, but Rahm managed to shoot back, "This isn't a crisis, it's a pimple on the ass of the U.S.-Israel friendship," just as Obama entered his office.

More disconcerting still was my confidential briefing of Israel's nine consuls general in the United States. Carelessly falling back into my historian's mode, I quoted a State Department comment to the effect that Israeli building in East Jerusalem threatened the future of U.S.-Israel ties. The last time this happened, I reminded the consuls, was in 1975, when a disagreement over the peace process led then-president Gerald Ford to "reassess" America's relations with Israel. Several listeners on the line hurried to call *Haaretz,* which rushed to headline "Oren: Worst U.S.-Israel Crisis in 35 Years." Another disleak, it leapt into the American media.

Sunday came and, with it, the morning talk shows. Dennis Ross had indicated that the administration would use the occasion to defuse the crisis atmosphere. But when asked by NBC's Tom Brokaw to comment on Israel's construction of "1,600 new settlements," David Axelrod called them an "insult" and an "affront." Pressed by interviewer Jake Tapper as to whether he regarded Israel as an asset or a liability, Axelrod simply ducked the question.

In his indifferent attire and bushy mustache, Axelrod could pass for a high school science teacher. Behind the avuncular exterior, though, lay a take-no-prisoners political mind closely aligned with the president's. Appreciative of that access, I sought a conversation with him at that week's Gridiron Club dinner. Notorious for its off-color musical sketches put on by the press corps and for the lacerating speeches delivered by party leaders and sometimes by the president himself, the Gridiron is also renowned for between-the-tables politicking. So, when Virginia's copacetic governor (later senator) Tim Kaine volunteered to help, I asked him to arrange a sidebar with Axelrod.

We met in the shadows of the kitchen exit, each of us in a white tie and tux. I urged him to find a way out of a situation that I feared might become dangerous for Israel, but Axelrod calmly brushed this aside. Instead, he accused me of urging congressmen to hold on until 2012, that Obama would never get reelected. The charge of interfering in internal American politics could have rendered me persona non grata and resulted in my expulsion from the United States. "That's utterly untrue," I repeatedly responded, but Axelrod ignored my denials.

"I wouldn't take it too seriously," Senator Joseph Lieberman said the next day, quieting me with warm counsel and a cold beer. "It's just Chicago politics." In the basement of Joe's Georgetown house, between walls covered with comforting photographs of his wife, Hadassah, and their children and grandchildren, among the mementos of his thirty-five years of public service, I found solace and wisdom. Originally a Democrat, a 2004 candidate for vice president, he was the only American Jew ever to be nominated for national office. Nevertheless, Lieberman had angered some of his supporters by becoming an independent and joining Republicans John McCain and Lindsey Graham as one of the "Three Amigos," pursuing a muscular foreign policy. For me, there was no substitute for a personal friendship with Joe, a man who knew Washington thoroughly and cherished Israel—"founded by Jews," he once quipped, "who weren't going to take crap from anyone after the Holocaust, not even from each other." Now, still shaken by my conversation with Axelrod, I reminded the senator of Truman's famous adage, "If you want a friend in this town, get a dog." Senator Lieberman clinked his beer bottle on mine and smiled his half-sagacious, half-mischievous smile. "Well, I guess that makes me your dog."

Other officials called in to lend support. "Don't take that bullshit," New York senator Chuck Schumer said to bolster me. "Stick to your guns and don't give an inch." But the press ridiculed Netanyahu, labeling him arrogant and inept. *The New Yorker* again claimed that he called Rahm Emanuel and David Axelrod "self-hating Jews," while the Republicans railed against Obama for abandoning Israel. In an attempt to soften the onslaught and restore some bipartisanship, I agreed to write an op-ed for *The New York Times*. My deadline was in four hours, two of which I spent gazing bleary-eyed into a blank screen. Where to begin? I had to uphold the alliance, deny it was experiencing its worse crisis in thirty-five years, recall the moratorium, restate our position on Jerusalem and our dedication to peace, and remind readers that even the best of friends can sometimes disagree—all in eight hundred words.

The article, "For Israel and the United States, Disagreement Not a Crisis," appeared the next morning, March 17, but I had no time to read it. Rather, I ran to an interview with Charlie Rose, rushing onto the set without even stopping for makeup. Impeccably thoughtful in his questioning, Charlie probed the depths of the current U.S.-Israel malaise, yet I managed to stay on message. There was no crisis. Period. Yet my appearance said otherwise. "You looked all beat up," Yossi Klein Halevi phoned from Israel to tell me. My mother sounded more concerned. "Please, Michael, promise me you'll get some sleep."

But rest, much less slumber, remained unthinkable as rumors of an Obama peace plan now proliferated. "The history of Arab-Israel diplomacy is littered with such plans," I told Dennis Ross, and again I sensed he concurred. Together, we listed ways of averting similar wrangles in the future, among them restoring the "no surprises" principle, preserving direct communications between the president and the prime minister, and pledging to keep all further disagreements out of the public eye.

Yet the administration seemed uninterested. It still insisted that Netanyahu agree to its demands while, in the press, unnamed White House sources accused Ross of dual loyalty and of acting as the prime minister's advocate. I, too, was criticized by some in the Prime Minister's Office for exceeding my authority in trying to find a way out of the morass. Support, though, came from an unexpected source: the defense minister. "A bad ambassador is one who sits and does nothing," Ehud Barak told me. "You are simply doing your job."

Barak's *firgun* never felt timelier, for I soon learned that Netanyahu had decided to address the AIPAC conference in Washington on March 22. Obama, compelled by the health-care debate to cancel a visit to Indonesia, would be in the capital that day. The two leaders simply had to meet. I called several senior administration officials and asked them how they would define a successful session between the two. Their answers were uniform: "Bibi should tell the president where he's going on the peace process—what's his end game." But the White House remained noncommittal about scheduling the summit's time and format. The estrangement became palpable after Netanyahu, to the cheers of ten thousand AIPAC enthusiasts, defiantly declared that "Jerusalem is not a settlement. It's our capital."

Later, the prime minister and his entourage retired to the embassy to await word from the White House. Ehud Barak turned to my young head of office, the effervescent Moriya Blumenfeld, and asked for a glass of whiskey and the biggest lock in the building. This he set to disassembling with a screwdriver while we debated the tenor of the prime minister's meeting with the president.

A majority opinion held that the administration had come out swinging at Israel, precipitated a crisis, and appreciated only strength, which Netanyahu should show. My voice was virtually alone in calling for prudence. Responding rashly to the provocations would only play into the hands of those who wanted to transform support for Israel into a partisan issue, I argued. "Your policy should be rope-a-dope," I said, referring to Muhammad Ali's boxing strategy of deflecting blows until his opponent wore out. "Ignore the jabs and save your strength for when it really counts." The discussion dragged on well past midnight, until finally the invitation to the White House arrived, for seven o'clock that evening.

The limo ride afforded me another opportunity to remind Netanyahu of the need to go the extra mile in placating the president. But the absence of any protocol officers or even Marine guards to receive us outside conveyed a mood of coolness rather than conciliation. The prime minister immediately adjourned to the Oval Office for his face-to-face with Obama, leaving their teams to linger once again in the Roosevelt Room.

While Barak fiddled perilously with an antique clock, I called my colleagues' attention to the Frederic Remington sculptures of buffalo and George Catlin portraits of Native Americans that oddly recalled the world that America nearly destroyed. Similarly, I pointed out the photographs of the president that lined the hallways and the battle ribbons—Yorktown 1781, Gettysburg 1863, Iwo Jima 1945—draped around every flag. I asked them to imagine the Prime Minister's Office decorated with pictures of Netanyahu or Israeli banners marked with "Conquest of Sinai 1956" or "Siege of Jerusalem 1948," but they could not. I asked a secretary for some snacks and received some crackers and cheese—minimal fare that Barak nevertheless devoured.

After an hour or so, Obama and Netanyahu emerged in pleasant humor. But then the president addressed the prime minister and his team and said, "I have an assignment for you." By this he meant that we were supposed to work out a schedule for meeting his demands, including the construction freeze. We floated alternative ideas until 9 P.M., when Obama announced that he was retiring upstairs. Michelle and their two daughters were out of town and he wanted to get to bed early. Netanyahu asked if we could remain and work with General Jones, Dennis Ross, and deputy NSC director Tom Donilon. Another two hours passed, and at 11 P.M., Netanyahu requested to see the president again, in private. The president descended from his quarters with rolled-up shirtsleeves and reconvened with Netanyahu for another thirty minutes. The rest of us—Israelis and Americans—remained poring over various drafts until 2:30 A.M.

That was when, after dragging myself into my car, I heard the radio announce that Israel had been snubbed. The news noted that there had been no official photograph of Obama and Netanyahu, no joint communiqué, not even an official dinner—worse, the headlines claimed, Obama had dined with his wife and daughters, leaving Netanyahu and his advisors to starve. To a ravenous press I had to explain that this had been a working meeting, not a state visit, arranged at the last minute. The first family was not even present in the White House, I added. There was no snub, and no crisis certainly.

And yet the memory of those crackers, of those unrealistic demands on Netanyahu, needled me. So, too, did the realization that the snub headline, though most likely spun by the White House, could just as well have sprung from Jerusalem. In contrast to the past, when the friendship of the U.S. president augmented an Israeli prime minister's popularity, Obama's hostility toward Netanyahu actually bolstered the prime minister in the polls.

Still, the media harped on Netanyahu's "shabby" reception at the White House, how he was treated like a "third world dictator," and "humiliated, demeaned, and devastated." U.S.-Israel relations, *Haaretz* editorialized, had reached an ultimate low. In fact, they descended further.

In pursuit of his nonproliferation agenda—another *kishke* issue—Obama convened a Nuclear Security Summit in Washington on April 12–13. Forty-seven world leaders attended but not Netanyahu. The nuclear issue was singularly sensitive for Israel. Though our longstanding policy remained that we would never be the first nation to introduce nuclear weapons to the Middle East, Israel feared international pressure to reveal its nuclear capabilities. The administration sought to allay Netanyahu's concerns, assuring him that Iran, and not Israel, would be singled out for criticism. But the prime minister remained wary of attempts by Egypt and Turkey to pass anti-Israel resolutions at Obama's summit and unsure of the president's determination to block them. And so, instead of going to Washington himself, Netanyahu sent Atomic Energy Minister Dan Meridor—Sallai's brother—to represent Israel. Meridor and I spent much of the two days chatting with German chancellor Angela Merkel, Jordan's King Abdullah, and Italy's rakish prime minister, Silvio Berlusconi, who raved about a certain Alitalia flight attendant. In the end, Israel was not singled out at this summit. Only at the next one.

Gathering in New York in May, representatives of the 189 signatory countries of the Non-Proliferation Treaty specifically cited Israel—and ignored Iran—in demanding a nuclear-free Middle East. Israel favored disarming the region of all massively destructive weapons, but only *after* the achievement of peace. Obama nevertheless hailed the summit for promoting "balanced and practical steps." Jim Jones, the national security advisor tried to walk the statement back by pledging that "the United States will not permit actions that could jeopardize Israel." Still, Obama's initial willingness to support the singling out of Israel on its most delicate security issue seemed to confirm Netanyahu's deepest apprehensions.

Trust was further eroded when General David Petraeus, commander of all U.S. forces from Afghanistan to the Persian Gulf and America's most celebrated soldier, was quoted saying that Israel's conflict with the Palestinians cost America "blood and treasure" in the region. The remarks, purportedly made on the very day that Israeli rescue workers landed in earthquake-stricken Haiti, deeply insulted Israeli civilian and defense leaders. In a later conversation with me, Petraeus denied making the remark. But then, in closing his Nuclear Summit, Obama declared that "the need for peace between Israelis and Palestinians and the Arab states remains as critical as ever," and "when conflicts break out . . . that ends up costing us significantly in . . . blood and treasure."

Alone in the embassy's Aquarium, I agonized over those words. Israel had not only the failure of peace on its hands, according to the administration, but the suffering of America's unemployed and the sacrifices of its soldiers. The vicious sludge that was just then coating the Gulf of Mexico—the spillage of billions of barrels of BP oil—evoked my own pitch-black mood. I wondered whether I would last out the year in my post.

Earlier that morning, I appeared on CNN's *State of the Union* and the host, Candy Crowley, asked me to describe the state of the U.S.-Israel alliance. I smiled at her and replied, "Great!" It was the only response I ever regretted making on TV. Brooding back at the embassy, I wondered whether there was a limit even to diplomatic falsehoods. Just then, Lior Weintraub ambled into the room. Grinning, my chief of staff uttered the only two words that at that lightless moment could have made me laugh, the very words that I should have spoken to Candy Crowley. "Unbreakable," Lior said. "Unshakable."

Fish and Fighters

"My district already has twenty-five percent unemployment and Israel's going to jack it up to thirty percent," Illinois congressman Donald Manzullo, a Republican, practically shouted into the phone. "You've impounded nine containers—nine—of our frozen Asian carp."

My first year in office had posed successive and seemingly unsurpassable challenges. I had to maneuver through the embassy's politics, minimize leaks, maintain bipartisan bridges, straddle divisions in the American Jewish community, create a diplomatic persona, and preserve open channels between two governments at odds on multiple issues. I had internalized crucial lessons—be cautious on conference calls, for example, and never go on TV without makeup. My appreciation of Congress as a counterweight to federal criticism of Israel deepened, and I doubled the time I spent weekly on the Hill. But none of the year's instructive experiences prepared me for this. Fish.

I tried to calm the congressman, assuring him that I would do my utmost to free the embargoed fillets, but my options were in fact few. America signed its first-ever free-trade agreement with Israel back in 1985, but the treaty exempted certain Israeli products liable to be eradicated by their cheaper American counterparts. Apples, avocados, and oranges fell into this category, and, so, too, did the carp cultivated by Galilean farmers. Which was why four hundred thousand pounds of the frozen Illinois fish were denied entry to the Promised Land.

Still, in view of the possible diplomatic damage, I thought Israel should make this one exception, and told that to the Ministers of Trade and Finance. Congressman Manzullo, meanwhile, ramped up the pressure. He phoned me incessantly, using increasingly acrimonious tones, and complained to the secretary of state. "You think finding Middle East peace is hard," Hillary blithely told reporters. "I'm dealing with carp!" Netanyahu called to question me, "What's all this carp stuff?" I urged him to focus on Israel's critical issues and leave the fish to me.

Days of effort passed before a compromise was finally achieved. On a one-time, nonprecedent basis, the nine containers were unloaded in Israeli ports. A now-composed Congressman Manzullo called to thank me and to ask, "Why do you Israelis need so much carp?" Realizing that his question was genuine, I explained that the Jewish people would soon celebrate Passover, when they traditionally eat gefilte fish. "Carp, Congressman, is the main ingredient."

Gefilte fish, together with *matzah* and chicken soup, was served at the maiden White House seder, which the Obamas held with senior advisors, selected staffers, and friends. Daughters Malia and Sasha recited the Four Questions reserved for the youngest attendees and searched for the hidden shard of *matzah*—the *Afikomen*. The theme of the night, recalling the dreams of antebellum slaves, was the exodus to freedom. The press nevertheless speculated whether, in light of the tension between the administration and Israel, the president ended the seder with the usual pledge, "Next year in Jerusalem."

At the Residence, Sally and I also held our first ambassadorial seder, together with my parents and our children. Noam, black-and-blue from his IDF Special Forces training, flew directly from the field to join us. Around the glowing table, we sat with Dennis and Debbie Ross, several ambassadors, and senior Clinton advisor Ann Lewis. We listened to Dr. Haleh Esfandiari, an international authority on Iran whom I first met at Princeton. While visiting her mother in Tehran in 2007, Haleh was arrested by Iranian agents, who charged her with subversion and jailed her for eight months in the notorious Evin prison. The story of Haleh's modern exodus from captivity to liberation moved everyone around the table to tears. It reminded me of that underground seder I attended in the Soviet Union a quarter century before, of the unafraid Jews who sang "Hatikvah"—"To be a free people in the Land of Zion"—while the KGB led me away.

Passover brought no freedom from U.S.-Israel tensions, though. Ronald Lauder, philanthropist and president of the World Jewish Congress, published a full-page letter in *The Wall Street Journal* questioning whether Obama's friction with Israel represented an attempt to appease the Muslim world and squeeze the Jewish State into indefensible borders. New York's cantankerous former mayor Ed Koch, an outspoken Obama supporter in the 2008 elections, now accused the president of "making Israel into a pariah" and of "throwing Israel under the bus in order to please Muslim nations." Even Elie Wiesel, whom Obama described as his personal friend and moral advisor, publicly assailed the White House for pressuring Israel on Jerusalem, "the world's Jewish spiritual capital."

Rumors meanwhile circulated of administration attempts to topple Netanyahu and of White House insinuations that the prime minister was secretly scheming with Republicans. Veteran White House correspondent Helen Thomas, the eighty-nine-year-old role model of women journalists and staple of the Washington press corps, called for the expulsion of Jewish Israelis. "Tell them to get the hell out of Palestine," the sour-faced Thomas, born to Arab parents, hissed. "Go home [to] Poland, Germany, America, and everywhere else."

The atmosphere, it seemed, could not have grown more noxious. Until, suddenly in late April, the venom turned to nectar. Obama convened the first-ever meeting between a president and the Jewish members of Congress, telling his thirty-seven guests of "the unbreakable bond of friendship" with Israel, America's "key strategic ally in the Middle East." General Jones, after opening with a joke that many in his mostly Jewish audience found vaguely anti-Semitic, recovered by praising America's alliance and "special relationship" with Israel and "the shared values, deep and interwoven connections, and mutual interests," binding the two countries. Secretary of State Clinton similarly cited her "deep personal commitment to . . . promoting Israel's future." And for the first time, she invited me for a private meeting at the State Department, where she inquired about—and I confirmed—Netanyahu's commitment to peace.

The "love offensive," as the press dubbed it, continued. After addressing the crowd at the embassy's celebration of Israel's Independence Day, David Axelrod assured me that, as the son of a lifelong Hadassah member, he would never work for anyone not devoted to Israel. And while interviewing with Charlie Rose, Rahm Emanuel described Obama and Netanyahu as "friends" who enjoyed a "very good, totally honest," and "very constructive" relationship. I gasped so audibly on hearing these words that I barely noticed him describing the U.S.-Israel ties as "unbreakable and unshakable."

Several theories circulated explaining the love offensive's objectives. The proximity talks with the Palestinians had started, some observers said, and the administration sought Israeli goodwill. Others cited polls that showed the growing unease with the Democrats among pro-Israeli voters. Factions within the White House, meanwhile, accused one another of picking the fight with Israel and of adopting a "never waste a good crisis" approach to the Biden visit spat. Clinton later wrote that Rahm Emanuel argued for a tough stance "right out of the gate" against Netanyahu, who would "otherwise walk all over us." I cared less about the reasons for the turnaround or those responsible for it. I merely appreciated the respite.

Taking advantage of that lull, I delivered the 2010 commencement speech at Brandeis University. Founded as America's elite Jewish university and named for the chief justice whose blending of American patriotism with Zionism so influenced my own, Brandeis's invitation indeed moved me. Though 150 students, among them several J Street activists, protested against my appearance, five thousand others signed a petition supporting it. Now I sat alongside fellow honorees Dennis Ross and Paul Simon on a sweltering dais, sweat streaming under my robe.

"I wasn't much of an athlete or even a student," I told the audience, recalling my early childhood challenges. "I was a three-letterman, but the three letters were *A-D-D*." But then I went on to talk about overcoming obstacles, not the least of which was getting through paratrooper training. Even then, I admitted, I still had to be shoved out of the plane. "Be courageous," I concluded. "Be strong. And though you may just once in a while need the littlest push, jump."

Even while speaking these words, I wondered if I could take my own advice. The reprieve from U.S.-Israel tensions would end soon, I knew. The creation of a Palestinian state remained crucial for Obama, as did nuclear nonproliferation, and the outreach to Iran. Other hazards included partisanship in Washington, the fractured Jewish community, and an often-adversarial press. There were the vagaries of Israeli politics and the potential for upheaval in the Middle East.

And then there was me. Just as rowing and marathon running had not prepared me for the unimaginable rigors of the IDF, all that I had done to ready myself for this job—the writing, the speaking, the interviewing on TV—had fallen far short of what succeeding at it required. Beyond the daunting physical demands lay the emotional and psychological strains of coping with virtually relentless tensions between the two countries I loved. How long, I asked myself, could I continue?

The question vexed me even as Paul Simon, the sublime composer, singer, and sixties icon, received his honorary doctorate. Wizened now and looking frail, he replaced his mortarboard with a porkpie hat, took up his guitar, and sang "The Boxer." Apart from "The Star-Spangled Banner," what other song is so beloved by Americans of all ages? Simon's voice, still as supple as a teenager's, gripped the thousands of students and family members who spontaneously broke into song.

I sang, too, all the while reminding myself why I had sought the ambassador's job to begin with. I remembered the need to keep America and Israel—like the two halves of my identity—together in spite of their wrangles. The world needed them united, I recalled, and the two nations needed each other. I sang and remembered, and the words to Paul Simon's song seemed to assure me. The scarred boxer, reeling with dishonor and rage, repeatedly vows to quit. "I am leaving, I am leaving," he cries. "But the fighter still remains."

YEAR OF
AFFLICTION

THE FULL MOON CAST A SHIMMERING BEAM OVER THE SEA, JUST OFF the prow of the *Mavi Marmara*. The temperature on this night— May 30, 2010—was tepid and the water calm as the passenger liner plied southward at a steady 7.2 knots. At that speed, the ship would come within sight of its destination after daybreak, in another few hours. To pass the time, the hundreds of people on board chatted with one another, slept, or prayed. Until, that is, on the horizon, a host of beacons neared.

The night exploded in a blaze of searchlights and rotors. Morena speedboats swarmed around the *Mavi Marmara* and Black Hawk helicopters hovered above. Passengers on deck, aroused, dropped heavy objects down at the far smaller *Morenas*. Shouting "Allahu Akhbar"— God is great—they slung iron balls at the choppers. The intercom buzzed on the bridge. "This is the Israeli Navy," an IDF captain informed the liner's skipper. "You are approaching an area that is under a naval blockade. The Israeli government supports delivery of humanitarian supplies to the civilian population in the Gaza Strip and invites you to enter the Ashdod port." The responses, spoken in two different accents but with identical vehemence, were "Go back to Auschwitz," and, "We're helping the Arabs against the U.S. Don't forget 9/11."

With no choice but to prepare to board the ship, the *Morenas* extended ladders up to the *Mavi Marmara*'s lowest deck. But powerful fire hoses repulsed them. The Israelis next fired stun grenades and paintballs to clear the rails, and helicopters lowered ropes. One of these lines was intercepted, but another allowed a fifteen-man team of Shayetet 13—Israeli Navy SEALS—to rappel onto the upper deck. They were instantly overwhelmed by dozens of attackers wielding knives, axes, iron bars, and at least one gun. The Israelis were beaten, stabbed, and shot; three of them, thrown over the side, fell several decks below. One suffered multiple skull fractures and the other a gaping knife wound. Both were taken prisoner and beaten further.

In quarters too close for either tear gas or rubber bullets, the commandos fired paintballs and bean bags against their attackers. But these nonlethal means proved useless in saving the team from imminent harm. Following procedures standard in both the IDF and the U.S. military, the Israelis asked their commander for permission to use their sidearms. They shot—first in warning, then to disable, and, finally, when still threatened, to kill.

In Honor and in Shame

That bloodshed represented the failure of weeks of intense diplomacy. Information reached the embassy that a large flotilla was gathering to break the Gaza blockade. Supporters of Hamas had launched similar convoys in the past only to be intercepted by the Israeli Navy and turned back without incident. But this flotilla would be different. Set to sail from Turkey, apparently with Prime Minister Erdoğan's blessing, its size and composition were unprecedented. Its seven hundred participants—radical leftists and Islamic extremists—included several European parliamentarians. Also on board was Haneen Zoabi, the only female Arab member of the Knesset. The flotilla's centerpiece was the four-thousand-ton *Mavi Marmara,* as long as a football field and too large to be stopped safely by the technical means available to either Israel or the United States. Any attempt to blow off its propeller or snarl it in a net could sink the entire ship.

While striving to devise a way to stop the flotilla, Israeli leaders again debated the pros and cons of the Gaza blockade. This was deemed essential to prevent Iran from smuggling rockets to Hamas and to maintain pressure on the organization. The terrorists still fired dozens of rockets at Israeli towns and continued to hold Corporal Gilad Shalit, denying him Red Cross visits or communications with his family. Where Israeli officials differed was over the embargo's extent and efficacy. Some pressed for banning all nonessential items— cilantro, for example—to fan public disaffection with Hamas. Others preferred to void only the construction materials that Hamas could use to rebuild its bunkers. Most agreed on the need to strengthen

Abbas, who secretly supported the blockade as a way of weakening his Hamas archenemies.

Publicly, though, Abbas condemned Israel's policy as did much of international opinion. Consequently, many Israeli decision makers would have preferred to treat the flotilla as a one-time exception and let it pass unimpeded. But, unfortunately, international law determined that maritime blockades must either be abandoned or uniformly enforced—if necessary by military means.

I saw little benefit for Israel in the "cilantro boycott" or in secretly helping Abbas while he overtly denounced us. Denying Hamas the ability to renew its military infrastructure made more sense to me, but the political costs would skyrocket if Israel came to blows with the flotilla. Obama opposed the blockade and enjoyed very friendly relations with Erdoğan, who conformed to the Cairo speech's ideal of an authentically Muslim, democratically elected leader. By maintaining a blockade that Obama disliked and Erdoğan detested, Israel was likely once again to lock horns with the United States.

To avert that clash, I turned to my Turkish counterpart, Namik Tan, who had previously served as Ankara's ambassador to Israel. A warm-spirited man, he was committed to preserving his country's connections with mine in the months before the flotilla. Namik joined me in planning events to celebrate the centuries-long friendship between Turks and Jews.

Yet no display of goodwill in Washington could slow the decline in Turkish-Israeli relations. After years of unsuccessfully appealing for acceptance into the European Union, Turkey had turned back to its Middle Eastern and Islamic roots—a strategic pivot that precluded overly friendly ties with Israel. By 2010, Turkish television was broadcasting an action series about Turkish babies kidnapped by the Mossad. Deriding Israel as "the main threat to peace in the Middle East," Erdoğan canceled the Turkish army's annual joint maneuvers with the IDF. From four hundred thousand, the number of Israelis annually vacationing in Turkey plummeted to near zero.

None of this kept Namik Tan and I from working together and hoping for a breakthrough. Those hopes dwindled, though, on May 22, when the *Mavi Marmara* rendezvoused with five smaller protest ships in Istanbul. Some 640 nautical miles away—ninety hours' sailing time—Hamas officials in Gaza erected a holiday marquee to greet the triumphant flotilla.

Two days later, while driving home from the Brandeis commencement, I received an intriguing call from Ambassador Tan. "Could the flotilla dock in Israel's southern port of Ashdod?" he asked. "Could representatives of the Red Crescent meet it there, take control of any humanitarian cargoes, and transfer them to Gaza?" Tan needed an answer quickly—Erdoğan was flying to Iran—and I got him one. The Israeli government agreed. Some aid packages could even be delivered to our prisoner in Gaza, Gilad Shalit. Tan sounded delighted and I felt enormously relieved. But then, within forty hours, he phoned again. Erdoğan had called off the deal, the ambassador said. The flotilla would proceed as planned.

I braced for what seemed likely to be an unpleasant event—a kerfuffle, in Washington parlance. Israel did not collect intelligence on Turkey, regarding it as a friendly country. As a result, I learned only belatedly that the Mavi Marmara had been purchased and refurbished specifically for the flotilla by the IHH, a Turkish Islamic extremist group listed as a terrorist organization by Israel and the Netherlands and accused by the United States of aiding al-Qaeda. I saw—again, too late—footage of the sixty IHH members gathered on the dock and chanting, "Muhammad's army is returning to Khaybar," a reference to the Prophet's massacre of Arabian Jews. Days would pass before I heard how the IHH had boarded the Mavi Marmara separately from the other passengers, without inspection, wearing gas masks and protective vests. They sequestered the upper deck, where the Israelis were expected to land.

That landing was set for the night of May 31—America's Memorial Day. Before going to sleep, I briefed several reporters and touched base with the NSC. Israel each day facilitated the transfer of one hundred truckloads of aid into Gaza, I emphasized, where there was no humanitarian crisis. The flotilla had one purpose: to break the blockade and facilitate the transfer of Iranian arms to Hamas, a racist organization that opposed the peace process and pledged to kill all Jews. Still, I expressed confidence that the flotilla would be turned back peacefully, without any resort to force. Before shutting off the lights, I put in a final call to Lior Weintraub and reminded him to wake me if anything unusual happened.

At that moment—I would later learn—additional Shayetet 13 teams descended onto the Mavi Marmara's upper deck and were similarly set upon by the IHH members. The Israelis had to defend themselves as well as locate their wounded comrades held below. An hour-long video smuggled out by one of the Western journalists aboard showed IHH casualties—all men, most of them bearded—being carried down the stairs with gunshot wounds to the knee or near the heart. Though equipped with a state-of-the-art press room, the ship appeared to have no sick bay, no infusions, respirators, or even stethoscopes. A woman is heard pleading over a loudspeaker to an Israeli cruiser nearby, "We need help. We have many injured people." Forty minutes passed before the commandos completed Operation Sky Winds and fully secured the ship. By that time, forty-six protesters were wounded and nine—including a dual Turkish-American citizen—lay dead.

Those were the ghastly statistics that Lior reported to me after I groped for the phone near my bed. In addition to the horrendous casualty count, my chief of staff told me of the mass demonstrations in Istanbul, where tens of thousands of protesters chanted, "Murderous Israel, you will drown in the blood you shed," and tried to overrun the Israeli consulate. Erdoğan accused Israel of "inhumane state terrorism" and recalled his ambassador from Tel Aviv. But the rancor was hardly confined to Turkey. In Iran, President Ahmadinejad predicted that the flotilla episode heralded the "end of the existence of the heinous and fake Zionist regime." Even West Bank leader Mahmoud Abbas, the blockade's clandestine champion, declared a three-day mourning period for the "massacre" of innocent Turks, and offered Palestinian citizenship to the flotilla's participants.

Listening to Lior, I recalled how Washington pundits were always asking how candidates would react to a 3 A.M. phone call. My response was curt. "Call Dan Arbell," I instructed him. "Call my secretaries. Tell everybody to meet me in the embassy as soon as possible."

The previous year had taught me some basic lessons in crisis management and I immediately applied them, triaging tasks. The first was to contact the prime minister. Netanyahu was in Ottawa that morning, on a state visit to Canada, and planning to fly down to Washington. A meeting between him and Obama, I anticipated, would have capped the administration's "love offensive" with Israel and perhaps put the alliance on firmer footing. That opportunity vanished, though, when Netanyahu informed me of his imminent return to Israel. The White House seemed less than heartbroken. Obama "expressed deep regret at the loss of life," and stressed "the importance of learning all the facts . . . around this morning's tragic events." The president, I imagined, scarcely relished smiling at the cameras and shaking Netanyahu's hand while blood still ran on the *Mavi Marmara*.

The flotilla incident provided another example of the administration's uncanny ability to stay on message. In contrast to Israel, where ministries issue uncoordinated statements, the tightly centralized Obama White House controlled the content of every response from the State Department to the Democratic-led Congress. "We expect the Israeli Government to conduct a prompt, impartial, credible, and transparent investigation that conforms to international standards and gets to all the facts surrounding this tragic event," declared Secretary of State Clinton. House Speaker Nancy Pelosi similarly called for "a credible and transparent investigation," as did Senate Foreign Relations Committee chairman John Kerry. All reactions reiterated the need for a comprehensive Israeli-Palestinian peace.

While not surprised, I nevertheless found the administration's reaction to the flotilla disappointing. After upholding a blockade designed to fight Hamas and bolster the Palestinian Authority, after its soldiers were mauled by armed Islamic extremists, Israel might have expected stauncher backing from its ally. But, then again, I reminded myself that the president always opposed the blockade, that Turkey was also America's ally and Erdoğan, Obama's friend. And though our Special Forces acted in self-defense, something surely went wrong on the *Mavi Marmara*. Why, for example, after their first attempts to board the boat were repulsed, did our commandos continue to descend to the deck rather than break off contact and rethink their tactics? Still, the White House might have honored Israel's request to veto the Security Council condemnation of the incident. Instead, the U.S. delegation merely worked to soften the resolution's language and to prevent another Goldstone-like report. For that, at least, I felt grateful.

Gestures at the UN could not, however, hide the main contention between Obama and Netanyahu. "No foreign judges," Netanyahu instructed me before I set off to the White House to fulfill my morning's second task. This was to object to any American demand for an international probe of the flotilla incident. But no sooner did I enter the West Wing than I learned that that was exactly what the president demanded. Amid the ceremonial swords and pistols that appointed his office, General Jones informed me that without an "international component" in Israel's inquiry, the United States could not protect the IDF from charges of war crimes. I countered that Israel, just like the United States, took pride in its world-class judiciary and rejected any attempt by foreign bodies to pass judgment on its troops. The administration remained adamant, though. An exclusively Israeli inquest would not salve world opinion, which was livid over the flotilla.

The difficulty of the first two tasks—canceling Netanyahu's Washington visit and trying to deflect America's insistence on an international investigation of the IDF—shrank before that of the third. Reentering the embassy before noon, I collided with a massif of media reports impassibly critical of the operation.

The New York Times dedicated its entire op-ed page to deploring Israel. Historian Tony Judt, a British-born Jew and former Zionist who later opposed Israel's existence, accused Israel of endangering the U.S.-Turkish alliance, jeopardizing America's standing in Afghanistan, Central Asia, and the Arab world. In one of his last pronouncements before dying of ALS, Judt called for the end of Israel's special relationship with the United States. "The time has come to . . . treat Israel like a 'normal' state and sever the umbilical cord," he wrote. Pulitzer Prize–winning novelist Michael Chabon marshaled the IDF's "unprecedented display of blockheadedness" to refute the Jews' claim to intellectual prowess. "Now, with the memory of the *Mavi Marmara* fresh in our minds, is the time for Jews to confront, at long last, the eternal truth of our stupidity as a people." Even ardent Israel defenders—and personal friends—assailed the Shayetet 13's actions. Leon Wieseltier, my brilliant erstwhile colleague at *The New Republic,* decried the assault on the *Mavi Marmara* as "a stupid gift to the delegitimators."

The sheer mass of these critiques astounded me. By comparison, the accidental killing of fourteen Afghani women and children by U.S. forces that same week hardly merited a mention in the American press, much less entire pages of commentary. But more painful for me was the rush to condemn Israel for enforcing a policy essential to its civilians' security and the success of the peace process—all before the IDF released the operation's details.

Yet obtaining those facts proved frustrating for me as well. The army was loath to release videos of its finest troops being clubbed and tossed over the *Mavi Marmara*'s guardrails. Invaluable hours slipped by before I heard that the other boats in the flotilla had surrendered without violence and been safely towed to Ashdod. More time passed before word arrived that the IHH members in fact carried no humanitarian aid for Gaza, only video clips—filmed in advance—showing their arrest by actors dressed as Israeli soldiers, plus more than a million dollars in cash. Only on the next day did I learn that cartridges collected from the deck as well as the bullet extracted from the leg of one of our soldiers were of a caliber not used by the Shayetet. In addition to attacking with "cold weapons" such as bats and knives, the IHH also fired guns.

The second I received this information, I rushed it over to Congress. Several dozen legislators, all Democrats, listened as I expressed regret for the flotilla's casualties but explained Israel's need to resist any attempt to pry open the sea-lanes to Gaza. Those channels would not be used to ship humanitarian aid, I stressed, but Iranian rockets for Hamas. "We, too, want a free Gaza," I later wrote in *The New York Times,* "a Gaza liberated from brutal Hamas rule as well as an Israel freed from terrorist threats."

Such arguments, however compelling, could not dispel the impression of Israeli cold-bloodedness. Altering that image necessitated an out-of-the-box approach. So I accepted an invitation to interview on *The Colbert Report.*

This was a hazardous gamble. A wildly popular comedy talk show, the *Report* was also the graveyard of public figures who, with the help of the ingenious Stephen Colbert, made national fools of themselves. Having previously interviewed with Jon Stewart and Bill Maher, I knew the risks—knew that the guests, unlike the emcees, were unscripted and could not request a retake. I understood that I was on the show to be pilloried, and that the best I could expect was to suffer Colbert's poking fun at me and perhaps get in a point or two. Yet I saw no other venue for reaching the millions of young Americans for whom such shows provided a major news source.

Playing a half-deranged, right-wing pundit, Colbert indeed tried to goad me into making misstatements about the flotilla. I joined in the live audience's laughs, even when at my own expense, and strove to stay on message. But, then, offering me a mug marked with "World's Greatest Friend of Israel," he quoted the haggish Helen Thomas telling Israeli Jews to go back to Poland and Germany. "If anything, the Palestinians should go back to where they came from," Colbert said. "Do you agree?" Here was the most fatal trap and, with slightest affirmative, I could have tumbled into it. Instead, I nodded and said, "No. There's room for both of us to share this homeland—Palestinians living in their homeland, Israelis living in their homeland in a position of permanent, legitimate peace."

My performance on Colbert may have mitigated, if only marginally, the flotilla's public relations fallout. Eventually, the news cycle moved on to other stories. General Petraeus replaced General Stanley McChrystal, fired by Obama for criticizing him in *Rolling Stone* magazine, as commander of U.S. and NATO forces in Afghanistan. Helen Thomas resigned. Supreme Court nominee Elena Kagan, when asked by Senator Lindsey Graham about her whereabouts at the time of the Christmas Day bombing attempt, responded, "Like all Jews, I was probably at a Chinese restaurant." Behind the scenes, though, there was no relief from the melee that erupted on the decks of the *Mavi Marmara*. On the contrary, the controversy only deepened.

Israel still insisted that it alone would investigate the flotilla episode, without external adjudication. Detailed inquiries were indeed filed by the IDF and a civilian commission. These reconstructed the events leading up to the clash—including my contacts with the Turkish ambassador—as well as the operation itself. The jurists, though critical of some of the government's decisions, nevertheless upheld the legality of the Gaza blockade and recognized the commandos' need to defend themselves. Under American pressure, Netanyahu agreed to include two international observers on the civilian panel. But Turkey rejected all of Israel's conclusions and the White House endorsed an official UN probe. Isolated, facing another Goldstone-like calumny, Israel buckled and cooperated with the UN.

Then, a miracle happened. The UN investigation, headed by former New Zealand prime minister Geoffrey Palmer, affirmed most of Israel's claims. Though the IDF employed "excessive and unreasonable" force aboard the *Mavi Marmara,* the flotilla had acted recklessly in challenging a legal blockade. Palmer called on Israel to express regret for the incident and to pay compensation to the bereaved Turkish families, but he also called on Turkey to mend its differences with Israel.

Israel accepted the Palmer Report but Turkey rejected it. Worse—Erdoğan threatened to try IDF commanders for atrocities and to dispatch his navy against Israel's exploration of natural gas deposits off its coast. Though Israel quickly repatriated all of the flotilla's participants without leveling charges, and even released the *Mavi Marmara,* Turkey accused Israel of torturing the IHH members and manhandling the ship. Even my friend Namik Tan—painfully, for me—joined in the allegations of war crimes. Turkish-Israel relations had run smoothly, he claimed, until Israel scuttled the flotilla.

But threats and condemnations did not suffice for Erdoğan, who now demanded that Netanyahu apologize for Israel's actions, publicly and unconditionally. Israeli leaders assumed the White House would reject these stipulations—the United States did not apologize for killing Pakistani troops along the Afghan border—but they assumed wrongly. In a poignant conversation with the prime minister, Secretary of State Clinton stressed that maintaining Erdoğan's goodwill represented a strategic U.S. interest. Turkey's cooperation was vital for America's deployments in Iraq and Afghanistan as well as for the efforts to curb Iranian nuclearization and achieve Israeli-Palestinian peace. The apology, Hillary made clear, was also a matter of personal importance to Obama.

Back in Israel for consultations, I sat across from Netanyahu as he received the secretary's request. Clinton can be intensely persuasive, and I wondered whether the prime minister could resist her beseeching. But he did. Israeli leaders could not apologize, he explained, and leave Israeli soldiers to face war crimes charges alone. Moreover, saying sorry to Erdoğan, who never ceased vilifying Israel and bolstering terrorist groups seeking its destruction, would send a wrong message to other Middle Eastern adversaries. "We live in a tough neighborhood," he said.

I agreed with him. The time for making amends with Ankara might someday arrive, but not now, with Israeli commandos still hospitalized and their officers reluctant to travel abroad for fear of being arrested as war criminals. "He who apologizes is neither a valued friend nor a feared foe," Bernard Lewis, the renowned Princeton professor, once told me. "In the Middle East, no one gets credit for a preemptive cringe." But Netanyahu did give in to the administration's pressure and ease the Gaza blockade. Now, not only cilantro crossed the border, but also construction materials, supposedly monitored by the UN.

Seventeen months later—after five years' imprisonment—Gilad Shalit regained his freedom. The price was unprecedented: 1,027 Palestinian prisoners released from Israeli jails. The Obama administration bristled at the deal, which, it claimed, strengthened Hamas at Abbas's expense and included several terrorists known to have killed Americans. But the exchange also troubled many Israelis, my family included, as we watched the Palestinians hail as heroes the murderers of 569 of our countrymen. Some of those former inmates, we knew, would return as active terrorists and kill more civilians. But in Israel, where every soldier is everybody's son, the sweetly timid Shalit—an honorary citizen of Baltimore, New Orleans, and Pittsburgh—felt like family. Along with anxiety and anguish, his homecoming also evoked joy.

In retrospect, I asked myself whether the Gaza blockade justified its political costs or how Israel might have handled the flotilla differently. Could Israel have found one legal loophole and let the *Mavi Marmara* pass? Should Israel have collected intelligence on the IHH? Monday morning quarterbacking—an American term untranslatable into Hebrew—is a luxury in which statesmen can rarely indulge. The facts, though, remained irrefutable: Israel's image suffered a grievous blow and relations between Washington and Jerusalem were once again strained. Though the Israeli Navy kept a vigilant watch for Iranian arms ships bound for Gaza, thousands of advanced rockets reached Hamas through the tunnels from Egypt, where Hosni Mubarak's regime mostly looked the other way. Not only Israeli border towns like Sderot were now within missile range, but downtown Tel Aviv and even the outskirts of Jerusalem. The scene was set for the next showdown with Hamas, to be fought not on the high seas but in the neighborhoods of Israel's major cities.

"You serve in honor and in shame," Yossi Klein Halevi, who doubled as my closest friend and spiritual sustainer, reminded me. "In honor and in shame—it's the highest privilege." Still, I wondered about the honor of Israel in sustaining the almost daily rocket strikes from Gaza and the Obama administration's continuing appeals for an apology to Turkey. The former situation, I knew, would eventually provoke a large-scale IDF response, while the latter aggravated the president's pent-up frustrations with Netanyahu. Either one could erupt into crisis.

The problem was that I had zero time to prepare for such exigencies. My second year in office began with Israeli commandos descending on the *Mavi Marmara* and would go on to confront successive crises in the U.S.-Israel alliance. In addition, there would be man-made and natural disasters together with a rash of personal ordeals—truly a year of afflictions. And swiftly they followed. That 3 A.M. call from Lior Weintraub was still resounding in my mind when the 6 A.M. news in Israel announced that I had contradicted long-standing government policy and tweaked the rawest of bilateral nerves.

09185-016

The cliché is true: the crisis that smacks hardest is the one least foreseen. While interviewing me on a Washington, D.C., radio station about the flotilla incident, my host abruptly changed topics and asked me: "What do you have to say about Jonathan Pollard? Doesn't the fact that he spied for Israel against the United States mean that Israel is not a faithful ally?" I might have paused briefly before responding, struggling to recall whether any Israeli official had ever briefed me on Pollard, much less set out our policy. "Jonathan Pollard worked for a rogue organization in the Israeli intelligence community twenty-five years ago," I answered. "We apologized for it and we hope he's let free."

In the relentless public and discreet diplomacy that followed, I completely forgot that exchange. And I still had difficulty remembering it when wakened by an Israeli broadcaster telling listeners that Jonathan's wife, Esther, had denounced me for "putting out lies." An instant later, the phone rang with a call from Israel's cabinet secretary, Zvika Hauser, a lawyer who often handled sensitive legal matters. Zvika calmly informed me of a letter to Esther sent by the first Netanyahu government in 1998, which assumed full Israeli responsibility for Pollard's spying activities in the United States. This was no rogue operation. "So, Zvika," I responded, "what's our policy on Pollard?" As imperturbable as he is intelligent, the secretary for once seemed stumped. "Don't you know?"

I immediately published a clarification: "Though the unit that operated him no longer exists, Mr. Pollard worked for and on behalf of Israel, and the ambassador hopes for his early release." The crisis moment passed, but rather than relieved, I felt sickened.

Over the course of twenty-five years—while I was married, raising children, building a vibrant life—Pollard sat behind bars. For seven of those years, he was locked in solitary confinement. After divorcing his first wife and accomplice, Anne, who served a five-year sentence, Pollard married Esther. Relentlessly, she campaigned for him, conducted a hunger strike, and criticized Israeli officials—me, most recently—for failing to stand up sufficiently for his cause. The Pollards were even reluctant to receive me at the Federal Corrections Complex in Butner, North Carolina, unless the visit hastened Jonathan's release.

The Pollard affair was a re-inflaming wound in American-Israel relations. Like the IDF's deadly attack on the USS *Liberty*, a navy spy ship, during the Six-Day War, it perpetuated allegations of Israeli perfidy and evoked some of the darkest preconceptions about Jews. While writing my book about the war, I had scrupulously researched the *Liberty* incident and ruled it a tragic mistake in which Israeli forces reasonably believed the vessel was hostile. By contrast, Pollard deliberately and knowingly committed espionage against the United States, and at Israel's explicit behest.

Pollard's story has been extensively, if divergently, documented. All versions agree that he was raised in a giving Jewish home. All acknowledge that Pollard became fascinated with Israel at an early age and remained so throughout his undergraduate years at Stanford. Academically gifted, the sources concur, he secured work with U.S. Navy intelligence near Washington. Starting in 1984, Pollard began passing classified papers to Israeli Defense Ministry handlers who, in turn, paid him tens of thousands of dollars. Exposed the following year, Pollard sought asylum at the Israeli embassy only to be denied entry and arrested. He was tried for conveying national defense information to a foreign state and for conspiracy to commit espionage. As part of a plea bargain, Pollard admitted his guilt and believed he would receive a lighter punishment. But while in jail, Pollard interviewed with Wolf Blitzer, then a reporter for *The Jerusalem Post*. "I want to be very clear," the prisoner purportedly told Blitzer, "I do not believe the operation was a mistake." Such remorseless statements, U.S. authorities held, violated his agreement with the court. Pollard received a life sentence.

From those mutually accepted facts, though, the story splits into two, irreconcilable, narratives. The first portrays Pollard as delusional, dishonest, corrupted by drug abuse and monetary greed. Accordingly, he attempted to sell U.S. secrets to other countries besides Israel, cost the lives of American agents, and caused long-term damage to the United States. Given the enormity of his crimes—so this school concludes—Pollard's punishment was just.

The second account asserts that Pollard, though misguided, acted nobly to provide Israel with intelligence vital to its security. As he told Blitzer, "I simply got sick and tired of standing idly by and observing Jews die." He did not offer his services to other countries or hurt American interests. Indeed, the harm ascribed to his actions was in fact caused by another double agent who actually helped frame Pollard. Charged with conveying classified information to a foreign government—a lesser offense than spying—Pollard received a life sentence rather than the standard six to eight years. His plea bargain went ignored. Pollard was singled out as a Jew working for the Jewish State, an ally. Had he acted for France or Italy, the second school maintains, he would have been freed years go.

Over the course of Pollard's quarter-century incarceration, the gulf between these two versions deepened. After initially disassociating itself from Pollard, Israel granted him citizenship in 1995. Israelis increasingly viewed him as a principled Jew who sacrificed his freedom for his people, a soldier who must not be abandoned in the field. His image—bearded, bespectacled, his *kippa*-crowned pate hemmed by ringlets—gazed from Israeli billboards and kiosks. At the intersection near my Jerusalem neighborhood, young demonstrators displayed banners demanding "Bring Jonathan Home!" And addressing Israeli audiences, someone invariably asked me, "If America is such a friend, why doesn't it liberate Pollard?"

In America, though, sentiments about Pollard were split. While U.S. intelligence circles still rejected any reduction of his sentence, a number of former senior officials—among them Secretaries of State Henry Kissinger and George Shultz and CIA director James Woolsey—called for clemency. The most divided on the issue, though, were American Jews. While many community members, especially the more politically conservative and religiously observant, rallied for Pollard's freedom, others upheld the verdict. "Pollard is no hero of Israel," Martin Peretz, the avidly pro-Israel editor emeritus of *The New Republic*, blogged. "He was paid for his filthy work . . . [and] his moral profile is truly disgusting."

Such revulsion reflected, at least in part, American Jewry's lingering fear that the Pollard affair exposed it to accusations of dual loyalty. "Pollard['s] . . . hope that he will yet be able to immigrate to Israel . . . clearly indicates that his loyalty to Israel transcends his loyalty to the United States," Secretary of Defense Caspar Weinberger testified in 1987. Many American Jews still cringed at the memory of Julius and Ethel Rosenberg, both Jews and the only Americans to be executed for espionage after World War II, who were prosecuted and sentenced by American Jews. Indeed, Pollard's supporters accused the half-Jewish Weinberger of seeking the harshest possible punishment in order to deflect charges of conflicted loyalty from himself. The issue remained so sensitive that, more than two decades later, the liberal online Jewish magazine *Tablet* still grappled with it. "Pollard's continued incarceration appears . . . to be intended as a statement that dual loyalty on the part of American Jews is a real threat to America," *Tablet* editorialized, "and a warning to the American Jewish community as a whole."

For me, as an Israeli and as a Jew raised in America, the Pollard issue aroused potent emotions. On the one hand, I had little sympathy for the dual-loyalty fears—my twin identities, rather, complemented each other—and even less for the "friends don't spy on friends" mantra sounded by Pollard's detractors. America's aerial surveillance of Israel since the 1950s was well-known, along with its eavesdropping of IDF communications during the Six-Day War. A former IDF intelligence officer, Yosef Amit, spent seven years in an Israeli prison after reportedly being recruited by American agents. The Israeli press even alleged that Israel offered to exchange Amit for Pollard.

On the other hand, Pollard, roughly my age, was disconcertingly familiar. Like me, he suffered anti-Semitism as a youth, bore the burden of the Holocaust, and exulted in Israel's rebirth. "There was no difference between being a good American and a good Zionist," he explained to Blitzer. "American Jews should hold themselves personally accountable for Israel's security." But Pollard's life choices, unlike mine, had led him down unlawful paths. If not for those choices, he, too, might have been a free man in the Land of Zion. Instead, he became federal inmate number 09185-016.

None of my personal feelings were relevant, though, nor was either of the versions of Pollard's story. As ambassador, the only pertinent facts were that Pollard was an Israeli citizen for whom the State took responsibility. The episode also gave rise to repeated claims by "anonymous U.S. intelligence sources" that Israelis still spied on America—allegations that the White House knew to be utterly untrue but never refuted. Those reasons alone bound me to work for Pollard's release. His case, I knew, weakened the claim of closer-than-ever security cooperation between the United States and Israel. As long as Pollard remained a prisoner, a pall hung over the alliance.

Paradoxically, my ill-informed response to a Washington radio interviewer helped spur the Israeli government to review its position on Pollard and redouble its efforts on his behalf. Equipped with new instructions, I took to the Hill, where Senators Chuck Schumer and Arlen Specter and Congressman Barney Frank and thirty-nine of his colleagues had already come out in favor of freeing Pollard. In addition to legislators, I met with former intelligence heads, with community leaders, and journalists. I never asked for a pardon—Pollard was guilty of his crimes and Israel remained culpable—but rather for clemency based on humanitarian grounds. Having served many times the usual sentence for someone who committed similar offenses, Pollard was suffering from serious illnesses and deteriorating physically.

Many individuals and organizations mobilized to secure Pollard's freedom and, in the first week of 2011, their determination bore fruit. Five hundred leading American clergymen, Christians and Jews, wrote to President Obama exhorting him to follow the biblical injunction to seek justice and end Pollard's imprisonment. Professor Charles Ogletree—"Tree"—the Harvard Law School professor who mentored Barack and Michelle Obama during their student days, also asked the president to show leniency. I had met with Tree several times to explore ways of strengthening Israel's ties with African-Americans, and was delighted by his principled stance.

Finally, on Wednesday, January 5, I entered the West Wing carrying a manila envelope, blank except for Israel's blue menorah seal. Inside, was a personal letter from Netanyahu to Obama. This recalled the long record of requests from Israeli leaders regarding Pollard, their commitment to never repeat his wrongful actions, and their concern for the prisoner's health. "I know that the United States is a country based on fairness, justice and mercy," Netanyahu wrote, again asking for clemency. "The people of Israel will be eternally grateful."

The earnestness of these entreaties might have well yielded results, yet the American position stayed fixed. Though eligible to appear before a parole board in 2015, Pollard would remain incarcerated in Butner. At no point did I receive the slightest indication of any U.S. government willingness to even consider letting him go. Speculating on the reasons why became one of my thornier tasks in speaking to incredulous Israelis back home.

The primary reason, I told them, was the persistent opposition of the American intelligence community. Though most of its officials were too young to have served at the time of Pollard's arrest, they retained their predecessors' resentment of a security-cleared analyst who had taken the oath and violated it. "Deal with whatever you want to—the peace process, Iran," an American once close to intelligence circles advised me. "But stay away from Pollard."

I further described to Israelis the dissonance between the American and Israeli perceptions of Pollard. The person whom Israel viewed as a hero was, for the United States, a traitor. Why, many Americans asked, should Pollard go free while more than two million of their countrymen, many of them blacks and Hispanics convicted of drug crimes, remained jailed? The Pollard issue also continued to divide American Jews. Especially sensitive were those in government, even congressmen who voted consistently in support of Israel. Some believed that Pollard should be let go but hesitated to say so publicly. Others remained unflinchingly opposed. One senior member of the National Security Council told me over breakfast, "As an American Jew, I believe Jonathan Pollard should get out of prison. . . ." He paused to take a bite of his bacon. "In a coffin."

Finally, I related to Israelis the repellent fact that Pollard was a bargaining chip. As early as 1998, during peace talks, President Clinton proposed releasing Pollard to compensate Netanyahu for interim concessions that Netanyahu might make to the Palestinians. Dennis Ross, who favored freeing Pollard on humanitarian grounds, nevertheless advised the president to save the Pollard "chip" for a more comprehensive agreement. "It would be a huge payoff for Bibi," Dennis said. "You will need it later, don't use it now." The deal fell through, but the United States still regarded his release as an incentive for Israeli concessions. Asked if Pollard might be traded for Israeli gestures to the Palestinians, State Department spokesman P. J. Crowley admitted that "[w]e don't rule out the possibility that this issue will be decided within a wider perspective . . . of advancing peace in the Middle East."

I explained the reasons for Pollard's continuing imprisonment yet Israelis remained puzzled. Their bewilderment deepened after the FBI uncovered a sleeper cell of ten Russian spies in the United States that, only days later, was exchanged for four American agents held by Moscow. WikiLeaks—the publication of declassified documents by the renegade editor Julian Assange—intimated that the United States spied on a number of friendly countries. Subsequent revelations embarrassingly substantiated that fact. But the disclosures also showed that Washington still believed that it was targeted by Israeli espionage—despite Jerusalem's adamant denials.

I, meanwhile, continued to probe American decision makers, present and past, about their attitudes toward Pollard. His plight still stirred many emotions in me—pity, confusion, anger—but, above all, the frustration of my inability to relieve it. Throughout 2010, I remained ready to visit him in Butner, but received no response. His chances for release I feared, were slight, and years might pass before he could replace his prison number, 09185-016, with the citizen's ID issued to him by Israel. The best hope, I concluded, lay in peace talks in which Pollard's freedom might be a matter of price, not principle. If only the Palestinians returned to the table.

Partners for Peace?

To our frustration, the Palestinians seemed further from that table than ever. Though the end of the ten-month moratorium on new building in the settlements was approaching, Mahmoud Abbas still refused to negotiate with Netanyahu, confining himself to the proximity talks through U.S. envoy George Mitchell. The Palestinian leader also composed a list of preconditions—an end to Israel's demolition of Palestinian houses, its arrest of terror suspects, and the removal of its checkpoints—that first had to be met. Most critically, Abbas insisted that Israel recognize the June 4, 1967, lines as the borders of the future Palestinian state.

Netanyahu rejected all of these demands, especially regarding the 1967 lines. According to those boundaries, the Western Wall, part of the Jerusalem–Tel Aviv highway, and the heights above Ben-Gurion Airport, would all be outside of Israel. Previous prime ministers had agreed to "land swaps" with the Palestinians. But no understanding had ever been reached over the size of the swaps—the Israelis wanted significant exchanges, the Palestinians mere adjustments—and the very word *swap* remained repellent to Netanyahu. Rather, he held that the talks begin immediately, without preconditions. "I'm ready to meet President Abbas, today and tomorrow and the next day, in any place," he declared. "I'm prepared to go to Ramallah."

Ideally, I thought, Abbas and Netanyahu could be confined in some remote Maryland farmhouse, far from the press, and compelled to talk. That was the secret to the Egyptian-Israeli peace treaty, concluded after thirteen intensive days at Camp David in 1978, and twenty years later to the Wye Plantation Memorandum hammered out between Netanyahu and Arafat over the course of a week. In both cases, the parties entered the discussions determined to avoid the concessions they eventually made. Isolated from the public, forced to interact, leaders could accept conditions they once considered unthinkable. I still suspected that Abbas, like Arafat at the 2000 Camp David Summit, would bolt before signing any permanent peace. Yet the possibility existed of forging interim agreements and, if nothing else, demonstrating once again that Israel had exhausted all diplomatic options.

But the chances of getting Abbas and Netanyahu into that secluded estate seemed distant in the summer of 2010. Rather than pressuring the Palestinians to drop their preconditions, the administration focused on portraying the settlement freeze as fulfilling part—but not all—of the president's demands of Israel. The White House stated, "We look forward to discussing additional measures with Prime Minister Netanyahu when he next visits Washington."

That stopover was scheduled for July 6, and in preparation for the tête-à-tête, I once again did the rounds—Rahm Emanuel, Dennis Ross, David Axelrod—asking them to describe what a good Obama-Netanyahu meeting might look like. The answers I received were discouraging. The moratorium was insufficient and more concessions were expected. "The onus of proving commitment to peace is on our shoulders," I updated the prime minister, "not the Palestinians'. We should not expect gratitude for gestures that the White House believes we should have made long ago."

My analysis must have upset Netanyahu, for Uzi Arad, the national security advisor, called the next day to convey the dreary mood in Jerusalem. "Iran, Turkey, Hezbollah, Hamas, international delegitimization, and now this, the president," he moaned. I tried to remind Arad of the gloomier periods in Israeli history—the War of Independence, the eve of the Six-Day War. "Yes," Arad sighed, "but Israel's leaders back then could at least see a light ahead."

Fortunately, in contrast to these dark predictions, the next Netanyahu-Obama meeting seemed almost dazzling. Obama emerged from the eighty-minute discussion praising the alliance with Israel and extolling his guest as a peacemaker willing to take risks. "I've trusted Prime Minister Netanyahu since I met him before I was elected," he told Israeli TV. Netanyahu similarly gushed. "The reports about the demise of the special U.S.-Israel relationship aren't just premature," he said, paraphrasing Mark Twain. "They're just flat wrong." Journalists noted the positive body language of the two and how Obama personally escorted Netanyahu to his car. They quoted me saying that, unlike our previous unphotographed visit to the White House, this time "there were more cameras than at the Academy Awards."

But the change was more than theatrical. Rather than harping on Israeli concessions, the conversation dealt with the confidence-building measures—CBMs—including large-scale West Bank development projects, with which Israel could induce Abbas to negotiate. Netanyahu pressed for immediate implementation of the CBMs and for the earliest possible resumption of the peace process. "We have real willingness to move forward," he assured Obama. "We need to overcome skepticism and proceed quickly."

If relieved by this sudden improvement of tone, I was surprised the next day when, speaking at the Council on Foreign Relations in New York, Netanyahu said that peace could be achieved within a year. "Were you serious about that?" I asked him when he got back in his car. "One year?" The prime minister shrugged. "I could do it in three months, if Abbas would negotiate seriously."

That "if" remained cardinal in my mind. I never ceased doubting Abbas's willingness to engage with us sincerely, just as I never ceased believing in the Obama administration's quenchless demand for Israeli concessions. Nevertheless, perhaps from lack of sleep, Netanyahu's stay left me feeling giddy. Suddenly, the White House was no longer talking settlements but embracing the prime minister's vision of a one-year peace process. "I need a Palestinian partner," he told Chris Wallace at Fox News. "You can't be a trapeze artist that wants to connect with the other guy and there's no one there. Abbas has got to step up to the plate," Netanyahu said, mixing metaphors if not his meaning. And for once Obama seemed to agree. He invited Abbas to attend a peace summit—to fly through the air, as it were, or enter the batter's box—convening in Washington on September 1.

• • •

The night before, Hamas terrorists ambushed an Israeli vehicle near Hebron. They approached the car and kept firing their Kalashnikov rifles through the windows until all four of the people inside were dead. One of them was a pregnant woman.

The Palestinian Authority condemned the murderers and quickly captured the gunmen, then just as swiftly freed them. The State Department praised the condemnation but ignored the release. Anxious to get back to talks, Israel also downplayed Abbas's action, all the while opposing preconditions.

Implicitly, at least, all parties agreed that nothing should dull the luster of Obama, Netanyahu, and Abbas seated together on a State Department stage, flanked by Jordan's King Abdullah and President Hosni Mubarak of Egypt. To the crackle of hundreds of press cameras, the participants delivered their opening remarks. Obama exulted: "Though each of us holds a title of honor—President, Prime Minister, King—we are bound by the one title we share. We are fathers, blessed with sons and daughters. So we must ask ourselves what kind of world do we want to bequeath to our children?" Abbas, by contrast, was blunt, reiterating his demand for a settlement freeze and for rectifying the "historical injustice" that occurred in 1948. He referred to the Palestinians as victims and Israel's prime minister—pettily, I thought—as "Mr." Then it was Netanyahu's turn.

When fine-tuning the speech, I suggested that it begin with "Shalom. Salaam. Peace." Ron Dermer dismissed the idea, saying "he doesn't do touchy-feely." But Netanyahu, extemporizing, began with all three words. He looked straight at the Palestinian leader and declared, "President Abbas, you are my partner for peace. And it is up to us, with the help of our friends, to conclude the agonizing conflict between our peoples." Solutions, not excuses, were Israel's goal, he asserted, peace and not "a blame game where even the winners lose." He spoke eloquently, even by Netanyahu standards. "Thousands of years ago, on these very hills where Israelis and Palestinians live today, the Jewish prophet Isaiah . . . envisaged a future of lasting peace. Let us today . . . realize that ancient vision." Which was amazing, since the text was in Hebrew. Later, I asked him why, after Abbas spoke in his native Arabic, he opted for an off-the-cuff translation. "I saw all those cameras out there," the prime minister replied. "I realized I was addressing the world."

The leaders adjourned for a working dinner while their teams gathered around a long oaken table and ate, mostly in silence. The mood was stilted: Palestinians arrayed on one side, Israelis on the other, with minimal interaction between us. The historian in me was keen to see Saeb Erekat, the bullish Palestinian negotiator, my age and American-educated, who held the spotlight for twenty years without uttering—I often heard said—a single truth.

The compensation for that excruciating meal came later, when I rejoined the principals. I paid my respects to Jordan's Abdullah, a reluctant monarch who was reputedly happier grasping the handlebars of his Harley along the Big Sur coast than he was clutching the reins of his shaky desert kingdom. I chatted with former British prime minister Tony Blair, whose son, Euan, had been my student at Yale. Tony was now the special envoy for the Quartet, the international peacemaking mechanism, and exuded an irrepressible optimism about the process. And there was Mubarak, who, when I first met him while working for the Rabin government in the early 1990s, struck me as burly and robust. Now, an illness-stricken eighty-two-year-old with hair dyed an improbable black and a face caked with makeup, he looked almost mummified.

Finally, there was Abbas. Short, round-shouldered, insalubrious-looking from his smoking habit of two packs per day, he seemed withdrawn and visibly discomfited by the festivities. American diplomacy would have to be at its pinnacle, I thought, to maneuver him into making peace. Netanyahu appeared to be doing just that, wrapping his arm around Abbas and cajoling him. A lengthy history linked the two men, and they might have seemed like old friends except for Abbas's mirthless expression. The prime minister called me over and introduced me to the Palestinian president. I extended a warm hand and in return received a curt, begrudging grip. Then, still half-hugging him, Netanyahu wheeled Abbas in the direction of the hall where the face-to-face negotiations would ensue.

But the talks produced no progress. Abbas once again wanted to discuss borders first while Netanyahu responded that Israel could not discuss borders without knowing how those lines could be defended. Abbas claimed that he could not discuss the West Bank "pie" while Israel cut out slices for settlements. Netanyahu retorted that the Palestinian leader could not cherry-pick the core issues—settlements among them—to be decided in advance of negotiations.

"The bride and the groom don't really want to get married," my chief of staff, Lior Weintraub, wisecracked, "They just don't want to disappoint the parents." Optically, at least, Lior was right: neither Abbas nor Netanyahu wanted to be seen as opposing Obama. And their reluctance mounted as the moratorium's September 30 termination approached.

Netanyahu believed that Obama had agreed that the moratorium was a one-time gesture to the Palestinians, and that Abbas would seize on any excuse not to negotiate. Then, suddenly and without informing Israel, Obama called for extending the moratorium. No explanation was offered us, though I suspected the motive was less strategic than ideological. Settlements, even under arrangements helpful to the peace process, were simply unacceptable to the president. "It's a monumental historical mistake," a dumbfounded Netanyahu told me. Abbas, who previously dismissed the freeze as insignificant, now threatened to quit the talks unless it was renewed.

So the settlement issue harnessed by the administration to drive the peace process once again derailed it. Clinton made clear that the United States could not keep the Palestinians in the talks, and prevent the European Union from ganging up on Israel, without a four-month extension. "It'll be a shame to see a two-thousand-year project die because of four fucking months," Rahm Emanuel cautioned me, but Netanyahu held firm. There would be no extension. And the next round of negotiations, scheduled to convene in Jerusalem on September 14, was likely to be the last.

That day, Dan Shapiro met Ron Dermer and me and asked, "What can we do to make this less painful for you?" We were sitting in the refreshment tent outside of the Prime Minister's Residence in Jerusalem. Flaccidly lit and lined with somber 1950s paintings, the building resembled the Prime Minister's Office, which Condoleezza Rice once likened to "a little run-down high school." The only color inside came from the American and Israeli flags and their Palestinian counterpart—red, green, and black—included as a gesture to Abbas. He posed with Clinton and Netanyahu before filing into the prime minister's cramped office for a fruitless debate about the length of Israel's military presence in the Jordan Valley.

A more substantive discussion, perhaps, took place in that refreshment tent, where Dan suggested quid pro quos for extending the freeze. Several ideas were exchanged before the NSC official mentioned jets—specifically, the ultra-advanced F-35 Joint Strike Fighter (JSF). The aircraft were still in development but Israel planned to purchase nineteen of them, at the staggering total cost of $3 billion. "How many JSFs would it take," Dan wondered, "to buy us several more months of moratorium?"

Netanyahu was furious that we even conducted the conversation—"You violated the first rule of negotiating," he snapped at us: "never open a second track." But the haggling nevertheless continued over the next two weeks as Ehud Barak and Shimon Peres held last-ditch discussions with American leaders in the United States and George Mitchell shuttled frantically around the Middle East—all, ultimately, for naught. As pressure mounted on Israel to extend the moratorium, Abbas could sit quietly and watch.

"While the rival Israeli team is playing against the American referees," David Rothkopf pithily observed, "the Palestinian team can eat popcorn in the stands." To this, I added a football analogy of my own. "Abbas is like a quarterback who runs down the clock and then demands overtime." Remembering his refusal to respond to Prime Minister Olmert's 2008 offer of a Palestinian state in the West Bank, Jerusalem, and Gaza, I still doubted whether Abbas would ever be a serious partner for peace. His goal, rather, was to quietly back Israel in fighting his rivals in Hamas while accusing Israel of war crimes in international forums. Throughout, he could count on American and European leaders to keep meeting Palestinian demands without requiring any concession in return. Israel would be increasingly isolated. Not surprisingly, when the moratorium expired on September 30, the Palestinian president immediately quit the talks.

While the controversy surrounding the moratorium continued, I kept a breakneck schedule of high-level meetings in New York, Washington, and Jerusalem, and High Holiday remarks at ten different synagogues. Imprudently, at the end of October, Sally and I tried to take our first vacation since entering office. Yoav, our eldest, still an American citizen and a fluent Chinese speaker, was working at the U.S. pavilion at the Shanghai Expo. He hosted us there and took us on a breathtaking tour across the China expanse, all the way to the Tibetan border. There I received a phone call from my assistant, Moriya, at the embassy. Netanyahu would meet Biden in three days, she said, in New Orleans. Puddle-jumping to Beijing, huddling over coal-burning stoves between flights, I landed in the Big Easy three days later, at midnight, one hour before the motorcade left to meet the prime minister.

The venue was again the Jewish Federations' General Assembly, and Biden was at his loquacious best, assuring the crowd that supporting Israel "is in our own naked self-interest" and would remain so "as long as there's a breath in me." The vice president played down the peace process, as did Netanyahu in his speech. But then, while returning to the hotel, I received word that Israel's Housing Ministry had publicized a new building project beyond the 1967 lines in Jerusalem. This violated a pledge we made to inform the administration well in advance of any such announcements and the timing once again seemed designed to embarrass Biden. Tony Blinken, the vice president's foreign policy advisor, called me and asked, "How could you do this to Israel's best friend?" The son of a Holocaust survivor and a person of singular intelligence and warmth, Tony icily warned, "It's your decision to build in Jerusalem, but you should know that it will have strategic implications for our relationship."

The State Department expressed its "deep disappointment" with the announcement and Obama labeled it "unhelpful," which prompted Netanyahu to reiterate that "Jerusalem is not a settlement. Jerusalem is our capital." The pattern was drearily familiar, yet it did not deter Clinton from making a final effort to resume the peace talks. She offered an additional $150 million in aid to the Palestinian Authority and, on November 11, conferred with Netanyahu at New York's Regency Hotel.

Though wan from another of her multicountry tours, the secretary seemed indefatigable as she labored through seven hours of back-and-forth with Netanyahu and our respective teams. "This is a hefty chunk of history we have to lift here," the prime minister said. "Let's not put it all on a few houses." Clinton later recalled her amazement at the Israelis' candor, our willingness to argue with one another, even with the prime minister, in front of the strictly hierarchical Americans. She remembered that cutting Hebrew slang word for sucker. "The last thing any Israeli wants is to be a *freier*," she told us. "But the Palestinians don't want to be *freiers*, either."

Thereafter, the conversation quickly bogged down in a lawyerly debate between George Mitchell and Yitzik Molcho over how many housing projects could be "grandfathered"—permitted to continue—in the event of an additional freeze. The rest of us just looked on stultified until, with uncharacteristic thunder, Dan Shapiro smacked the table with both fists and shouted, "This is stupid! We all know what we want, so let's just cut a deal!" Everyone—Netanyahu, Clinton, Mitchell, Molcho—gaped at him for a second and then numbly nodded, "okay." I quietly slipped Dan a note: "That was your finest moment."

We forged a text in which Israel froze settlement building for an additional ninety days and received, free of charge, twenty F-35 Joint Strike Fighters. Also, in the event that Abbas tried to obtain UN recognition of a Palestinian state, the administration pledged to cast its veto in the Security Council. I tried, unsuccessfully, to get Pollard's release as part of the arrangement, but still left the Regency that night with a sense of breakthrough.

Israel's select security cabinet, though, was far less enthused. Led by the highly respected Benny Begin, most of the eight ministers argued against selling Israel's right to build in its homeland for any amount of jets. Netanyahu nevertheless stood by the arrangement. But then, once again bewilderingly, the White House backed out.

Various reasons were given, including Obama's realization that the Palestinians would agree to negotiate but only about the next three-month extension. Indeed, the entire process would be about freezes rather than about core issues. Yet clearly the president was also perturbed by press reports that Israel's cooperation could only be secured with military hardware worth billions.

The impact, for Israel, was calamitous. Editorials—apparently fanned by official sources—suggested that the F-35s had been an Israeli demand, rather than an American offer. The cover of *Time* magazine, sporting a flower-festooned Star of David, claimed that "Israel Doesn't Care About Peace." I fired back in the *Los Angeles Times* that, while refusing to succumb to the despair of six decades of strife, most Israelis never stopped believing in the two-state solution. "For Israelis who don't have to imagine what it's like to live in a perpetual war zone, that vision of peace is our lifeline."

To Netanyahu, though, I adopted a more adamant tone: "Why are you letting them beat up on you like this, calling you a blackmailer?" The prime minister consequently issued a statement explaining that the decision not to endorse the ninety-day package was Obama's, not his, and that Israel remained ready to take steps "without precedent" to return to the talks. But his words could not change the impression of Israeli intransigence and greed.

Peace-wise, 2010 ended much as it began, with the disputes over Jerusalem and settlements highlighted and the possibility of direct talks dimmed. Former president Bill Clinton blamed the impasse on hawkish Russian Jewish immigrants to Israel, and *New York Times* columnist Tom Friedman warned that, because of its stubbornness on peace, Israel was "losing America." Neither claim was true. Support for peace was strong among all Israelis, former Russians included. Proportionally, more Israelis backed a two-state solution than did Americans. And pro-Israel sentiment in America continued to rise.

Abbas, meanwhile, threatened to resign his post and, alternatively, to seek a Security Council condemnation of Israel's West Bank construction. "Beware," I admonished Dan Shapiro, "you may end up vetoing your own policy at the UN." My warning would prove depressingly prescient, but the incident that distressed me most that season was the one I never foresaw. And it touched on two of Israel's most fateful issues.

DNA

In the thick of the fall's ultimately failed diplomacy, I managed to halt for about half an hour in the Residence in Washington to greet three hundred guests at our Rosh Hashanah reception and offer some upbeat remarks about the U.S.-Israel alliance. Remembering how, the previous year, a Democratic congresswoman criticized me for not mentioning the president's name, this time I did so, repeatedly. Then, wishing everyone a joyous year, I dashed off to catch a plane for Tel Aviv and rejoin the peace effort. I arrived to learn that right-wing commentators were calling for my resignation. Israel's ambassador, they claimed, had become a propagandist for Obama.

One of the invitees to the reception, a Democratic Party activist, had circulated an email highlighting my references to Obama and quoting me praising the president for twelve pro-Israel policies. The email went viral, enraging conservatives. But their ire was the least of my anxieties. Along with the distortions and embellishments of what I said were several references to sensitive defense matters that I would never have mentioned in public and on which the activist had clearly been briefed. Two of the claims were simply untrue and potentially harmful to Israel's security.

The first of them was "President Obama has restored Israel's QME." Those three letters are arguably the most crucial in U.S.-Israel relations. They stand for Qualitative Military Edge, shorthand for one of the most far-reaching military commitments made by America—or by any power—to a foreign state in modern times.

Contrary to myth, the United States and Israel were not always linked strategically. Presidents Truman and Eisenhower scarcely supplied a bullet to Israel, and Kennedy only sold it some antiaircraft missiles. But then, in the Six-Day War, Israel defeated several Soviet-backed armies, and President Johnson suddenly saw the Jewish State as an invaluable ally. Soon American Phantom jets began replacing French Mirages in the IDF's arsenal, and Patton tanks supplanted British Centurions. Assistance quadrupled after the 1973 Yom Kippur War, during which the United States airlifted more than fifty-five thousand tons of arms and supplies to hard-pressed Israeli troops. The change was palpable on the battlefield. In contrast to the Arabs' Kalashnikovs, Israeli soldiers now bore M-16s. My pup tent in the paratroopers, as well as my ammunition packs and entrenching tools, were all stenciled "U.S. Army."

By 1990, Israel had been designated a "major non-NATO ally" of the United States and the largest recipient of its military aid. That year, I participated in the first joint exercise—code-named Juniper Cobra—which, at that stage, involved U.S. and Israeli officers playing war games around a table. In time, though, the cooperation expanded to include large-scale field exercises and advanced weapons development. Our home was always open to the grateful sailors of the U.S. Sixth Fleet, who relished their Israeli port of call.

America's commitment to Israel's defense climaxed in President Bush's offer to provide the Jewish State with $30 billion of military aid over a ten-year period. Roughly 75 percent of these funds were spent in the United States, stimulating its economy and creating tens of thousands of jobs. Israel, in turn, shared its world-class intelligence and cyber-knowledge with America. Among other vital supplies, Israel produced the high-tech bandages carried by U.S. troops and the interactive helmets worn by all U.S. combat pilots.

The alliance's path was never bump-free—an Israeli attempt to sell arms to China in 2005 infuriated the otherwise sympathetic

Bush—but the relationship nevertheless intensified. A year later, Pentagon and IDF planners began drafting a formula that contained the commitment's spirit and substance. Congress then voted that document into a law guaranteeing Israel:

> The ability to counter and defeat any credible conventional military threat from any individual state or possible coalition of states or from non-state actors, while sustaining minimal damages and casualties, through the use of superior military means . . .

This was the Qualitative Military Edge—QME—the DNA of the U.S.-Israel alliance. The purpose was not only to enable the Jewish State to defend itself, by itself, against any attack, but also to furnish Israelis with the security needed to make concessions. As much as it girded Israel for war, QME empowered Israelis to make peace. But now, in 2010, that double helix was in danger of unraveling.

The reason was huge American arms sales to Arab states, including $60 billion worth of F-15 fighters, attack helicopters, and Joint Direct Attack Munition (JDAM) bombs to Saudi Arabia. Though most of the recipient regimes were only technically at war with Israel, the 1967 and 1973 conflicts proved how quickly passive foes could turn into effective combatants. Moreover, given the region's inherent instability, massive American-supplied arsenals could fall overnight into radical hands, as happened in the 1979 Iranian Revolution. Consequently, the U.S. weapons packages—unprecedented not only in their size but also in their sophistication—threatened to empty QME of all meaning.

And Israel was virtually powerless to prevent it. How, at the height of the recession, could Israelis ask the American people to sacrifice myriad jobs and tens of billions of dollars in national income? How could Israel's ambassador in Washington openly question the administration's claim that "our commitment to Israel's qualitative military edge has never been greater"? Asked on live television whether Israel was concerned about the Saudi sale, I fell back on that time-honored diplomatic adage: when in doubt, dodge. "Security relations between the United States and Israel are exceptionally close," I responded, "and we know how to make our interests known to the White House."

But transactions that immense could not remain secret for long. Nearly two hundred Congress members from both parties sent a letter to Secretary of Defense Robert Gates inquiring how the United States could sell so much weaponry to the Saudis and still preserve Israel's QME. Could the aircraft be positioned farther from Israeli airspace, the legislators asked. Such suggestions could be raised by Congress but not publicly by Israel. The Saudis were liable to be offended and take their business elsewhere. The world has no shortage of arms suppliers, and, as much as American jets in Arab air forces worried Israel, the purchase of foreign jets—not subject to QME considerations—worried us even more.

So the deliberations on QME moved into the innermost rooms of the Pentagon and the Executive Office Building. An Israeli team headed by Major General Amir Eshel, a plucky fighter pilot and the IDF's strategic planner, and the wise but curmudgeonly General Amos Gilad, the Defense Ministry's senior political advisor, visited Washington repeatedly for often-heated discussions with Dennis Ross and other NSC officials. Part of the problem was how to measure QME in an era in which the classic metrics—pilot proficiency, territorial depth—were rendered less relevant by the advent of drones and long-range missiles. Compounding these difficulties was the administration's determination to shield its arms dealings from Israeli eyes, denying Eshel and Gilad access to the confidential QME report that, by law, the White House had to submit to Congress. More than once, I listened as Eshel and Gilad exited these meetings grumbling, "Awful, simply awful."

But, as often occurs in diplomacy, prickly issues were smoothed by congenial rapports. For all his grumpiness, Gilad gained the confidence of Under Secretary of Defense Michèle Flournoy, another of the administration's seemingly limitless corps of Harvard and Oxford graduates, a redoubtable person who, though at first standoffish, eventually acknowledged Israel's genuine QME concerns. Another personal connection ran through Admiral Mike Mullen, the chairman of the Joint Chiefs of Staff, and Major General Benny Gantz, the embassy's defense attaché. Tall, taciturn, the image of a Special Forces commander, Gantz developed a close friendship with Mullen, who, far shorter and bespectacled, looked less like a warrior than a poet. At Gantz's going-away party, Mullen whispered to me that he was in a rush and could stay only a few minutes. I arranged to have him speak first, and he did, praising Gantz and extolling Israel, for more than half an hour.

Together, Gilad and Flournoy and Gantz and Mullen worked to redress the imbalance in Israel's QME. Defense Minister Ehud Barak also swept through the capital repeatedly for QME-related discussions. The White House announced a grant of $205 million for Iron Dome, Israel's revolutionary antiballistic system. The United States integrated its sophisticated radar and missile defense capabilities with Israel's and offered to sell it the F-35 jet. But the F-35s would not be delivered for several years, and the presence of hundreds of advanced and lethally armed Saudi warplanes only a few minutes' flying time from Tel Aviv still disconcerted Israelis. Such concerns unnerved Netanyahu in a July 6 meeting with Robert Gates.

The defense secretary had long harbored a visceral dislike of Netanyahu. As a security advisor to George H. W. Bush twenty years earlier, Gates was offended by then deputy foreign minister Netanyahu's "superficiality," his "glibness . . . his arrogance and outlandish ambition," and recommended that he be banned from the White House. Though a self-described "very good friend and supporter of Israel," and enormously fond of Ehud Barak, the secretary still bristled at the prime minister. Netanyahu, Gates maintained, was intransigent on the peace issue and "ungrateful" for U.S. military aid.

That animus was discernible in the Blair House reception room, where Netanyahu promptly took Gates to task for the Saudi sale. "It poses a serious threat to Israel," he said bluntly. "We need a new understanding with the United States on how to counterbalance it." Gates, an éminence grise not known for easygoingness, visibly stiffened. So, too, did Michèle Flournoy and Mike Mullen, who were also present. Gates replied by citing the administration's unprecedented backing for Israel's defense and the benefits of supplying the Saudis with American—rather than foreign—arms. "How long will those planes work without U.S. support?" he snapped. "And when did the Saudis ever attack Israel?" The secretary quoted the Middle Eastern axiom, "The enemy of my enemy is my friend," to which Netanyahu replied—"acidly," according to Gates—"No, in the Middle East, the enemy of my enemy is my frenemy."

Following our upbeat meeting with Obama at the White House, the tension with Gates was jarring. Outside the room, I learned from Flournoy and Admiral Mullen that the secretary felt blindsided by Netanyahu. Ehud Barak, they explained, had assured Gates that Israel would not object to the Saudi sale and was feeling more confident about its QME. "You guys should get your stories straight," they advised me. Barak, it seemed, had once again placed me in a janitorial role, sweeping up.

Frankly, I agreed with Netanyahu. I recalled all too poignantly the instability of Arab states and the times when Israel's frenemies turned overnight into aggressive foes. It vexed me deeply to read in that activist's email how, at my Rosh Hashanah reception, I had praised President Obama for restoring Israel's QME.

Yet the email's second claim was even more untrue—and more dangerous. According to the activist, I assured my guests that Israel was delighted with the administration's position on Iran. "President Obama and his team are spending more time on this issue than almost any other issue facing our country today," I allegedly said. If unconcerned about QME, I was also supposedly blithe about another three letters that had become DNA-like in U.S.-Israel relations—HEU, meaning highly enriched uranium.

The Twenty Percent Solution

"Rarely in modern history have nations faced genuine existential threats," I once wrote in *Commentary* magazine, then asserted that Israel uniquely confronted many potential cataclysms on a daily basis. Three of them, alone, were posed by Iran's nuclear program. The first arose from Iran's attempt to produce a bomb that it could place atop one of the many missiles it already possessed and which could hit any city in Israel, "a one-bomb country," according to a former Iranian president. The second mortal danger derived from Iran's status as the world's largest state supporter of terrorism. If Iran got the bomb, so would the terrorists who did not need a missile to deliver it, but merely a ship container. And lastly, once Iran acquired military nuclear capabilities, Turkey, Egypt, and Saudi Arabia would develop them as well, locking Israel into a fatally unstable neighborhood. Apart from Israel, I concluded in *Commentary*, "it is . . . impossible to find an example of another state in the modern epic that has faced such a variety of concurrent existential threats."

Helping Israel to surmount those perils together with the United States remained my core objective. I remember hearing Prime Minister Rabin back in the early 1990s explain that peace with the Palestinians would enable Israel to meet the ultimate challenge. The radical Islamic regime of Iran, he revealed, was covertly working to produce nuclear bombs.

Under the Nuclear Non-Proliferation Treaty (NPT), Iran was prohibited from developing such weapons. Inspectors from the International Atomic Energy Agency (IAEA) were supposed to expose such illicit activities. But Iran had grown adept at evading these monitors and expert at importing industrial machinery, tunneling equipment, even auto parts that could be dually used to make nuclear arsenals.

Secretly, Iran began testing the centrifuges needed to spin uranium to weapons grade. In 2001, it constructed a vast underground enrichment plant near Natanz in central Iran and tried to conceal it from inspectors. Finally, after years of hesitation, the Bush administration publicized Iran's lies and accused it of attempting to build a bomb. But, while placing Iran in his "axis of evil," an Iraq- and Afghanistan-wearied Bush was unwilling to embark on yet another Middle Eastern war. A U.S. intelligence estimate published at the end of 2007 suggested that Iran had long ceased working on a weapon. Just then, a North Korea–supplied nuclear site was discovered in Syria, but Bush refused to bomb it, leaving the task—purportedly—to the Israelis.

But could the IDF take on Iran? Far more distant than Syria, and with multiple facilities, Iran represented a formidable challenge for Israel's air force, equipped with fighter jets rather than strategic bombers. One hundred Israeli F-15s and F-16s maneuvered over the Mediterranean in June 2008 in what many observers interpreted as a warning to Iran. But while an Israeli action might at best set the Iranians back, it could also ignite a regional conflagration. The specter of tens of thousands of Iranian, Syrian, and Hezbollah missiles devastating Israeli cities was also nightmarish. Yet what choice did Israel have? As Yossi Klein Halevi and I wrote in *The New Republic,* "A Jewish state that allows itself to be threatened with nuclear weapons will forfeit its right to speak in the name of Jewish history."

The optimal solution, then, was diplomatic. Starting in 2006, the Security Council passed five resolutions calling on Iran to suspend its nuclear program and open its plants to international inspection or else face sanctions. All transactions liable to assist Iran with its nuclear project were prohibited. But Israel believed that these sanctions had to be painfully ratcheted up and combined with a credible military threat. Iranian leaders had to internalize that the many billions they had already spent on the nuclear project—and the additional billions it would cost—were wasted. Just short of grasping their atomic weapon, the ayatollahs had to know, Iran would be bombed.

Formally, at least, this was also the American position. "An Iranian nuclear weapon is unacceptable to the United States," President Obama declared, and opaquely warned that "all options remained on the table." My public statements similarly emphasized the common U.S. and Israeli goals of preventing Iran from nuclearizing. But beneath this outward confluence of policies yawned several chasms.

Some of these clefts were structural. America, a very large and supremely armed country located far from the Middle East and not threatened with national annihilation by Iran, could afford to take chances on the nuclear issue that tiny and less powerful Israel, situated in Iran's backyard and slated by its rulers for destruction, could not. While Defense Secretary Gates could say that the Iranians "have the intention of having nuclear weapons," but did not yet make the "formal decision" to produce them, Israelis acted on the assumption that the Iranians had long ago determined to weaponize. Gates, who opposed the 2007 action against Syria, told CNN, "The reality is that there is no military option that does anything more than buy time . . . three years or so." Back in 1981, Israeli jets bombed the Osirak reactor with the goal of gaining a one-year respite from the Iraqi nuclear threat. Iraq never produced an atomic bomb. A three-year delay in Iran's nuclear activities could be, for Israel, an eternity.

Beyond their geographic and tactical differences over Iran, though, the United States and Israel were also divided conceptually. While Netanyahu doubted that Iran would concede its nuclear program without first enduring crippling sanctions and confronting a serious military threat, Obama remained committed to the principle of engagement. By entering a "meaningful dialogue," the president said, and opening its facilities to international inspectors, Iran could "rejoin the community of nations." Until then, the United States would pursue a dual-track policy of pressuring Iran while still holding out the offer of talks.

I knew too well the inherent dissimilarities between America and Israel but still wrestled with the conceptual gap. Obama's bar for Iran, I thought, was far too low. The ayatollahs had merely to admit international inspectors to Natanz and all of their lies about their nuclear program, their sponsorship of world terror, and the suppression of their own people would be forgotten. So too would Iran's stated determination to obliterate Israel. "It is the mission of the Islamic Republic of Iran to erase Israel from the map of the region," said Iran's Supreme Leader Ayatollah Ali Khamenei. "Israel is a hideous entity which will undoubtedly be annihilated."

In impugning the justice of Obama's assertion, made in this 2009 Cairo speech, that "any nation—including Iran—should have the right to access peaceful nuclear power," I also questioned the efficacy of simultaneously coercing and engaging Iran. "It's difficult to build up steam in a steam room if you keep the door open," I once observed to Stuart Levey, the Treasury Department's undersecretary for terrorism and financial intelligence. For seven years under two administrations, Stuart forfeited a lucrative law career to scour the world for loopholes in the UN sanctions, and my sauna analogy made him wince. The policy nevertheless continued, enabling Iran—so Israel saw it—to play for time, dragging out negotiations while the centrifuges spun.

Yet no gulf more fathomlessly separated Washington from Jerusalem than the possibility of military action. "One night of strategic bombing will restore all your lost prestige in the Middle East," I heard Ehud Barak tell American leaders on more than one occasion. "The Iranian nightmare is a full-blown American attack." But the response Barak received was silence. Long entangled in two exhausting Middle Eastern wars, Americans scarcely needed a third against Iran that they feared would prove more depleting. Nor did Washington welcome an Israeli attack that the White House believed would embroil U.S. forces in the almost-certain Iranian retaliation and spike the price of Persian Gulf oil. Without exception, virtually every administration official I met in this period insisted that striking the nuclear facilities would rally Muslims around the ayatollahs and spur, rather than deter, their drive for nuclear weapons. Perhaps more than the prospect of an Iranian bomb, I realized early in my term, Obama feared the impact of a preemptive Israeli strike.

That fear helped motivate the president's staff to maintain an intimate dialogue on Iran with their Israeli counterparts. I participated in all of these discussions and understood—we all did—that they also represented another hug to keep tabs on Israeli thinking on Iran. Still, the exchanges were exceptionally friendly, professional, and frank. The Americans assured us that they had no intention of reviving the Cold War concept of containment—that is, allowing the Iranians to make a bomb and then threatening to nuke them if they used it. Similarly, we heard that the United States was confident of knowing in real time whether the Iranians moved to break or sneak out of the international inspection system and quickly enrich their stockpile to military levels.

These assurances did not entirely assuage the Israelis, though, many of whom wondered whether the administration would be content to contain an Iranian ability to break out. Even this capacity, they feared, would trigger the dreaded Middle East nuclear arms race and weaken Israel's deterrence power over Hezbollah. Japan, too, had the means to break out and quickly make atomic bombs, but Japan-like capabilities in Iran's hands were nearly as deadly as a weapon. Israeli officials warned that the ayatollahs would wait for the moment when the world's attention was diverted elsewhere—to a war or a natural disaster—and then rush to place their newly spun uranium 238 inside a bomb. They would then mount this on one of the intercontinental ballistic missiles that they already possessed and that could reach any Israeli city.

Such scenarios did not, however, indicate deep differences between the Israeli and American readings of the Iranian program. On the contrary, the intelligence communities of both countries tracked the same developments and derived very similar conclusions. There was little disagreement over the size and speed of Iran's nuclear "clock." Unfortunately, there was little chance of synchronizing the other two clocks in the room. When it came to Iranian nuclearizing, America's clock was large and slow, while Israel's remained small and rapidly ticking.

The Israeli clock rang alarmingly in the summer of 2009 when intelligence revealed the existence of yet another massive, secretly constructed nuclear facility in Fordow, near the Iranian holy city of Qom. Israel had long warned about the possibility of such "immune and redundant" sites—difficult to attack and detect. Fordow, built under a mountain and equipped with one thousand centrifuges, confirmed Israel's gloomiest fears.

Obama condemned this latest Iranian attempt at deception, which, he warned, might "lead to confrontation." But the policy of engagement endured. The goal, according to Dennis Ross, was to offer Iran a confidence-building "freeze for freeze" deal, in which UN sanctions would be temporarily suspended in return for a time-limited cessation of Iranian enrichment. Another proposal aimed at preventing Iran from upgrading its stockpile of 3.5 percent low-enriched uranium (LEU) to 20 percent—far closer to weapons grade—supposedly for use in cancer-treating isotopes. The idea was to transfer most of the stockpile to Russia and France which would refine the isotopes and return them harmlessly to Tehran. Such measures, Dennis argued, would "set back Iran's nuclear clock," and yield more time for negotiations.

But the Iranians had no real intention of negotiating. Meeting with representatives of the Security Council's five permanent members and Germany—the P5+1—in early October 2009, the Iranians rejected both "freeze for freeze" and the isotope package. "The Zionist regime and its [Western] backers cannot do a damn thing to stop Iran's nuclear work," Iranian president Ahmadinejad trumpeted. Defiantly, Iran unveiled plans to build ten new enrichment plants.

Tehran's unwillingness to compromise caught the administration off guard. "Mr. Ahmadinejad may not recognize . . . that this is a very real deadline for the international community," announced White House spokesman Robert Gibbs. But the secretary of state denied the existence of any firm timetable and even eschewed the word *deadline*, stressing that America remained ready to negotiate. In a 2010 memo later leaked to *The New York Times,* Secretary of Defense Gates complained of the absence of any "comprehensive, realistic strategy to stop Iran from assembling all the major parts it needs for a nuclear weapon."

Yet, if out of synch on its statements on Iran, the White House was painstakingly disciplined in its attitude toward Israeli preemption. Publicly, the president and vice president stressed Israel's right to defend itself against any Middle Eastern threat. "Israel is a sovereign country and can best decide how to protect its citizens," went the administration's official line. Off camera, though, the message was "Don't you dare." While willing to wield the Israeli military threat to intimidate the Iranians and prod the P5+1 into supporting tightened sanctions, Washington quietly quashed any military option for Israel. When, at the Pentagon, I probed U.S. defense officials about the meaning of "all options on the table," I was answered brusquely, "Make no mistake about it, the way Israel handles the Iranian issue will determine the future course of your relations with the United States."

Meanwhile, the Iranian program progressed unimpeded. Thousands of new centrifuges churned out enough LEU for two nuclear devices. Some of the machines were reconfigured to enrich to 20 percent, and on February 11, 2010—Iranian Revolution Day—Ahmadinejad announced that the Islamic Republic had now become "a nuclear state." If it decided to, he boasted, Iran could enrich to 100 percent.

The White House once again seemed shocked by the news. Despite subsequent claims that it never expected the negotiations to succeed, the Obama administration scrambled to deal with their failure. Suddenly, the P5+1 had to be galvanized into a unified front armed with sanctions. "Iran had become a kind of national security black hole," Gates remembered, "pulling into its gravitational force our relationships with Europe, Russia, China, Israel, and the Arab Gulf states." The interests of India and Japan, which imported much of their oil from Iran, had to be reconciled with those of Brazil and Turkey, which sought to assert their independence from American policy making. German manufacturers and Swiss banks had to be persuaded to forfeit their lush Iranian accounts.

All of this took time, which Israel did not necessarily have. "We can't coordinate our clocks to the Iranian nuclear clock, which is running faster," Netanyahu told Biden in their November 2009 meeting in New Orleans. The prime minister had shown restraint while Obama's attempts to reconcile with Iran ran their course. He even held back Ehud Barak, who adopted a more militant stance. The following month, while addressing an AIPAC audience in Chicago, I was called offstage by an urgent phone call from Washington. Israel's defense minister had come out against the isotope compromise package, saying it violated Security Council resolutions demanding the cessation of all Iranian enrichment. Deputy National Security Advisor Tom Donilon was furious and demanded that Barak issue an immediate clarification. I got Barak on the line, convinced him to publish a retraction, then went back and resumed my speech.

Now, as 2010 began, Netanyahu's patience was thinning. Demanding the imposition of "crippling sanctions," he likened the Iranian program to a "fast-moving train" outrunning the international community's "beaten-down car." His motorized metaphor did not reflect Israel's dilemma as much as that of a cattle driver. Over the heads of the P5+1, Netanyahu had to crack the whip of threatened

IDF action against Iran without actually lashing its back. And he had to keep cracking without losing the powers' belief that he *could* thrash Iran.

Nevertheless, the P5+1's sluggish pace persisted and six months passed before the Security Council approved another sanctions resolution. Even these strictures, which further targeted the nuclear program and the Islamic Revolutionary Guards, fell short of the all-out embargo of Iran's economy that Israel favored. And even then, Obama made clear, "these sanctions do not close the door on diplomacy."

Not surprisingly, the Iranians once again slammed that door in Obama's face. They arrested three young American backpackers and imprisoned them for spying. They began fueling a Russian-made nuclear energy plant at Bushehr and hosted an international tour—off-limits to Americans—of the heavy-water facility at Arak. The regime brazenly hampered international inspections of nuclear sites and further tested long-range missiles. The Iranian military, *Haaretz* reported, tried out nuclear triggers at its Parchin base southeast of Tehran, and then sanitized the area.

Diplomacy, nevertheless, continued, and with equally futile results. Two more sessions of P5+1 talks—in Geneva in December 2010 and in Istanbul one month later—produced no more progress than the previous rounds. "The United States has never entered a serious war, and has never been victorious," Ahmadinejad vaunted, and accused America of conducting the 9/11 attacks to justify global aggression. "We have documents proving that Washington is the root of world terrorism."

More than the peace process, more even than QME, the Iranian issue compelled me to tread cautiously. It wedged me between a prime minister who believed it his historic duty to defend Israel against an imminent mortal threat and a president who saw that same danger as less lethal, less pressing, and still addressable through diplomacy. "Dealing with Iran requires strategic thinking of the highest order," Israeli security advisor Uzi Arad often reminded me. Dealing with Iran also necessitated the utmost degree of diplomatic tact. Stepping into television studios, I could almost hear the eggshells cracking.

While emphasizing the homicidal madness of Ahmadinejad and the ayatollahs—their Holocaust denial and fetish for terror, their

genocidal rants—I had to sidestep the fact that Washington was willing to overlook their insanity in exchange for a nuclear deal. I had to
swear that American and Israeli leaders were on the same page regarding Iran when, in reality, they often worked from different books. I had
to point out the multiple perils to Israel posed by a nuclear-enabled
Iran but without admitting any fear. "Iranian rulers could accomplish
in a matter of seconds what they denied Hitler did—kill six million
Jews," I told Jeffrey Goldberg in an Aspen Ideas Festival interview,
only to receive a reproachful phone call from Ehud Barak. "Israel can
defend itself," he said. "Period." I had to maintain Israel's overriding
interest in a negotiated solution—after all, we had the most skin in the
game—while doubting the possibility of reaching one. And I had to
dodge the same question, over and over, on TV: when is Israel going to
attack Iran? "That's too hypothetical," I responded, or, "we're not
there yet." Just once, I hungered to reply, "Three P.M., next Tuesday."

Mostly, though, I had to say nothing. By the beginning of 2011,
reports of covert Israeli actions against Iran emerged in the media.
Nuclear scientists were assassinated in the streets of Tehran and ultra-
sophisticated computer viruses were said to have wormed their way
into Iranian centrifuges and caused them to self-destruct. Such acts,
journalists speculated, averted the risks of striking Iran militarily
while setting its nuclear program back indefinitely.

Again and again, I was asked to comment on these reports, and
each time tersely but honestly answered, "I really know nothing."
Complicating my task was the alleged American role in the operations.
While firmly disassociating itself from the assassinations, the White
House kept silent regarding assertions that the United States and Israel
had collaborated on the cyberattacks. David Sanger, a dogged *Times*
reporter, suggested that the administration viewed cyber-cooperation
with the Israelis as a way to rein them in militarily—in short, as another *chibbuk* hug.

"Think of the campaign against Iran as a ten-story building," I
often heard Israeli intelligence officials tell visiting American leaders.
"You are willing to climb only to the second floor, while we're willing
to go on the roof." That image summed up Israel's quandary. The
White House openly opposed some of Israel's purported actions
against Iran but then denied reports that it had teamed up with the
Israelis on others. And the administration's willingness to cooperate
with Israel—according to Sanger—may have aimed more at staying

the hands of the Jewish State than delaying the steps of Iran. While I had no problem fielding questions about Israel's responsibility for the operations, I was ambivalent about shrugging off those regarding America's.

In the end, it hardly mattered. For all their storied successes, the supposed secret ops failed to halt Iran's nuclear program. While the number of centrifuges topped ten thousand, Iranian engineers dashed to produce more advanced models capable of quadrupling the output. With no solution in sight, Iran's 20 percent stockpile—the foundation of the HEU necessary to produce a nuclear weapon—mounted.

As a child in Cold War America, I had participated in nuclear air raid drills in which our teachers instructed us to huddle under our desks and hold our coats over our heads. I retained haunting memories of those exercises and the siren's spooky wail. Now, many decades later, I reexperienced that fear, compounded by the fact that at stake was my family's fate and the future of the Jewish people.

Conflagration

Sirens indeed sounded across northern Israel on December 2, 2010, though not because of any attack. Rather, the alarms rang in response to the deadliest fire in Israel's history. Within hours, immense flames engulfed much of the Carmel mountain range and roared toward the city of Haifa.

The blaze decimated woodlands that took generations to cultivate and which Israelis rightly prized. One of the only areas on earth to enter the twenty-first century with more trees than it finished the nineteenth, the Jewish State regarded reforestation as a testament to its own rebirth. Jews throughout the world remember dropping coins in the *puskhe*—Yiddish for charity box—for Jewish National Fund conservation and receiving gift certificates of Israeli saplings planted in their honor. And like many American Jewish kids, I sincerely believed that somewhere in Israel stood trees with my name on them. I came to know better, but continued to rejoice in Israel's forest-furred slopes. Which is why Palestinian arsonists routinely ignited them, scorching both our hills and our hearts.

Whether set by terrorists or ignited by negligent teens—the cause was never fully determined—the Carmel fire destroyed more than trees. Charging at more than five hundred yards per minute, fifty-foot walls of flame trapped a bus carrying Prison Service officers trying to evacuate Palestinian inmates in a high-security correctional facility located in the fire's path. The conflagration made no distinction between Jews, Arabs, and Druze. Forty-four people were killed, including Israel's highest-ranking female police officer and a sixteen-year-old volunteer.

And Israel quickly exhausted its means of extinguishing the blaze. Supplies of retardant—the carrot-colored powder dispersed by air—ran out, and Israeli firefighters were overwhelmed. The wildfire ravaged the Carmel Nature Reserve, Israel's jewel, and blackened the edges of outlying communities. Some seventeen thousand people were evacuated. Urgently seeking assistance, Netanyahu phoned the heads of thirty states, and a great many—Greece, Cyprus, Russia, Spain, Britain, and the Netherlands—responded. Even Turkey and the Palestinian Authority sent help. But still the inferno leapt, descending on densely populated neighborhoods.

Thousands of miles away, in Washington, the flickers emanated not from the embers of incinerated forests but rather from the decorations sparkling on the South Lawn. The multicolored glow played on the White House's walls as I entered the president's annual Hanukkah reception. Even in crisisless times, the event seemed, to me, surreal. Between the holly wreathes, mistletoe, and spangled trees that seasonally bedeck the Lincoln Room, Jewish leaders—many of them wearing *kippas* and even black Hasidic hats—nibbled latkes. The irony struck me when I first attended the party, during the Bush years, and it might have tickled me again but for the disaster devastating northern Israel. Instead, the syncretic glare of Hanukkah and Christmas lights merely sickened me.

Just outside the gate, my cellphone rang. Netanyahu, on the other end, sounded as I never heard him before, truly frightened. "We need firefighting planes, big ones. Go to the president now and ask for help." I informed him that, fortuitously, I was just entering the White House and would soon see Obama. "Quickly," the prime minister urged me. "The fire's nearing Haifa."

Once inside, I found the beneficent Susan Sher, the first lady's chief of staff, and informed her of the situation. "No problem," she said. "Let's go." Susan took me to the library where the president was preparing for photo ops with the guests.

"Mr. President," I began, "Prime Minister Netanyahu just phoned me. A catastrophic fire is burning in northern Israel. Dozens of people are dead, sir, and Haifa's threatened. The prime minister has instructed me to ask you for your urgent help. Israel needs you."

Obama, as usual at ease in his evening suit, seemed to stiffen. He leaned toward me as I spoke, nodded gravely, and then pivoted toward Reggie Love, his personal aide. "Reggie," the president said without hesitation. "Make a list with Ambassador Oren. Get Israel whatever it needs."

I sincerely thanked the president and conferred for a few minutes with Reggie. The physically imposing but soft-spoken former basketball star wrote furiously as I ticked off our pressing requirements: retardant, special firefighting units, and, above all, "scoopers." The last were planes, some as large as 747s, capable of sucking in thousands of cubic meters of seawater and releasing them over flaming forests. "Scoopers, right," Reggie assured me. "I'm on it."

Forgoing the party, I left the White House for my Residence and yet another cheerfully incongruous event. As part of my continuing outreach to influential American communities, I organized a dinner with prominent LGBT leaders, among them press commentators and administration officials. The idea was to highlight Israel's accomplishments in the area of gay and lesbian rights—the IDF, for example, never enforced the equivalent of "don't ask, don't tell." Celebrated Israeli singer Ivri Lider, a creative and ultracool role model for gay people worldwide and, as it happened, a relative of mine by marriage, was the guest of honor. Together with Angela Buchdahl, the first Asian American rabbi and a cantor whose singing voice validated her first name, Ivri led us in singing traditional songs about dreidels and eight-day miracles. The ambience was truly luminous, but as we lit the menorah, I remained fixated on distant, monstrously larger flames.

Excusing myself from my own table, I phoned the chief firefighter of California and the Quebec company that leased fire-extinguishing planes, frantically seeking scoopers. The search went on long after the guests departed, by which time I had completed a self-taught crash course in combating forest fires. Discovering that North Carolina possessed one of America's three available scoopers, I recalled that among my guests that evening were Kathy Manning and Randall Kaplan, a Greensboro couple dedicated to Democratic and Jewish causes. I woke them in their hotel room and asked them to contact the office of North Carolina governor Bev Perdue and request to borrow the state's scooper. They did, without hesitation, at 2 A.M., only to hear that the scooper was grounded for lack of parts.

I next rushed back to the White House, to the West Wing situation room set up especially for dealing with the Carmel disaster. Reggie Love faithfully carried out his presidential instructions. Representatives of the NSC and the Pentagon sat around a table issuing orders to scour U.S. military warehouses for seventy tons of retardant and to fly C-130 Mobile Air Fire Fighting Systems (MAFFS) from west of the Rockies to northeast of the Nile. Of the eleven planes in the United States, Israel received eight. A team of Hotshot crews—firefighting commandos trained to parachute into mountainous terrains and battle blazes on their own—hurriedly left Boise, Idaho, that night en route to Tel Aviv.

After dawn, I learned that, just after the Hanukkah reception, President Obama had secretly flown to Afghanistan. Landing in Kabul, the first call he made was to our situation room. And the first question he asked was "Did Israel get its planes?"

Israel got its planes, though they arrived after the fire was already extinguished. But the retardant did reach Israel in time for the operation, as did the Hotshots. Together with other caring countries, Americans helped put out a fire that, if left unquenched, might have left swaths of Israel smoldering. "The United States intends to pursue a full-court press in offering assistance to Israel," Obama promised Netanyahu in a ten-minute condolence call. Though he may have missed the basketball allusion, the prime minister appreciated the sentiment and thanked Obama warmly.

Three weeks later, I walked the hairpin mountain turn where walls of fire had closed on the Prison Services bus. The asphalt was cracked from the heat. Carbonized stubs of what had once been five million trees studded the landscape. An Israeli forest ranger showed me where, beneath the ashes, charred bodies had been found intertwined. "Look," he said, pointing to a nearby ridge combed by helmeted conservationists. "They've already started replanting."

Walking back from that deadly bend, I reflected on the complex turns in the U.S.-Israel alliance. Subjected to ceaseless strains, the bonds between America and Israel once again proved resilient. Like the Carmel forest, it, too, would regenerate. At that moment, Israel could not have had a better ally—truly a *ben brit*, son of a covenant—than Barack Obama.

The Carmel disaster further confirmed my initial assessment that the president, contrary to common conservative belief, was not anti-Israel. On the contrary, he was intensely supportive of a specific version of Israel—the Israel of refuge and innovation. But the Israel he cared about was also the Israel whose interests he believed he understood better than its own citizens and better than the leaders they chose at the ballot box.

I turned away from the place where defenseless human beings had been consumed, unaware that, elsewhere in the Middle East, another immolation was imminent. Unlike the Carmel disaster, though, this fire would not be doused. Rather, it would race, unsuppressed, across the entire region, burning down structures that had existed for decades, even centuries, igniting—it seemed—history itself.

Wintry Spring

His name, Mohammed Bouazizi, would soon be forgotten, but not his act. Slapped, spat at in the face, and berated by a police officer on December 17, 2010, the twenty-six-year-old Tunisian fruit vendor poured gasoline over his body and set himself on fire. As Bouazizi expired, Tunisia erupted. Thousands of protesters, many of them mobilized by social media networks, rioted in the streets, burning shops and overturning vehicles. More than two hundred people were killed over the next two weeks as the rampage expanded into a popular revolt. Finally, his security forces overwhelmed, President Zine al-Abidine Ben Ali, Tunisia's dictator for more than two decades, fled the country. For the first time in modern history, the citizens of an Arab state had risen up and toppled an autocratic ruler.

The success of Tunisia's "jasmine revolution" sparked elation throughout the United States. Momentarily overcoming partisanship, both Democrats and Republicans jointly praised the insurrection. The media covered it obsessively, with reporters unabashedly rooting for the rebels. Though once dismissive of his predecessor's democracy agenda in the Middle East, President Obama now embraced it. "I applaud the courage of the Tunisian people," he declared. "The United States of America . . . supports the democratic aspirations of all people."

But what Americans hailed as the start of a Middle Eastern march toward freedom, Israelis feared was a crack in the regional order. In contrast to Obama's support for change, Netanyahu expressed his "hope that there will be quiet and security [and] that stability will be restored." Americans perceived Bouazizi's suicide as a protest against despotic rule and a desperate plea for freedom. Israelis, noting that the police officer who publicly assaulted the vendor was a woman, saw his fiery death as a means of purging humiliation. The violent tension between honor and shame, so central to Middle Eastern cultures and tragically familiar to Israel, was alien to most Americans. Interpreted in the United States as a revolutionary quest for liberty, Tunisia's uprising looked to Israelis like a traditional demand for dignity.

The tremors radiating from Tunisia threatened further ruptures between the United States and Israel. In speaking before American audiences, Israeli ambassadors rarely receive a question they have never been asked repeatedly before—"Why does Israel build settlements?" for example, or "How come your PR's so bad?" But after one campus speech, some precocious student surprised me by inquiring, "What's more difficult for you, explaining Israel to Americans or America to Israelis?" I paused, pondering my answer, then confessed out loud what I had never fully admitted to myself. "Hands down, it's much harder explaining America to Israelis."

Apart from complex issues such as the territories and Jerusalem, Americans basically understand Israel. A people that returns to its homeland after two thousand years, establishes a Western-style democracy, and defends itself against genocidal enemies—that narrative is readily grasped throughout most of the United States. But Israelis have difficulty understanding America's missionizing zeal and the belief—hardwired into the nation's identity—that the United States was created not only for its own good but for all of humanity's. They recoil from the American tendency to impose its reality on the Middle East. The notion that the region secretly longs for American-style freedom is simply incomprehensible to Israelis.

"Are they mad?" Amos Gilad, the Defense Ministry's advisor and seasoned Arabist, shouted into the phone when I conveyed the American response to Tunisia. "This is the Middle East, for God's sake, not Manhattan!" I explained that, just as rescuing a Jewish community from danger was embedded in the Israeli narrative, so too did the Tunisian revolt resonate among Americans as a modern-day Lexington and Concord. Gilad's response nevertheless remained deafening: "Madness!"

I understood America, but I agreed with the Israelis. A neoconservative friend once branded me a racist for denying that Arabs craved democracy. I responded that he, my friend, was the real bigot for setting the United States as the highest form of governance to which all peoples, irrespective of their customs, must aspire. But while I intellectually sided with Israel's reading of Middle Eastern protests, I prayed that America's was right. Rather than cleansing shame and restoring honor, I hoped that the Tunisian vendor's self-immolation represented a shackled man's outcry for rights.

The dissonance between the American and Israeli viewpoints deepened in late January 2011, when riots broke out across Egypt. In Alexandria, Suez, and Ismailia, Egyptians confronted helmeted police who repelled them with tear gas and water cannons and beat them with batons. The core of Egypt's meltdown, though, was located in Cairo's Tahrir (Freedom) Square, ironically named for the 1952 revolution that brought Colonel Nasser and other officers, including Hosni Mubarak, to power.

First tens, then hundreds of thousands of Egyptians, many of them unemployed young men, converged on the square, demanding political reform and economic opportunities. By the month's end, an Internet-declared "Day of Rage" and "Friday of Anger" mobilized an estimated one million demonstrators. Government buildings were burned, innumerable protesters arrested, and six hundred people killed. With Egypt's colors—red, white, and black—painted on their faces, the people repulsed successive waves of security forces' assaults and even a surreal charge of pro-Mubarak tour guides mounted on horses and camels. Still, the rebellion swelled. The call was no longer for an end to emergency laws and police brutality, but for Mubarak's ouster. His military regime, deemed "stable" by the State Department only two weeks earlier, tottered.

Yet Egypt's massive army merely looked on. As tanks surrounded Tahrir Square, Israeli intelligence analysts debated whether Egyptian troops would step in to save their patron, Mubarak. But the military, "acknowledging the legitimate rights of the people," announced that it "has not and will not use force." The generals, it seemed, struck a deal with the demonstrators, jettisoning the president in exchange for retaining the army's lucrative budget.

But the question remained: who would rule Egypt? The protesters, a hodgepodge of liberals, nationalists, and Facebook-savvy activists personified by Google marketer Wael Ghonim, espoused no unified political program or leadership. Only the Muslim Brotherhood, founded in 1928 and galvanized around the vision of a global Islamic caliphate, offered an amply funded and hierarchical alternative. The Brotherhood, Israeli analysts agreed, would wait for the mob to bring down the government and then swiftly snatch up power. "Israel has long proudly called itself the only Middle Eastern democracy," I briefed reporters. "And we'll be happier still to be one of many Middle Eastern democracies. But we've seen it happen before in Iran, Gaza, and Lebanon. What begins as a secular, progressive revolution ends up as an Islamic radical coup."

The prospect of Egypt's takeover by an organization dedicated to Israel's destruction, the mother movement of Hamas, terrified Israelis. Yes, Mubarak was corrupt, and yes, under his rule, anti-Semitism in Egypt became rampant and weapons flowed into Gaza. But Mubarak also upheld the Camp David Accords, which, for thirty years, guaranteed Israel's stability and facilitated its economic development. Peace freed the IDF to repel other threats rather than grapple with the thousands of advanced tanks and hundreds of fighter jets and as many as 1.5 million soldiers in the Egyptian army. "The people of Egypt will decide their own fate," Netanyahu remarked. "But we want the Egyptian government to remain committed to the peace." The prime minister maintained a calm demeanor, even while El Al airlifted four hundred Israeli tourists from Cairo and the Israeli embassy evacuated all diplomatic families and nonessential personnel.

By contrast, in the United States, the sight of bearded and white-robed agitators around Tahrir's fringes aroused little anxiety. Nothing—not the beating by Egyptian thugs of CNN correspondent Anderson Cooper or the mass sexual assault on CBS reporter Lara Logan—dampened the press's frenzy. Extolling the overturn of "Paleolithic tyrants" by "new societies," *The New York Times* welcomed the "post-Islamist revolutions" waged by "young Muslims demanding freedom, representation, and the rule of law." *New Yorker* editor in chief David Remnick attested that "the historic moments of . . . oppressed peoples emerging as one from their private realms of silence and fear are thrilling." *The Washington Post* lauded "the radiant sunrise" that "could forever transform the Arab world's most populous country . . . and reshape a region where autocracy has nourished extremism and terrorism." Sameh Shoukry, Egypt's urbane ambassador—later, its foreign minister—was relentlessly assailed by American anchormen for standing up for his government. And after each interview, I called him to tell him, "Hang in there." Yet my words of encouragement were overpowered by a media "preparing," in the *Post*'s words, "for a new and more democratic Middle East."

Such exuberance could not be overlooked by the press-sensitive Obama administration. Shortly after the outbreak of unrest, the president called Mubarak and reportedly threatened to cut U.S. aid to Egypt unless far-reaching reforms were promptly enacted. "What's needed right now are concrete steps that advance the rights of the Egyptian people," the president told reporters, and called for "political change that leads to a future of greater freedom . . . for the Egyptian people." Mubarak responded first by announcing broad political and economic measures and then by declaring he would not seek re-election. But neither statement relieved Washington's pressure. "An orderly transition must be meaningful, it must be peaceful, and it must begin now," Obama said emphatically on February 1. Three days later, he reiterated: "The only thing that will work is moving an orderly transition process that begins right now."

In all of modern Middle East history, no single English word has reverberated more thunderously than President Obama's "now." Years later, Arab dignitaries I encountered still spoke about it rancorously. "Nobody will ever believe a word America says anymore!" a leftist member of the Knesset called and shouted at me. "Obama's just killed the Israeli peace camp!" Flagrantly brutal and corrupt, Mubarak was nevertheless America's loyal friend for more than thirty years. And after a single week of demonstrations that, though highly publicized, involved a fraction of Egypt's 85 million inhabitants, the United States abandoned him. That single act of betrayal—as Middle Easterners, even those opposed to Mubarak, saw it—contrasted jarringly with Obama's earlier refusal to support the Green Revolution against the hostile regime in Iran. Other American allies in the region took notice. So, too, did America's foes.

On February 11, Mubarak resigned. Later he was arrested and put on trial for the premeditated murder of protesters. A sea of flags rippled over Tahrir Square, where countless Egyptians rejoiced. The reaction in the White House seemed no less exultant. Together with National Security Advisor Uzi Arad, I heard the news of Mubarak's overthrow while discussing the Egyptian situation with senior National Security Council officials. They appeared delighted by the events in Cairo—high-fives were exchanged—and credited themselves for remaining "on the right side of history." Obama issued a statement averring that "the spirit of peaceful protest and perseverance that the Egyptian people have shown can serve as a powerful wind of . . . change," and that the transition "must bring all of Egypt's voices to the table." Turning to Dennis Ross, I mentioned that, to an Israeli ear, "all voices" sounded like the Muslim Brotherhood. He assured me that the administration had no intention of engaging the Islamic radicals.

I doubted that. The president's Cairo speech—that foundational document—offered America's hand to Muslim leaders who were rooted in Islam and democratically voted into office. The Brotherhood met that criteria and would win at the polls, Israeli experts were certain. But even that process would take time as the chaos in Egypt, and along Egypt's borders with Israel, deepened. And while part of me longed to share in our neighbors' jubilation, the fears for my own neighborhood prevailed. The three regional powers—Iran, Turkey, and now Egypt—all former friends, were now arrayed against us. That anxiety weighed on me as Arad and I entered Dan Shapiro's oddly cramped office, where much of one wall was taken up with a photograph of Mubarak. It showed the soon-to-be-deposed Egyptian president standing in the Oval Office and glancing at his watch. Arad quipped, "There's a leader wondering how much time he has left in power." When I next returned to Dan's office, the photo was gone.

As the revolution swept over Egypt, a blizzard buried Washington in ten inches of snow. Thousands of households lost power but Middle Easterners rose to seize it. America's capital wallowed in winter while an Arab Spring appeared to bloom.

In Algeria and in Jordan, thousands of protesters crammed the streets, clamoring for change. The Pearl Roundabout in the capital of Bahrain became another Tahrir Square, where demonstrators erected tents and battled security forces. The people of Yemen, one of the region's poorest countries, demanded the resignation of President Ali Abdullah Saleh, in office as long as Mubarak. Desperate to avoid the Egyptian leader's fate, the rulers of those countries swiftly quashed the revolts, shooting thousands, while taking pro forma steps at reform. Iran derided these measures and cheered the rebels on, then ruthlessly suppressed the largest domestic demonstrations since 2009.

The Obama administration, meanwhile, scrambled to keep up. After rushing to secure Mubarak's fall, the White House appeared to halt and even backtrack. While generally calling for restraint and promoting reforms, it refrained from supporting regime change in Algeria and Jordan, and counseled peaceful transition in Yemen. But on the Bahraini island—home to the U.S. Navy's Fifth Fleet—America remained largely silent while Sunni troops charged over a causeway from the Saudi mainland to crush the mostly Shia insurgents. Likewise, the demonstrations in Tehran roused no reaction from Washington.

The administration's inconsistency was bewildering, yet at times I could commiserate. The Arab Spring, which from a distance appeared to be a uniform movement, was, viewed more closely, a melee of tribal and ethnic rivalries, religious tensions, and factional strife. Strangely, I found myself defending Obama to reporters who began to question the vagaries of his approach. "There's no cookie-cutter response to these uprisings," I told them. "No one-policy-fits-all." But the president, no less anomalously, seemed perfectly at ease with his decisions. "I think we calibrated it just right," he said, and advised Arab leaders that "to stay ahead of change, you have to be out in front."

But the administration shrank from the forefront when the Arab Spring reached Libya. Previously, relations with the oil-flushed desert country and its loony but lethal dictator, Muammar Gaddafi, improved markedly under Obama. The two met briefly at a G8 summit in July 2009, posing for a handshake, after which a succession of high-ranking State Department officials visited Tripoli. In February 2010, representatives of twenty-five American companies led the first U.S. trade mission to Libya in nearly four decades.

A year later, though, a merciless civil war pitted Gaddafi's hyperequipped army against poorly armed and fractious rebels. Snipers, artillery, and helicopter gunships fired at demonstrators, killing thousands. Denouncing the violence as "appalling," Obama issued a directive designed to "loosen the dictator's grip on power" by freezing his assets. "Muammar Gaddafi has lost the legitimacy to lead and he must leave," the president said, but he took no further steps. Both the U.S. embassy in Tripoli and the Benghazi consulate remained open.

Instead, France took the lead. Early in March 2011, the preeminent French philosopher and public intellectual Bernard-Henri Lévy brazenly slipped into Libya, made contact with rebels, and put them into contact with President Nicolas Sarkozy in Paris. "The blood of the people of Benghazi will stain the flag of France," Lévy warned. Later, he helped convince Hillary Clinton of the urgency of rescuing Libyans from their own ruler. The result was a Security Council authorization for a NATO no-fly zone over Libya. Following the French contrails, American jets and cruise missiles pulverized government troops.

Throughout, the White House insisted that the goal was to prevent a massacre, not change Libya's regime, but the war was clearly aimed at Gaddafi's downfall. "Brotherly Leader," as he crowned himself, appealed to Obama—"our son"—for a cease-fire, reminding him that "democracy and building of civil society cannot be achieved . . . by backing . . . Al Qaeda in Benghazi." Yet the airstrikes continued and, on April 30, took the lives of Gaddafi's son, Saif, and three of his grandchildren. Beaten back to Sirte, his birthplace, the ruler and 140 of his henchman were captured, tortured, and shot.

"The death of Muammar Gaddafi showed that our role in protecting the Libyan people, and helping them break free from a tyrant, was the right thing to do," Obama said. The intervention served as a "powerful reminder of how we've renewed American leadership in the world." But in *The New Yorker*, an unnamed White House advisor characterized the president's policy—memorably—as "leading from behind."

And in Syria, where a slaughter indeed took place, Obama chose not to lead at all. As in Libya, the Syrian Spring uprising was preceded by a sharp upturn in the country's relations with the United States. After restoring diplomatic ties with Damascus, the administration proactively worked to draw dictator Bashar al-Assad out of Iran's orbit and into a diplomatic process with Israel. House Speaker Nancy Pelosi, who once declared that "the road to peace is a road to Damascus," journeyed to the city in 2009 and was followed by John Kerry, chairman of the Senate Foreign Relations Committee. Other Congress members, mostly Democrats but also several Republicans, made the voyage and returned to tell Secretary of State Clinton that Assad was a reformer. The reaction of most Israelis echoed that of General Amos Gilad: "A reformer? Are they mad?"

The American assessment of Assad changed abruptly in the first week of March 2011. The arrest and torture of fifteen children for spray-painting anti-Assad graffiti on a wall in the southwestern Syrian city of Daraa sparked popular demonstrations against the regime. At first peaceful, the protests swiftly turned deadly after Assad's army dispersed them with live fire. The disturbances nevertheless spread—to Damascus and Aleppo and twenty other cities, leaving a thousand civilians dead. The Arab Spring, which began in Tunisia as a campaign for dignity, and was devolving in Egypt into a showdown between nationalists and militant Islamists, in Syria soon escalated into a civil war between an Alawite-led, Iranian-backed regime and its mostly Sunni, Saudi-supported opponents. And though violent elsewhere in the Middle East, only in Syria did the Arab Spring produce a bloodbath.

Yet toward Syria, oddly, the administration's policy was the most ambivalent. To be sure, the White House and the State Department regularly condemned the mass murder, arbitrary arrests, and wholesale torture taking place throughout the country. "We strongly oppose the Syrian government's treatment of its citizens," stated Press Secretary Jay Carney. "History is not on the side of this kind of action." But Obama also denounced the protesters' violence and insisted that the opposition was too disorganized to merit American aid. The president refrained from calling for Assad's ouster and, initially at least, exempted him from sanctions placed on other Syrian officials. Unnamed administration sources repeatedly informed *The Wall Street Journal* that Israel wanted to preserve Assad's rule, compelling me each time to issue a denial and clarify that, on the contrary, the fall of Iran and Hezbollah's Syrian ally was a patent Israeli interest. One could conclude, even in 2011, that while Israel welcomed Assad's demise as a deathly blow to Iran, the Obama administration, looking to reconcile with Tehran, was less eager to hasten his departure.

Only later, together with the European Union, the Arab League, and the "international community"—which excluded Russia and China—did the United States ramp up sanctions on Syria and oppose its membership in the UN Human Rights Council. Not until the summer, after many thousands of deaths, did the administration determine that "Assad has lost his legitimacy," and declared that "Assad must go."

• • •

"We're waiting for the Arab Spring to take a spring break," a State Department expert on Arab affairs told me. I agreed: "We're waiting for the Arab Awakening to take a nap." Yet neither of us received a respite from the turmoil roiling the Middle East. As an historian, I could appreciate this epic moment. Not since the Napoleonic invasion of Egypt in 1798 or the collapse of the Ottoman Empire near the end of World War I had the region been so irrevocably altered. "It's 1917," I heard Netanyahu remark. "Only there are no Europeans to oversee the Middle East." As an Israeli, though, the Arab Spring aroused mixed emotions in me—frustration and fear, certainly, but also hope.

The frustration stemmed from Israel's inability to participate in the optimism-bordering-on-elation that the Arab uprisings sparked in Americans. I watched incredulously as TV commentator Fareed Zakaria praised Obama for removing Mubarak in a single week whereas Reagan and Clinton took years to oust Marcos in the Philippines and Suharto from Indonesia. "But those transitions were successful!" I hollered at the screen. I watched columnist Tom Friedman boast of the Syrian protesters' chant of "silmiya, silmiya"—peaceful, peaceful—and anchorman Anderson Cooper assure a panicked woman under fire in Libya that "the whole world cares right now" and would never forget her. "*Silmiya,* who's he kidding?" I thought, and predicted that America would indeed forget that poor Libyan woman. I wondered how, in America's eyes, vicious dictators like Gaddafi and Assad ever had the legitimacy to lose.

Israel's pessimism, in turn, was regularly attacked in the media. Dismissing Netanyahu's "predictable warnings," a *New York Times* editorial asserted that "Egypt's Facebook-adept youth are not lining up behind the Muslim Brotherhood, itself scarcely a band of fanatics," and that Israel should welcome "the first peace between a Jewish and an Arab democracy." Writing in *The Washington Post,* veteran peace negotiator Aaron David Miller described Mubarak as the "one pharaoh that Israelis wish had stayed on the throne," and Tom Friedman wrote that "the children of Egypt were having their liberation moment and the children of Israel decided to side with Pharaoh." Post columnist David Ignatius pulled me aside at a diplomatic dinner and derided Israelis for "never seeing the positive side of anything" and not sharing in the Arabs' joy. Coming from this debonair and fair-minded friend, a bestselling novelist as well as keen political analyst, David's criticism disturbed me. But David was also a mensch, and at another reception a year later, he apologized to me, admitting, "You guys were right."

Being right, though, proved of little help to Israel in meeting the newfound dangers it confronted. The country's so-called Peace Border with Egypt, unfenced and lightly patrolled, suddenly became a battlefield as terrorists, exploiting the breakdown of order in Sinai, attacked passing Israeli vehicles and fired rockets at Eilat. Islamic radicals were rallying in Cairo as well, and becoming increasingly prominent among the Syrian rebels. "Look at the Islamist banners they're flying," I pointed out to a roomful of ABC journalists, only to be rebuked by one of them, a Jordanian, for trying to taint the rebellion. But reports out of Syria substantiated the growing role of jihadist groups and their advances toward Assad's chemical weapons arsenal, the Middle East's largest.

Most harrowingly, the Arab Spring diverted attention from Iran's supply of rockets to terrorist organizations and its dispatch, for the first time, of warships through the Suez Canal. The ayatollahs undoubtedly took note of the NATO intervention in Libya, which gave up its nuclear weapons program in 2004, and redoubled their quest for a doomsday option. "If Gaddafi had not surrendered his centrifuges and were now surrounded in his bunker with nothing left but a button," I asked in a *Wall Street Journal* op-ed, "would he push it?"

Yet, while posing many perils to Israel, the Arab Spring also created opportunities. It resulted in the removal of the deranged Gaddafi, and loosened the Syrian keystone in Iran's strategic arc with Lebanon. Arabs everywhere were protesting, but for their own sakes, not for Palestine. They proudly waved their own flags, and did not burn Israel's. The doctrine of linkage that cast the Israel-Palestinian conflict as the core of every Middle Eastern dispute could at last be debunked. The way was opened—theoretically, at least—for a new chapter in U.S.-Israel understanding.

Indeed, the Arab world's convulsion should have made American and Israeli officials cling more forcefully to their ties. In a region proffering nothing but upheaval, Israel represented stability. Alone among Middle Eastern states, it remained technologically, scientifically, and militarily robust, fiercely democratic, and unreservedly pro-American. And for an Israel lashed by Middle Eastern storms, the United States was both beacon and anchor. The alliance had rarely appeared so vital.

"We've lost the entire Middle East, so now what do we do?" I asked Dan Shapiro over lunch. I had a miserable cold and could barely get the words out without coughing. My illness, it seemed, was symptomatic of our common malaise. Together, Israel and the United States had to rethink all of their assumptions about the Middle East and together try to devise solutions. "This is the time to rebuild trust between America and Israel," I said through sniffles. "We don't have to agree on everything, but we can still coordinate our response." Dan nodded, and offered me a tissue. There was nothing more to say. With history so incoherently weaving, we all had to determine the direction it was heading and which side of it was right.

Through the Dust Darkly

On January 5, 2011, Republican legislator John Boehner took the oath as Congress's sixty-first Speaker of the House of Representatives. Renowned for smoking filterless Camels and retaining a year-round tan, the quiet Ohioan was also noted for crying in public. "That's not a tan," Obama once said, roasting him, "it's rust." Boehner indeed wept as he assumed America's third-most-powerful office. But for all those tears, the moment capped the Republicans' retaking of the House in the largest midterm election victory since the 1940s. The Tea Party, initially dismissed as insignificant by my congressional liaisons, proved to be a potent component in the GOP's victory, which also swept most state and gubernatorial contests.

One Democrat who nevertheless retained her seat was Gabrielle Giffords, an engaging representative from Arizona. Three days after Boehner's swearing-in, a crazed gunman burst into a rally she was holding near Tuscon, killed six people, and wounded twelve, including Giffords. Shot point-blank in the head, she survived in part thanks to an Israeli-made high-tech bandage applied by medics on the scene. Even then her recovery required many excruciating months and would never be complete. A shattered America listened as the president, quoting from the book of Job, gleaned meaning from meaningless pain and urged divided politicians to begin a "national conversation . . . in a way that heals, not in a way that wounds." Commenta-

Presenting my credentials, July 2009. Instead of hearing my "elevator speech," the president spent most of the event schmoozing with my parents (between Obama and me).

White House

Laughing with Lior Weintraub (left), my first chief of staff, and Deputy Chief of Mission Dan Arbell. We laughed because the embassy's petty concerns—press leaks and management issues—paled compared to the tens of thousands of terrorist rockets aimed at Israel, the moribund peace process, and Iran's race for the bomb. We laughed bitterly, knowing that the three of us, sometimes alone, had to safeguard Israel's vital alliance with America.

With Rahm Emanuel, Obama's first chief of staff and, later, mayor of Chicago. Rahm lost part of a finger in an accident which, President Obama said, cost him half of his vocabulary. In spite of his tart words and often strident criticism of our policy, I valued his friendship, his candor, and his commitment to Israel.
Brooke Collins/City of Chicago

Senior White House advisor David Axelrod was the guest speaker at the embassy's Israel Independence Day celebrations, 2010. An advocate of a hard-line policy toward Netanyahu, David could be tough with me as well. Regarding the prime minister, I suggested to him, "Try love."
Shmuel Almany/Embassy of Israel to the U.S.

Outside of the First Lady, Valerie Jarrett was the most powerful woman in Washington. In a very centralized administration, she stood within the innermost circle as the president's closest advisor. Few Israelis, though, ever heard her name, much less appreciated her influence.
Shmuel Almany/Embassy of Israel to the U.S.

Greeting Secretary of State Hillary Clinton at Ben Gurion Airport.
Formidable and seemingly inexhaustible, she also displayed an unflagging wit.
"I've been phoning you and phoning you," she exclaims to me here, after weeks
of not responding to my calls. "But you never return my messages!"
Shmuel Almany/Embassy of Israel to the U.S.

Iranian Night with Israeli singer Rita.
Shmuel Almany/Embassy of Israel to the U.S.

Anti-Israel protestors accosting me on the stage at the University of Texas.
People often asked me how, in such tense situations, I managed to keep my cool.
In addition to thirty years' experience coping with hostile crowds, I often recalled
tougher times—such as the day I transferred from my high school's "dumb class"
to Honors English. Mostly, I was disappointed. These were the students
I came to engage and, possibly, educate.
Embassy of Israel to the U.S.

A Holocaust denier and fierce advocate of Israel's destruction, Iranian president
Mahmoud Ahmadinejad tours a nuclear plant with thousands of newly installed centrifuges.
These could enrich uranium to a weapons grade, threatening Israel's existence and
triggering a Middle East nuclear arms race capable of destabilizing the world.
Office of the Presidency of the Islamic Republic of Iran/Getty Images

Erupting in December 2010, the Carmel forest fire—the worst conflagration in Israel's
history—destroyed five million trees, displaced seventeen thousand people, and killed
forty-four. Whatever disagreements Obama had with Netanyahu disappeared as the
president immediately responded to the prime minister's urgent request for aid.

Wikimedia Commons

Together with U.S. Chief of Protocol Capricia Marshall, receiving Benjamin Netanyahu at the airport. Part commando, part politico, and thoroughly predatory, the prime minister had a grim view of Jewish history and an Old Testament temper. I gave him loyalty, honesty, and the advice he did not always relish hearing.

Embassy of Israel to the U.S.

Off-and-on talks between Prime Minister Netanyahu and Palestinian Authority President Mahmoud Abbas, here mediated by Secretary of State Clinton, brought the sides further from—rather than closer to—peace. Abbas ultimately forged a unity pact with Hamas and sought to achieve Palestinian statehood through the UN, without giving Israel peace. The Obama administration nevertheless placed the bulk of the blame on Israel's settlement policy.

Drew Angerer

The holiest place in Judaism, the Western Wall became the scene of escalating tensions between the Ultra-Orthodox establishment and liberal women—many of them from the United States—who prayed in nontraditional ways. The controversy threatened to strain relations between Americans, who viewed the issue as a matter of freedom of religion and women's rights, and Israelis, who saw it as a question of law and security.

AP Photo/Michal Fattal

In the Capitol Rotunda, addressing the annual Day of Remembrance. Back in the 1970s, Israel gave American Jews the courage to confront the Holocaust, yet they often forgot America's failure to save European Jewry. Rather than standing and saluting at such ceremonies, I asked myself, why weren't we rending our garments in shame?

Embassy of Israel to the U.S.

"A man at ease inside his body," I told Sally.
And a leader, I concluded, "more about ideology than policy."
Embassy of Israel to the U.S.

tors from both parties deemed the speech worthy of Dr. Martin Luther King.

Keeping up with this whirlwind, analytically and emotionally, would be trying for any ambassador. As Israel's envoy, though, I had to gauge the impact of the Republicans' victory on vital issues such as the peace process and Tehran's nuclear program. Though foreign-policy making is a presidential prerogative, the House could exert its influence by, for example, suspending aid to a recalcitrant Palestinian Authority or by intensifying sanctions on Iran. There were dozens of freshman congressmen to meet and new Foreign Affairs, Armed Services, and Appropriations Committee chairmen to engage. And, at the height of this hustling, there was the need to stop and grapple with tragedy. I knew Gabby Giffords, a Jewish woman firmly committed to Israel, as well as her husband, astronaut Mark Kelly, who attended my high school. The Tucson shooting—perhaps more than any of the arbitrary massacres that sporadically traumatize Americans—stunned me.

The relentless march of such events raises a kind of dust that can blind even the most observant ambassador. The task is to somehow anticipate long-term trends—to see through the soot—and chart the road ahead. Squinting, as it were, in early February, I discerned the future path of the peace process. President Obama, I wrote to Netanyahu, would soon unveil a major diplomatic initiative and set out his vision of peace.

My case, logically at least, was weak. After suffering such a stinging midterm defeat, while wrestling with the Arab Spring, why would the president risk alienating more Americans and churning up what had become—paradoxically—the Middle East's calmest corner? What, moreover, were the chances for success? I once heard Obama say, "Mediating between Israelis and Palestinians is harder than mediating between Democrats and Republicans." Why did he believe that this effort, more than serial failures of the previous twenty years, would prevail?

The cable sent to Netanyahu listed several motives for the initiative. There was Obama's need to bolster his progressive base after its electoral setback as well as to maintain the momentum he believed he had gained by smartly managing the Arab Spring. Mentioned also was the threat, frequently cited by the White House, that the Europeans would soon advance a plan much less amenable to Israel. And while the people of the Middle East were demonstrating for themselves, rather than against the Jewish State, the president still regarded a peace deal as key to the region's stability.

But my letter omitted two additional reasons. The first was that this most centralized of administrations had difficulty multitasking, and that once he had finished focusing on health care and change in the Arab world, the president would return to Israel-Palestine. The second reason related to Obama's undiminished determination to achieve a peace accord. That goal, I believed, remained deeply embedded in his worldview, a *kishke* issue.

Still, the exact contents of Obama's plan remained unknowable. The two-state solution would be central, certainly, as would a resolution of the refugee and Jerusalem disputes. But the capstone would be recognition of the 1967 lines as the basis for peace. This, the president would likely say, would merely express the obvious and reiterate long-standing U.S. policy. In reality, though, America's embrace of the 1967 lines would undermine the Terms of Reference so fastidiously forged by Hillary Clinton. That TOR talked of "the Palestinian goal of an independent and viable state based on the 1967 lines"—that is, not the Israeli or American goal. Endorsing those borders, even with mutually agreed land swaps, meant granting an immense concession to the Palestinians while they refused to even enter peace talks. It meant tying those talks to lines that, in broad areas in and around Jerusalem and along the Jordan Valley, no longer existed.

Obama's attachment to the 1967 map persisted despite the publication of secret documents—the "PaliLeaks"—from the 2008 peace talks between Abbas and Olmert. These records revealed that, in a future two-state solution, the Palestinian leader was willing to concede parts of the West Bank and East Jerusalem to Israel. Yet, rather than take advantage of this information to reduce tensions with Israel, the White House continued to condemn Israeli construction in some of the very areas that Abbas offered to forgo. Ideology, it seemed to me, still took precedence over an effective U.S. strategy for peacemaking. Instead of taking Abbas to task for not negotiating and for opposing construction in neighborhoods Israel would ultimately retain, the administration rewarded him.

On January 18, the PLO mission to Washington for the first time was allowed to display a Palestinian flag. The upgrade in the mission's status, according to Palestinian envoy Maen Erekat, represented a significant step toward Palestinian statehood. But Ileana Ros-Lehtinen, the newly appointed chairwoman of the House Foreign Affairs Committee, denounced the move as a "scheme to manipulate international acceptance . . . of a Palestinian state while refusing to negotiate directly with Israel." In any event, the Palestinians repaid the gesture a few days later by ignoring American objections and seeking a Security Council condemnation of Israeli settlements.

Sometimes the only thing worse than being a false prophet is being an accurate one. Months before, I had warned administration officials that someday they would have to veto their own settlement policy in the UN. The resolution, sponsored by 130 of the organization's 192 members, and supported by fourteen of the Security Council's states, threatened America's role as the honest broker in the peace process. "We believe strongly that New York is not the place to resolve the . . . outstanding issues between the Israelis and the Palestinians," said Secretary Clinton. U.S. ambassador to the UN Susan Rice worked furiously to convince the Palestinians to rescind or at least temper the resolution. The Palestinians refused and the voting date was set for Friday, February 18.

But would the United States exercise its veto power? Within my glassed-in suite at the embassy, opinion was divided. Deputy Mission Chief Dan Arbell bet that the United States would not oppose the Palestinians, while Chief of Staff Lior Weintraub wagered that it would. I remained uncertain. Senior NSC and State Department officials warned me that a "no" vote would ignite anti-American violence throughout the Middle East. A million Egyptian protesters would burst out of Tahrir Square and overrun the nearby U.S. embassy. When I suggested that Arabs who could now demonstrate against their own leaders might care less about settlements, the answer I received was adamant: "It's a fact. Americans will be massacred."

That certainty no doubt influenced Obama's fifty-minute phone call with Abbas on the evening before the vote. In return for dropping the resolution, the president offered to support a Security Council "investigative mission" to the region to report on the settlements. He would renew America's demand for a total freeze on Israeli construction in the West Bank and East Jerusalem. And he was ready to declare his support for a Palestinian state based on the 1967 lines with mutually agreed swaps. Israel was never consulted about this conversation nor even informed. While acknowledging that Obama and Abbas had talked, the White House spokesman insisted the subject was Egypt.

Answering the phone at the Residence that Thursday night, I could barely hold the receiver to my ear. The Prime Minister's Office had learned of Obama's offer to Abbas from UN sources, not the United States, and was outraged. I was instructed to immediately call congressional leaders and tell them that, by endorsing the Palestinian position on the 1967 lines, the White House had overnight altered more than forty years of American policy. Israel felt abandoned, I was to say. And that is no way to treat an ally.

Before carrying out these orders, I informed Dan Shapiro at the NSC of what I was about to do. He protested, as expected, yet I felt it important not to keep the White House in the dark. The rest of the night was spent contacting senators and congress members from both parties, all of whom seemed shocked. This resulted in a bipartisan letter to the president stating that "it should not be the practice of the U.S. to be conducting backdoor deals . . . that weaken the strategic interests of . . . one of our closest allies." Anti-Israel organizations, meanwhile, urged the president to back the UN resolution, as did J Street. The brassy New York Democratic representative Gary Ackerman, an early J Street supporter, berated the "befuddled" group for being "so open-minded. . . . that its brains have fallen out."

Ironically, Abbas rejected Obama's concessions and, for the first and only time in his presidency, the United States cast its veto in the Security Council. At pains to explain why the administration opposed the condemnation of the settlements that it had repeatedly denounced, Ambassador Rice reasoned that resolving the fundamental issues dividing Israelis and Palestinians was their job, not the UN's. She simultaneously delivered a blistering criticism of a policy that "has undermined Israel's security and corroded hopes for peace and stability in the region . . . violates Israel's international commitments, devastates trust between the parties, and threatens the prospects for peace." The White House was angry—more with Israel than at Abbas—and while Israel won, our victory seemed Pyrrhic.

Worse than the fracas following Biden's visit to Israel and the tensions generated by the settlement freeze, the controversy surrounding the Security Council vote—though largely hidden from the public—

was dire. This time the president kept Israeli leaders in the dark while dealing with issues vital to their national security. The prime minister had incited Congress against the White House. And I felt utterly crushed. Having set out with the goal of maintaining trust between Washington and Jerusalem, I found that objective more distant than ever.

Just how remote became clear in my conversation with Susan Rice three weeks later. I met Susan early in my term, when she came to the Residence for breakfast. Though she was reputedly prickly, I found her to be affable and patently smart, as I helped her plan a trip to Israel. I suggested that she visit Yemin Orde, a youth village on Mount Carmel named for the pro-Zionist British general Orde Wingate, whom I always admired. The village is home to a number of young Ethiopian immigrants who touched Rice emotionally, she later told me. Now, in her office opposite UN headquarters in New York, she sat brooding and peevishly tapping her forehead with her finger. "Israel must freeze all settlement activity," she said bluntly. "Otherwise the United States will not be able to protect Israel from Palestinian actions at the UN." My suggestion—posed in the most velveteen tone—that the American practice of allowing the Palestinians to pocket concessions deprived them of a reason *not* to go to the UN, was angrily rebuffed. So, too, was my speculation that Israel might have preferred a U.S. abstention on the vote rather than the American offers to Abbas. "If you don't appreciate the fact that we defend you night and day, tell us," Rice fumed, practically rapping her forehead. "We have other important things to do."

So, apparently, did the Arabs, who went on protesting against their rulers and completely ignored the Security Council vote. Disproving the alarmists, no American embassy was touched, much less torched. The only criticism came from the Palestinian Authority, which called for a "Day of Rage" against the United States. "The time has come to spit in the faces of Americans," boiled Ibrahim Sansour, an Arab member of the Knesset. "Obama can go to hell."

The terrorists, meanwhile, targeted only Israelis. At 10:30 P.M. on March 11, two teenage Palestinians infiltrated the Itamar settlement near the West Bank city of Nablus. Armed with knives and a rifle, they broke into the Fogel household, slashed the throat of eleven-year-old Yoav, strangled four-year-old Elad, nearly decapitated three-month-old Hadas, and stabbed and shot their parents, Ruth and Ehud.

The Fogel family massacre horrified Americans. The White House condemned it "in the strongest possible terms," and called on the Palestinian Authority to do likewise. But the shock was short-lived. A right-wing, religious community, Itamar was widely associated with the rising settler violence against Palestinians—the uprooting of olive trees, desecrating of mosques, and even alleged shootings. Considered illegitimate by the Obama administration and illegal by the UN, the settlements were subliminally considered fair targets by a growing body of international opinion, including progressive sectors of the United States. To Dan Arbell and Lior Weintraub at the embassy, I confided my sense that the entire settler population had become "Fogelized"—branded as occupiers who essentially had it coming to them. Increasingly, I feared, all Israelis would become "Fogelized," deserving of the rockets fired at us.

The Fogel atrocity made a single headline in American papers and was swiftly replaced by stories about the economy's recovery and the NFL players' strike. Tornados whorled across southern states, inflicting more than three hundred deaths, and famed actress Elizabeth Taylor passed away. Virtually unregistered by the press was the announcement by Mahmoud Abbas of a reconciliation agreement between his al-Fatah organization and Hamas.

The decision incensed Netanyahu—Hamas terrorists had just shot an antitank missile at an Israeli school bus, killing a student—but Obama's reaction was subdued. He merely indicated that he expected any future Palestinian unity government to advance the peace process. That reaction did not surprise me, having speculated back in 2008 that a President Obama could someday recognize a Fatah-Hamas Palestinian government. Still, the refusal to distinguish between Hamas and al-Qaeda needled me. Both were jihadist organizations sworn to kill all Jews, to crush Western civilization, and replace it with a medieval caliphate. I was disappointed and yet nothing could diminish my joy when, on the evening of May 2, my Residence phone rang once again.

Brooke Anderson, NSC chief of staff, said to me simply, "We got him."

"Dead or alive?" I laconically asked.

"Dead."

"Mazal tov."

I hung up and turned to Sally, who was sitting nearby. "They got him," I said, to which she likewise replied, "Mazal tov." Somehow, we both understood Brooke's message, but when I woke up Netanyahu's staff—it was 3 A.M. in Israel—no one quite fathomed. "Got who?" And their reaction, when I told them, was a breathless "Wow."

Osama bin Laden was dead. Two hours after I updated Jerusalem, President Obama appeared on national television and informed the world. "The United States has conducted an operation that killed . . . a terrorist who's responsible for the murder of thousands of innocent men, women, and children," he announced. "We are once again reminded that America can do whatever we set our mind to."

And all of America rejoiced. Crowds spontaneously gathered at Ground Zero in New York, and college students, many of them wrapped in the Stars and Stripes, chanted "U-S-A! U-S-A!" outside of the White House. The exultation over bin Laden's death was another aspect of American culture that was difficult to explain to Israelis, who never celebrate their adversaries' deaths. Yet the people of Israel, too, shared in America's pride. "The battle against terrorism is long and relentless and resolute," Netanyahu, congratulating Obama, declared. "This is a day of victory for justice, for freedom, and for our common civilization." Largely unheard in all this commotion was the reaction of Hamas, which condemned bin Laden's killing as "the continuation of the American oppression of . . . Muslims," and prayed that "the soul of this Arab warrior rests in peace."

The elimination of bin Laden was a triumph for Obama. His call to send in the SEALs was courageous—"gutsy," Defense Secretary Gates later described it—and demonstrated the president's willingness to make high-risk decisions. The iconic photograph of the White House Situation Room during the operation shows him seated low, in a corner, leading seemingly from behind, but leading nonetheless. Around that fateful table sat twelve other individuals, all of whom I personally knew to be formidable. That team, and not just the man who led it, would firmly resist any Israeli attempt to counter an Obama peace plan.

And such a proposal, I concluded, was more imminent than ever. Bin Laden's death had emboldened Obama—rightly, perhaps—to take on new Middle East initiatives. These would likely be unveiled in the president's speech on the region, scheduled for May 19. Netanyahu would arrive in Washington the following day to meet with the president and then address a joint meeting of Congress, at the invitation of Speaker Boehner. I had kept the administration informed about Boehner's offer, which the White House did not oppose, but hardly welcomed. Any presidential reference to the 1967 lines, and a prime ministerial rejection of it, could bring those tension to a head. The events of the previous months—America's veto at the UN, the Fatah-Hamas pact—had indeed kicked up much dust. And ahead, I glimpsed only darkness.

Six Days in May

"We're not sure that the peace process will be mentioned, but even if it is, the section will be very short," senior White House advisors assured me on Wednesday, May 18, 2011, on the eve of Obama's nationally televised address. Titled "U.S. Policy in Middle East and North Africa," the text would furnish a vision of America's future relations with a revolutionary Middle East, an epic follow-up to the historic Cairo speech two years earlier. Israel and the Palestinians were simply not the focus, the advisors said.

I wanted to believe them. Mahmoud Abbas had just published an op-ed in *The New York Times* announcing his intention to declare a Palestinian state unilaterally in the UN and then sue Israel in international courts for illegally occupying that state. The Palestinian leader who renounced violence now revealed that his opposition was largely tactical. Terrorism could not defeat Israel, only stain the Palestinians' reputation and divert global attention from settlements. But a policy designed to isolate, delegitimize, and sanction Israel could bring about its downfall. Lawfare, rather than warfare, became Abbas's weapon of choice.

Yet, in turning to the international courts, Abbas not only threatened Israel, he violated long-standing Palestinian commitments to the United States. These obligated the Palestinian Authority to seek peace only through negotiations. On the eve of February's Security Council vote on settlements, he rejected Obama's offer to embrace the Palestinian position on borders and forced him to veto his own policy. Why, then, would the president now concede the 1967 lines and once again reward Palestinian ill will?

That question recurred to me as I viewed the speech on my office television. My invitation to the event, held at the State Department, had been lost in the embassy's email—fortunately—for I, alone among the ambassadors present, could not have clapped. Instead, I watched as the president praised the bin Laden operation and pledged to support Middle East democracy, and then devoted a full quarter of his remarks to the peace process. Obama reiterated his belief that the status quo was not sustainable, that the Palestinians living west of the Jordan would eventually outnumber the Jews, and that "technology will make it harder for Israel to defend itself." He called for the resumption of talks on security and territory as well as efforts to find a "fair and just" solution to the Jerusalem and refugee issues. But then, at last, came the long-dreaded sentence: "We believe the borders of Israel and Palestine should be based on the 1967 lines with mutually agreed swaps."

The Internet headlines instantly flashed: OBAMA ENDORSES THE '67 BORDERS. The rest of the speech, intended to be one of the most memorable of his term, was roundly ignored. The Palestinian Authority, joined by the Quartet, applauded the 1967 reference, and Republicans condemned it as "throwing Israel under the bus." But the most vehement response came from Netanyahu. Speaking about his scheduled meeting with Obama the following day, Netanyahu said that he would "expect" the president to reaffirm that Israel would never return to the 1967 lines, that Israeli forces would remain in the Jordan Valley, and that Palestinian refugees would not be resettled in Israel. "The Palestinians . . . must recognize Israel as the nation state of the Jewish people, and any peace agreement with them must end all claims against Israel," Netanyahu said expectantly. And I expected sparks.

I already saw fire in Netanyahu's eyes the following dawn after his plane landed at Washington's Dulles Airport. He paused at the top of the stairs, glaring. In place of his usual wave and smile was a grim expression that barely disguised his fury. In the two years since my appointment, I had come to know that anger well—a monumental rage capable, it sounded, of cracking a telephone receiver. But I also gained a more intimate and nuanced perspective of Netanyahu. He is one of the world's most complex, seasoned, divisive, and hounded leaders, and perhaps its loneliest.

His résumé reads more glowingly than even the most sterling of the Obama administration's CVs. It includes Netanyahu's service in Sayeret Matkal, the IDF's equivalent of the Delta Force. The chances of making it into the Unit, as it is popularly known, much less completing its agonizing training, are exceedingly limited. Netanyahu not only finished the course, he became an officer. Once, during a television interview in Israel, the producer introduced himself to me as another Unit veteran. "I can't stand Bibi," he said. "But he was not only an exceptional officer, he was a courageous one." Participating in numerous operations behind enemy lines, wounded in action, Netanyahu also fought in the Yom Kippur War and achieved the rank of captain.

Accepted at Yale and studying at Harvard, he graduated from MIT with an honors BA in architecture and a master's degree in management. He became a successful analyst at the Boston Consulting Group and would remain, at heart, an economist. For a solid hour once, I listened nearly openmouthed as Netanyahu and Bill Clinton theorized about the mechanisms of markets. Next, Netanyahu became a statesman—first an eloquent deputy chief of mission at the Israeli embassy in Washington, and then a media-savvy ambassador to the UN. Returning to Israel in 1988, he entered politics. He distinguished himself as a foreign minister and finance minister, twice headed the government, and was now closing in on Ben-Gurion's record as Israel's longest-serving prime minister. All that, plus Netanyahu was a published author, a superb orator in Hebrew and English, conversant in French, a serious reader, and, in his heyday, famous for his good looks. Who would not be impressed by that résumé, if not intimidated?

And yet respect and fear were far from the only emotions the prime minister evoked. "Recalcitrant, myopic, reactionary, obtuse, blustering, pompous"—were just some of the adjectives that, according to journalist Jeffrey Goldberg, senior White House officials attached to Netanyahu. In the left-leaning Israeli press, especially, vilifying him was close to a national pastime. "He panics quickly in the face of every lurking shadow and every insinuated threat," carped political columnist Ben Caspit. "He plays against himself and always ends in a tie." For Netanyahu, TV analyst Raviv Druker observed, "it's always the world against Netanyahu." Nahum Barnea, Israel's equivalent of Tom Friedman, wrote most cuttingly, "He's not so big that he can afford to be so small."

But the real Tom Friedman was no less censorious. For him, Netanyahu was "annoying" and "disconnected from reality" and, most commonly, "arrogant." No less than their Israeli counterparts, American commentators—almost all of them Jewish—were fiercely indisposed toward Netanyahu. Joe Klein, of *Time,* decried him as "outrageous . . . cynical and brazen." For *The New Yorker*'s David Remnick, Netanyahu was "smug and lacking diplomatic creativity," a firebrand who posed a risk "to the future of his own country." In *The New Republic,* Leon Wieseltier described him as a "gray, muddling, reactive figure . . . a creature of the bunker." When I suggested to Leon that his hatred of Bibi had become pathological, he merely shrugged and admitted, "Yes, I know, it's pathological."

The antagonism sparked by Netanyahu, I gradually noticed, resembled that traditionally triggered by the Jews. We were always the ultimate Other—communists in the view of the capitalists and capitalists in communist eyes, nationalists for the cosmopolitans and, for jingoists, the International Jew. So, too, was Netanyahu declaimed as "reckless" by White House sources and incapable of decision making by many Israelis. He was branded intransigent by *The New York Times,* yet *Haaretz* faulted him for never taking a stand. Washington insiders assailed him for being out of touch with America, and the Tel Aviv *branja*—the intellectual elite—snubbed him for being too American. The Israeli right lambasted him for spinelessness, the left for intractability, the Ultra-Orthodox for heresy, and the secular for pandering to rabbis. All agreed in labeling Netanyahu disingenuous, imperious, and paralyzed by paranoia—qualities not uncommon among politicians.

Nevertheless, Netanyahu remained in office, virtually unopposed. In Israel's often cutthroat political culture, that achievement would be remarkable enough, but was even more astounding in light of Israel's precarious political system. Unlike the U.S. president's four-year term, an Israeli prime minister's can be ended at any time by a no-confidence vote. The commander in chief of the U.S. armed forces is the president, but the IDF's commander is the Israeli government, which the prime minister has to persuade to act. "Your worst day in Washington is Bibi's best day," Ron Dermer periodically reminded me. In contrast to Obama's cabinet, often described as a Lincoln-like "team of rivals," Netanyahu's contained multiple ministers actively seeking to unseat him.

For years, though, none succeeded. No other politician could engender the sense of security that Israelis, for all their grousing about Netanyahu, needed to feel at night when tucking in their children. The majority of Israelis still could not trust anybody else to manage a war, meet the Iranian nuclear threat, and prevent a Gaza-like Hamas state from arising in the West Bank. "One way or another," one Israeli pundit told me, "every election for the past twenty years has been about Bibi." And each time, he had won. Benjamin Netanyahu might not always be loved—not by his people, not even by his own party—but neither could he be replaced.

This was the Netanyahu I had come to know, a man of mighty contradictions. Less than a modern Jew, he reminded me of an ancient Hebrew, a biblical figure with biblical strengths, flaws, appetites, valor, and wrath, scything his foes with rhetorical and political jawbones. Uncannily robust, he retained in his sixties the physical heft and endurance of a Sayeret Matkal captain, only rarely revealing the depths of his exhaustion. Though he tried to get five hours of sleep each night—"Someone's got to drive," he said—Netanyahu rarely got more than four, and was frequently awakened by emergencies.

Pundits often tried to plumb the origins of Netanyahu's outlook, especially the influence of his father, Benzion. A hard-line Zionist historian who nevertheless spent many of his 102 years in the United States, Benzion chronicled the racist roots of anti-Semitism from antiquity through the Inquisition and the Holocaust. That gloomy view of Jewish fate—to be hated for who we are irrespective of how we hide it—darkened the son's worldview, analysts said. Though Netanyahu dismissed such insights as "psychobabble," the images of Masada, Auschwitz, and looming Jewish apocalypses permeated his speeches and even our private talks. "The world sees Israel as the most powerful Middle Eastern state," he once told me, "but that could change overnight, rendering us very vulnerable."

Another influence on his life was his brother, Yoni, the dashing Sayeret Matkal commander who lost his life rescuing Jewish hostages hijacked by terrorists during the 1976 Entebbe Operation in Uganda. Yoni, who would remain young, handsome, and iconic, joined Benzion in setting another bar—the armchair therapists alleged—that Netanyahu could never reach. But no one swayed the prime minister more than his wife, Sara, so the papers claimed. Politically outspoken, a working child psychologist and mother of two, she might be expected to serve as an inspiration for Israelis, especially women. Instead, Sara supplied lurid headlines about her alleged mistreatment of staff members, her overspending, and undue influence on policy.

I never met Benzion or, of course, Yoni, though their photographs hung prominently in Netanyahu's private office. By contrast, I knew Sara, but our contact was limited to the times when she entered the room where her husband and I were mulling over a speech. She offered comments and usually seconded my efforts to make the text less militant. On another occasion, while she was visiting Washington and riding to her only meeting with Michelle Obama, Sara's limo stopped short and pitched her into the front seat, severely gashing her foot. But she refused medical attention and refrained from mentioning the injury at the White House. When I asked her why, she explained that she wanted the conversation's focus to be solely on family, not on her foot. She struck me as strong-willed, fiercely committed to her husband, and never to be crossed. More than those of his late father and brother, the photographs of Sara dominated the prime minister's walls.

So did Churchill's. Like that old-fashioned Englishman, I discerned, Netanyahu was not quite a man of his time. He hated political correctness—futilely, I tried to get him to say "humanity" rather than the "mankind" that feminists resented. He despised the word *paradigm* and shunned all computers and cellphones. Like Churchill, he believed in the power of language, disdained slang and most expletives, and adhered to the British Bulldog's dictum that any good point should be hit repeatedly "with a pile driver—a tremendous whack." And like Churchill warning the world of the looming Nazi threat, Netanyahu viewed himself as a man with an historical mission. Destiny had tasked him with saving the Jewish people, irrespective of the personal price. "I spoke about the Iranian nuclear threat when it was fashionable and I spoke about it when it wasn't fashionable," he declared. "I speak about it now because when it comes to the survival of my country, it's not only my right to speak, it's my duty."

Ever mindful of the opportunity he gave me to achieve a lifelong dream, I liked Netanyahu, but I never became his friend. Rendered suspicious by years of political treacheries, he appeared not to cultivate or even need friendships. *Firgun* was not his forte. And yet, I still empathized with his loneliness, a leader of a country that had little respect for rank and often less for those who wore it. A person, reputedly, of indulgences, he seemed to derive no joy from them, but rather ate and drank with a grim resolve and resignedly smoked his cigars. Except when watching the TV series *Breaking Bad*, Netanyahu never seemed to relax. Rather, he presided over unremitting crises, domestic and foreign, that would break most normal men.

Which was why making him laugh could feel like an act of kindness. Whenever I told him an off-color joke or gave him a funny line for a speech, he kept repeating them and guffawing, sometimes for hours. And along with levity, I gave him loyalty. And honesty. In the face of that Old Testament temper, I offered advice he did not always relish hearing.

One of my recommendations was to conciliate rather than confront Obama, to roll with the president's punches rather than try to outsock him. I believed that Israel needed to maintain the bipartisan support and widen the diplomatic leeway we might later need in war. And preserving the alliance remained my paramount priority. Netanyahu, though, insisted that by giving in on peace issues, Israel would undercut its credibility on the most pressing threat of all: Iran. But in addition to his strategic thinking, my approach ran counter to Netanyahu's personality—part commando, part politico, and thoroughly predatory.

That combination, perhaps, deterred me from telling Netanyahu the most difficult truth of all. Simply: that he had much in common with Obama. Both men were left-handed, both believed in the power of oratory and that they were the smartest men in the room. Both were loners, adverse to hasty decision making and susceptible to a strong woman's advice. And both saw themselves in transformative historical roles.

Their similarities, perhaps as much as their differences, heightened the chances for friction between the president and Netanyahu, I could have told him. But I did not. Rather, as the prime minister descended the stairs to the tarmac that early May 20 morning, I merely said, "Welcome to Washington, sir," and extended my hand. This he gripped and pulled me toward him. With his eyes still flaring, he recalled the cable I sent him months back predicting the president's speech. "You called it right," he whispered.

• • •

An elegant Federal-style structure built in the 1830s, Blair House serves as the official pension of the president, who lives directly across the street. Visiting dignitaries usually stay for two nights, though in view of Netanyahu's protracted visit, the U.S. chief of protocol, the whimsically named but hypercompetent Capricia Marshall, gave us four. Inside, Blair's décor—the candelabra, wainscoting, and brocade—casts an air of antique grace. Weather permitting, decision makers prefer to confer in the trellis-lined courtyard. That is where the prime minister's advisors congregated around him, hunched on wrought-iron chairs, and tried to avoid a crisis.

Or at least mitigate one. Already piqued by Netanyahu's "expectations" of the president, the NSC's Dan Shapiro warned me that confronting Obama over the speech would be "a terrible, terrible mistake." But Netanyahu was incensed over what he regarded as a flagrant violation of trust and could not—as his advisor Ron Dermer put it— "simply roll over." The statement he had prepared to deliver to the president said as much, and I understood my role just then was to take its tone down as many decibels as possible. Hours of fervid debate passed in that courtyard before the prime minister agreed to address his rebuke to the Palestinians, rather than to the president.

Adjourning to the White House, Obama and Netanyahu conferred for two hours alone in the Oval Office, leaving their teams to wrangle in the Roosevelt Room. Secretary of State Clinton assured us that she and her staff had worked hard to insert pro-Israeli positions into the president's speech, which did not even mention Hamas. But the Israelis were still incredulous as to why Obama would want to award Abbas for kicking him in the teeth. I predicted that the Palestinians would simply pocket America's latest concession and then seek UN recognition of an independent state based on 1967 lines. "As in the settlement issue," I once again wagered, "the United States will have to veto its own policy."

The discussion might have grown heated but, just then, the protocol officers entered and invited us to join the principals in the Oval Office. Netanyahu was seated on the edge of his chair and gesturing emphatically at the president. "For there to be peace, the Palestinians will have to accept some basic realities," he began. With his chin propped on his fist, Obama glared as dozens of reporters noted his constricted body language. Netanyahu listed those realities: No return to the 1967 lines, which were half as wide as the Beltway and ignored the large Jewish neighborhoods built beyond them. No negotiations with Hamas, which he called "the Palestinian version of al-Qaeda." No resettling of Palestinian refugees within the Jewish State. Classic Netanyahu, his memorized comments repeated the Jewish legacy of "expulsions, and pogroms and massacres and the murder of millions." Israel, he concluded, remained committed to peace, but "we don't have a lot of margin for error because history will not give the Jewish people another chance."

Crammed in among the press corps, I listened to the prime minister and thought—Pollyannaishly—that the showdown was averted. To my ear, Netanyahu sounded firm but not preachy, and focused exclusively on the Palestinians. As if to reinforce that impression, he and Obama subsequently strolled for twenty minutes across the South Lawn, chatting amicably. Following them at a respectable ambassadorial distance, I heard them refer to each other, as they always did, as Barack and Bibi, and saw the president put his arm around his guest. "Goodbye, my friend," he said.

Only back at Blair House did I learn that the White House was livid. During Netanyahu's remarks, it seemed, Bill Daley, Rahm Emanuel's recent replacement as chief of staff, hissed in Ron Dermer's ear, "Is your boss in the habit of telling off his hosts?" I could imagine Obama's advisors meeting him after his South Lawn stroll and complaining of Netanyahu's unpardonable offense. For the first time in history, they probably raged, a foreign leader had entered the Oval Office and publicly lectured the president.

Within minutes, the word *lecture* clamored from every headline, along with *arrogance* and *affront*. In his memoirs, David Axelrod wrote how congressional and world leaders sometimes resented Obama for "telling them why acting boldly was not only their duty but also served their political needs" Clearly Obama did not appreciate being on the receiving end of such counsel. The result was precisely the crisis I had tried to avoid. The sole task now was to limit its damage.

Leaving Netanyahu and his staff in the courtyard, I phoned every administration official I knew. "If we'd known that your prime minister was going to insult the American people and the president of the

United States we would never have invited him," Bill Daley scolded me. "Yes, you can go to Congress and be hugged by the Republicans, but know that you've got this president for six more years and know that you've got a problem."

Still, I went on phoning, trying to find a way of defusing, or at least containing, the crisis. "What if the prime minister just walked over to the White House and joined the president for a beer?" I suggested, recalling the time Obama shared a beer with the Cambridge police officer who had arrested Professor Henry Louis Gates. The proposal was curtly rebuffed. I nevertheless kept dialing until finally Tom Donilon, the new national security advisor, roared in my ear: "Stop phone-banking the White House!" Netanyahu, I learned, was guilty not only of lecturing Obama but of leaving out any mention of "mutually agreed swaps." Tom shouted, "He maliciously distorted the president's words!"

I had nothing but respect for Tom, and hearing his deeply incensed tone both hurt and startled me. Finally, I proposed that the prime minister put out a statement citing the positive points in the president's speech. This seemed to soothe Tom somewhat, and I thanked him for teaching me a new word, *phone-banking*.

Back in the courtyard, I had to convince Netanyahu and his team of the need to draft that communiqué. Though I expected more resistance, the prime minister clearly realized that he had gone very far indeed and needed to pull back. "It's true we have some differences of opinion, but these are among friends," the statement read. "President Obama has shown his commitment to Israel's security, both in word and in deed, and we're working with him to achieve common goals." Only once I saw the words online—close to midnight—did I finally relax and remember that May 20 was my birthday.

My reprieve, it seemed, was premature. That day's *Wall Street Journal* ran an op-ed by Dr. Dore Gold. A successful ambassador to the UN in the late 1990s, and a senior advisor to several Israeli prime ministers, Dore was part of the prime minister's entourage and present at the Oval Office "lecture." As if to respond to Tom Donilon's charges of distortion, the article addressed the question of swaps. But Obama, it argued, was gullible for believing that Abbas would agree to anything but "minuscule" swaps and would not use the president's words to force Israel back behind indefensible borders. "We want to get this straight," the next call from the West Wing upbraided me. "We invite this guy into the White House and he attacks the president?"

Dore and I had been friends since our Columbia days—we made *aliya* together—and I did my best to defend him. But I could not dispel the administration's belief that he wrote the article on Netanyahu's instructions. The crisis was reignited and threatened to roil out of control. The following morning, Sunday, Obama would address the AIPAC conference. "The president is going to take on the prime minister in front of AIPAC," Bill Daley warned me. "And if he gets booed, so what?" Bill might have been right: any dressing down of Netanyahu before that crowd was liable to unleash acrid reactions. Before me glared the specter of ten thousand Israel supporters jeering the nation's first African-American president. The organization would be indelibly tainted and the U.S.-Israel alliance damaged, perhaps irreparably.

Entering the cavernous Walter E. Washington Convention Center at 10 A.M., I waved at the densely packed audience, displaying optimism in spite of my inner fear. The next twenty-six minutes were some of my most stressful as I waited for Obama to strike back. But, to my immeasurable relief, the president's remarks were benign—Dennis Ross, I later learned, had helped calm him down. Rather than retaliate against Netanyahu, the president reiterated his commitment to the Qualitative Military Edge for Israel and its "unbreakable" bonds with America. Rather than taking Netanyahu to task on the issue of "mutually agreed swaps," the president merely clarified that "Israelis and Palestinians will negotiate a border that is different than the one that existed on June 4, 1967." The definition elicited a single boo that was instantly drowned out by the crowd's ovation, together with my audible sigh.

From the convention center, I rushed back to Blair House to help prepare two more speeches. The first, for AIPAC, was scheduled for the following evening, much to Netanyahu's ire. Unlike American presidents, who annually deliver the State of the Union message and can address their nation at almost any time they choose, Israeli prime ministers have no such stage. Their only opportunity is to speak abroad—often in English—in the morning, in order to be broadcast on Israeli prime time. Unfortunately, the prime minister's appearance closed the AIPAC conference and could not be moved. That lent even greater weight to his televised speech to the joint meeting of Congress, set the next day for 11 A.M., which was 8 P.M. in Israel.

Beyond providing access to the Israeli public, the joint meeting enabled Netanyahu to set out his views on the peace process and Iran, and to highlight the U.S.-Israel alliance. The speech-honing team took up position among the dusty volumes and colonial busts in the Blair House library. Time Warner's Gary Ginsberg again volunteered to help add "music" to Netanyahu's remarks. These contained several groundbreaking concessions, including recognition that a peace accord might leave "some Israeli settlements . . . beyond Israel's borders," and that with "creativity and with goodwill," the Jerusalem issue could be solved. But such largesse could easily be lost in bluster. "You're going to get beat up on this stuff at home," I advised the prime minister; "you might as well emphasize these gestures before Congress." The music was still being pumped in twenty-four hours later when, without sleep, we left for Capitol Hill.

In total, Congress has hosted more than one hundred joint meetings, for the heads of forty countries, but very few—Rabin and Churchill among them—more than once. This was Netanyahu's second address to the combined Senate and House, and the chamber was packed, the atmosphere electric. For a resplendent moment, the claim of across-the-aisle support for Israel was unassailable. Liberal and conservative members, progressives and Tea Partiers, together greeted Israel's leader. Less enthused with the moment were the Israeli journalists who, craning from the mezzanine, snapped photos of Sara Netanyahu.

I, too, was distracted. The Treasury Department had just announced the sanctioning of an Israeli-linked shipping company that was supposedly doing business with Iran. I suspected the timing of the statement might not be coincidental and I was trying to persuade Treasury officials to hold off, at least until after the speech. But an usher threatened to expel me from the hall for using a cellphone. I scarcely had time to give the thumbs-up to Sally and our son Yoav, watching from the gallery, when the prime minister ascended the rostrum.

"My friends, you don't need to do nation building in Israel. We're already built. You don't need to export democracy to Israel. We've already got it. And you don't need to send American troops to Israel. We defend ourselves." At his oratorical best, calm but firm, Netanyahu spoke. The speech had moments of humor—"Think you're tough on one another in Congress? Come spend a day in the Knesset"—as well as pathos: "Too many Israelis have lost loved ones. I lost my brother." He wished a speedy recovery to Palestinian prime minister Fayyad, who had recently suffered a heart attack, and repeatedly thanked Obama for his security support. There was indeed music, but also the hard reiteration of Israel's right to stand up against Iran and its demands for the demilitarization of any future Palestinian state. "It's time for President Abbas to stand before his people and say, 'I will accept a Jewish state,'" Netanyahu insisted. "Those six words will change history."

Slated to run a half hour, the speech lasted nearly twice that long as the members of Congress rose and applauded, rose and cheered—twenty-nine times. The ovations were seamlessly bipartisan and only once, when Netanyahu declared that "Jerusalem must remain the united capital of Israel," did I note that several Democrats refrained from clapping. With the echo of those bravos still resounding in our ears, the prime minister's entourage mounted the motorcade back to Blair House.

There, jubilance still characterized everybody's mood, it seemed, but mine. While Ron Dermer packed his suitcase, I reminded him how Israel was able to defeat the Second Intifada, starting in 2002, because of the "down payment" made by Ehud Barak by offering Arafat a Palestinian state in 2000. Appreciative of our effort to achieve peace, the world gave us the latitude to wage war. Another diplomatic deposit—the Disengagement from Gaza in 2005—a year later enabled Israel to fight against Hezbollah in Lebanon. And by proposing yet another Palestinian state to Mahmoud Abbas in 2008, Ehud Olmert put the money in Israel's diplomatic bank account necessary to battle Hamas. "What if we have to go to war again?" I asked Ron. "We'll be writing blank checks on an empty account."

My metaphor made sense to Ron, a Wharton and Oxford graduate in economics. But he was also a former football player, accustomed to taking hits, and he merely shrugged. The rest of the entourage, meanwhile, smiled, as they posed for formal photographs with the prime minister and witnessed his traditional signing of the Blair House guestbook. Throughout, I remained on the cellphone, soliciting reactions to the speech from congressional leaders, Democrats and Republicans alike. Both sounded surprised by Netanyahu's combative tone. "But what about the 'settlements beyond Israel's borders'?" I asked them. "What about the solution to Jerusalem?" Nobody re-called even hearing it. So much for music.

"I sure hope that Israel's Prime Minister, Benjamin Netanyahu, understands that the standing ovation he got in Congress," Tom Fried-man wrote, omitting the other twenty-eight ovations, "was bought and paid for by the Israel lobby." I called Tom the moment the article came online and urged him to retract it. "You've confirmed the worst anti-Semitic stereotype, that Jews purchase seats in Congress." But Tom remained impenitent. "For every call I've received protesting, I've gotten ten congratulating me for finally telling the truth," he said. "Many of those calls were from senior administration officials."

I had no reason to doubt Tom's claim. On the contrary, it merely confirmed what I already feared. Netanyahu, in the administration's view, had lectured the president and mobilized Congress against him. By embracing the 1967 lines, Israeli leaders felt, Obama validated the Palestinian position and violated their trust. The previous two years revealed severe strains in the U.S.-Israel alliance, but the events of the past six days had torqued those tensions to the snapping point. De-parting from Dulles Airport, Netanyahu again mentioned how I fore-saw the crisis and "called it right." For once, I wished I had called it wrong.

In Sunshine or in Shadow

To the saw of a fiddle and the trill of a flute, I exuberantly thumped my bodhrán. A lover of Irish music since my first trip to the Emerald Isle in the seventies, I returned in 2004 with my daughter Lia on her pre-army trip and traveled from pub to pub relishing jigs and reels. In the sea-slapped village of Dingle, we watched a young drummer pro-duce rapturous rhythms on his round, goat-skinned bodhrán (pro-nounced "booran" or "bowran"). "Someday I'm going to learn to play that," I swore to Lia. And I did.

Back in Jerusalem, I found Abe Doron, formerly of Mexico City and a veteran of six years' touring with *Riverdance*, Leprechaun-like and Israel's only certified bodhrán teacher. Those hours in Abe's mag-ical studio, adorned with djembes and darbukas, eventually enabled me to come home from a trying day, put on a Chieftains disk, and pound my stress away. By 2011, I could bring Abe and Evergreen—one of several Celtic bands that make Israel an Irish music mecca—to Washington, D.C., and beat my bodhrán with them before seventy Irish-Americans.

The event was another outreach to influential American communities. Treated to Kosher *ropa vieja* at the Residence, Hispanic leaders clapped to the malagueñas of David Broza, Israel's world-class Spanish guitarist and singer. Over a feast of luleh kebabs and salad shirazi, Iranian-Americans—Muslims and Jews—cried at the Farsi ballads of the Tehran-born Israeli superstar, Rita. There was an Israeli-Greek night, complete with souvlaki and Laïkó dancing, and several evenings with Arab and Israeli performers who proved that music can bridge the widest divides. Chinese ambassador Chin Wa and his wife laughed in delight as our son Yoav surveyed the rich history of Chinese-Jewish relations—in fluent Mandarin. Washington columnist David Ignatius, who was also present at the dinner, told me that it was the most extraordinary diplomatic moment he had witnessed in twenty years.

But this was my favorite reach-out by far: Irish night, with its gourmet fish and chips, its ample bottles of Jameson and Guinness on tap, and the Israeli musicians of Evergreen accompanied by the Israeli ambassador. Around candlelit tables sat union heads, Congress members, representatives of the administration, and, of course, my Irish counterpart, Ambassador Michael Collins. The special guest, though, was Martin O'Malley, who, when not governing Maryland, performed Irish music professionally. He praised me as "the best bodhrán player in the entire Washington diplomatic corps," and then led the audience in singing his enchantingly fitting composition, "Where Is My Tribe?"

Sally adored hosting these evenings, and Irish Night was no exception. She meandered from table to table, engaging in the effortless Washington conversation she had mastered, refilling mugs and shot glasses. She never ceased beaming. Long after the last invitee departed, we stayed up jamming with Evergreen. Then, around dawn, we changed into casual clothes and left for Sibley Hospital, where she would undergo surgery for breast cancer.

The two weeks since she received the diagnosis had been harrowing, though the intensity of our schedules prevented us from dwelling on it. Only now did reality smack. Even then, not until the surgeon approached me in the waiting room hours later did I admit how terrified I was. And relieved. The operation was thoroughly successful, the surgeon reported. Though further treatments would be needed, Sally's cancer was contained.

Sally's tumor had been detected in a routine examination by Dr. David Jacobs, an impish internist, quirky and cantankerous. David not only saved Sally but also kept me functioning, in spite of many sleepless nights and almost no weekends, with his arsenal of anti-cold and -fever medications. He did this entirely for free, 24/7, out of his unswerving love for Israel. But while staving off illness, David could not immunize me from the tragedies that inescapably plague ambassadors.

There was the family friend from Los Angeles whose son had vanished on a photography trip to Jordan. With the help of Israeli officials who interfaced with authorities in Amman, the young man's body was eventually located at the bottom of a Petra ravine. I had to make that phone call. Another call went to the parents of Kristine Luken, an American Christian who wore a silver Star of David over her heart. Palestinian terrorists kidnapped Kristine outside of Jerusalem, tore off her star, and plunged a knife where it had hung. There were Israeli families who lost loved ones in the United States and needed visas to attend the funerals, and Americans without passports who begged to bury a deceased parent in Israel. And, most painfully, there were the parents of missing Israeli soldiers who came beseeching Washington's help. Behind the white-tie dinners and glittering receptions—though I could never allow myself to show it—an ambassador frequently copes with gloom. Three years after discovering Sally's cancer in time, and an hour after winning big at blackjack, the sixty-three-year-old Dr. David Jacobs dove into a Las Vegas pool and died of heart failure.

One of my most dismal moments came at the end of my second year in office, on the day I emerged from a car into North Carolina air so steamy I could scarcely breathe. Fortunately, only a short walk separated the parking lot from the air-conditioned building where I filled out several forms and submitted to a series of physical pat-downs. Then, after passing through sophisticated detectors, I was escorted by an armed guard down cinder-block halls to a barren holding room. There, with his hands folded on a tabletop, smiling wistfully at me, sat Jonathan Pollard.

He rose to greet me, a man I recognized from the posters plastered on Jerusalem walls but looking older and sallower in person. We were not alone. Together with an Israeli consular representative and activists working for Pollard's release was his wife, Esther. A religious woman with her hair traditionally covered and her expression grim, she spoke of her husband's worsening health and kidney failure. After a few moments' chatting, the others stepped back and allowed Jonathan and me—our words recorded by a federal note taker—to talk.

Insisting on action from Israel, not visits, Jonathan had not met with an Israeli official in three years, yet we spoke like old Jerusalem neighbors. He talked about my books on the Six-Day War and America in the Middle East, and solicited my opinion of other historians in my field. His mind, unlike his appearance, was undiminished. His background, intellectual interests, and passion for Israel made him starkly familiar to me. But our realities could not have been more disparate.

Inevitably, we turned to those realities. "I have no good news," I told him candidly. Leaning forward, I updated him on the unending efforts on his behalf, none of which had proved fruitful. The previous month, I had asked the Justice Department for permission to allow Jonathan to visit his dying father. Later, I requested that he be able to attend his father's funeral. Both of my appeals were denied. "All I can tell you, is that the Government and State of Israel will never cease asking for clemency," I rasped. "Prime Minister Netanyahu and President Peres have raised the issue, and will continue to raise it, at every White House meeting."

Now it was Jonathan's turn to arch toward me and whisper. He spoke not about his own torment but Esther's. Tears welled in his eyes. I listened and wished nothing more than to offer him some filament of hope. But I had none. All I could promise was to keep working, keep pleading, and to visit him again whenever he wanted.

An hour later, I exited the Butner Corrections Complex and again collided with the impenetrable Carolina heat. I inhaled nevertheless, savoring the air of freedom. While Jonathan Pollard remained behind bars, I was at liberty to cross the parking lot and drive away, and return to my life in Washington.

Staggering into the Residence that evening, I fell into an armchair and remained there, listless. I remembered how, in the impossibly tense weeks leading up to the Six-Day War, then IDF chief of staff

Yitzhak Rabin had also collapsed into a chair at his home and found himself powerless to rise. Though not faced with a possibly cataclysmic war, I could still sympathize with Rabin. The past twelve months had been rife with crises: the flotilla incident and the Iranian nuclear controversy, the Carmel forest fire and the conflagrations sweeping the Middle East, the erosion of Israel's Qualitative Military Edge and the constant controversies ignited by the peace process. All that and Sally's ordeal—truly a year of affliction.

Then I recalled my initial doubts about how long I could last in my position. Now, two years later, I was still in office, battered perhaps but crisis-tested. I had grown into my role, gained the respect of the lion's share of my embassy, and was no longer ignored when U.S. and Israeli officials mingled in the Roosevelt Room. Those achievements would prove crucial, I knew, as the alliance faced fateful challenges. The two countries I loved needed to unite on issues vital to both and yet they remained separated ideologically and even strategically. Whether I could succeed in bridging those divides remained uncertain. Nevertheless, whatever the afflictions, an ambassador's job is to persist. And this ambassador, gripping the armrests and emitting a groan, rose and went back to work.

ROLLER
COASTER

As IF SOMEONE BLEW A WHISTLE, BY THE MIDDLE OF 2011, MOST OF the major players had changed. Whether in Israel or in the United States, the rigors of government—the sleepless weeks, the perpetual tensions, the inescapable scrutiny of the press—inexorably wear one down. Frequently, I would leave some White House meeting after midnight and see most of the lights burning. And many still burned after dawn. In Israel, too, the pace of public service could be grueling. "It seemed the Israelis never slept," Condoleezza Rice once observed. "They worked late into the night, making it convenient to reach them." But while Americans expect their presidents to take much-needed vacations, Israelis begrudge their prime ministers little more than a weekend. Nevertheless, the attrition rate is similarly high in both countries. Among senior officials, especially, the longevity rate is roughly two years.

Two years into the Obama administration, Tom Donilon replaced Jim Jones as the national security advisor. Right up to the end of his service, the general remained convinced that the peace process and Iran were "two sides to the same coin," and that the Palestinian issue had "broader implications that reached all the way to Afghanistan, Morocco, and Nigeria." Donilon seemed far less wedded to the "linkage" doctrine, and less inclined to criticize Israel. Indeed, he had that "warm spot in his heart for the Jewish State" that Israelis always search for in American leaders. My age almost exactly, soft-spoken, and deeply grounded in the administration—his wife and brother advised the Bidens—Donilon became the ideal interlocutor on sensitive issues ranging from the Arab Spring to Iran's nuclear program.

Donilon auspiciously came in, but, on the downside, Dennis Ross exited. Respecting the wishes of his long-patient wife, Debbie, he resigned after two years, leaving an unfillable void. Virtually alone among Middle East experts, Dennis was never "stovepiped" into specializing in a certain country or topic, but possessed a broad regional and historical view. And while he was never "Netanyahu's man in the White House," as his detractors claimed, Dennis did present the prime minister's perspective in internal administration debates and countered those advocating a tougher line toward Israel. Now that check was gone.

So, too, was Dan Shapiro. Rather than return him to civilian life, though, Obama appointed Dan as America's ambassador to Israel. Religiously observant and a Hebrew speaker, Dan regarded the assignment as the realization of a lifelong dream—much as I had mine. But just as congressmen occasionally introduced me as "our ambassador in Tel Aviv," many Israelis would be curious as to where Dan's first allegiance lay, with the United States or the Jewish people. Yet Dan, I was sure, would set them straight and represent Obama unreservedly. Indeed, irrespective of the alliance's strains, he soon became the most popular U.S. envoy in decades, embraced by the Israeli public. But his promotion was a letdown for me. Dan's replacement, Steve Simon, a former Orthodox Jew turned dapper apostate in pinstripes and suspenders, though highly intelligent, lacked his predecessor's access to the president. Israel lost another voice capable of speaking up for us in the Oval Office.

The whistle also sounded for George Mitchell, who returned to his native Maine. The Middle East, he learned, was not Northern Ireland, and Britain and the IRA not Israel and the PLO. The role of special envoy became less unique as others—Dennis Ross and Hillary Clinton—shuttled between Jerusalem and Ramallah. But the secretary of state also announced that she would not seek a second term in that office, and gradually distanced herself from the peace process.

This was another loss. In spite of the often-sharp differences between them, the secretary and the prime minister enjoyed an easy rapport based on long acquaintance and mutual respect. In addition to having that "warm place in her heart for Israel," I believed she also understood us even when we disagreed. Once, when she intimated that Israelis might be too prosperous and secure to feel the need to make peace—echoing a Tom Friedman claim—I complained to Dennis Ross. "As a Jew and a father, I'm offended by the suggestion I care more about my salary than my children's safety." I further recalled that when the Second Intifada denied Israelis any security, their support for a two-state solution was close to zero. "Now, with security restored, seventy percent of Israelis back a two-state deal." Dennis conveyed my reaction to the secretary. She never used that argument again.

While Clinton prepared to transition out at the end of Obama's first term, new deputy secretaries of state moved in. In place of Jim Steinberg came Bill Burns, a consummate diplomat and mensch. Into the outsize shoes of Jack Lew—future director of the Office of Management and Budget, White House chief of staff, and Treasury secretary—stepped Tom Nides, a former Morgan Stanley chief operating officer. Irreverent, hard-working, highly intelligent, and warm, Nides quickly earned my affection and trust.

These were substantive appointments, yet I could not help sensing that the State Department had been sidelined on many Middle Eastern issues. These were now in the White House's hands and in those of an even tighter circle of presidential advisors. Obama's initial "team of rivals" was being replaced by an intimate band of those who enforced his opinions. And deep within that inner loop stood Denis McDonough.

Replacing Donilon as deputy national security advisor, the tall, blond, and athletic McDonough was indefatigable—seemingly indifferent to food and rest—and categorically loyal to the president. His heart, unlike Donilon's, did not have "that warm place for Israel," but his head accurately conveyed Obama's thoughts. I needed to hear them, however blistering, and knew that I could always count on McDonough to give them to me ultra-straight.

And still, the whistle blew. Across the Potomac, it signaled the retirement of Defense Secretary Gates and his replacement by the former CIA director Leon Panetta. Though he worked unconditionally to reinforce Israel's defense, Gates remained allergic to Netanyahu, who he reportedly claimed was unappreciative of U.S. aid to Israel and indifferent to its growing international isolation. A warm Italian-American who, as a congressman, enjoyed wide American Jewish support, Panetta would not be as standoffish as his predecessor but would nevertheless preserve his policies. Admiral Mike Mullen, meanwhile, turned the chairmanship of the Joint Chiefs of Staff over to General Martin Dempsey. I developed a genuine affection for Mullen, but had yet to meet his successor. At Langley, General Petraeus moved into Panetta's CIA spot, and at Treasury, the veteran Iran sanctioner Stuart Levy switched off with David Cohen, who proved to be just as diligent in plugging sanction loopholes.

Just keeping track of these transformations, much less assessing their impact on the U.S.-Israel relationship, required enormous effort. Many of the relationships that I had established had to be rebuilt from scratch and in real time, as crises crisscrossed the Middle East. Access to the highest level of decision making, so vital to maintaining an already-strained alliance, also had to be regained.

And few contacts were more sorely missed than Rahm Emanuel. Now that he had left his White House chief of staff job for the mayoralty of Chicago, there was no one to call me in the middle of the night and reprimand my government, no one to pump a half finger into my chest—as he did at a swank reception shortly after Netanyahu's last visit to Washington—and bark, "You do not fucking come to the White House and fucking lecture the president of the United States!"

Rahm's critics continued to debate the degree to which he bore responsibility for the tensions between Washington and Jerusalem, but I never once questioned Israel's integral place in his soul. Just before leaving office, Rahm took his family to Israel for his son's Bar Mitzvah. I was able to arrange security as well as visits to several frontline IDF units and lunches with the troops. Exiting the stage after receiving an honorary doctorate from Yeshiva University, I was called aside for an urgent phone call from Rahm. "I've just been walking with my wife on the Tel Aviv beach and people just kept coming up to us and wishing us, 'Mazal tov! Mazal tov!' What a country!" Rahm was crying.

Yet the whistle blew not only in Washington, but also in the Jewish State. Uzi Arad, the brainy and mercurial national security advisor, stepped down in favor of the no less cerebral but unflappable Yaakov Amidror. A classic curmudgeonly ex-general, Amidror also sported a trademark right-wing beard and large knitted *kippa*. Behind that salty veneer, though, he could be surprisingly sweet and politically moderate. Elsewhere in the Prime Minister's Office, the shake-up brought in a new military secretary and a new chief of staff. Netanyahu refused to extend the term of Mossad chief Meir Dagan—he reportedly departed resentful—and appointed Tamir Pardo, whose quiet civil servant façade masked a daring record of Sayeret Matkal missions, including Entebbe. Major General Benny Gantz, the former defense attaché in Washington, became IDF chief of staff. I first met Benny a decade earlier during reserve duty, a tall, quiet, honest man—an American might imagine him living in a log cabin—and told Sally that someday he would command the army. For once, it felt good to be right.

Far less gratifying was the closest shake-up of all, within the embassy. Deputy Chief of Mission Dan Arbell left, as did Lior Weintraub, my chief of staff. The Foreign Ministry granted Lior an extra year in Washington as the embassy spokesman, but in the Aquarium—that glassed-in ambassadorial suite—I found myself suddenly alone. Dan's and Lior's replacements were neither as competent nor remotely as trustworthy, and there was no one to confide in, no one to play the devil's advocate role of *iphah mi'stabra*. Fortunately, two new office assistants arrived from Israel—Aviv Sarel, creative, charming, and proficient; and Lee Moser, a close friend of my eldest son. Lee, in particular, proved to be indispensable, possessed of a saber-sharp political mind and an effervescent personality that swiftly became renowned throughout Washington. Though only in their midtwenties and deceptively delicate-looking, Aviv and Lee effectively kept the Aquarium shark-free.

The constellation of American and Israeli officials revolved, but the stars at their centers stayed fixed. Benjamin Netanyahu, still managing an unwieldy coalition of Likudniks, Laborites, and religious party leaders, reached the height of his power. Most of the American and Israeli press still lambasted him daily for not exploiting that strength to make a breakthrough to peace and, alternatively, for brandishing his musculature before Iran. If not nationally loved, he remained politically unchallenged—as *Time* magazine begrudgingly crowned him, "King Bibi."

Barack Obama's standing, by contrast, crested. Given his near deification two years earlier, such a decline was inevitable. Further accelerating the president's descent was the intractable split between Democrats and Republicans, the incessant battles over health care, and the economy's languor. But his personality, too, played a part. Ever cerebral, he seemed to prefer contemplation to leadership—"the Analyst in Chief," critics called him—and ideas to hands-on action. The coldness I detected in his autobiography and the insularity he still displayed hampered him from establishing cross-the-aisle understandings or even enduring friendships within his own party. A similar chill distanced him from traditional American allies—not only Israel—whose ambassadors complained to me of the administration's unprecedented aloofness. "Obama's problem is not a tin ear," one of my European colleagues lamented, "it's a tin heart."

Throughout, I continued to observe Obama's ambivalence about America's place among nations and its use of power. Rhapsodic in his speeches about his countrymen's can-do approach, he evinced less enthusiasm about flexing their might. "Whether we like it or not, we remain a dominant military superpower," he declared. Such words—unimaginable in the mouths of John Kennedy, Ronald Reagan, or Bill Clinton—discomfited Israelis and others overseas who viewed as miraculous the fact that the world's greatest democracy was also its strongest state. Yet nowhere was Obama's reticence more pronounced, and the anxiety it aroused higher, than in the still-tumultuous Middle East.

Gone from Obama's public remarks were any further references to his Muslim family ties, his ability to bridge the Middle East and the West. Gone was his middle name, Hussein, which only his detractors remembered. Instead, while listening to him address four thousand guests at the National Prayer Breakfast, I heard the president speak for the first time of his profound Christian faith and refer to others on the dais as "my brothers in Christ." Though still insistent on calling jihadists "violent extremists" rather than radical Islamists, Obama authorized drone strikes that killed more than 2,400 Muslims, including hundreds of civilians. The Guantánamo camp for Islamist prisoners he pledged to close down remained obdurately open. The vision of a United States at peace with the Middle East was supplanted by the patchwork of American military intervention in Libya, withdrawal from Iraq, indifference to Syria, and entanglement with Egypt. The president who once praised the "true greatness of the Iranian people and civilization" now weighed congressional demands for intensified sanctions against Iran. And the Palestinians, on whom Obama lavished so much political capital, turned their backs on him and prepared to seek statehood in the UN.

Throughout, the president never ceased reaffirming his commitment to the Jewish State. "Israel's security will always be at the top tier of considerations of how America manages its foreign policy," he told a gathering of pro-Israel Democrats, "because it's the right thing to do, because Israel is our closest ally and friend." Omitting any mention of settlements or Jerusalem, Obama referenced the Arab Spring and the need for new approaches. "It's not going to be sufficient for us just to keep on doing the same things we've been doing and expect somehow that things are going to work themselves out." Obama's Middle East policies appeared to be heading in many directions at once, with untold ramifications for Israel.

In the summer of 2011, as a thicker-set but still game Netanyahu squared off against a grayer but no less subdued Barack Obama, I signed my second contract. The Israeli ambassador's term runs for two years—a respectable period followed by a deservedly prolonged rest—but can be extended for an additional year at the prime minister's request. When I asked him if he wanted me to stay on, Netanyahu grunted, "Yeah, yeah," and so I signed.

"Israeli Ambassador Michael Oren looks older and thinner than he did when he took office," began an interview with me in *The Washington Post*. My weight was indeed down—there was little time to eat—and my hair had skipped the gray stage and gone directly to white. It would grow hoarier still as the alliance entered a period of nerve-racking twists and dips. Visiting amusement parks as a child, I always shied away from the scarier rides, preferring the stable ignominy of merry-go-rounds. But now, as a third-year ambassador, I took my seat, strapped in, and braced myself for the diplomatic equivalent of a roller coaster.

Job 1:16

Dressed in brown uniforms indistinguishable from the Egyptian army's, wielding RPGs, machine guns, and grenades, twelve terrorists infiltrated into southern Israel. At four points along the unfenced Sinai border, they set up ambushes and, at midday on August 18, opened fire. Six Israeli civilians riding in passing vehicles were murdered, along with two soldiers who rushed to the scene. IDF units eventually shot all twelve of the attackers, but in the melee, five Egyptian troops also died. Though Israel could not determine exactly who killed the Egyptians, it nevertheless apologized to Cairo. The gesture failed to appease Egypt's interim military government, which promptly withdrew its ambassador from Tel Aviv.

Also unassuaged were the thousands of frustrated protesters still clustered in Tahrir Square. From demanding reforms and vengeance against Mubarak, they turned their anger toward a nearby building, the top three floors of which housed the Israeli embassy. One demonstrator climbed up a drainpipe seventeen stories to the roof, triumphantly tore off the Israeli flag, and hurled it to the ecstatic mob below.

Israeli warplanes, meanwhile, bombed terrorist sites in Gaza—the presumed source of the border attack—and Palestinian groups fired rockets at Israeli cities. Most of the missiles were intercepted in midair by Iron Dome. Contrary to Obama's claim that "technology will make it harder for Israel to defend itself," Iron Dome, developed and deployed in a mere four years, became the first antiballistic system in history to work in combat. Still, in spite of generous U.S. aid, only two Iron Dome batteries had so far been produced, not enough to shield the entire south. And with a success rate of 85 percent, a few rockets got through. One killed a civilian in Beersheba, where our daughter Lia was still studying.

But while dwelling on this peril, I suddenly had to grapple with Sally's. Every August, she and I returned to Jerusalem to attend her sister Joanie's memorial. This gave me an opportunity to hold direct discussions at the Prime Minister's Office, where, while working late, I learned that Sally fell ill. That night, she underwent emergency surgery for a ruptured appendix at the Hadassah Medical Center. Bloated, greenish, spiking a high fever, my wife was scarcely recognizable. I was frantic but the on-duty doctors told me not to worry, that they were there for her. As grateful as I was frazzled, I hugged them and asked them their names. Muhammad and Osama.

Later that week, when I returned to Washington, I told the story of the two Arab-Israeli doctors who treated my wife to the guests at the first-ever Israeli Iftar. The notion of hosting a Ramadan break-fast meal at the Residence first occurred to me in 2009, but arranging it required a two-year battle with Israeli bureaucracy and skittish security officials. No sooner was that completed, though, than the search for Muslims willing to participate began. Most of the Arab invitees declined, and I feared the guest book would remain blank. But then Farah Pandith, an extraordinary human being and the first woman to serve as the State Department's representative to the Muslim communities, accepted my invitation. So, astonishingly, did sixty-five others. They prayed on rugs spread on my dining room floor and ate halal-supervised kebabs prepared in the kitchen. We listened to Farah, together with White House anti-Semitism monitor Hannah Rosenthal, speak about the need for understanding in this time of strife. Imam Abdullah Antepli, Duke University's inspiring Muslim chaplain, delivered a stirring sermon about peace. And I spoke about Muhammad and Osama, the physicians who showed me new horizons of hope, and wished all those present, "Ramadan karim."

The Iftar, the first of three the embassy would hold, remained one of my proudest moments. But there was little time to revel in that pride due to violent events in Egypt. Rioters on September 9 returned en masse to the Israeli embassy, took sledgehammers to a newly built protective wall, and stormed to the upper stories. Inside were six Israelis—the deputy chief of mission and a security team—who were barricaded behind steel doors. Their families had been sent home at the outset of the Arab Spring, and the rest of the embassy staff, including Ambassador Yitzhak Levanon and some ninety others, were cloistered in unmarked suburban houses. Still, all were in danger and none more so than the six who listened as the hammers began smashing through steel.

Called to the embassy in the middle of that Friday night, I began liaising between the NSC and General Amos Gilad at the Defense Ministry. The United States offered its unconditional help and Anne Patterson, America's ambassador in Cairo, intrepidly fulfilled this commitment. Years later, Israeli diplomats still credited her with saving their lives.

Six Israelis needed to be extricated from the embassy. One way was via the roof, equipped with an escape ladder, but a mob had collected there, too. The only hope was to break through to the top floor with Egyptian Special Forces. The army, though present at the scene, watched impassively, while its generals simply refused to answer their phones.

I experienced this nightmare through the phone receiver, as the NSC updated me on the repeated efforts of Secretaries Clinton and Panetta to reach their Egyptian counterparts. President Obama also intervened. But still no Egyptian commandos. Netanyahu, meanwhile, passed anguished hours in the Foreign Ministry situation room speaking with the entrapped Israelis in Cairo. "We're coming to get you," the prime minister quietly assured the chief of security, a young man named Jonathan. "I'm with you and I won't leave you, ever." I relayed these developments back and forth between Washington and Jerusalem. I, too, sought to stay focused, monitoring the secret evacuation of Ambassador Levanon and his staff to Israel.

"The Special Forces will be there soon," the NSC's Steve Simon informed me. "Tell your guys inside not to open fire on them." I passed on this news to Gilad, who, in turn, informed me that only a single door now separated the rioters from the six. Jonathan and his men, highly trained, would surely shoot the first intruders to break into the embassy and would keep on firing until their ammunition ran out. "We're almost there," Netanyahu told them. "Stay calm." But I was fraught, picturing the dozens of people who would be killed, the Egyptians shot and the Israelis dismembered. I thought about the peace agreement that might never be salvaged.

The Egyptian commandos arrived, literally at the last moment, burst into the embassy, hastily disguised the six Israelis as demonstrators, and smuggled them out. They were saved—and the peace preserved—yet I had to wonder whether any rescue mission would have been mounted without American intercession with the Egyptian leaders. From Anne Patterson to the president, they had all been there, allies when we most needed them.

And in Egypt, we would need them still. Terrorists repeatedly blew up the Sinai pipeline that supplied Israel with natural gas, and Egyptian military forces, exceeding limits established by the peace treaty, concentrated near the Israeli border. The extremist Muslim Brotherhood was poised to dominate the Egyptian elections, scheduled for early 2012. If the organization won, it would extend massive aid to Hamas, the Brotherhood's branch in Gaza. At the same time, Syria remained riven by civil bloodshed that drove a half million refugees into Jordan. Iran exploited this chaos to transfer advanced missiles to Hezbollah terrorists in Lebanon and to accelerate work on its nuclear program.

This overwhelmingly bleak situation reminded me of the book of Job, specifically chapter 1, verse 16, in which successive messengers arrive to inform the biblical hero that his loved ones have died and his worldly possessions vanished. "While he was speaking, there came another," Job responds sparsely in ancient Hebrew. But the modern Israeli reader understands Job's reply as "I've barely learned of this latest catastrophe and already there's news of the next." Israel had not yet internalized one crisis when others erupted. These, too, tested Israel's ties with the United States, and few more intensely than UDI.

• • •

If the initials of the Qualitative Military Edge were the three most cardinal in the U.S.-Israel alliance and those of highly enriched uranium (HEU) the most dangerous, UDI—standing for Unilaterally Declared Independence—ranked among the most controversial. They stood for Abbas's effort to obtain UN recognition of Palestinian statehood, sidestepping the peace process and the United States. The Palestinian leader never forgave Obama for backing down on the settlements issue. "[He] suggested a full settlement freeze and I accepted," Abbas complained to *Newsweek*'s Dan Ephron. "We both went up the tree. But Obama came down with a ladder and he removed the ladder and said to me, jump." He further resented America's abrupt abandonment of Mubarak. "You will get chaos or the Muslim Brotherhood or both," he warned the administration. Having lost faith in the White House, Abbas once again planned to use Obama's own words against him. He spoke of the president's "promise," presented in his speech before the last UN General Assembly, to create a sovereign Palestine within one year. Now that year had passed and Abbas quoted Obama in seeking to receive, concession-free, the state he refused to achieve through negotiations.

"We are facing a political tsunami," warned Defense Minister Barak. He and Netanyahu viewed UDI as a Palestinian plan to sue Israel in international courts for illegally occupying a UN member state. The penalty could be sanctions on Israel, with devastating economic results. "2011 is going to be like . . . 1973," wrote *Haaretz* columnist Ari Shavit, evoking the specter of the Yom Kippur War. "A diplomatic siege from without and a civil uprising from within will grip Israel in a stranglehold."

Fortunately for Israel, the administration was determined to avoid revisiting the previous year's trauma of vetoing its own policy in the Security Council. American diplomats labored to prevent UDI from ever coming to a vote. Israel fully supported this position and, working in tandem with the State Department, I lobbied the ambassadors of rotating member states such as Gabon and Colombia. But while united in the fight against UDI, Israel and the administration were deeply split over how to react if it succeeded.

Even if the Security Council rejected the Palestinians' bid, other UN bodies might not. In that case, long-standing congressional legislation mandated the immediate closure of the PLO's Washington office, the cessation of U.S. aid to the Palestinian Authority, and the defunding of any UN agency that recognized Palestine. Israel strongly endorsed all three repercussions, which the White House just as vehemently opposed.

"You don't want the fucking UN to collapse because of your fucking conflict with the Palestinians, and you don't want the fucking Palestinian Authority to fall apart either," Deputy Secretary Tom Nides warned me at the State Department.

Exactingly civil in public, American officials, behind the scenes, often revel in four-letter words. Israelis, by contrast, usually avoid expletives, perhaps because biblical Hebrew supplied them with none. When in Washington, though, I spoke like a Washingtonian. "No, Israel does not want the fucking UN to collapse," I replied to Nides. "But there are plenty of Tea Party types who would, and no shortage of Congress members who are wondering why they have to keep paying Palestinians who spit in the president's eye. You don't want to cut off aid, you don't want to defund the UN or close the PLO office, so what will you do?"

Nides slumped into his Louis XVth chair and looked beat. The answer to my question was apparently "nothing."

I reported that to Netanyahu by paraphrasing an old movie we both remembered. "Being Palestinian," I said, "means never having to say you're sorry." The administration's response, less lyrical, appeared in a Jeffrey Goldberg article in which unnamed government sources said the White House would "oppose [UDI] in spite of Netanyahu, not to help him." The president's dislike of the prime minister, Jeff wrote, "has deepened in a way that could ultimately be dangerous for Israel."

On September 20, then, while rushing to New York to receive Netanyahu, I had every reason to expect another showdown. As anticipated, Abbas's speech to the General Assembly cited the Muslim and Christian connection to Palestine and ignored the Jews', quoted Obama's "promise" of the previous year, and called on the Security Council to recognize Palestine. Netanyahu, true to form, highlighted the Holocaust and the Iranian nuclear threat. More untypically, the prime minister concluded on a movingly musical note: "President Abbas, I extend my hand—the hand of Israel—in peace. . . . We are both sons of Abraham. We share the same patriarch. We dwell in the same land. Our destinies are intertwined. Let us realize the vision of Isaiah, 'The people who walk in darkness will see a great light.' "

But the starkest surprise came in Obama's remarks. After extolling the democratic victories of the Arab Spring and reaffirming the need for a negotiated two-state solution, the president launched into his most pro-Israel oration ever:

> Our friendship with Israel is deep and enduring. . . . [A]ny lasting peace must acknowledge the very real security concerns that Israel faces every single day. . . . Israel is surrounded by neighbors that have waged repeated wars against it. Israel's citizens have been killed by rockets fired at their houses and suicide bombs on their buses. Israel's children come of age knowing that throughout the region, other children are taught to hate them. Israel, a small country of less than eight million people, looks out at a world where leaders of much larger nations threaten to wipe it off of the map. The Jewish people carry the burden of centuries of exile and persecution, and fresh memories of knowing that six million people were killed simply because of who they are. . . . The Jewish people have forged a successful state in their historic homeland. . . . And friends of the Palestinians do them no favors by ignoring this truth. . . .

I was nonplussed, albeit in a positive way, as were other Israelis. Even Foreign Minister Liberman, not wont to compliment the president, praised his address as "the speech of an ally." And indeed an ally Obama seemed to be, conferring for an hour alone with Netanyahu at UN headquarters. I peeked into the room several times to glimpse the two leaders chatting shoulder-to-shoulder like pals. Part of me longed to believe it was true—that Obama had finally realized that Abbas would never negotiate and that Netanyahu, when embraced rather than dissed by the White House, would make an amenable partner. So, too, I wanted to believe that Netanyahu could build trust with Obama. Unfortunately, previous experience had taught me that such moments of fraternity proved to be just that, momentary, and that the core differences between the two leaders would resurface.

And they did, almost immediately. Checked by the Americans in the Security Council, Abbas turned to achieving his goal of unilaterally declared independence incrementally, by joining associated UN agencies. Of these he chose the most prestigious: the UN Educational, Scientific, and Cultural Organization, UNESCO. Congress promptly responded by defunding the agency, enraging the administration. Instead of rebuking Abbas, the White House took Israel to task for supporting the cut-off.

"UNESCO teaches Holocaust studies, for chrissakes," Tom Nides berated me. "You want to cut off fucking Holocaust studies?"

Israel did not, but the president thought he had already done enough by opposing the Palestinians' bid and did not need to punish them further. Instead, using his waiver powers, Obama prevented the shutdown of the PLO's Washington office and preserved most of America's aid to the Palestinian Authority. A furious Netanyahu announced the acceleration of Israeli building in East Jerusalem, which in turn triggered the usual State Department condemnations.

Finally, on November 8—one week after the Palestinians' acceptance into UNESCO—Obama met with French president Nicolas Sarkozy in Cannes. Sarkozy, whose early ardor for Israel had shriveled into an almost constant critique, called Netanyahu a liar. "You are fed up with him, but I have to deal with him even more often than you," Obama replied, unaware that he was speaking into a live microphone.

The incident again brought to mind the words of Job: "I've barely learned of this latest catastrophe, and already there's news of the next." And the back-to-back crises continued. The Egyptians arrested an Israeli-American, Ilan Grapel, charged him with spying, and began bargaining for the release of Egyptian prisoners in Israeli jails. Radical Israeli settlers vandalized a West Bank mosque and Ultra-Orthodox men spat at female Israelis outside of Jerusalem. Referring to these reports at the annual Saban Forum on U.S.-Israel relations, a senior administration official warned that Israel was en route to becoming another Iran. Though off the record, the remark so incensed Netanyahu that he instructed me to phone congressional leaders and remind them that women have served as the chief justice of Israel's Supreme Court, the Speaker of the Knesset, and the prime minister. The calls further annoyed the administration. But I had no time to deal with this fallout. With Job 1:16 in mind, I rushed back to the embassy to grapple with a potentially devastating assault from the press.

Hatchet Jobs

That same November, I received an email from a well-placed source within the production staff at *60 Minutes*. The famed CBS TV newsmagazine would soon air an item accusing Israel of forcing Christians to flee "the Holy Land," the source revealed.

This intelligence dispirited me. Since my adolescence, when it first debuted, I admired *60 Minutes* for its hard-nosed but entertaining format. But during my time in Washington, the show began displaying an increasingly anti-Israel slant. There were segments critical not only of the settlements but also of archeological digs in Jerusalem and even Israel's alleged cyber-operations against Iran. According to *60 Minutes,* the Iranians discovered the computer viruses that Israel planted in their nuclear facilities and then turned those "worms" against the West.

Disappointed by these segments, I went to see Jeffrey Fager, the program's executive producer and chairman of CBS News. Fager rebuffed any charges of bias, pointing out the program had positively profiled the Israeli Air Force and Hadassah Hospital. "Fair enough," I replied. But then that email from the *60 Minutes* source arrived informing me of a threat not only to Israel's image, but to its national defense.

Paradoxical though it may sound, the security of the Jewish State significantly depends on Christians. The United States is the most religiously observant of the world's industrialized nations. A significant percentage of Americans attend church each week, and though some churches are critical of Israel, the most crowded ones are not. On the contrary, the colonial-era notion that I first explored in my book *Power, Faith, and Fantasy,* that the "new Israel" of America and the "old Israel" of the Jews were indivisibly linked, continued to impact U.S. policy. By 2011, close to three-quarters of all Americans defined themselves as pro-Israel—more than twice as many as the evangelical and American Jewish communities combined. It never surprised me to encounter a congressman whose district contained few if any Jews but who nevertheless pointed at the Bible on his desk and told me, "God says I will bless those who bless you. Now how much do you need for Iron Dome?"

Israel's enemies were keenly aware of the importance of Christian support for Israel and labored to undermine it. They promoted the

2009 Kairos Document—issued by a group of West Bank Christians—that denied the right of self-determination to the Jews, designated Israel as a sin against God, and justified suicide bombing. In spite of these smears, Kairos remained a potent tool for driving Israeli-Christian wedges. These were widened by periodic reports—all proven groundless—of Christian suffering at Israeli hands. One spring morning, I awoke to an online article, "Dark Easter for Palestinian Christians," claiming that Israel had prevented West Bank Christians from attending church in Jerusalem. I quickly called the head of Israel's Internal Security Services, who assured me that tens of thousands of Palestinian Christians had entered Israel that Sunday. The story, planted by Palestinian propagandists, was a sham. Some of the websites retracted the story, yet still it went viral.

But none of these canards had ever been promulgated by a platform as broadly viewed as *60 Minutes*. Far exceeding any PR problem, such a slur posed a strategic danger to Israel by eroding its vital Christian support. What could be done? I could try to persuade the producers to cancel the project or at least present an accurate view. All else failing, I could attempt to delay the broadcast until after the football season, during which *60 Minutes* airs directly after the Sunday game and attracts a much wider audience. I could push it past the Christmas and Easter holidays, which would surely amplify any anti-Christian message. Or I could do nothing.

In baiting Israel, *60 Minutes* was merely mimicking the popular trend in much of the American media. Rarely did my day not begin with several critical press reports about Israel on issues ranging from the peace process and Iran to trends in Israeli society. I had to choose which items required a letter to the editor or merely a complaint to the ombudsman. In *Foreign Policy* magazine, now published by my college roommate, David Rothkopf, I refuted the charge that Israel was no longer a strategic asset to the United States ("Ultimate Ally") and no longer liberal ("Resilient Democracy"). Responding to all the allegations could have been a full-time job.

Most malicious was the op-ed page of *The New York Times*, once revered as an interface of ideas, now sadly reduced to a sounding board for only one, which often excluded Israel's legitimacy. The page's contributors accused Israel of ethnic cleansing, brutal militarism, racism of several stripes, and even "pinkwashing"—exploiting its liberal policy toward lesbians and gays to cover up its oppression of Palestinians. After a while, I simply gave up trying to debunk such lunacy. Only once, when an op-ed by Mahmoud Abbas suggested that the Arabs had accepted the UN's Partition Plan in 1947 while Israel rejected it, did I feel compelled to phone the page's editor, Andy Rosenthal.

"When I write for the *Times,* fact checkers examine every word I write," I began. "Did anybody check whether Abbas has his facts exactly backward?"

"That's your opinion," Rosenthal replied.

"I'm an historian, Andy, and there are opinions and there are facts. That the Arabs rejected partition and the Jews accepted it is an irrefutable fact."

"In your view."

"Tell me, on June 6, 1944, did Allied forces land or did they not land on Normandy Beach?"

Rosenthal, the son of a Pulitzer Prize–winning *Times* reporter and famed executive editor, replied, "Some might say so."

I urged him to publish a response by President Shimon Peres, who was present at Israel's creation. Rosenthal said that he already had an article by Knesset member Danny Danon. A rightist who opposed the two-state solution, Danon would only make Israel look more extreme, I knew, which is perhaps what Rosenthal wanted. "Hold off on Danon," I urged the editor. "I'll get you the Peres piece in time to go to press tomorrow."

That day, Sally and I attended our son Yoav's graduation from Columbia. Seated in the VIP section next to the famous *Alma Mater* statue, I could have enjoyed the pageantry and relished the view of my old dorm room in John Jay Hall. Instead, I text-messaged Peres. The result was his moving memoir of Israel's struggle for independence and its insuppressible yearning for peace. Just before deadline, I pressed the SEND button and sighed with relief.

The next day, the *Times* published Danon's article.

How to explain such chicanery? Israel was certainly not lacking for policies, such as settlement building, that were difficult if not impossible to portray positively to the press. Our frequent need to resort to force and the growth of religiously observant communities tended to paint us in less liberal colors. But displayed in my embassy office was a 1973 edition of *Life* magazine celebrating Israel's twenty-fifth anniversary. Back then, the Jewish State was far more militaristic and less democratic and tolerant. Yet *Life* praised it as a paragon of righteousness and creativity. Such adoration typified the media's depiction of Israel back then. Something obviously changed.

That something, according to former Associated Press reporter Matti Friedman, is the grossly disproportionate number of journalists assigned to covering Israel—more, Friedman writes, than "AP had in China, Russia, or India, or in all of the 50 countries of sub-Saharan Africa combined." Beyond the unbalanced numbers of correspondents, Friedman posits, is the biased story line they are forced to adopt. Investigations into Palestinian Authority corruption or Abbas's rejection of peace offers are simply quashed, while exposés of Israeli intransigence merit headlines. Friedman believes the reason is anti-Semitism, the willingness to associate Jews with the worst traits in today's world, namely, militarism, colonialism, and racism. Charges of Israeli trafficking in human organs, highlighted by *Time* and *The New York Times,* indeed evoke classic anti-Semitic tropes. And more than a few journalists are ill-disposed toward Israel. But there is also a more mundane reason for Israel's bad press: ratings.

Israel sells. Arabs massacring Arabs in, say, Syria, is a footnote, while a Palestinian child shot by Israeli soldiers is a scoop. The racist undertones are clear but the reality, irrefutable. And no one understands it better than the terrorists, Hamas and Hezbollah. If they fire at Israeli civilians, Israel will retaliate and invariably kill the Palestinian and Lebanese civilians behind whom the terrorists hide. The pictures will be gruesome, and if insufficiently so, the terrorists will manufacture them, exhuming bodies from morgues and graveyards. The staged images, picked up by editorless blogs, proliferate on the Internet. Many will be reproduced, uncritically, by the mainstream press.

Even *The Washington Post,* an august paper, can fall for the ruse. Once, after a round of Hamas-Israel fighting in Gaza, the *Post* ran a four-column-wide front-page photograph of a crying man surrounded by mourners and clutching a small shrouded body. The caption said that a Palestinian father grieves for his son "after an Israeli airstrike in Gaza City." I called the editor, a good friend, and asked about the photo's provenance. "I'm no expert," I said, "but the figures' positions are too symmetrical—a neat semicircle—and their expressions identical. Are you sure it's real?" The editor insisted that the photograph had been authenticated by its source, the Associated Press.

Some months later, an investigation by the UN (the UN!) determined that the infant was most likely not killed by the IDF but by a Hamas rocket. The *Post* apologized yet the harm to Israel's reputation was, once again, irreversible.

In addressing American audiences, someone invariably asked me, "Why is Israel's PR so bad?" I responded by admitting that, yes, Israel must do a much better job of explaining itself. Yet even if it did, the bad press would likely continue. No amount of spin can separate the public's prurient fascination with Israel from the media's hunger for ratings.

Still, could I ignore the knowledge that *60 Minutes* intended to portray Israel as hostile to Christians? Here, too, was a classic anti-Semitic theme culled, seemingly, straight from *The Merchant of Venice*. Here was a shameless attempt to libel the Jewish State, the only country in the Middle East with a growing, thriving Christian community. The damage to the U.S.-Israel alliance inflicted by such a segment could, at best, be mitigated or delayed. Did that relieve me of the duty of acting preemptively?

"Why, in view of the pervasive injustice against Christians in Middle Eastern Muslim countries, is *60 Minutes* singling out Israel?" I asked in a letter to CBS president and CEO Les Moonves. I listed just some of the atrocities committed against Christians in the region, including mass murders, expulsions, and the wholesale destruction of churches. In Israel, contrastingly, Christians served in the military, in the Knesset, and on the Supreme Court. Though discrimination did occur in Israel—one Orthodox Jewish mayor in the Galilee objected to public Christmas decorations in his town—Israeli Arab Christians were on average better educated and more affluent than Israeli Jews. Moonves, a delightful person, the grandnephew of Ben-Gurion's wife, Paula (Munweis), was very sympathetic but understandably reluctant to intercede in an internal editorial issue.

Instead, he recommended that I take my case back to Executive Producer Jeff Fager, which I did, posing the same questions: Why pick on Israel again and on such unfair grounds? Why had not one Israeli official been asked to interview for the piece? But, in addition to protesting, I suggested ways of making the segment more balanced. Consult Israeli and Christian experts on the subject, I proposed, and provided several names. Make sure to disguise faces and even voices of the interviewed Christians, who will fear retribution from Muslim extremists. And supply regional context. The entire Middle East is roiling, I wrote, *except* for the Holy Land.

My note led to some acrimonious exchanges with Jeff and with correspondent Bob Simon, who took exception to my use of the term "hatchet job." Simon, who formerly lived in Israel and befriended Sally's parents, had spent forty days in Iraqi captivity in the Persian Gulf War. He was a celebrated correspondent. When it came to Israel, though, its settlements and building in Jerusalem, Simon had an agenda. Pointing this out prompted *60 Minutes* to review the project—so the inside source updated me—and push the broadcast past the football season, Christmas, and Easter. But, in the end, the episode would run and feature a single Israeli responder—me.

I had never intended to be interviewed and sought the opinion of the Prime Minister's Office. In view of my outreach efforts to American Christian communities as well as my past experience as Israel's advisor on church affairs, it was decided that my voice would, in fact, be strongest. The situation was unwinnable, but the defeat might still be mitigated.

A veteran now of hundreds of interviews, many of them hostile, I was shocked by Simon's venom. For more than one and a half hours—my longest grilling ever—he accused Israel of forcing Christians to flee the Holy Land. I fought back by recalling that in Israel, alone in the Middle East, the Christian population had not diminished but actually grown by 1,000 percent. Why, I asked, had Simon confined his definition of the Holy Land to the West Bank while some of Christianity's most sacred sites—the Sea of Galilee, Nazareth, the Hill of the Beatitudes—were located in Israel. Why was Gaza, where Christians had been brutalized by Hamas, excluded? Why had he not inquired into the reasons for the shrinkage of the once-great West Bank Christian populations of Ramallah, Jericho, and Bethlehem after 1995, when Israel transferred those cities to Palestinian Authority control? And why, if Israel's policies since 1967 were so suffocating, had the West Bank's Muslim population at least tripled?

Simon ducked these questions and countered with his own—not about Christians at all but my attempts to preempt the segment's production. "I've been doing this a long time," Simon claimed, "but I've never gotten a reaction before from a story that hasn't been broadcast yet." I knew that this was flagrantly untrue. Recent press reports revealed Nancy Pelosi's efforts to prevent *60 Minutes* from investigating her investments. But I was not going to drag the House minority leader into a taped debate with Bob Simon. Instead, I replied point-blank, "There's a first time for everything."

"Christians in the Holy Land" aired on April 22, 2012. Sally and I watched it at the Residence, together with two of our closest friends, bestselling novelist Dan Silva and his wife, NBC *Today* show producer Jamie Gangel. We sipped wine and braced for the worst. As bad as I anticipated, the segment was above all pathetic. Ignoring my advice that the West Bank Christians be interviewed incognito, Simon questioned them in an open panel featuring only figures notorious for their anti-Israel stands. Clergymen like Nazareth's Father Gabriel Naddaf, who claimed "those who want to destroy the Jewish State are signing the death warrant on the last free Christians in the Holy Land," and who called on the "seekers of peace [to] end your witch hunt of the only free country in the region," went unheard. Rather, *60 Minutes* blamed Israel's West Bank security barrier for the Christians' flight and accused the Jewish State of cleansing the Holy Land of Jesus's followers. The Kairos Document, branded anti-Semitic by the left-leaning Central Conference of American Rabbis, was described as a document of "hope, love, and faith."

Of course, all of the questions I asked Simon were edited out, while my responses were cut-and-pasted in ways that would have fascinated any class on journalistic ethics. But I was heartened to see that much of Simon's time was devoted not to vilifying Israel but to attacking me for trying to block the broadcast. The Prime Minister's Office later congratulated me on my diversion. "What bullet won't you take for the State of Israel?"

Other viewers, though, were not in a congratulatory mood. Many thousands of them bombarded *60 Minutes* with protest letters. The segment, they pointed out, lied by saying that the security barrier completely surrounded Bethlehem (it does not), and purposefully overlooked the hundreds of documented cases of anti-Christian abuse by Palestinian Muslims. The term they most frequently attached to the piece—without any prompting from me—was "hatchet job."

None of the protests pointed out the inaccuracy that I, as an historian, found the most offensive. One of the clergymen interviewed by Simon described Christianity as "made in Palestine." But Jesus, of course, who lived in Judea, never heard the word *Palestine,* which was coined by the Romans a century after his death.

Clarifying such distortions required time that I did not have. Several congressmen, formerly staunch Israel supporters, expressed uncertainty to me about aiding a country which, according to 60 *Minutes,* oppressed Christians. Bob Simon, meanwhile, further pressed his agenda by producing a segment on Iron Dome. This, I told my staff, would cast doubt on the system's success but nevertheless blame it for facilitating Israel's aggression against Gaza and occupation of the West Bank. And Simon's segment did exactly that. Iron Dome, it suggested, did not intercept 85 percent of Hamas rockets, as Israel claimed, but far less, yet the system still provided the protection Israel needed to devastate Gaza. A Palestinian professor explained—unintelligibly—how shielding Israelis from Hamas rocket fire enabled them to build West Bank settlements. "Forget the Israel-bashing," I told Jeff Fager, with whom, in spite of everything, I remained on cordial terms. "Any report that predictable is just bad journalism."

Simon would be killed in a car crash in 2015, but the struggle for Israel's image slogged on. Victories were often measured by our ability to limit loss. While some solace could be derived from the fact that backing for Israel in the United States steadily increased—a statistic reflecting America's skepticism toward the media as much as its affection for the Jewish State—the relentless press criticism helped fuel a global movement of delegitimization. On campuses and in front of town halls, radical protesters bore signs demanding "BDS"—the boycott, divestment from, and sanctioning of Israel. Where conventional Arab armies and terrorists had failed to achieve their goal of destroying Israel, BDS aimed to succeed by devastating Israel's economy and isolating its citizens internationally.

Standing up for Israel in the media, battling BDS, often cast me back into my old Don Quixote role. These were struggles that could rarely be won entirely, only less damagingly lost. Yet, old-fashioned and illogical as it often seemed, I felt duty-bound to keep fighting. The press attacks on Israel and the campaign to delegitimize it internationally would continue. The windmills would churn and somebody had to tilt at them.

So I continued sallying, sometimes in situations that would have made Cervantes, that master of the human comedy, laugh. I had to pull columnist George Will out of a baseball game—like yanking Hemingway out of a bar—to correct one misattributed quote, and berate blogger Josh Rogin for recording a public talk between Jeffrey Goldberg and me in a synagogue, on Yom Kippur. Most miffing was the book *This Town,* a pillorying of well-connected Washingtonians by *The New York Times*'s Mark Leibovich. The only thing worse than being mentioned in Mark's bestselling book was not being mentioned in it. I merited much of a paragraph relating how, at the Christmas party of media grandees Ben Bradlee and Sally Quinn, I "hovered dangerously over the buffet table, eyeing a massive Christmas ham." But Nathan Guttman, a reporter for *The Jewish Daily Forward,* changed the word "eyeing" to "reaching for," insinuating that I ate the ham. Ironically, the embassy employed Nathan's caterer wife to cook gala kosher dinners.

George Will graciously corrected the quote and Josh Rogin apologized. *The Jewish Daily Forward* printed a full retraction. Yet, in the new media age, old stories never vanish. A day after the *Forward*'s faux pas, I received several angry phone calls from around the United States. "You should be ashamed of yourself!" they remonstrated. "The Israeli ambassador eating *trief*? In public? On Christmas?" I tried to defend myself—"I didn't eat it, I eyed it"—but fruitlessly. Those calls reminded me that, more complex than many of the issues I faced in the press, and often more explosive, was the minefield of American Jewry.

We Are One?

Viewing an American University art exhibition dedicated in my honor, the last thing I expected was to be accosted by a ninety-year-old Jewish woman whose head barely reached my belt. "I like you, but I don't like everything your country does," she growled.

"Excuse me, ma'am," I courteously replied, "but do you like everything your country does?"

"No." She wagged her finger in my face. "But your country must be perfect."

That one remark encapsulated what was for me the deepest and most painful divide. For a person who viewed himself as personifying an alliance, the rifts between the U.S. and Israeli governments often felt physically agonizing. More tormenting still were the widening gaps between Israel and American Jews.

From an early age, I had an abiding—Freud would call it oceanic— love of the Jewish people. Whatever our differences, I insisted, and however disparately we practice our religion, we still belonged to the same tribe. A rambunctious, endlessly argumentative tribe, to be sure, that once drove Moses to grouse, "Why, God, did you saddle me with this stiff-necked people?" But we were also a boundlessly creative and caring tribe, and I could not imagine anyone not being thankful for belonging to it. When the American Jews of my youth contributed to Israel under the banner "We Are One," I believed it.

I believed it even during the desperate period leading up to the 1967 Six-Day War, when, with Israel's existence endangered, tens of thousands of American Jews went out to demonstrate—against the Vietnam War. I still believed it decades later, after some prominent American Jews embraced Yasser Arafat and others repudiated Zionism entirely. I believed it in spite of knowing that only a third of American Jews ever visited Israel and many of those would cancel their trips at the first whiff of crisis. I believed it while, as an historian, I learned about the American rabbis who once denied the validity of a Jewish nation and the mainstream Jewish organizations that opposed the State's rebirth. Much as I cherished Israel, I embraced Jewish peoplehood. Both were fractious, flawed, and more than occasionally maddening, but their very existence was a blessing, I believed, a miracle.

Which was why I felt cleaved by the expanding gulfs between them. When I was growing up, many liberal Jews looked to Israel to fill the spiritual vacuum left by their flight from Orthodoxy. Others saw it as the means of expiating their guilt for failing to rescue their European Jewish families from the Nazis. For all, Israel seemed a source of celebration. This was the Israel of the breathtaking Paul Newman playing Ari Ben Canaan in the Hollywood epic *Exodus,* the Israel of the saccharine Sabra liqueur, and of the requisite horas at every Bar and Bat Mitzvah and wedding. American Jews may not have marched for Israel before the Six-Day War, but they danced for it zealously afterward.

Yet the American Jewish community was evolving and in ways that often distanced it from Israel. In the seventies, American Jews answered Elie Wiesel's challenge to confront the Holocaust. Countless millions of dollars were donated to fund research on the Final Solution and to construct the United States Holocaust Memorial Museum, astride the National Mall. Israel—its victories, its spirit—emboldened American Jews to embark on this introspective process, but for some of them, the Holocaust began replacing Israel as the centerpiece of Jewish identity.

A generation passed and new genocidal narratives—Cambodian, Serbian, Rwandan—emerged. No longer comfortable with defining themselves solely in tragic terms, younger American Jews searched for a fresh source of self-affirmation. This was *Tikkun Olam*. Meaning, literally, "Repair the World," the concept derived from the medieval Kabbalistic idea of reconnecting with the divine light of Creation. But, in its twenty-first-century American Jewish interpretation, *Tikkun Olam* became a call to rescue humanity. For liberal American Jews, especially, *Tikkun Olam* served as Judaism's most compelling commandment, almost a religion in itself. Addressing synagogues, non-Jewish politicians dependably mentioned the term and mangled it into *Tekan Oleem* and *Tik Konolum*. And like the Holocaust before it, *Tikkun Olam* tended to sideline Israel as the focal point of American Jewish purpose. How can we donate to the Hebrew University in Jerusalem, liberal Jews increasingly asked, when children went hungry in Honduras?

This drift away from an Israel-centric American Jewish identity distressed me. Of course, I welcomed the willingness of American Jews, who once only whispered about it behind closed doors, to publicly reckon with the Holocaust. But, for me, the annihilation of the six million remained a uniquely Jewish catastrophe whose recurrence was best prevented by Israeli power. By contrast, the U.S. Holocaust Memorial conveyed a universalist message that stressed tolerance as the cure for future genocides. While Native, African, and Latin Americans designed national museums to showcase their cultures, American Jews erected a monument to the suffering they did little to prevent. When, as ambassador, I addressed the annual Day of Remembrance ceremony in the Capitol, I rose with hundreds of American Jews as the U.S. Army band played "National Emblem, Trio" and an honor guard marched into the Rotunda bearing the flags of those units that liberated concentration camps. Silently I asked: why are we standing at attention rather than rending our garments in shame?

Similar ambivalence characterized my feelings about *Tikkun Olam*. Here, on the one hand, was an outstandingly prosperous community recalling its humble origins and responding to Judaism's ancient, compassionate appeal. And yet, in fulfilling their commitment to aid the world, what resources would American Jews retain for assisting our own people? Honduran children were indeed needier than the Hebrew University, but did one charity have to eclipse the other? Feed the Hondurans—so I felt—but also support the students who were, after all, our family.

Ultimately, though, neither refocusing on the Holocaust nor reenergizing *Tikkun Olam* could dilute the lure of the melting pot. Assimilation, according to surveys, soared, with as many as 70 percent of all non-Orthodox Jews marrying outside the faith. The younger the Jews, statistics showed, the shallower their religious roots. The supreme question asked by post–World War II Jewish writers such as Bernard Malamud and Philip Roth, "How can I reconcile being Jewish and American?" was no longer even intelligible to young American Jews. None would feel the need to begin a book, as Saul Bellow did in *The Adventures of Augie March,* with "I am an American, Chicago born." Bred on that literature, I saw no contradiction between love for America and loyalty to my people and its nation-state. But that was not the case of the Jewish twenty-somethings, members of a liberal congregation I visited in Washington, who declined to discuss issues, such as intermarriage and peoplehood, that they considered borderline racist. Israel was virtually taboo.

For Israel had also changed. From the spunky, intrepid frontier state that once exhilarated American Jews, Israel was increasingly portrayed by the press as a warlike and intolerant state. That discomfiting image, however skewed, could not camouflage the fact that Israel ruled over more than two million Palestinians and settled what virtually the entire world regarded as their land. The country that was supposed to normalize Jews and instill them with pride was making many American Jews feel more isolated and embarrassed.

I shared their discomfort and even their pain. Yet I also wrestled with the inability of those same American Jews to understand Israel's existential quandary, that creating a Palestinian state that refused to make genuine peace with us and was likely to devolve into a terrorist chaos was at least as dangerous as not creating one. I was frustrated by their lack of anguish in demanding Israel's withdrawal from land sacred to their forebears for nearly four millennia. "Disagree with the settlers," I wanted to tell them, "denounce them if you must, but do not disown them, for they—like you—are part of our people."

But did all Israelis share in that sense of peoplehood? Hardly. I learned this on my first day on Kibbutz Gan Shmuel, when, while watching me unpack my prayer shawl, my teenage Israeli peers broke out laughing. "What's so funny?" I stammered. "Aren't you Jewish?" They snickered, "Jewish? No! We are Israeli!" They were the descendants of the late-nineteenth- and early-twentieth-century Zionists who believed they were forging a Jewish state but, in reality, founded a Hebrew-speaking Israeli nation with its own culture, cohesiveness, and ethos.

Those pioneers never came to grips with an America that defied their definition of Diaspora life as a cultural and political dead end. Their point of reference was Alfred Dreyfus, the French captain who, though thoroughly assimilated, was accused of spying in 1894 and sentenced to Devil's Island. Covering the Dreyfus trial, encountering mass anti-Semitic protests, the journalist Theodor Herzl concluded that Jews could never be a part of Europe but rather must leave and establish their own Jewish state. Herzl and the early Zionists could not have conceived of the sight that I came to regard as commonplace—of six Jews, three Israelis and three Americans, sitting in the White House and discussing Middle East peace.

Similarly, those early Zionists could not have foretold the question I would one day pose to my son Noam, now an officer in the IDF. "Who do you feel you have more in common with, your Bedouin sergeant Mahmud, or your cousin Josh in Long Island?" And no pioneer could have predicted Noam's answer. "Are you serious?" he shrugged. "Mahmud slept in the dirt with me. Mahmud fought for this country."

So, it seemed, we drifted. Numbers of American Jews resented Israel for not living up to its original promise. Many Israelis—the world's only Jews without a compound identity—looked down on an American Jewry that preferred comfort to sovereignty. Pressed with the monumental question of Jewish survival, both communities claimed to provide utopian solutions. Once, while assisting then-

Israeli president Ezer Weizman to draft a "New Covenant of the Jewish People," I approached American Jewish and Israeli leaders with a compromise. American Jewry would recognize making *aliya* as a means of ensuring Jewish continuity and Israel would acknowledge the legitimacy of Jewish life in America. Brushing aside my urgings, neither side would sign.

Yet, in spite of all this estrangement, still I believed, "We are one." And the reasons were simple. A collaborative effort, Israel emerged from the unity between its citizens and American Jews. Lovingly, often lavishly, American Jews enriched the social, educational, artistic, and scientific soil from which Israel's creativity blossomed. Their names graced Israel's playgrounds and libraries, its theaters and laboratories, even its ambulances. They defended Israel, sometimes as soldiers on its battlefields, more often as advocates on their campuses. Proportionally small but politically dynamic, American Jews brought their devotion to Israel into the ballot box, bore it into the halls of Congress and through the White House's doors.

Israel, in turn, sent hundreds of young volunteers to serve Jewish communities across the United States. Many thousands of young American Jews visited Israel in order to reinforce their Jewish identity. Our daughter, Lia, then a sergeant in the Golani Brigade, accompanied a bus of these Americans to Jerusalem, and called home sobbing.

"Why are you crying?" Sally asked her.

"Because we're entering Jerusalem."

"But Lia, you live in Jerusalem," Sally reminded her. "You were born in Jerusalem. Why are you crying?"

"I'm crying," Lia wept, "because we're *all* crying."

And so I believed that these competing utopians—Israelis and American Jews—could munificently coexist. But that faith did not relieve me of the need to seek help. Returning to the United States as Israel's ambassador in 2009, I scarcely recognized the American Jewish landscape I had left thirty years earlier. For guidance, I turned to Rabbi Steven Gutow, head of the Jewish Council on Public Affairs— the policy wing of the Jewish Federations—to Reform leader Rabbi David Saperstein, and to the legendary head of the Anti-Defamation League, Abe Foxman. "Help me navigate this," I asked them, and they obliged, pointing out the major players, the emerging organizations, and, especially, the politics. Still, even with such expert helmsmen, the path forward proved labyrinthine. Jewish oneness was indeed a miracle, I discovered, but maintaining it became more than a full-time job.

I forget whose idea it was—fortunately not mine—to put Jewish Democrats and Jewish Republicans in the same room with Israel's prime minister. The great rapprochement was to take place at Blair House during Netanyahu's July 2010 visit to Washington. Representatives of the National Jewish Democratic Coalition (NJDC) and the Republican Jewish Coalition (RJC) in equal numbers quietly filed into the dark brocaded dining room. They took their seats around the elliptical table, the NJDC fittingly on Netanyahu's left and the RJC to his right. I remarked on this lightheartedly and began to praise this display of bipartisan support that represented a strategic Israeli interest. But I never finished my thought. Suddenly the two delegations began screaming at each other, shaking their fists and pounding the table. The chandelier tinkled menacingly above us. Netanyahu merely looked on, dumbfounded.

"Hold on! Hold on!" I shouted and hammered that poor table the hardest. "The democratically elected leader of Israel is here and you may just want to ask him a question!"

The chastised representatives fell silent and finally acknowledged Netanyahu's presence, but their near brawl demonstrated that Washington's political schizophrenia also split American Jews. Though a decisive majority of them still voted Democratic—and percentage-wise supported Obama more than any ethnic group except for African-Americans—an increasingly upscale and vocal bloc leaned Republican. Together with gambling magnate Sheldon Adelson, right-wing Jews appeared alongside Republican governors Rick Perry and Mitt Romney, former House Speaker Newt Gingrich and businessman Herman Cain, and other presidential contenders. While Florida congresswoman Debbie Wasserman Schultz, a feisty young Jewish liberal, became head of the Democratic National Committee (DNC), Adelson donated at least $100 million to the GOP.

Walking the partisan fissure between American Jews often felt like a high-wire act, and a wobbly one at that. Rebuked at a liberal rabbinic assembly for not attending the J Street convention, I was equally reproofed by several national Jewish leaders for meeting with J Street's board. Jews opposed to Israel protested outside a New York synagogue where I spoke, claiming that I was anti-Obama, and several members of a Baltimore synagogue booed me for praising the president as pro-Israel. For some, the mere fact of Netanyahu's conservatism and known friendship with Adelson was enough to brand me, his ambassador, as a closet Republican. For others, my utter refusal to come out in favor of Gingrich or Romney—much as Ambassador Rabin endorsed Nixon in 1972—labeled me an Obama supporter.

The precariousness of the Israeli-American Jewish trapeze was highlighted at the end of 2011, when Jeffrey Goldberg broke a story about a series of Israeli Ministry of Absorption videos designed to convince Israelis living in the United States to come home. The YouTube clips, one of which depicted a little Israeli-American girl confusing Hanukkah with Christmas, conveyed an incontrovertible—and, for American Jews, unconscionable—message: only Israel can safeguard Jewish identity. Within minutes of going online, Goldberg's report sparked outrage throughout the American Jewish community. Leaders called me quite literally screaming and CNN hauled me before the cameras to explain Israel's insult. I immediately phoned Netanyahu, wakening him late on Friday night, and told him that the videos had to be removed, now. He agreed and the campaign instantly ended. But the resentment of some American Jews remained, as did the incredulousness of many Israelis who could not understand the umbrage those videos aroused.

Though sometimes dizzying, my high-wire balance at least came with a net named the State of Israel, to where I would someday return. But no such safety mechanism existed for AIPAC, an entirely American organization headquartered in Washington. According to conspiracy theories, the American Israel Public Affairs Committee buys politicians and acts on Israel's instructions. Neither charge is true. In fact, AIPAC educates legislators about the Middle East and endorses those most supportive of Israel. Under the rock-steady directorship of Howard Kohr, AIPAC members view themselves as Americans working to strengthen the United States by solidifying its ties with Israel—by promoting military aid, opposing terror and the Iranian nuclear threat, and upholding the principles of a stable Israeli-Palestinian peace. AIPAC's detractors credit it with creating an artificial U.S.-Israel friendship that undermines America's interests. But the opposite is true.

Starting in the 1970s, the rise of the alliance elevated AIPAC, formerly an obscure group, into one of America's most influential lobbies.

Indeed, during my first three years in Washington, participation in AIPAC's annual Policy Conference nearly doubled, to twelve thousand. It boasted of hosting more congressmen than any event except for the State of the Union address and of serving the world's largest kosher banquet. Believing in the lobby's prowess, foreign countries often assigned their diplomats to Jerusalem—I met several who spoke Hebrew—before posting them to Washington. The louder the conspiracy-mongers shouted "cabal," it seemed, the faster AIPAC burgeoned.

Which should have been superb news for American Jews. Instead, AIPAC became the target for community members on the right and left wings. Ultraconservatives faulted the group for placing bipartisanship ahead of its support for Israel and for refusing to take on Obama. "How could you sell out the Republican caucus, when we were advocating exactly what Bibi Netanyahu was!" a senatorial aide railed to *The New Yorker*'s Connie Bruck. But, with the same vehemence, left-wingers derided AIPAC as irredeemably Republican and directly controlled by the Likud. "Mr. Sharon has Mr. Arafat surrounded by tanks," Tom Friedman wrote back in 2004, "and Mr. Bush surrounded by . . . pro-Israel lobbyists—all conspiring to make sure the president does nothing." Depending on whose opinions were solicited, AIPAC could either be spineless or overbearing, self-serving or mindlessly loyal. If adversarial on all other issues, Jews on both ends of America's political spectrum at least agreed on berating AIPAC.

I, too, was caught in this crossfire. Yes, AIPAC sometimes fell out of step with Israel—it endorsed the two-state solution before Netanyahu did—and its outspoken positions on Middle East peace and security more than occasionally irked Obama. Yet I could not understand how anyone who remembered American Jewish powerlessness during the Holocaust would shun Jewish power today. I could not fathom why, with Democrats and Republicans at constant loggerheads, anyone would shatter a rare congressional consensus. And I could not comprehend any Jew opposing the U.S.-Israel alliance that AIPAC championed. Each time those twelve thousand Policy Conference attendees greeted me with a standing ovation, I could only blush and applaud in return. And whenever AIPAC came under partisan attack, I felt personally—and perhaps too viscerally—stung.

• • •

The political lines cut deeply through the American Jewish community, but they were hardly the most lacerating. Once cloistered in Russian shtetls, European ghettos, and Middle Eastern *mellahs,* Jews over the past two hundred years were exposed to the winds of modernity. From a generally observant people, they came to differentiate themselves as Orthodox, Conservative, or Reform, or, more commonly, as unaffiliated. Previously united as a religion and a nation—like the Japanese, only global—Jews began to distinguish between the two, especially in the United States, where most claimed to feel totally American. In Israel, meanwhile, an Ultra-Orthodox establishment monopolized life-cycle events—weddings, funerals, births—and strictly controlled who could convert and which food was kosher. Though many Israelis resented this status quo, opting for civil marriage ceremonies in Cyprus, relatively few mobilized to change it. The synagogue that numerous nonpracticing Israeli Jews never attended was Orthodox.

Bridging those schisms stretched me emotionally if not physically, and in ways immeasurable to most non-Jews. Take, for example, the case of the hundred thousand non-Jewish Israelis, relatives of the million Jews who made *aliya* from the former Soviet Bloc, who wanted to convert to Judaism. To assist them, the Knesset in 2009 considered a law to expedite the traditionally protracted process. In return for securing its agreement, though, Israel's Orthodox Rabbinate demanded that the State cease recognizing the conversions conducted by Conservative and Reform rabbis in America. These, in turn, protested vehemently to the Israeli government, accusing it of discrimination. For months I shuttled between American rabbis and senior Israeli ministers, desperate to prevent a fracture, but neither side would budge. Crisis seemed imminent when, in the spring of 2010, Prime Minister Netanyahu received a letter from eight Jewish senators. Any attempt to deny the validity of the Reform and Conservative movements, the senators warned, would permanently impair U.S.-Israel relations. The proposed conversion law instantly vanished.

The near-collision between American and Israeli Jews over the conversion issue exposed me to the troubling rifts between them. What the former saw as matters of religious freedom and pluralism, the latter viewed as issues of governance, legality, and even national security. Informed by feminism and the civil rights movement, American Jews demanded equal rights. Scarred by wars and bearing sovereign responsibilities, Israelis insisted on stability and respect for its powerful Orthodox electorate. And so the breach widened and on no site more precipitously than the Western Wall.

The largest remnant of the Temple destroyed by the Romans in the year 70, the Western or Wailing Wall—*HaKotel,* in Hebrew— abuts the Temple Mount, Judaism's most hallowed site. Shortly after its capture by Israeli paratroopers in 1967, the Wall came under the aegis of Israel's Orthodox rabbis. In keeping with their tradition, the Wall was divided between a men's prayer section and a significantly smaller area for women. On either side, modest dress codes were strictly enforced. But then, starting in 1988, members of Women of the Wall, a Jewish feminist group, began worshipping in the women's section while wearing the phylacteries and prayer shawls reserved by Orthodoxy exclusively for men. The women read aloud from the Torah, a practice also proscribed by the Wall's rabbis. Consequently, some male worshippers cursed and spat at the activists and even threatened them physically.

This triggered a twenty-year battle in which Israel's government and Supreme Court bandied the Wall issue between them. Israeli police officers meanwhile adopted increasingly forceful policies toward the activists, who, they feared, would set off a riot. Though they rarely made Israeli headlines, Women of the Wall nevertheless tweaked one of the most sensitive U.S.-Israeli nerves. Many of the group's members, and the bulk of its foreign supporters, were American. And, once again, what Israelis viewed through the lens of law and public order— most of Jerusalem's shrines, including the al-Aqsa mosque and Christianity's Church of the Holy Sepulchre, enforced similar status quo arrangements—Americans saw from the perspectives of freedom of speech and religion as well as women's rights.

The Western Wall controversy, spiritually and politically, divided me. Raised in the Conservative movement in New Jersey and a member of a Reform congregation in Jerusalem, I cherished Jewish pluralism. For that reason, the marriage of our son Yoav to Ayala Sherman was a mixture of joy and frustration. Both grew up in the same progressive synagogue, but they could not be officially wed in Israel, which did not recognize Reform nuptials. Instead, the two first underwent a civil ceremony at the Residence in Washington. Supreme Court justice Elena Kagan—after momentarily forgetting the rings but not for a second her infectious wit—pronounced them husband and wife. Later, under an Israeli chuppa in the presence of their lifelong rabbi, Levi Weiman-Kelman, Yoav stomped on the glass and kissed his stunning bride. But while cheering "Mazal tov!" with the rest of our guests—among them Israeli president Shimon Peres—I could not help regretting the refusal of the State I served to validate my son and daughter-in-law's Jewish vows.

Yet I still had to separate my personal ire from my ambassadorial duties. I had to support the Israeli police in executing their interpretation of an Israeli Supreme Court ruling upholding the Western Wall's status quo. And I had to avoid a violent confrontation in which one of the Women of the Wall, most likely an American, could be injured. Such a catastrophe would be condemned not just by eight Jewish senators but by all of Congress and the White House.

Remembering my experience with the conversion law, I called Prime Minister Netanyahu and other relevant cabinet members and stressed that the Western Wall was not merely a Jewish or a PR issue but a potential crisis maker in our alliance with the United States. Over the course of 2011 and into 2012, I spent countless hours discussing the issue with Reform and Conservative leaders, pressing them to agree on what was and was not permissible behavior in our most sacred space. I met with Women of the Wall as well as the Orthodox leaders who opposed them, and beseeched the Israeli police to show restraint. Nevertheless, by the fall of 2012, hundreds of liberal Jews, among them notable Americans, marched to the Wall, where thousands of Ultra-Orthodox demonstrators waited to confront them. Several Women of the Wall were arrested, raising outcries from congregations across the United States.

The symbol of our faith and unity, the retainer of our most sacred mount, the Wall now threatened to divide us. But, then, just as the opposing sides neared the precipice, they all seemed to pull back. A local Jerusalem court ruled in favor of the Women of the Wall and instructed the police to protect rather than restrain them. The Orthodox, Reform, and Conservative rabbis finally agreed to the compromise I proposed for designating the archeological garden at the Wall's southern end as an area for egalitarian prayer. Natan Sharansky, now the head of the Jewish Agency—the world's largest Jewish NGO—secured the government's support. Narrowly, a devastating breakdown of the Jewish people was averted.

But that story never made the mainstream American media. The headlines, rather, called attention to the alleged erosion of human rights in Israel, its oppression of Palestinians, and misuse of military force. And with alarmingly few exceptions, those stories were authored by Jews.

Among the most common anti-Semitic canards is that Jews control the press. A pernicious myth, it nevertheless reflects the disproportional number—relative to their share of the U.S. population—of Jewish journalists. Most days, the op-ed pages of leading newspapers can look like a quarrel between members of a raucous Jewish family, a *mishpoochah*. One could imagine Tom Friedman arguing with David Brooks, Jeffrey Goldberg, and Charles Krauthammer or Roger Cohen taking issue with Richard Cohen, Paul Krugman, or Frank Rich, with Mort Zuckerman occasionally joining the fray. Television is no different, with nationally known names like Jake Tapper, Wolf Blitzer, Barbara Walters, and Jon Stewart proudly identified as Jews.

But the presence of so many Jews in print and on the screen rarely translates into support for Israel. The opposite is often the case, as some American Jewish journalists flag their Jewishness as a credential for criticizing Israel. "I'm Jewish," some even seem to say, "but I'm not one of those Jews—the settlers, the rabbis, Israeli leaders, or the soldiers of the IDF." The preponderance of Jews in the U.S. media often means, simply, that Israel is subjected to scrutiny and standards imposed on no other foreign nation.

Of the multiple press critiques of Israel that confronted me each morning, a high percentage were mounted by Jews. Reporting about the Women of the Wall in December 2012, *Times* bureau chief Jodi Rudoren, a friend and fellow member of my Jerusalem synagogue, linked the issue to the Diaspora Jewish objection to Israel's settlement policies and "laws that are seen as antidemocratic or discriminatory against Arab citizens." The article appeared on the front page, as did an investigation into tax-free American donations to settlements—printed purposely on the morning of Netanyahu's arrival in Washington—and a "scoop" on Israel's dominance in the human organs trade. These and other unflattering dispatches were written by Jews working for a paper long under Jewish ownership.

But *The New York Times,* which historically displayed a conflicted approach to Jewish issues—during World War II, it infamously played down the Holocaust—was scarcely the only platform for American Jewish criticism of Israel. *The New Yorker* and *The New York Review of Books,* both Jewish-edited, rarely ran nonincriminating reports on Israeli affairs. Jews throughout the American media were generally more disturbed by the accidental killing of Palestinians by the IDF than by the bombing of Iraqi or Afghani civilians by their own army. My experience with *60 Minutes*'s Bob Simon showed me how opposition to settlements could move an American Jew to damage Israel strategically.

Still, the majority of American Jewish journalists would not, I discovered, define themselves as anti-Israel. On the contrary, they cared intensely about the Jewish State but were increasingly troubled by its policies. Ruth Marcus of *The Washington Post,* a member of the synagogue I attended as ambassador, exemplified this attitude. Her columns dealt exclusively with domestic affairs, yet she devoted one of them to Ultra-Orthodox discrimination against Israeli women. The cases, though indeed disturbing, were localized and even had parallels in Orthodox neighborhoods in New York. But Ruth's op-ed precipitated several others on the topic, painting the image of an Israel steeped in intolerance. Referring to these reports, Secretary of State Hillary Clinton evoked the legacy of Rosa Parks, the young African-American woman who stood up for civil rights in the racist South. Senate Majority Leader Harry Reid made a personal and pain-filled call to me. "I have always defended Israel and always will," he said, "but not if our common values are compromised."

The pinch I felt reading articles censorious of Israel sharpened into a stab whenever the names on the bylines were Jewish. Almost all of the world's countries are nation-states, so what, I wondered, drove these writers to nitpick at theirs? Some, I knew, saw assailing Israel as a career enhancer—the equivalent of Jewish man bites Jewish dog—that saved several struggling pundits from obscurity. Others seemed to disdain Israel the way upper-class American Jews of German ancestry once scorned the poor Jewish immigrants from Eastern Europe, the Yiddish-speaking "rabble" who allegedly made all Jews look bad. Others still, largely assimilated, resented Israel for further complicating their already-conflicted identity. Did some American Jews prefer the moral ease of victimhood, I asked myself, to the complexities of Israeli power? Was no Israel better than an Israel that fell short of their dreams?

Pondering these questions, I could not help questioning whether American Jews really felt as secure as they claimed. Perhaps persistent fears of anti-Semitism impelled them to distance themselves from Israel and its often controversial policies. Maybe that was why so many of them supported Obama, with his preference for soft power, his universalist White House seders, and aversion to tribes. After all, the cover of a late 2011 edition of *New York* magazine crowned "The First Jewish President." That was true if being Jewish in America meant recoiling from military power, territorialism, nationalism, and a sense of tribe.

And yet, for all my disappointments and frustrations with some American Jews, I could never let my emotions interfere with my job. In addition to the spiritual ties, the shared values, and common strategic interests, the bonds between Israel and the United States rest on American Jewish–Israeli solidarity. I not only believed that "we are one," I had to ensure that we remained so.

So, while reaching out to diverse ethnic communities, I extended both hands to my own. I met with the progressive rabbis of the Bay Area, some dressed in multicolored robes, and with Ultra-Orthodox leaders who were uniformly garbed in black. I met with groups who refused to sing "Hatikvah" either because it failed to mention the Palestinians or because it omitted reference to God. I was the first Israeli ambassador to greet gatherings of Israeli immigrants to the United States. As one who had given up his U.S. citizenship to pursue an Israeli dream, it was strange to address those who, for financial or family reasons, had forfeited that dream to become Americans. But they remained avidly committed to Israel, and Israel, I believed, should embrace them.

The "American Jewish community," I came to realize, is a misnomer. American Jews belong to many communities, not all of them mutually accepting. And just as I strove to reach out to various ethnic groups, so, too, I worked to bring American Jews into dialogue not only with Israel but, firstly, with one another. The result was a series of *tisches*—"tables," in Yiddish—convened at Israeli consulates around the United States. Under these neutral Israeli auspices, Jews

from all religious and political movements could candidly, if sometimes loudly, interact.

At the same time, I visited dozens of synagogues of all orienta-
tions, always bringing the same message. Pursue *Tikkun Olam,* I said;
fix the world, but do it together—American and Israeli Jews—
providing food for the hungry and hope for the chronically ill. I talked
frankly about what we could expect from one another. American
Jews, I held, should uphold Israel's right to defend itself and to exist
as the Jewish State. They should respect the responsibility that Israelis
bore by choosing their leaders democratically. Israel, for its part, must
acknowledge American Jewish pluralism and behave as the nation-
state of all the Jewish people. "From one another," I concluded, "we
must expect open minds and compassionate hearts, patience, and a
willingness to listen."

But how many really heard? For all my hundreds of speeches and
innumerable hours of talk, American Jewish criticism of Israel seemed
only to surge. Israel's Orthodox rabbinate appeared to do its utmost
to alienate Israel's nonreligious majority and even to estrange Orthodox rabbis in the United States by refusing to honor their conversions.
At times, the sheer intolerance of Jew for Jew made me want to
scream, "J'accuse!" echoing Émile Zola's anguished attack on French
anti-Semites during the Dreyfus trial. I wanted to rail at those Jews
who failed to recognize that they belong to the luckiest Jewish generation in centuries, who live at a time when our exiles have been repatriated, our prisoners freed, and our two great nations allied. I wanted to
accuse them of that most narcissistic of sins: ingratitude.

I was grateful, then, whenever I entered an auditorium filled with
American Jews who cheered me as Israel's representative. I had to remind myself that, though not published on front pages or featured on
the nightly news, this solid majority of Jews still stood united behind
our State. And occasionally, I needed no reminder, such as with the
extraordinary people at Temple Beth 'El.

I traveled there on a rainy weekend, at the request of Rabbi Capers
Funnye, Michelle Obama's cousin who often advised me on Israel's
relations with African-Americans. "You've done so much for me," I
said to him over coffee in his native Chicago. "What can I do for you?"

Heftily built with a gaze as heartwarming as it was strong, Rabbi Funnye smiled at me and asked whether I would visit Philadelphia's Temple Beth 'El, which was celebrating its sixtieth anniversary. He smiled again when I unhesitatingly replied, "Done."

The modest structure, located in a less-than-fancy section of Philly, indicated little about the spiritual opulence inside. Sally and I ran through the wintry drizzle and into an ecstatic reception led by Rabbi Debra Bowen and her husband, Earl. The daughter of Beth 'El's founder, Debra lovingly led a congregation unlike any I had ever encountered, and not only because it was entirely African-American. Both men and women were dressed mostly in white, and remained in the synagogue throughout the entire Sabbath, worshipping, singing, feasting, and studying. Though a rock band accompanied many of the prayers, the ritual followed Jewish tradition and the young people— unlike me at their age—read from the Torah in flawless Hebrew. Their joy in their Jewishness was unbridled. Stirred by their elation, I told Debra and her community that we, as one people, shared a sacred homeland that no one could ever take from us. We danced together and *davened* together. Sally and I departed, hoarse and emotionally speechless, leaving behind an enlarged, framed photograph of elite IDF soldiers in training. Two of them were African and next to them, with gritted teeth, ran Noam, our son.

I later hosted Debra and Earl at our Residence and escorted them to a White House reception. They persisted in believing that I had done some favor for them and Beth 'El, but the reverse was true. They gave me fortitude and reinforced my faith. They reminded me, if I had momentarily forgotten, that we are indeed one.

Jewish unity grew even more essential as Israel faced its most fearsome challenge in decades. The Iranian nuclear program was still accelerating and nearing a point where fateful decisions might have to be made. Yet American Jews for the most part remained impassive. Three young women from a New Jersey Jewish high school mounted a button-and-poster campaign called "No Nukes for Iran." Hoping to rekindle the activism of the Free Soviet Jewry movement that electrified me as a youth, I brought these intrepid teenagers to Capitol Hill, introduced them to Netanyahu, and supported their efforts nationally. The American Jewish response was largely silence.

So, too, was that of the American rabbis whom I asked to address the Iranian threat in their sermons. Some of the rabbis said that the issue was too "divisive" to raise at services—as if the threatened annihilation of millions of Jews could somehow be contentious. I asked them to plant a "No Nukes for Iran" banner on their synagogue lawns, beside those proclaiming "We Stand with Darfur." Again, the rabbis demurred. One of them, a world-renowned scholar, inquired—without irony—"And if I fly such a flag, who will protect my congregation?"

Zones of Immunity

"Who will protect the embassy?" I asked Netanyahu on October 11, 2011. The prime minister had just informed me by phone of a foiled Iranian plot to bomb the Israeli legation. The terrorists also targeted Saudi Arabia's ambassador to Washington, planning to murder him with a bomb while he dined at his favorite restaurant, Cafe Milano. Posing as a drug dealer, an undercover U.S. agent asked the ringleader, an Iranian-American named Manssor Arbabsiar, whether he cared about the innocent guests who would also be killed at the popular Georgetown bistro. "They want that guy done," Arbabsiar replied, "and if a hundred go with him, fuck 'em."

The "they" cited by Arbabsiar was Iran's elite al-Quds Force, in charge of overseas operations directly authorized by the regime's Supreme Leader. In a conspiracy plausibly lifted from a boilerplate spy novel, payment for the assassinations passed through an Iranian-American used car salesman to hitmen working for a Mexican drug cartel. Felicitously, the FBI managed to thwart the bombings in time, but untold threats still lurked. Who, I wondered, would protect my staff?

"Don't worry," Netanyahu promised me, "we've got you covered."

Subsequently, my security detail doubled, but so, too, did my anxiety. By selling drugs internationally and laundering the profits through used-car dealerships, Iran had financed terrorist attacks in twenty-five cities throughout the world. Now that list included America's capital. Such brazen aggression should have precipitated an instant U.S. military response. Instead, President Obama called the Saudi king—not Netanyahu—telling him, "This plot represents a flagrant violation of fundamental international norms, ethics, and law." Such abstractions,

I assumed, did not appease the desert monarch. And they certainly failed to mollify me. If the administration balked at retaliating for an attempted massacre only blocks from the White House, I asked myself, would it strike nuclear facilities six thousand miles away?

All Israelis wrestled with that question. Would—or, rather, could—Obama act? They read how the president told Jeffrey Goldberg—his go-to journalist on issues of Jewish concern—that "[w]e've got Israel's back." They read how he pledged to Goldberg, "When I say we're not taking any option off the table, we mean it," and "I don't bluff." They heard administration spokespeople say that the U.S. military was fortifying its presence in the Persian Gulf and developing offensive plans so that the president would have "every possible arrow in his quiver." Sensitive to such nuances, Israelis registered the change in the administration's official line, from "a nuclear-armed Iran is unacceptable to the United States" to "the United States is determined to prevent Iran from acquiring nuclear weapons." In our intimate dialogue with American officials dealing with Iran, Under Secretary of State for Political Affairs Wendy Sherman reassured us that the administration was placing "a constant squeeze on Iran's major economic artery," and pursuing "an unrelenting crescendo of pressure." Ardent about her work, proud of her Jewish heritage, Sherman promised us that "Iran won't get a 'get out of jail card' free."

Such guarantees satisfied a large number of Israelis, including major public figures and most of the press. President Peres asserted that "Obama is not just saying this to keep us happy. This time we are not alone." Former Mossad chief Meir Dagan, interviewed by *The Jerusalem Post*, précised every Israeli's question: "If we are not going to trust the U.S. president, then who are we going to trust?"

And some Israelis had a categorical answer. "We cannot bind our security to America's willingness to act," Defense Minister Ehud Barak confided to interlocutors at the White House. "The greatest danger is self-delusion." While appreciative of our intimate dialogue with the United States, Israel security officials still assumed that it doubled as a *chibbuk*—a hug—to keep us close. Wendy Sherman, some of those same officials recalled, presided over the 1994 Framework Agreement on North Korea's nuclear program. This "good deal," as President Clinton called it then, based on intrusive international inspections, "made the world safer" and enabled North Korea "to rejoin the community of nations"—precisely the words Obama used with Iran. Eight years later, Israelis remembered, North Korea exploded its first nuclear weapon.

Against the mostly verbal evidence that Obama would use force against Iran, skeptical Israelis adduced his promises to reach out to its regime and to end Middle Eastern wars. For every denial that the president was not bluffing, the administration signaled its reluctance to tussle with Tehran. A month after the Cafe Milano episode, Iran and Hezbollah reportedly arrested and executed at least twelve CIA agents in Lebanon, and the administration again reacted with silence. By contrast, when assassins eliminated another Iranian nuclear scientist— the deed similarly ascribed to the Mossad—the White House quickly issued a statement that "condemned this kind of violence." No sooner did *Newsweek* report that the United States sold fifty-five "bunker buster" bombs to Israel than a high-ranking U.S. military official denied that the ordnance was meant for Iran. Anonymous sources leaked to *The New York Times* the outcome of a secret war game in which an Israeli assault on Iran caused "hundreds of American casualties." Others accused Israel of negligently exposing to Iran the codes for secret U.S.-Israeli cyberattacks. "Sonofabitch," *Times* reporter David Sanger quoted Vice President Biden exclaiming. "It's got to be the Israelis. They went too far."

Most damaging to the "Obama will do it" argument was a series of interviews given by Secretary of Defense Leon Panetta early in 2011. After revealing that Iran might be no more than a year away from producing a nuclear weapon, Panetta told *The Washington Post*'s David Ignatius that his "biggest worry" was the likelihood of an Israeli attack. This, he indicated, would likely take place in the spring. And when it did, the United States might not come to Israel's aid. "We would have to be prepared to protect our forces in that situation," Panetta told CBS's *Face the Nation*. "And that's what we'd be concerned about."

Why, Israelis asked, even if the IDF were preparing to strike, would our allies want to alert the Iranians? Why, if it sought to avoid war, would the White House allay the war fears that drove much of the world to cooperate with the sanctions?

Over the course of 2011, the sanctions against Iran kept escalating. Most of the ratcheting up was performed by robust legislators such as Ileana Ros-Lehtinen and Ted Deutch in the House, and in the Senate by Robert Menendez and Mark Kirk, who heroically persisted despite suffering a stroke. The sanctions targeted Iran's oil industry and ability to do business internationally. The results exceeded even the most sanguine Israeli estimates. Iran's oil exports fell by as much as 80 percent and the value of its national currency plummeted. Iranian businessmen were reduced to bartering for imported goods and a generation of young Iranians was rendered jobless. For the first time since 2009, the possibility arose that the Iranian people might again take to the streets and tear down the Islamic regime.

The sanctions succeeded in harming Iran's economy yet the administration resisted congressional attempts to expand them. One reason, officials told me, was America's need to maintain a united front with the P5+1 and especially with the Russians and the Chinese, who balked at any additional twisting of Iran's arm. But another explanation held that the president believed he could negotiate an agreement with the Iranians, and feared that further sanctions would drive them from the table. "We have a multi-vector approach," the State Department averred, "a combination of pressure and talks." A pattern recurred in which the White House pushed back on sanctions bills and then, once they passed, took credit for them. "When I came into office, Iran was united and the world was divided," Obama boasted. "And now what we have is a united international community that is saying to Iran, you've got to change your ways."

Throughout this period, quietly, Israel embarked on a large-scale enhancement of its military capabilities. The cost reportedly ran into the billions. According to the Israeli press, the IDF maneuvered warplanes over Sardinia in early November 2011 and successfully tested a long-range missile. Purposely quoting Obama, Netanyahu reiterated that "Israel must be able to defend itself, by itself, against any threat."

Of all the questions I confronted as ambassador, none was more fateful, more sensitive, and fraught than that of "will Obama act?" Whether publicly, in the media, or behind closed doors, I was constantly pressed to provide an answer. Formulating one required countless hours of careful listening to experts both inside and outside the administration, identifying trends, and piecing together a picture of Obama's long-range policy. For every think-tank type who guaranteed me that the president would never send U.S. planes against Iran, senior officials promised me that he would. "Never underestimate this guy," Vice President Biden, pulling me aside at a reception, rasped. "Push comes to shove, he will pull the trigger."

In fact, I learned that the White House was host to three schools of thought on Iran. The first held that the United States should support an Israeli attack that, carried out surgically by IDF tactical jets, would cause less collateral damage than a massive strike by U.S. strategic bombers. By contrast, the second school preferred an American strike, which, since the Israelis were anyway likely to drag the United States into a confrontation, would at least complete the job. But others predicted that the Iranians would retaliate for any aggression by blocking the Straits of Hormuz, passageway for a fifth of the world's oil supply, and threatening those U.S. forces still stationed in the region. As Deputy Assistant Secretary of Defense Colin Kahl later wrote, "Any war with Iran would be a messy and extraordinarily violent affair, with significant casualties and consequences." My former colleague at Georgetown, Kahl spoke for the third and most dominant school.

And still my research continued. Foreign diplomatic sources informed me that, in spite of his stated rejection of any containment of an Iranian bomb, Obama would settle for capping Iran's ability to make a bomb within one year—the so-called threshold capacity. Other analysts claimed the president regarded Iran as an ascendant and logical power—unlike the feckless, disunited Arabs and those troublemaking Israelis—that could assist in resolving other regional conflicts. I first heard this theory at Georgetown back in 2008, in conversations with think tankers and former State Department officials. They also believed that Iran's radical Islam was merely an expression of interests and fears that the United States could, with sufficient goodwill, meet and allay.

Such ideas initially struck me as absurd. After all, even irrational regimes such as Nazi Germany could take rational steps to reach fanatical goals. But Obama, himself, now began describing Iran's behavior as "strategic" and "not impulsive." The ayatollahs, he told Jeffrey Goldberg, "have their worldview, and they see their interests, and they respond to costs and benefits. . . . [They] are not North Korea." Suddenly, it seemed plausible that an America freed of its dependence on Middle Eastern oil and anxious to retreat from the region could view

Iran as a dependable ally. The only hurdle remained that pesky nuclear program.

Finally, after many months of attentiveness, I reached my conclusion. In the absence of a high-profile provocation—an attack on a U.S. aircraft carrier, for example—the United States would not use force against Iran. Rather, the administration would remain committed to diplomatically resolving the Iranian nuclear issue, even at the risk of reaching a deal unacceptable to Israel. And if Israel took matters into its own hands, the White House would keep its distance and offer to defend Israel only if it were counterstruck by a hundred thousand Hezbollah missiles.

My hypotheses were harsh, especially in light of the nineteen thousand centrifuges now possessed by Iran and its rising stockpile of 20 percent–enriched uranium that could be quickly upgraded by those devices to the 90 percent level needed for nuclear weapons. Brushing aside the IAEA's warnings about the military nature of Iran's nuclear program, President Mahmoud Ahmadinejad proclaimed that "we will not budge an iota from the path we are committed to." Supreme Leader Khamenei pledged that "the United States and its pawns, the Zionist regime . . . will be smashed from the inside"—that is, struck by further terror. That was the hair-trigger atmosphere in the first half of 2012, as Iran prepared to enter "the zone of immunity."

The term was Ehud Barak's and it defined that situation in which Iran, having amassed a sufficient quantity of fissile material, moved its nuclear program underground. There, in a small room hidden inside a country half the size of Europe, the Iranians would pack a spherical nuclear device with fifty-five pounds of 90 percent–enriched uranium and prime it with a detonator and a "pusher" designed to maximize the blast. The process, once preventable by striking the Fordow and Natanz sites, would now be virtually impossible to stop. Neutralizing the "zone of immunity" would require carpet-bombing most of Iran.

At this juncture, precisely, the positions of the United States and Israel could not have been more irreconcilable. Obama believed that bombing Iran would strengthen the regime, set back its nuclear facilities only a few years, and provide it with an excuse for weaponizing. Netanyahu, by contrast, held that that military action would discredit the ayatollahs, much as the Entebbe raid had helped bring down Ugandan dictator Idi Amin. The president reasoned that air strikes could not destroy Iran's nuclear knowledge, while the prime minister countered that, without centrifuges, that know-how was useless—"a pilot without a plane can't fly," he said. The administration predicted that tightened sanctions would drive Iran away from the negotiating table, but the Israeli government insisted that sanctions, alone, would keep it there. Washington warned that war with Iran could ignite a regional firestorm. Jerusalem countered that inaction toward Iran would result in the nuclear armament of many Middle Eastern states and the undermining of global security. Iran, according to Obama, was a pragmatic player with addressable interests. For Netanyahu, Iran was irrational, messianic, and genocidal—"worse," he said, "than fifty North Koreas."

Around these precipices I stepped, cautious to stress publicly that America and Israel were determined to deny nuclear weapons to Iran, even if we differed over how to achieve that goal. Off the record, I briefed reporters about the mounting need for a credible military threat against Iran, emphasizing that, paradoxically, the larger that threat the smaller the chances anybody would have to use it. I reminded them that Israel neutralized the nuclear reactor in Iraq and was blamed for the destruction of Syria's site, but neither case resulted in war. In fact, I stressed, nobody knew for certain what would happen if Iran were attacked, only the results if it were not. Terrorists would get atomic arms, the entire Middle East would go nuclear, and the word *nonproliferation* would become meaningless.

I spoke to the journalists on deep background—not for attribution—knowing that my remarks would nevertheless reach and displease the administration. The already-simmering controversy over Iran would soon boil over. While answering press queries on Iran's zone of immunity, I began to question my own.

Ducks and Bombs

Exposure was indeed a concern on the bone-chilling dawn of Sunday, March 4, 2012, as I waited on the tarmac of Andrews Air Force Base. The prime minister would soon arrive for his annual AIPAC speech and his ninth meeting with the president. Media attention focused on both events, anticipating headlines about Iran. I braced myself for that breaking news as much as I did against the wind until Netanyahu's plane finally touched down.

"You're not the first Israeli leader to face this situation," I began, after bundling into his limousine. The purpose was to bolster him for what might be a tough conversation with Obama, and produced the handiest tool I knew: history. "In 1948, Ben-Gurion had to decide whether or not to declare the State and then be invaded by Arab armies. Those armies again surrounded Israel in 1967, and Eshkol had to decide whether or not to strike first. In both cases, the Americans urged them, 'Don't act now, give us more time for diplomacy.' And both Ben-Gurion and Eshkol replied, 'No, Israel's existence is threatened and we must defend ourselves.'"

Netanyahu nodded gravely. "Good precedents," he said softly, almost absently, but he would cite them several times in his subsequent press interviews.

The motorcade wound its way through Washington's specially barricaded intersections, passed the camera-snapping tourists who thought they were photographing Obama. Delivering the prime minister and his entourage at Blair House, I left to hear the president's speech at AIPAC. Before another record-topping crowd of pro-Israel activists, Obama reaffirmed his willingness to use force against Iran, while also underscoring his preference for diplomacy. "Already, there is too much loose talk of war," he said to tepid applause. "Now is not the time for bluster."

These words seemed to presage a confrontational meeting at the White House the next day. Netanyahu presented Obama with a gift of the book of Esther—read on the Purim holiday celebrated that week—about Jewish survival from a Persian existential threat. And yet the discussion dealt with virtually all the outstanding Middle Eastern issues except Iran. At the traditional luncheon, the Israeli team talked about the need for greater American support for the moderate Syrian opposition and for less backing for Egypt's Muslim Brotherhood. Obama restated his request for an Israeli apology to Turkey over the 2010 flotilla incident. "He's not living in the sixteenth century," Obama said of Turkey's strongman. "We could do much worse than have a bunch of Erdoğans in the Middle East."

Later, the two leaders left for their one-on-one session in the Oval Office, where they undoubtedly tackled the nuclear issue. Still, they emerged three hours later virtually beaming. Obama told reporters that the United States will "always have Israel's back," and Netanyahu declared that "America accepts and understands Israel's position on Iran."

No snubs, no lectures—the press remained disappointed until the following night, when Netanyahu delivered his AIPAC speech. The prime minister opened by rebuking those who claimed that the Iranian nuclear program, with its fortified facilities, its highly enriched uranium, and intercontinental missiles, was peaceful. "If it looks like a duck, walks like a duck, then what is it?" he rhetorically asked. "That's right, it's a duck. But this is a nuclear duck." The audience laughed and applauded, but then went silent when Netanyahu quoted from a declassified U.S. document that I had given him. It described how, in 1944, American Jewish leaders beseeched the Roosevelt administration to bomb the rail lines to Auschwitz. The answer was "no." Such an operation, the War Department explained, would be "of doubtful efficacy . . . and might even provoke more vindictive action by the Germans." The parallels with Iran were patent.

The "nuclear duck" passage went digitally viral, spliced in with snippets of an affronted Daffy Duck huffing, "I've never been more inthulted in my life!" Gary Ginsberg, the Time Warner executive who again helped fine-tune the speech, made me a T-shirt emblazoned with a madcap duck bronco-riding a nuclear warhead that evoked the classic film *Dr. Strangelove*. But the reference to Auschwitz had darker reverberations. The brilliant scholar Robert Satloff, head of the prestigious Washington Institute for Near East Policy, called me, exasperated. "Do you realize what your boss just did?" Rob chided me. "He made Obama into Roosevelt."

Rob's comparison would have been less problematic if Obama had reciprocally viewed Netanyahu as Churchill. But, rather than acting like historic allies, the United States and Israel lashed out at each other like adversaries. Ehud Barak delayed the holding of the largest-ever U.S.-Israel military maneuvers. Pentagon sources told Jeffrey Goldberg that Barak's decision was designed to signal American approval for an attack. Refuting this claim, Joint Chiefs of Staff chairman General Martin Dempsey stated that the United States would not be "complicit" in any Israeli action against Iranian facilities, which action, he estimated, would only set them back a few years. I did my best to explain to the press that the postponement of the joint exercise was for technical, not political, reasons. And a few years was a long time in the Middle East, I added, citing the changes wrought in the single year since the Arab Spring. "Diplomacy hasn't succeeded," I told Bloomberg News. "We've come to a very critical juncture where important decisions do have to be made."

Decisions were indeed made by the P5+1, which, on April 16, resumed negotiations with Iran. Convening first in Istanbul and then in Moscow, the delegates attempted to work out an arrangement based on the reduction of Iran's 20 percent–enriched stockpile. "Iran's window to seek and obtain a peaceful resolution will not remain open forever," the administration routinely declared. The window remained ajar well into June, but admitted no progress.

Meanwhile, Iran's disposition hardened. Tehran stated flatly that it would never cease enrichment, never close the subterranean Fordow facility, and never allow international inspectors into the Parchin military site, suspected of conducting nuclear tests. Iran developed new nuclear fuel rods and test-fired missiles into the Persian Gulf. Challenging Obama's claim that Iran was more isolated than ever, Ahmadinejad convened representatives of the 120 Non-Aligned Movement nations, together with UN secretary-general Ban Ki-moon, who voted unanimously in favor of Iran's right to enrich uranium. "With the force of God behind it," the Iranian president prayed, "we shall soon experience a world without the United States and Zionism."

Iran's rhetoric against Israel and the Jews also intensified. Ahmadinejad compared the Jewish State to a mosquito and a cancerous tumor—"an insult to humanity"—and his vice president, Mohammed-Reza Rahimi, blamed the Talmud for the global drug trade. Addressing a defense conference in Tehran, military chief Major General Hassan Firouzabadi proclaimed that "the Iranian nation is standing for its cause and that is the full annihilation of Israel." A report commissioned by Supreme Leader Khamenei called for launching an all-out war against Israel within two years, using long-range Iranian missiles capable, the paper claimed, "of destroying Israel in less than nine minutes."

These vicious Iranian words soon translated into murderous action. Starting in February 2012, when an al-Quds Force operative blew off his own legs while trying to bomb an Israeli diplomatic target, Iran masterminded a series of terrorist attacks worldwide. Mossad and foreign intelligence networks subsequently managed to thwart similar strikes against Israelis in Kenya, South Africa, Cyprus, Azerbaijan, and Georgia. But not all of Iran's aggression could be stopped. A car bomb wounded the wife of Israel's military attaché in New Delhi. Then, on July 18—exactly eighteen years after Iranian explosives killed eighty-five people at a Jewish center in Buenos Aires—Hezbollah terrorists struck a bus carrying Israeli tourists in Burgas airport in Bulgaria. A bomb planted in the luggage compartment blew burning bodies out of the bus, killing seven and wounding thirty-three.

If intended to deter Netanyahu, Iran's genocidal threats and terror campaign only intensified his fury. Characteristically quoting Churchill, he warned of the "slumber of democracies" in the face of looming dangers. He took issue with the P5+1 talks, accusing them of giving Iran a "freebie," and enabling the centrifuges to keep spinning. He demanded an end to all enrichment by Iran, the removal of its entire stockpile, and the complete dismantling of Fordow. On Canadian television, the prime minister said, "Iran will not stop unless it sees clear determination by the democratic countries of the world and a clear red line."

Yet, among the democracies, only Israel appeared poised to react to that red line's crossing. Throughout July and August, the press highlighted IDF preparations. Some of these reports even claimed that Israeli jets were stationed secretly in Azerbaijan and Saudi Arabia. Defense Secretary Panetta and General Dempsey both came to Israel—*rushed* might be the better word—to soothe and embrace us. Panetta's predecessor, Robert Gates, warned that "an American or Israeli military strike on Iran could . . . prove catastrophic, haunting us for generations." California senator Dianne Feinstein, chairwoman of the Senate Select Committee on Intelligence, complained to me about the reported practice jump of three hundred Israeli paratroopers. "It's part of your buildup," she charged. "I assure you, Madame Chairman, Israel's airborne are not about to take Tehran," I calmly replied. But, inside, my trepidation mounted.

For months I had listened to Ehud Barak warn that history will brutally judge us—Israelis and Americans both—for estimating that one or two years remained before Iran broke out to nuclear militarization when, in fact, the dash had already occurred. And once completed, the heavy-water facility at Arak would require less than a year to produce a plutonium bomb. Repeatedly, I heard Israeli national security advisor Yaakov Amidror describe the process as "It's too early, too early," and then, with a clap of his hands, shout, "Oops, it's too late!" Like North Korea, Iran would surprise the allies by wakening them one day with the news of a successfully tested nuclear device.

In terms of the Iranian program's pace, even weather-wise the summer of 2012 indeed seemed the last opportunity to attack. Yet the very thought of such an operation left me deeply conflicted. On the one hand, I unstintingly believed that Israel had the right and the duty to defend itself—that, by eschewing further diplomacy and deflecting existential threats, Ben-Gurion in 1948 and Eshkol in 1967 had both acted prudently and morally. I knew that maintaining our long-term deterrence power, even more than our daily security needs, was a paramount Israeli interest. On the other hand, though, there was the possible cost, even to my own family. Lia, our daughter, was getting married in Jerusalem that summer and already my relatives were phoning me frantically, asking, "Is it safe to come? We know you know." I did not, in fact, know, and assuming an almost unbearable onus of responsibility assured them that, yes, everything would be fine.

That was more than I could say about the U.S.-Israel alliance. By the summer, the two countries were openly quarreling about Iran. At a mid-August meeting in Caesarea with House Intelligence Committee chair Mike Rogers, Netanyahu expressed exasperation with Obama's policy. "There is no definition of when the knife cuts into the American flesh," he complained. "American policy now is not to stop Iran but to stop Israel." He urged the United States to define what it saw as Iran's "threshold capacity," and to make clear at which point it would act. "For the first time since Nagasaki and Hiroshima, you can get Nagasaki and Hiroshima in Tel Aviv."

I was present at the talk along with Dan Shapiro, who performed his ambassadorial duty by defending the president. The Israeli press turned this into an open altercation with Netanyahu, which I emphatically denied. But I could not gainsay Rogers, a Republican and burly former FBI agent, who later described an "agitated" and "elevated" discussion. "Bibi's at his wit's end . . . with the administration," he told Detroit radio back home. "I've never seen anything like it."

Even less refutable was Secretary of State Clinton's September 9 statement to Bloomberg. "The sanctions . . . are . . . by far the best approach to take at this time," she said. "We're not setting deadlines." The remark appeared directed at Netanyahu's "red line" demand, and the prime minister shot back by accusing the White House of giving Iran precisely what it wanted—time to enrich while endlessly negotiating. "Those in the international community who refuse to put red lines before Iran don't have a moral right to place a red light before Israel."

The confrontation reminded me of the earlier spats over the peace process. Back then, I advocated for a "rope-a-dope" approach, involving absorbing the administration's criticism. My friend David Rothkopf once quipped to me, "The administration gets tough with Israel for being impolite on settlements, and shows flexibility with Iran for building nuclear weapons," and I thought: if only we could show flexibility on the peace process, we could get tougher on Iran. I also doubted the efficacy of responding publicly to every administration statement on Iran, particularly if the source was not Obama. Quietly, I agreed with Foreign Minister Liberman, who preferred to keep our differences with America confidential and who, quoting from *The Good, the Bad, and the Ugly,* said, "When you have to shoot, shoot. Don't talk." But Netanyahu obviously concluded otherwise. Israel, he felt, had to maintain the pressure on foreign decision makers—Americans included—and the impression of our readiness to act.

That policy, though, had two unanticipated consequences. The first, in the United States, related to the approaching 2012 presidential elections and allegations that Netanyahu's outspokenness on Iran was intended to weaken Obama and bolster his Republican opponent, Mitt Romney. *The New York Times* claimed that Netanyahu had personally briefed Romney on the Iranian issue and consulted with him about ratcheting up sanctions. The report was untrue: Netanyahu had made a short courtesy call to Romney, as well as to the other Republican candidates, after his last meeting with Obama. Iran was never discussed. Yet the accusation stuck and amplified with each tit-for-tat on the nuclear issue. "Understand, what Americans see through the lens of elections, Israelis see through the prism of an existential threat," I tried to explain to journalists—in vain, for the debate only escalated. "Netanyahu would be wrong to root for Romney," Jeffrey Goldberg opined. "Barack Obama is the one who's more likely to confront Iran militarily, should sanctions and negotiations fail." To which Bret Stephens in *The Wall Street Journal* retorted, "We will not have another war in the Middle East . . . if President Romney orders Iran's nuclear sites bombed to smithereens."

My efforts to keep the Iran issue clear of the elections brought me to the White House office of Deputy National Security Advisor—and close Obama counsel—Denis McDonough. "Morning, everyone," he said pepping up his sleep-deprived staff. "What are we doing for America today?" Rather than remaining in the air-conditioned interior, he took me for a stroll across the South Lawn, where the temperature hovered above a hundred. Yet the svelte and energetic McDonough scarcely sweated. After we had mutually inquired about our children, he refreshingly turned to me and said, "Let's face it, we don't give a shit about one another's kids. The bottom line is that Bibi and the president are practical men—nothing's personal here—and nobody should delude himself that the president won't act." Then, employing a metaphor that only an ex-American would understand, McDonough assured me that "America wants to move the ball steadily up the field, run down the clock, and make a touchdown."

I reported the gist of McDonough's words to Jerusalem—the president expected the prime minister to trust him on Iran—but they were lost in a rancorous din. The second unintended result of Netanyahu's pronouncements on the nuclear issue was to spark a public shouting match over the question of an Israeli preemptive strike. This, opponents of the operation argued, would ignite a desperate war with Iran and its regional allies—Syria and Hezbollah—and isolate Israel internationally. Relations with America would be perilously and perhaps permanently strained. For that exorbitant price, Israel would gain only a few years' delay in Iran's nuclear activities. In the long run, critics predicted, military action was liable to accelerate the program.

Leading the opposition was Meir Dagan, the former Mossad chief, who accused Netanyahu and Barak of "adventurism" and "shallowness" in dealing with Israel's security, and warned of another Yom Kippur War–like catastrophe. "Attacking Iran is the stupidest idea I've ever heard," he said. The press quoted the widely respected former IDF chief of staff Gabi Ashkenazi deeming any Israeli action at this time a "strategic mistake." Yuval Diskin, the past head of Israel's Internal Security Service—the renowned Shin Bet—denounced both the prime minister and defense minister as "messianic."

Among the most strident of these voices was that of another esteemed former IDF chief—himself born in Tehran—Shaul Mofaz. "Netanyahu is sowing panic in the public in order to divert its attention from social issues," he warned. Just after landing in Israel for consultations in August, I received instructions to appear on a televised panel that night and offer a counterweight to Mofaz. Only a few months earlier, while he briefly brought his Kadima Party into the coalition, I hosted Mofaz in Washington and brought him to meet the president. Now, stopping at a restaurant en route to the studio and changing into a suit, I prepared to debate him on national TV. "Obama has recognized Israel's right, as a sovereign country, to defend itself," I began, sluggish with jet lag. But Mofaz snapped, "Bibi is jeopardizing the lives of our children!" The other panelists, agreeing, piled on.

The list of security figures opposing Netanyahu lengthened and then peaked with the addition of Ehud Barak. Speaking to the press on September 8, the defense minister appeared to pull back from his previous combativeness on Iran. "In spite of . . . maintaining Israel's right to act independently, we have to remember the importance of our partnership with the U.S. and we should do everything possible not to harm it." A few days later, Barak flew to Chicago—reportedly without Netanyahu's knowledge—for a confidential conversation in the mayor's office with Rahm Emanuel. Cynical commentators in the Israeli press speculated that Barak, whose poll numbers indicated he would not be reelected, no longer felt compelled to support Netanyahu. All observers concurred that, when it came to Iran, the prime minister now stood virtually alone.

I joined him in the flagstone courtyard of the Prime Minister's Residence in the last week of September. Also present was chief advisor Ron Dermer and Gary Ginsberg, of Time Warner. Together, we sat to draft Netanyahu's crucial UN General Assembly speech. I knew the subject would once again be Iran, but was unprepared for the angle.

"I'm going to draw a red line around twenty percent enrichment," Netanyahu explained. "Right now the Iranians have about 180 kilograms and in a matter of a few months, at most, they can expand that to the 250 kilograms they need for a nuclear arsenal. Think of the uranium like gunpowder. You pack it into a bomb and light the fuse. But if you can't fill the bomb all the way, it won't go off. At the point when the Iranians have enough twenty percent uranium to fill the bomb nearly to the top, that's where I'll draw the red line."

We looked at him quizzically. "Let me show you," he said. A skilled draftsman from his MIT architecture days, Netanyahu took a piece of paper and a felt-tipped pen and drew a cannonball freestyle. He even added a little fuse. "Here," he indicated and, exchanging the black pen for a red one, drew a line at 90 percent of the shell.

"Why don't you show the drawing during your speech?" Gary suggested, but Netanyahu merely smiled.

"They'll compare it to Yosemite Sam," he predicted and proceeded to draw a decent likeness of the mustachioed, gun-toting Looney Tunes character.

"No, Mr. Prime Minister," I respectfully replied. "They'll compare it to Wile E. Coyote."

On Thursday, September 27, Netanyahu stood at the marbled jade podium of the UN General Assembly and delivered his toughest speech yet on Iran. He dismissed the containment policy—"For the ayatollahs, mutually assured destruction is not a deterrent, it's an inducement"—and denied that diplomacy had achieved any slow-down in Iran's nuclearization. "Red lines don't lead to war, red lines prevent war," he posited. "Faced with a clear red line, Iran will back down." Then, unfolding a chart, he showed the bomb. Prepared by a graphic artist rather than drawn by the prime minister, the bomb indeed looked cartoonish, complete with a sparkling fuse. Yet nobody in the packed hall as much as giggled as Netanyahu produced an extra-thick red pen and drew his 90 percent line.

Later, in the VIP suite, Netanyahu received a call from Obama. An audibly relieved president thanked him for the speech, which he deemed courageous and statesmanlike. The two leaders chatted about other subjects as well, all amiably, again referring to each other as "Barack" and "Bibi" and "my friend." Clearly Obama understood as we did that the red line speech marked not only the upper limit of Iranian enrichment, but the peak of Israel's threatened attack on Iran. This would now not take place, as so many feared, before the U.S. elections.

Outside, the media zoomed in on Netanyahu's bomb sketch. Opinions were divided over whether it represented an ingenious attention-grabbing device or a slick PR trick, much like the "nuclear duck." True to predictions, the prime minister was not likened to the gun-slinging Yosemite Sam, but to Wile E. Coyote, haplessly holding a fizzling bomb while, with a triumphant "beep beep," an Iranian Road Runner escaped.

A vastly more serious debate centered over whether the red-line concept could succeed. Several analysts warned that Iran could now expand its entire program right up to the line and then, in a single movement, cross it to create not one but twenty bombs. But another school noted that Iran's production of 20 percent–enriched uranium ceased well short of the 250 kilogram mark, and that the red line actually worked. Either way, the reality remained that Iran continued to operate thousands of centrifuges, thicken its stockpiles, and construct long-range missiles. Iran still imperiled Israel's existence.

And I was left ambivalent. Part of me agreed with my friend Ari Shavit, who, in his bestselling book *My Promised Land,* lamented Israel's failure "to mobilize all of its powers to contend properly with its most dramatic challenge." Part of me worried about how our restraint in the face of Iranian dangers might be interpreted by other hostile forces. But some part of me experienced relief. Instead of enduring a major crisis, Israel enjoyed one of its quietest summers ever. Lia and her adoring betrothed, Yair, married under a sun-gilded *chuppa* overlooking the Jerusalem hills. President Peres again honored us with his presence. Together, my American and Israeli families danced ecstatically until dawn.

Eased as an Israeli father, I was also becalmed as Israel's ambassador. More than a half century before, I recalled, during the Suez Crisis, the IDF attacked Egypt only a few days before the U.S. elections. An enraged President Eisenhower condemned and nearly sanctioned Israel. President Obama might have reacted with similar fury had Israel preempted Iran before November 2.

Commentators later posited several explanations for Israel's forbearance. Some suggested that the loud debate within Israel put the Iranians on high alert and eliminated the advantage of surprise. Others claimed that analysts close to the prime minister predicted a Republican victory, which, they held, would provide for closer U.S.-Israeli cooperation on Iran. And then there were those who insisted that Netanyahu lacked the courage to act and that he was all along bluffing. I was content to say the president had asked for "time and space" to deal with Iran diplomatically, and, ally-like, the prime minister had consented.

• • •

A month later, I received an inquiry from *The New York Times*'s Mark Landler, one of the finest journalists I knew. Reports were circulating of secret face-to-face talks between American and Iranian representatives, Mark informed me, and asked for Israel's reaction. A quick dial to the Prime Minister's Office procured the answer: Israel welcomed any steps to resolve the Iranian nuclear threat diplomatically. I duly passed this on to Mark, but, in midsentence, my phone indicated another incoming call from Jerusalem. Putting Mark on hold, I heard a completely different response. Getting back to the understandably irked correspondent, I dictated Israel's new official line. Landler wrote:

"Israel's ambassador to the United States . . . said the administration had not informed Israel, and that the Israeli government feared Iran would use new talks to 'advance their nuclear weapons program. . . . We do not think Iran should be rewarded with direct talks, rather that sanctions and all other possible pressures on Iran must be increased.'"

This back-and-forth between Landler and Jerusalem would have been awkward enough if conducted in the Aquarium, behind my desk. Unfortunately, the conversation took place on the water, through the cellphone that I always kept, waterproofed and secured, in my single scull. I was rowing on the Potomac, in the bay between Arlington National Cemetery and the Lincoln Memorial, directly in the path of yachts and ferries. One hand held the phone and the other intensely clasped my oars to keep the boat from capsizing. I explained Netanyahu's anxiety over U.S.-Iranian negotiations that were liable to result in a dangerous deal for Israel. I fought to sound calm, all the while watching the wakes—both real and metaphoric—churn closer.

How You Doin', Shimon?

Whenever someone asked me, "Are you enjoying your job?" I immediately thought of the Iranian issue, media criticism of Israel, and the American Jewish maze, and laughed. Then, after regaining my composure, I spoke about the privilege of serving my country and upholding the world's most precious alliance. "And, yes," I admitted, "I do sometimes have fun. I get to hang out with Shimon Peres."

In fact, I got to hang out with not one Shimon Peres but three.

First, there was the political Peres, the Labor Party apparatchik who in the 1970s championed some of the most radical settlers, and then, starting in the early 1990s, spearheaded the peace process. This was the Peres rejected by the majority of Israelis, who associated him with backstabbing intrigues and who consistently denied him the premiership. I, too, resented this Peres, especially during the Second Intifada, when, with Israeli buses blowing up, he persisted in downplaying Arafat's role in terror.

But then there was the second Peres, the historical Peres. The Peres who had made *aliya* alone, milked cows, and tended sheep before becoming Ben-Gurion's right-hand defense man during the War of Independence and Israel's tenuous first decade. This was the Peres who championed the Dimona nuclear reactor, who put the world's greatest power into the hands of the world's most vulnerable people.

Finally, there was the presidential Peres. Nearing ninety, he had at last gained what he always coveted—the love of Israel's people. Though nominally the head of state, the Israeli president's function is largely ceremonial. It includes accepting diplomats' credentials, approving the appointment of Supreme Court judges, bestowing national awards, and pardoning prisoners. Most substantively, the president oversees the dissolution of the Knesset and, after elections, determines which party is likeliest to form the new coalition. For that reason, and because he (or, theoretically, she) is chosen by the Knesset, the president is most often a politician. Peres was indeed that, but, once ascending to the presidency, he became incalculably more. He became the mirror of Israel's best image of itself, an internationally admired statesman, an icon.

I got to sit with all three. With President Peres, I discussed international and, especially, American affairs. I pressed the historical Peres about his role in clandestinely acquiring arms for Israel in 1948, about the buildup to the 1956 Suez Campaign, when France, rather than the United States, was our principal ally. The master of the diplomatic *tour d'horizon,* the sentimentalist who adored reminiscing about Guy Mollet, Christian Pineau, and other French politicians of the 1950s, Peres could talk for hours. And we did, over breakfast each time I returned to Israel, in his hotel room whenever he visited America, and in limousines to and from airports. We talked books, we talked ideas, and, in talking with the historical and presidential Peres, I quickly forgot Peres the politician.

Netanyahu, though, could not. While the two men, after decades of rivalry, begrudgingly respected each other, Peres and the prime minister were often at odds. Unwilling to remain within his symbolic role, the president ran a shadow government with positions openly divergent from Netanyahu's. On the peace process, Peres called for freezing settlements indefinitely and for accepting the principle of a Palestinian state on the 1967 lines with swaps. Never understating the danger posed by the ayatollahs, the man who opposed Israel's 1981 bombing of the Iraqi reactor was now not about to support a similar strike against Iran. Rather, Peres urged Israelis to demonstrate restraint and place their trust in Obama.

And Obama, not surprisingly, appreciated him. From the eve of my appointment until the end of my term, America's president repeatedly welcomed Israel's to the White House. Their conversations, warm and mutually deferential, touched on all the pressing Middle Eastern issues. Consistently, Peres asked for Jonathan Pollard's release and, just as regularly, Obama demurred. At some point, the pair always adjourned for a prolonged one-on-one talk. Free of the usual fear of hiccups and kerfuffles, I enjoyed these meetings, yet they placed me in a dilemma. As much as I cherished my friendship with Peres and deferred to his preeminent rank, I was sworn to preserve Netanyahu's trust. But trust did not always characterize his relationship with Peres, whom he suspected of pursuing an independent foreign policy. Here was another high-wire act I had to execute, serving my president and updating my boss, one diplomatic foot planted carefully after the other.

Outside of Washington, though, accompanying Peres was, quite simply, fun. No sooner had I seen Netanyahu's plane off from icy Andrews Air Force Base in March than I boarded another flight to California and a rendezvous with Peres. At the DreamWorks headquarters, Steven Spielberg and Jeffrey Katzenberg convened the major studio heads to listen to Peres hold forth on Middle East and global affairs, even neurology. "The human brain understands everything around it, but does not understand itself," Peres observed. "Brain science is our next great frontier." He posed for photos with Billy Crystal and Barbra Streisand, then rushed to a reception for Hollywood stars hosted by media mogul Haim Saban and then another gathering of Hispanic leaders held by actors Andy Garcia and Eva Longoria. At each event, Peres revealed the secret of Jewish success: "Dissatisfaction." Jetting back to New York, I watched him on *The View* charm Barbara Walters and Whoopi Goldberg by inviting them to join his Facebook page. "Won't you be my friends?" he pouted. Later, I sat with Peres as he tried for a fervid hour to convince a subdued Woody Allen to situate his next film not in Paris or Barcelona, but in Tel Aviv.

Assisted by his dedicated and mostly female staff—my office called them, affectionately, the "Peresites"—the president could be difficult to keep up with. Ever gracious, he was impossible not to like. With his corona of silver hair reminiscent of Ben-Gurion's, his elegant suits, perspicacious eyes, and paternal air, he was the embodiment of the éminence grise. Despite his heavy Polish accent in Hebrew, English, and French, he succeeded in fashioning supple turns of phrase. I often jotted down these "Peresisms," listing among my favorites, "Egypt is not a river with a country, it is a country with a river." And, "You can't come to the Arab Spring dressed in wintry clothing." And, "The Middle East is divided between holy places and oily places." Then, finally, my favorite, something that only Peres could say in public: "There are two things you must never do in front of a camera: make love and make Middle East peace."

None of these Peres experiences could cap the White House ceremony on June 13, 2012, when he received the Presidential Medal of Freedom. Awarded for "an especially meritorious contribution to . . . world peace," this was America's highest civilian distinction. Some cynical journalists saw the event's timing—six months before the U.S. elections—as a transparent ploy for the Jewish vote or even a slap to Netanyahu in reprisal for his recalcitrance on Iran. Yet I saw the sentiment as genuine, reflecting Obama's abiding respect for Peres. That esteem, however, did not inhibit the administration from denying entry to several members of the honoree's entourage.

That decision reached me at Blair House while I was working round-the-clock on Peres's speech. Israel's president was visibly upset—these were some of his closest friends—and asked me to call the White House. I did, and heard how these individuals had criticized Obama on television or committed some other offense that necessitated their omission from the guest list. One of the stricken names belonged to retired general Doron Almog. The son of Holocaust survivors, he had lost a brother in the Yom Kippur War and five close family members in an Intifada suicide bombing. Together with his educator wife, Deedee, Doron was also the founder of a Negev village dedicated to treating severely autistic children, among them their son, Eran. But radical European groups branded Almog, a decorated veteran of the Entebbe raid, a war criminal for his role in combating Hamas. The sight of Doron and Deedee in the East Room might be offensive to those leftists, the administration apparently feared.

Outraged, I phoned Jack Lew, the former deputy secretary of state and now Obama's chief of staff, with whom I always spoke frankly. "Just know, Jack, who you're blackballing," I explained. "Tomorrow's headline in Israel won't be, 'Peres Gets Freedom Medal,' but 'Obama Insults Israeli Hero.'" The ever-sage Lew instantly understood. The Almogs, at least, were admitted.

These bumps notwithstanding, the evening went smoothly—in fact, stunningly. Included among the more than 140 attendees were former secretaries of state Henry Kissinger and George Shultz as well as Bill and Hillary Clinton. Israeli violinist Itzhak Perlman serenaded us with a minuet and Obama toasted us, "L'Chaim!" In Peres, the president said, "we see the essence of Israel itself—an indomitable spirit that will not be denied." Peres replied by accepting the honor in the name of "the pioneers who built homes on barren mountains, on shifting sands. Who sacrificed their lives for their country." Seated between Sally and Secretary Clinton, I beamed as the last leader of Israel's founding generation—if not our Madison, our Monroe—"paid tribute to . . . the Jews who dreamed of, and fought for, a state of their own." I took pride in the fact that I helped the president to write his words about America's eternal bonds with Israel and the imperative quest for peace, though I failed to dissuade him from mentioning "brain science."

The next day, at the Residence, we hosted our largest-ever reception. There to honor Peres were his adoring children and grandchildren, Yitzhak Rabin's daughter Dalia, and hundreds of admirers from Israel and across the United States. Speaker after prestigious speaker rose to praise him. Then came my turn. And what could I, after all those accolades from world leaders, possibly add? So I told how, twenty years earlier, when we were living in the desert community of Sde Boker, the then foreign minister came to lay a wreath on the grave of his mentor, Ben-Gurion. Walking toward the hallowed site, he was stopped by a feisty eight-year-old who waved at him and cheered, "Hey, Shimon, how you doin'?" And rather than ignoring the kid and proceeding with the ceremony, the foreign minister took the boy aside and chatted with him for several minutes. "That boy," I told the guests, "was our son Yoav. And that minister is the man we extol today, a man who, at the heights of political power, found time for an eight-year-old child."

Later that night, at a private dinner with his staff, Peres praised me as "a man completely without ego." I was moved and grateful for this opportunity not only to touch, but to befriend, history. But history, by nature, does not wait, and while the past accomplishments of one president were feted, the future of another would soon be sealed. As Peres's plane took off for Israel, I pivoted on the tarmac and started grappling with the next controversy: Israel's alleged interference in the 2012 U.S. elections.

Polls Apart

Among its awe-inspiring achievements, Israel's democracy stands supreme. Older than more than half of the world's democracies, a member of that select club of countries—such as the United States, Britain, and Canada—that have never known a second of nondemocratic governance, Israel is unique in having withstood pressures capable of crushing most democratic systems. Yet, during elections, Israel's scrappy Athenian-style democracy turns Spartan. The campaigns, strictly controlled financially and lasting roughly three months, feature a single hour of nightly television ads that hardly anyone watches. Whether it's because democracy in Israel arose less out of ideals than from political necessity—the only way that multiple Zionist parties could achieve anything—or because so many issues are life-or-death, election time is not happy. There are no balloons, no ribbons, no conventions with streamer-hatted delegates hoisting placards. "If Americans celebrate democracy, then Israelis endure it," I once wrote in *The New York Times*. "Voting in Israel feels like playing an extreme version of Russian roulette, a bullet in every chamber but one."

That pistol was fully loaded—for me, at least—as America entered its 2012 elections. Throughout the previous three years, much of the U.S. and Israeli media promoted a narrative in which Netanyahu actively stumped for the Republicans. The press pointed to the prime minister's friendship with Sheldon Adelson and his close association with House Majority Leader Eric Cantor, the only Jewish Republican congressman and history's highest-ranking elected American Jew. In its preference for free markets, its antipathy to political correctness, and militant stance on Iran, Netanyahu's worldview indeed resembled the GOP's. "Wouldn't Netanyahu prefer an administration closer to his own beliefs?" journalists often asked me. "Could he afford another four years of public spats and not-so-secret disagreements with Obama?"

Such questions were, in fact, irrelevant. Israel must never interfere—or even appear to intercede—in any American election, I maintained, much less one for the presidency. Choosing a chief executive, even one known to have contrarian views on Israel, remained a categorically internal American affair. Hewing to that rule, though, did not mean refraining from prognostications about which of the contenders would prevail. The winner in 2012, I had long predicted to Jerusalem, would be Barack Obama.

That conclusion reflected less my assessment of the president's record than my gauging of America. During my period in Washington, the once-WASPy United States became a nation with a white and Protestant minority and a Supreme Court presided over by Catholics and Jews. Single-parent families outnumbered traditional nuclear families and Hispanics now accounted for nearly a quarter of all K–12 students. Obama still succeeded in harnessing these transformations and cobbling together coalitions from diverse constituencies—liberals, students, immigrants, and minorities. Preserving civil liberties remained an overriding concern for a sizable number of American Jews who were, to quote one embittered conservative, "more pro-choice than pro-Israel." The Republicans, by contrast, appeared determined to alienate all of these interest groups.

I submitted my evaluation, but not everyone in the Prime Minister's Office agreed. "Mosaic politics never work" was one answer I received. Others cited polls indicating a guaranteed Republican landslide. Nevertheless, I stuck by my forecast, all the while laboring to avoid the minutest impression of favoritism. Yet, as the election cycle accelerated, that task grew nearly impossible.

The race was close and hinged on several key states, including Florida, with its sizable Jewish population. The pro-Israel vote could, then, become pivotal. Though the Democrats accused the Republicans of making Israel into a wedge issue, they were the first to post a YouTube clip with snippets of Netanyahu and me praising the incumbent. A Republican version soon followed. Speaking before American Jewish donors in New York, Obama purportedly said that "if Netanyahu lived in the United States, he'd probably be a Republican." The remark deeply upset the prime minister, who saw it as a deliberate attempt to divide American Jews on the Israel issue. "How would he feel if I described him to Israelis as a Laborite?" he asked me. The front page of *The New York Times* posited that Netanyahu and Republican front-runner Mitt Romney enjoyed "a warm friendship, little known to outsiders, that is now rich with political intrigue." The article traced the relationship to the mid-1970s, when both men worked at the Boston Consulting Group. A closer reading, though, revealed that the two overlapped at BCG for exactly one month. I protested the piece in a letter to the editor, but without effect. In the public's eye, Netanyahu and Romney were now best friends, and the only question was which party initiated the story, Republican or Democrat?

The matter was rendered largely moot on July 29, when Romney landed in Israel. He met with Netanyahu, Peres, and Palestinian prime minister Fayyad, and prayed at the Western Wall—all without incident. From the beginning, though, the tour triggered friction. Attributing Israel's high-tech success to "Providence" and the "hand of culture," Romney drew accusations of racism from the Palestinians, who also condemned his call to recognize Jerusalem as Israel's capital. Left-wing Israelis criticized him for snubbing the head of the Labor Party opposition, which they described as Israel's version of the Democrats. A fund-raising event inadvertently scheduled on a Jewish fast day had to be postponed to the next morning but then continued to draw fire when American donors contributed $1 million to the Romney campaign. "We have a solemn duty . . . to deny Iran's leaders the means to follow through on their malevolent intentions," Romney said, clearly rebuking Obama. "We must not delude ourselves into thinking that containment is an option." From Washington, Vice President Biden acridly dismissed the remark as "just another feeble attempt by the Romney campaign to score political points at the expense of this critical partnership."

The heightened tension crested the following night when the Netanyahus hosted Romney and his wife and their son, Josh, for a private dinner. "It's standard practice for the prime minister to meet with visiting presidential candidates," I told reporters, and reminded them that then opposition head Netanyahu had similarly met with Senator Obama in 2008. But the intimacy of the gathering was striking and difficult to explain away. Even the pro-Israel *Tablet* magazine alleged that Romney's visit—the "brainchild" of Ron Dermer, a former Republican advocate—was carefully coordinated by the Prime Minister's Office. The fact that Netanyahu had declined invitations to attend additional Romney events, including the fund-raiser, could not dispel the image of Israeli interference in American politics.

Determined not to deepen that impression, I walked fine lines around the Romney visit. Protocol-bound to accompany the candidate to Israel, I carefully limited my participation in his itinerary. The trick was to balance that caution with my curiosity about the squarely built, soft-spoken Romney and his amiable and almost absurdly good-looking family. I enjoyed discussing Middle East affairs with Dan Senor, Romney's astute foreign policy advisor, who once interviewed me for his book, *Start-Up Nation,* about Israel's high-tech miracle. But I could never cease glancing over my shoulder for the camera that would catch me "colluding"—so the headline would claim—with the Republicans.

Instead, I got lambasted by the right for expressing "profound gratitude" to Obama for signing the U.S.-Israel Enhanced Security Cooperation Act, passed by both houses of Congress, and for allocating an additional $70 million to Iron Dome. "Such an expression is . . . so inappropriate, that one has to wonder whether Oren didn't intend subtly to raise questions as to its sincerity," speculated my friend Bill Kristol in the conservative *Weekly Standard*. "Oren signals that his absurdly overdone fawning before Obama isn't to be taken too seriously."

Israel, I now understood, was unlikely to emerge unscathed from the 2012 elections. At best the damage could be minimized by keeping out of them entirely. So, prohibited by schedule conflicts from attending both the Democratic and Republican national conventions, I went to neither. Nevertheless, at the Democratic summit in Charlotte, North Carolina, starting on September 4, DNC chairwoman Debbie Wasserman Schultz of Florida told Jewish donors that I had complained to her about Republican efforts to transform Israel into a wedge issue. Such an assertion was, of course, untrue, but cherishing my friendship with Debbie, I gave her time to issue a retraction. Instead, she denied having made the remark, prompting Fox News to broadcast a video of it. Finally, as the Israeli news cycle approached, I had no choice but to respond. "I categorically deny that I ever characterized Republican policies as harmful to Israel," I said in a press statement. "Bipartisan support is a paramount national interest for Israel, and we have great friends on both sides of the aisle."

The dustup with Debbie was troubling for me, but far less than the debate that erupted on the convention floor over the question of Jerusalem. Los Angeles mayor Antonio Villaraigosa, a great friend of Israel, tried to reinsert into his party's platform the phrase "Jerusalem is and will remain the capital of Israel," which the administration had ordered removed. Villaraigosa's move sparked bitter choruses of nos and required three contentious votes to pass. AIPAC praised the restoration but Romney denounced it as a further sign of Obama's perfidy toward Israel. "The Democrats have accused Republicans of making Israel a political football by painting Mr. Obama as an unreliable partner," observed the *Times*'s Mark Landler. "But it is the Democrats who have tripped up on Israel at their convention this week."

And the electoral tensions around Israel continued to climb. During one of the presidential debates, Obama compared his trip to Israel in 2008 to his rival's more recent visit. "I didn't take donors. I didn't attend fund-raisers. I went to Yad Vashem, the Holocaust museum there, to remind myself the nature of evil and why our bond with Israel will be unbreakable." The Iranian nuclear program also crept into the contest. "Let's look at this from the view of the ayatollahs," said Republican vice presidential candidate Paul Ryan. "They see this administration trying to water down sanctions in Congress. . . . They're moving faster toward a nuclear weapon; they're spinning the centrifuges faster. They see us saying . . . we need more space with our ally Israel." In response, Vice President Biden derided Ryan's position as "malarkey," cited Netanyahu's bomb drawing as proof that Iran did not yet have a weapon, and reminded voters that "the president does not bluff." When, only days before the election, *The Sunday Times* of London reported that Israeli jets bombed a missile factory in the Sudan, anonymous sources described the raid as a "dry run for a forthcoming attack on Iran's nuclear facilities." The possibility of a preelection Israeli strike was once again thrust into the race.

Frequently at first, then almost daily, I received phone calls from Democratic leaders angry over alleged Israeli canvasing for Romney. Barbara Boxer, the veteran California senator and cosponsor of the U.S.-Israel Enhanced Security Cooperation Act, railed at me so furiously that I literally had to hold the phone from my ear. New York's

Chuck Schumer similarly hollered, "The elections are in six weeks, for chrissakes, can't you guys just stop criticizing Obama?" All my reassurances that Israel was not interfering in the elections, not campaigning for any candidate, and not criticizing Obama, failed to persuade the senators.

The bleak situation grew darkest on September 11, when the White House announced that the president would not meet with Netanyahu during the coming UN General Assembly session. The reason, according to spokesman Tommy Vietor, was that the two leaders would be in New York on different days. But Netanyahu's offer to travel to Washington was also spurned. Republican senators John McCain and Lindsey Graham quickly jumped on the snub, saying, "the White House's decision sends a troubling signal to our ally Israel about America's commitment at this dangerous and challenging time." Paul Ryan lashed out at Obama for having sufficient time to interview with Barbara Walters on morning television but not enough to meet Netanyahu.

Leaping into my cleanup mode, I ascribed the entire affair to scheduling problems. "The president is very busy and the prime minister's time is very narrow," I told CNN's Anderson Cooper. "Nobody was out to snub anybody." But this argument, too, proved unconvincing. Later that month, after Netanyahu's arrival in New York, I left the hotel for an exclusive interview on Fox. Just outside the studio, though, I learned that I would appear on a split screen with America's former ambassador to the UN John Bolton, a virulent decrier of Obama. Interviewed alongside me, he would have attacked the president and placed me in the partisan position of defending him. "Either take me off the split screen or forget the interview," I told the producers. They relented and I interviewed alone, harmlessly. But walking out of the building, I was accosted by Bolton. With a bushy mustache and bookish spectacles, he cast a refined, even academic image. Yet he physically lunged at me—so fiercely that my security detail stepped in to restrain him—and jeered, "You're afraid to go on a split screen! You know what you are? You're a weenie!"

"How'd it go?" Netanyahu inquired when I returned to his hotel suite.

"I don't know," I numbly replied. "I've just been called a weenie."

I had, in fact, been called many things during the previous contentious months, and only wanted these elections to be over. The night at last arrived—a typical night for America's democracy, bright with celebrations. After interviewing with Araleh Barnea—Israel's Walter Cronkite—I went party hopping, all the while keeping my eye on the screens as the voting results came in. Between announcements, I phoned Netanyahu and prepared him for what looked like a certain Obama victory. Finally, at a hip Microsoft/Bloomberg reception, I stood with veteran political pollster Mark Penn and watched the Florida count. "That's it," Mark said. "It's over." I excused myself to make one last call. "Congratulate him, publicly and personally," I recommended. "As quickly as possible."

Far more than those of 2008, the 2012 elections were transformative. The seismic event of four years earlier might have been a one-time tremor, but this outcome showed that the "tectonic shifts" I once described were permanent. The race, I remarked to David Rothkopf, was essentially a contest between the 1960s and the 1980s. Obama, though only a child in the sixties, nevertheless represented the multicultural, egalitarian, and Great Society ideas of that revolutionary decade. Romney was a college student in France at the time of the 1968 revolt, but spent it handing out Bibles. He stood for the traditional values and free enterprise of the Reagan era. The sixties won. If soured on hope, the country was unready for another change. It had yet to recover from the economic crisis, to overcome traumatic Middle Eastern wars, or to extricate its politics from polarization. An irreversibly altered America once again chose Obama.

Obama, too, remained unchanged. "We will . . . try and resolve our differences with other nations peacefully," he declared in his second inaugural address, "not because we are naïve about the dangers we face, but because engagement can more durably lift suspicion and fear." While respecting overseas alliances, he said, "We will renew those institutions that extend our capacity to manage crisis abroad." In other words, the United States would continue to reach out to Iran and other Middle Eastern adversaries and work collaboratively through the UN. "We will support democracy from Asia to Africa, from the Americas to the Middle East," pledged the reelected president, irrespective of the leaders that democracy produced.

Listening to these words, I thought, perhaps only I was different. In contrast to four years ago, when I stood shoulder-to-shivering-shoulder with millions of well-wishers on the Washington Monument lawn, now I gazed out at that crowd from the Capitol steps, where I sat, under official inauguration blankets, among diplomats and Congress members. That night, instead of preparing college lectures, I danced with Sally at Rahm Emanuel's Chicago party, to the blues of Buddy Guy, whom she first heard perform forty years earlier at the Fillmore. I attended receptions with Obama confidants David Axelrod and Valerie Jarrett, and with Ambassador Susan Rice and Senator John Kerry, both of them in line to be named the next secretary of state. I felt better placed to preserve and, if possible, strengthen the alliance, to help America and Israel meet the challenges of a still-roiling Middle East. While Americans celebrated their democracy, the peoples of that region failed to achieve theirs. Rather, they descended further into revolution, anarchy, atrocities, and war.

Sandstorms

At 9:40 on the night of September 11, 2012, a wave of some 150 black-clad terrorists attacked the U.S. consulate in Benghazi, Libya. Hurling grenades and firing RPGs and machine guns, the jihadis penetrated the compound and set it ablaze. Two Americans, including Ambassador J. Christopher Stevens, died from smoke inhalation. An additional two—former Navy SEALs—were killed and several were wounded at a nearby CIA annex. The Libyan Spring, once hailed by the White House as a "powerful reminder of . . . renewed American leadership in the world," became an epitaph to America's vulnerability.

News of the assault reached Washington that afternoon. I had met Chris Stevens in his previous postings in Jerusalem and at the State Department's Bureau of Near East Affairs, and his violent death shocked me. But, grappling with the combined tensions generated by Iran and the presidential elections, I barely had time to dwell on the loss. My main concern was the administration's initial reaction to the attack, which, Press Secretary Jay Carney claimed was a spontaneous response to a rabidly anti-Islamic movie, *The Innocence of Muslims,* that portrayed the Prophet as a homosexual pedophile, a womanizer, and a thug. Media sources immediately claimed that the film's producer was Israeli. Though the allegation soon proved false, I prepared for the possibility that Israel would be blamed for four American deaths.

That Sunday, Susan Rice appeared on the morning talk shows. Though evidence mounted that Libya's branch of al-Qaeda staged the attacks, the ambassador still denied that the protest was premeditated. Like an earlier disturbance outside the U.S. embassy in Cairo, the Benghazi bloodshed resulted from "this hateful video."

Convening my staff in our special "Cohen of Silence" room, I explained the logic behind the administration's response. The attack had to be described as spontaneous, I said, because Obama had succeeded in Libya and defeated al-Qaeda. And Muslim rage invariably rose from some earlier Western offense. When in doubt, I concluded, always refer back to the president's Cairo speech of 2009, which ascribed such anger to colonialism, the Cold War, globalization, and Western-style modernity.

Nevertheless, as she came under fire for her explanations of Benghazi, I empathized with Rice. "It's not fair," I commiserated with her; "none of us write our talking points and we shouldn't be personally blamed for them." And yet, the administration's handling of Benghazi was symptomatic of its difficulty in dealing with the upheaval now sweeping the entire Middle East. From its first uniform flowering, the Arab Spring had devolved into multiple sandstorms.

America's inability to cope with these siroccos perplexed many observers, above all the Arabs. One of the peculiar privileges of Israel's ambassador in Washington is the ability to meet with Arab personages and diplomats off the record and, for the most part, far from public view. With the notable exception of the Saudi ambassador, virtually all of my Arab counterparts were willing to speak. These were exceptional people, appointed solely for their ability to excel in American circles. Counterintuitively, a disproportionate number of them were women, including one—the Bahraini—who was Jewish. Also unusual given the moribund state of the peace process, I became especially close to Palestinian figures in town, hosting them at the Residence, maintaining warm relations with them even when some were cold to one another. In all cases, their conversations with me were frank and quite friendly, and characterized by acute disappointment.

The letdown followed the Cairo speech, with its promise of a new age of amity between America and Islam. Thereafter, it surprised me to learn, Obama disenchanted many Arabs by—of all things— demanding an Israeli settlement freeze. "You don't turn on your allies, even if they're my enemies," one Palestinian activist explained to me.

The president next appeared to back down on the settlement moratorium demand, rendering him even less dependable in Arab eyes. But the deepest disillusionment arose from Obama's handling of the Arab Spring. The president at first coddled Gaddafi and then aided his killers, cosseted Assad and then applauded the insurgency against him, and courted Mubarak only to cast him out. Such a leader could not be esteemed. And the eagerness with which Washington sought a nuclear deal with Iran—a regime actively working to undermine Middle Eastern governments while brazenly provoking America—only deepened Arab mistrust.

I often wondered if Arab ambassadors shared my difficulty in explaining America to their countrymen back home. At my Residence, I threw a dinner party for Israeli National Security Advisor Yaakov Amidror and Washington's foremost strategic analysts, among them former senior officials. Though not given to emotion, Israel's poker-faced national security advisor visibly blanched on hearing my guests still insisting that "Arab parents want the same thing for their children as we do," and that the "Libyan people will always remain grateful for the freedom they received from America." But such bromides were not confined to the capital. In his *New York Times* column, Tom Friedman praised Yemen for promoting "the most unique post-revolutionary political process" and making "a stable transition to democracy." Obama, too, touted the country's success. Yemen would eventually be overrun by an Iranian-backed Shia insurgency, forcing U.S. diplomatic and military personnel to evacuate. "Why won't Americans face the truth?" one frustrated Israeli ex-general exclaimed to me. "To defend Western freedom, they must preserve Middle Eastern tyranny."

Most challenging to explain to Israelis was Obama's support for Egypt's Muslim Brotherhood. Contrary to the assurances I had received that the administration would not engage the Islamist movement, the State Department formally initiated ties with Brotherhood leaders in January 2012. Six months later, after the election of the movement's leader, Mohammed Morsi, to the presidency—by just over 51 percent of the vote—those contracts became an embrace. Deputy Secretary of State Tom Nides led a delegation of one hundred American businessman to Cairo to shore up the new government financially. Jay Carney, meanwhile, labored to cover up for Morsi's statements denouncing Obama as a Zionist and vilifying Jews as warmongers, apes, and pigs. "U.S. policy is focused on actions, not words," the press secretary said. The fact that Morsi rejected any contacts with Israel's government and openly supported the Brotherhood's Palestinian wing, Hamas, did not prevent the White House from inviting him for an official visit.

To Israelis left incredulous by these events, I recalled America's regard for any government—even of Islamic extremists—elected democratically. I noted Morsi's background as a Ph.D. student and lecturer at California universities, his idiomatic English, and familiarity with the United States. I cited the Cairo speech and how Morsi, like Turkey's Erdoğan, fulfilled Obama's vision of American backing for freely chosen and authentically Muslim leaders.

None of these explanations were compelling, I knew, and became less so as the Arab whirlwind further swirled out of America's control. In Syria, where the civil death toll topped one hundred thousand, reports emerged of Assad's use of chemical weapons. On August 20, President Obama for the first time articulated what would come to be seen as his red line with regard to such armaments. If it noticed "a whole bunch of chemical weapons moving around or being utilized," he said, America might consider a military response. Evidence of chemical attacks continued to surface, though, and Obama duly responded with threats. "The world is watching," he warned Assad on December 3. "If you make the tragic mistake of using these weapons, there will be consequences, and you will be held accountable."

Yet Assad remained impervious and Obama refrained from taking significant action to depose him. The Syria opposition was divided between radical groups close to al-Qaeda and pro-Western moderates. Secretary of State Clinton, Defense Secretary Panetta, and CIA Director David Petraeus all supported U.S. efforts to arm and train the moderates. Israel warned that thousands of foreigners were joining the radicals and might soon return as homegrown terrorists to the United States. Obama nevertheless remained adamant. "This idea that we could provide . . . arms to . . . an opposition made up of former doctors, farmers, pharmacists . . . to battle . . . a well-armed state backed by Russia, Iran, [and] Hezbollah, that was never in the cards," he told the *Times*. Though U.S. intelligence officials had originally given Assad two months to survive the insurgency, two years later he was still in power and pushing back the rebels. Instead of ousting the Syrian dictator, the United States withdrew its diplomatic personnel from Damascus. Assad responded by declaring U.S. ambassador Robert Ford persona non grata.

The situation in Egypt was no less disappointing. Morsi repaid the administration's support for him with a trial of ninety foreign democracy advocates—among them a number of Americans—and by assigning himself absolute powers. In doing so, he showed scant interest in, or even understanding of, Washington's attempts to rescue Egypt's economy. "To us real democracy means that every citizen has the right to live, work and worship as they choose," Hillary Clinton said after her first meeting with the Egyptian president. "Real democracy means that no group or faction or leader can impose their will . . . on anyone else." Yet, while she departed Alexandria, Egyptian Christians cursed the secretary for backing the Brotherhood and pelted her motorcade with tomatoes and shoes.

Landing in Israel, she promptly met with Avigdor Liberman. For several years, during which its representatives sat with Assad and Gaddafi, the administration boycotted Israel's democratically elected foreign minister, recoiling from his right-wing views. My insistence that Liberman was powerful and pragmatic and, if engaged, potentially helpful in the peace process, was ignored. Eventually, though, Clinton came to understand Liberman's worth and seemed to enjoy interacting with this blunt former Moldavian. Following her Egyptian ordeal, in particular, the secretary seemed relieved to see him. She even laughed when Liberman quipped, "The Brotherhood is to democracy what cannibals are to vegetarianism." Clinton, in turn, told him of rumors circulating in Cairo that the United States was plotting to detach Sinai from Egypt and give it to the Palestinians. The minister grinned and chuckled. "Not a bad idea."

"Not a bad idea." Defense Minister Barak laughed on hearing the same story from Clinton. Netanyahu practically howled, "We'll have to look into this!" But the escalating dangers Israel faced from the Arab Spring were far from jocular. Egyptian tanks in numbers well in excess of those established by the peace treaty were advancing into parts of Sinai, evoking terrifying Israeli memories of the Six-Day and Yom Kippur wars. The possibility that Syria's massive chemical arsenal would fall into radical rebel hands also denied Israelis sleep. There was no way of neutralizing those stockpiles from the air without releasing toxic clouds, and no way of seizing them without sending in thousands of Israeli troops. Elsewhere, in Libya, a hoard of shoulder-fired antiaircraft missiles—MANPADs—went missing. Some of these reappeared in Gaza, threatening IDF helicopters, just as Hamas rocket fire at Israel intensified.

In fact, the bombardment had never really stopped. Violating the 2009 cease-fire, Hamas and other terrorist groups maintained a steady "drizzle"—*tiftuf,* in Hebrew—of rockets and mortar shells on southern Israeli towns. After the Muslim Brotherhood's 2012 victory, that drip became a downpour. On October 24 alone, Hamas fired eighty projectiles at Israel. This time the rockets struck deeper—at Ashdod, Ashkelon, and north of Beersheba. Some 1.5 million Israelis, including two of my children, came in range. Accompanying the barrages were ground attacks against Israeli patrols that succeeded in wounding a number of soldiers, one critically, and Hamas attempts to tunnel under the border. A full-scale military confrontation, perhaps more devastating than the last round, loomed.

Gearing up for that clash, I phoned journalists and informed them, "Israel is under massive fire and must react. When it does, please don't report that Israeli leaders woke up one day and decided to attack Gaza. Remember the context." Beyond the likely press blowback, I was concerned about whether Israel possessed enough Iron Dome units and interceptors to protect its citizens. The costs were enormous—roughly $55 million per battery—and Israel urgently needed more. On the advice of the staff of Oklahoma senator Jim Inhofe, I wrote an op-ed on how the defense system not only saved lives, but prevented wars by giving Israeli leaders time to work out a cease-fire. I purposely placed the piece in *Politico,* the Capitol's insider paper, under the headline, "Investment in Iron Dome Is an Investment in Peace." The next morning, the phone in my office rang repeatedly as legislator after legislator called to ask how much aid Israel needed to defend itself.

But that assistance, however generous, would not reach Israel in time for Operation Pillar of Defense—a reference to the divine cloud that shielded the ancient Jews fleeing Egypt—launched by the IDF on November 14. It began with the elimination, by air-to-ground missile, of Hamas chief of staff Ahmad Jabari. The terrorists responded with thousands of rockets, some of which struck the outskirts of Tel Aviv and Jerusalem, killing three civilians. Israeli warplanes replied by bombing Hamas and Islamic Jihad targets in Gaza. The images were dispiritingly familiar: black smoke rising from Palestinian neighborhoods, Israelis dashing for shelters, world leaders urging restraint. The terrorists once again hid behind their own civilians while trying to kill Israeli civilians, and then cried "war crimes," when innocent Palestinians were killed.

And, once again, I defended Israel against such charges. Watched over by my trusted driver, Val, I slept in my car outside of the Washington studios where I gave some forty interviews. In between, I wrote for the *Times* and *The Washington Post,* and updated administration officials and congressional leaders on the operation's progress.

Much of my attention focused on Senator Dan Inouye of Hawaii. A one-armed Medal of Honor winner from World War II, his experience with racism against Japanese-Americans in that period made him an unflagging supporter of Israel. As the seniormost senator—third in line in succession to the president—and chairman of the Appropriations Committee, the gentle but powerful Inouye had always championed aid for Israel's missile defense. But repeated media reports that Iron Dome was failing to destroy incoming missiles prompted Inouye to call me and ask, "Can't your people get those things to work?" I explained that Iron Dome ignored rockets that it calculated would fall harmlessly in open areas and intercepted only those certain to hit neighborhoods. The system once again registered a success rate of 85 percent, I assured the senator. "Good," Inouya replied. "Keep firing 'em."

Iron Dome did in fact save lives and generate time for diplomacy. If not for the interceptors, dozens of Israelis would have been killed and the seventy-five thousand reservists called up by the IDF would have invaded Gaza, resulting in untold Palestinian deaths. Iron Dome gave Hillary Clinton time to reach the area and begin the search for a cease-fire.

"We were back on the high wire," she wrote in her memoirs. Clinton's last major mediating efforts as secretary indeed seemed acrobatic as she shuttled tirelessly between Cairo and Jerusalem. The task was to force Morsi to decide between his roles as Brotherhood chief and president of Egypt. He could not support Hamas and guarantee stability in the area. With tireless cajoling and pressure from Clinton,

Morsi chose Egypt. Eight days after it began, with six Israelis and 158 Palestinians dead, Operation Pillar of Defense ended.

The outcome left me relieved, ambivalent, and upset. I was grateful that the conflict had not raged on, escalating and claiming additional casualties. Life in Israel could return to its frenetic routine while Hamas-ruled Gaza stagnated. Yet, for the first time since the 1970s, I felt the frustration of not being able to protect my country in uniform. My duty, rather, was to stay in Washington, in front of the cameras and on the phone to policy makers. The response was inspiring. The American people and their representatives once again rallied to their ally. President Obama surpassed my expectations by coming out unequivocally in Israel's favor. "We are fully supportive of Israel's right to defend itself from missiles landing on people's homes and workplaces and potentially killing civilians," he declared.

But still, I remained disturbed. Under the terms of the cease-fire, Hamas could replenish and upgrade its missile stocks and decide when again to unleash them. The fighting could easily reignite. A bomb planted on a Tel Aviv bus on the operation's last day wounded twenty-eight people, further pressuring the Israeli government to act. Had the twenty-eight been killed, the army would have certainly invaded Gaza. And many Israeli soldiers would have willingly fought to uproot the terrorists and secure Israel's borders. Instead, before demobilizing, disgruntled reservists lay on the desert sand and with their bodies formed the Hebrew words, "Bibi is a loser."

Most distressing, though, was the American press, which, in spite of my forewarnings, portrayed the operation just as I feared, without context. Virtually unmentioned were the nearly seven hundred rocket attacks that preceded Israel's counterstrike. Once again, the media highlighted images of Palestinian suffering—some of them fabricated—and charges that Israel acted disproportionately against Hamas even as it fired from behind human shields. I trembled to contemplate the media backlash if Netanyahu had not held back and instead sent the IDF full force into Gaza.

Ultimately, the only good to come out of the operation lay in the U.S.-Israel alliance. From Obama's support for Israel's right to defend itself, congressional largesse for Iron Dome, and Secretary Clinton's commitment to achieving a cease-fire, the United States acted as Israel's ally par excellence. A year earlier, at the outbreak of the Arab

Spring, I had wondered if the turmoil in the Middle East would serve to strengthen our ties. Pillar of Defense substantiated those hopes.

But for how long? In spite of their confluent interests in the Middle East, America and Israel remained divided over the peace process and the Iranian nuclear program. The administration continued to support Morsi's Egypt, which refused to restore Israel's embassy in Cairo or return an Egyptian ambassador to Tel Aviv. And Obama still balked at intervening in the Syrian civil war, which threatened to spill over Israel's northern border and inundate Jordan with refugees. "When you have a professional army that is well-armed . . . fighting against a farmer, a carpenter, an engineer who started out as protesters . . . the notion that we could have . . . changed the equation on the ground there was never true," Obama explained to Jeffrey Goldberg.

I found the comment startling, and not only because it overlooked the ill-armed American farmers who fought against Britain's finest troops in 1776. It revealed the president's determination to withdraw from the Middle East irrespective of the human price. It admitted that America could no longer grapple with a region swept by such massive sandstorms. And the remark alarmed me by forgetting that Israel, unable to retreat, remained in that maelstrom's eye.

Last Lap

The last two years of my term in Washington had indeed been roller coaster–like. Yet many of the highest humps and sharpest descents still lay ahead. I encountered one of them only a few weeks after Operation Pillar of Defense, while driving to my parents' house for Thanksgiving, on—of all places—the New Jersey Turnpike. The number on my cellphone indicated that the Prime Minister's Office was calling.

"We have an urgent situation," I was informed. "Get to a diplomatic phone at once." Such a line, I knew, existed at the Israeli consulate on Second Avenue in New York. Glancing out my window at New York City, I replied that I could call back in half an hour, and asked Val, my driver, to turn into Manhattan.

And ran smack into the Thanksgiving Day Parade. How could I have forgotten? Unaware of where the parade ended, I feared that crossing to the East Side could take hours. So I bolted from the car and, with my security detail in tow, began running. Through the clouds of cotton candy munchers, beneath the ominous shadows of

Snoopy and Buzz Lightyear, and between rows of marching kilted men, I sprinted. A special crew had to be called into the consulate to meet me, though they hardly expected to greet a winded ambassador in his shirtsleeves.

"The Palestinian Authority is again applying for state status in the General Assembly," the message began. "Abbas will then go to the International Criminal Court and sanction us as an illegal occupier. The court is biased and won't accept our historic claim to the land or our need for secure borders. It'll deny us the right to defend ourselves." My instructions, consequently, were to contact key Congress members and urge them to threaten to cut off all UN funding if the Palestinians indeed turned to the ICC. "It's a matter of national survival."

Hustling back to the West Side left me little time to question my orders. Only after I had already made the first calls did I begin to have misgivings. Learning of my appeals to Congress would surely infuriate the administration and reverse the goodwill achieved during Pillar of Defense. The smarter move, I thought, was to contact the White House first, and only if necessary turn to the Hill. So instead of joining my parents for turkey—they prepared me a sandwich and a slice of pumpkin pie—I drove back to Washington, arriving at 4 A.M. I immediately phoned Netanyahu and explained my reservations. "I get it," he said. "Contact the White House."

But it was too late. Word spreads lightning fast in Washington and by 7 A.M. the White House already knew. Deputy National Security Advisor Denis McDonough was fuming. Still, he listened to my apology for not calling him before phoning the congressmen. We agreed to meet that same morning, despite the Thanksgiving weekend.

With the Jewish and Israeli national holidays, Israelis enjoy many more vacations than Americans. But Americans take their few days off seriously, and the White House was eerily deserted. In the Roosevelt Room—deathly quiet except for a drumming grandfather clock—McDonough, together with an NSC legal expert, sat stoically while I made Israel's case. "The ICC is a strategic threat," I explained. "We need a diplomatic Iron Dome." I mentioned existing legislation that protected U.S. soldiers and their allies from ICC-like charges. Would the United States threaten to sanction any country that sanctioned Israel?

With a directness sometimes painful but always appreciated, McDonough told me what I already suspected. The administration had gone far enough in opposing Abbas's unilateralism, he indicated, and would not take additional measures. The subtext was that as long as Israel adhered to its settlement policy, it should not expect above-and-beyond protection from the Palestinians. I thanked McDonough for interrupting his holiday, and hoped he and the legal expert could rejoin their families in time for leftover pie.

As expected, the Palestinians, supported by 138 nations, elevated their UN status from "nonvoting member" to "entity," enabling them to turn to the ICC. The United States, along with Canada, the Czech Republic, and several Pacific Island states, stood with Israel in opposing the measure. "The Palestinian people will wake up tomorrow and find that little about their lives has changed save that the prospects of a durable peace have only receded," said Ambassador Susan Rice. But further efforts to establish that "diplomatic Iron Dome" with the administration proved fruitless. And the announcement of the construction of three thousand apartments in East Jerusalem and the settlement blocs hardly augmented our case. "The U.S. Sticks with Israel and Israel Sticks it to the U.S.," shouted one headline. And though the new Palestinian entity did not turn to the ICC immediately, that threat dangled menacingly over Israel's head.

Yet, mistletoe, too, hung over heads, many of them covered with *kippas,* a few weeks later at the White House Hanukkah party. I was able to bring my younger sister, Karen, and to introduce her to Obama. He kissed her on the cheek, hugged her, and ribbed me, "She's better-looking than you are." Later, after listening to the Jewish choir of the U.S. Military Academy regale us with dreidel songs, we bundled over to the Library of Congress for the Jewish legislators' traditional Hanukkah gathering. Under the majestic Beaux Arts ceiling, the visiting IDF choir performed holiday favorites in Hebrew. Then, suddenly, the idea struck me. I ran with it to the evening's host, Debbie Wasserman Schultz—the Democratic convention drama was long behind us—and she exclaimed, "Let's do it!" Ten phone calls and much bureaucratic tape snipping later, the gray West Point tunics joined with the olive green fatigues of the IDF. Together, these young men and women sang "Jerusalem of Gold"—the theme song of the Six-Day War—and then stood at attention for "Hatikvah."

Surpassing that peak seemed almost inconceivable until the fol-

lowing week, when I held an overflowing goodbye dinner for Joe Lieberman. His retirement from nearly a quarter century's leadership in
the Senate was a landmark—and an irretrievable loss. Israel luxuri-
ated with friends in Congress, but few of its members were available
to Israel's ambassador at any hour and each day except, perhaps, for
the Sabbath that the Liebermans joyously observed. While regretting
his retirement, Sally and I also wanted to celebrate Joe and his wife
Hadassah's life contributions. So we set up a tent outside the Residence and filled it with nearly one hundred of the senator's admirers.

The event promised to be a decorous affair, with heartfelt speeches
by Jack Lew and Ehud Barak. But I could have kicked myself when
Lieberman leaned over and quietly asked if I had invited his best
friend, John McCain, to speak. "No," I said, "but I will right now."
McCain agreed, nonchalantly, and then, without a note, rose to address the audience.

"I have an important announcement to make," he began, squaring
his shoulders and gesturing with his signature stiff-armed chops. "I'm
converting to Judaism." The Arizona senator proceeded to explain
that, for the past eleven years, he had accompanied religiously observant Lieberman around the world. "We're in a Jerusalem hotel on a
Saturday, and I push the ninth floor but the elevator only goes to the
second and then the third. And I say, 'Hey, Joe, what's with the fuckin'
Shabbat elevator?' We go to dinner and I order a steak and Joe orders
salmon, and I say, 'Hey, Joe, what's with the fuckin' salmon?' And we
fly to Afghanistan, and I'm lying on the floor of the C-130, trying to
get some sleep, and hear someone mumbling over me. 'Hey, Joe,' I
said, 'what's with the fuckin' prayers?' And so," he concluded over
laughter that almost shook the Residence's already-shaky foundations, "I figure if I'm keeping all this Jewish commandment stuff anyway, I might as well convert."

The next day, still chuckling, Sally and I left for what would be our
first real vacation in nearly four years. Washington was all but closed
down for Christmas and we took advantage of the quiet to fly off to
Oaxaca, Mexico, to savor the art and the local mole.

While still in the cab to the hotel, my phone rang with news of the
horrendous murder of twenty children and six adults by a mad gunman at the Sandy Hook Elementary School in Newtown, Connecticut. I instantly called Netanyahu to draft a condolence letter for
President Obama and was assisting him still after the cab left us off in

the middle of a teeming Mexican street. Shortly thereafter, at the hotel, I learned that Hillary Clinton had taken ill, and again I alerted the prime minister. Then, at a restaurant, I received a message from Andrea Mitchell of MSNBC asking for Israel's help in locating correspondent Richard Engel, who had gone missing in Syria. Other calls followed—another confrontation between Israeli police and Women of the Wall—on the way to dinner. Finally, before I could order a meal, my chief of staff, Lee Moser, informed me that Senator Dan Inouye had died. His casket would lie in state in the Capitol and I, of course, had to be there to pay Israel's profoundest respects. So we got onto the next plane, which was too small to carry our suitcases, and returned to the United States. The luggage, sent by Israel's Foreign Ministry, followed via Mexico City and Jerusalem before reaching Washington four months later. By that time, I knew, there would never be a break from my job.

The roller coaster sped and, occasionally, it swooped. The last and steepest lap began at the outset of 2013, shortly after the inauguration. Such an ascent invariably presaged the most precipitous drop. Yet, after all the vacillations of the previous two years, through the ups and downs in the media and the American Jewish community and treacherous turns in the peace process and the Iranian nuclear issue, I welcomed the momentary respite. For a few moments—metaphorically—I could catch my breath while Obama planned his first presidential visit to Israel.

ALLY,
GOODBYE

SANITATION CREWS IN WASHINGTON WERE SWEEPING UP THE CON-fetti from the previous day's inauguration ceremony and pundits were still debating whether or not superstar Beyoncé lip-synched the national anthem, when Israel also went to the polls. Precipitated by a failure to pass the state's budget, rising opposition to Ultra-Orthodox exemptions from the IDF, and the inability of many Israelis to make a living, the 2013 elections shook up the country's politics as rarely before. If, in America, the recent presidential contest produced continuity, the Israeli race augured change.

By this time, I had spent nearly five years in the United States, and was often more familiar with National Football League standings than with most domestic trends in Israel. Still, I knew that the country, no less than America, was undergoing dramatic transformations. Once, just after landing at Ben-Gurion Airport, I cabbed to Tel Aviv's affluent Rothschild Street to speak with young people who had set up hundreds of tents in an act of social protest. They loved Israel, they told me, had served it proudly in uniform, and only wanted to live in it with economic dignity.

North of Rothschild Street, though, I encountered the other Israel—the start-up state where Apple, Google, Intel, and three hundred foreign high-tech companies maintained gleaming R&D offices. I witnessed evidence of a society becoming at once more liberal, with same-sex couples openly holding hands, as well as more religious. There were more Hasidic black hats on the heads of those refusing to serve in the military and more knitted *kippas* on those who did. I saw cafés brimming at all hours with leisurely customers while other Israelis labored even longer hours to get by. I saw a settler constituency swiftly expanding and peace groups whose numbers shrank in proportion to the Palestinians' refusal to negotiate. Returning to Israel, I saw a people who ranked among the world's leaders in health, happiness, and educational levels, but for whom cynicism and hardship was a fixture of life—a people at once flourishing and wearying of struggle.

Israeli democracy is acutely sensitive to such shifts and the 2013 contest reflected them. Netanyahu's Likud merged with Foreign Minister Liberman's Israel Our Home Party to form a decisive right-of-center bloc. After breaking with the Labor Party, a faction following Ehud Barak failed to gain a single Knesset seat. Tzipi Livni's Movement Party also lost power, impelling her to join the coalition. And two new parties emerged. The Jewish Home Party tapped into the rightward and religious swing, especially among young people, as embodied by its leader, Naftali Bennett, a Sayeret Matkal veteran and successful entrepreneur, the son of Americans who made *aliya*. The biggest winner, though, was There Is a Future—*Yesh Atid,* in Hebrew—which promised just that to financially strapped Israelis who could not afford an apartment. Its head, former TV talk show host Yair Lapid, proved that Israelis, too, could elect an Obama-like candidate. Whatever he lacked in political and managerial experience, Lapid made up for with eloquence and charisma.

Pausing to smile at the cameras, I dropped the anomalously low-tech envelope containing my ballot into the polling box set up at the embassy. I made a statement about the blessings of Israeli democracy and the responsibility that we, as voters, bore. I did not mention the challenges ahead—a second-term president with little to lose by pressuring us and a new Israeli government that was likely to be less centrist than the last. My worries I confided only to my innermost staff, to Chief of Staff Lee Moser and to my new spokesman Aaron Sagui, a sharp-witted and loyal young man who had replaced the otherwise irreplaceable Lior Weintraub. "That is why we get the big shekels," I told them.

But no amount of remuneration could salve my concerns as Jeffrey Goldberg again quoted Obama assailing Netanyahu's settlement policy and saying that "Israel doesn't know what its own best interests are." Then, on January 30, *The New York Times* reported that Israeli jets had struck the outskirts of Damascus and destroyed a Hezbollah-bound convoy of sophisticated antiaircraft missiles. Israel declined to comment on the claims, but U.S. administration sources leaked the news. Russia and Turkey promptly denounced the attack while Syria and Iran threatened retaliation.

Tensions reached another peak with the retirement of Secretary of Defense Panetta and Obama's decision to replace him with Chuck Hagel. Unusual for a midwestern Republican, Hagel was renowned for criticizing Israel. He once appeared to justify Palestinian suicide bombers as "desperate men [who] do desperate things when you take hope away," and described U.S. support during the Second Lebanon War as "irresponsible and dangerous." He refused to designate Hezbollah a terrorist organization and called for reconciliation with Iran and Hamas. A decorated Vietnam veteran, Hagel targeted AIPAC, which he controversially called "the Jewish lobby" and accused of intimidating Congress. "I'm not an Israeli senator," he defiantly declared. "I'm a United States senator." But as hard as he could be on Israel, Hagel was soft on Iran. During his confirmation hearings, he described the Iranian regime as "elected" and "legitimate" and supported Obama's "position on containment." Only after receiving notes from a senatorial aide did Hagel clarify that Iran "is recognized by the UN" and that "we do not favor containment." Such corrections could not, however, erase Hagel's record of opposing the Iranian sanctions.

The Hagel nomination not only reinserted the Israeli wedge between Democrats and Republicans but, for the first time, divided the pro-Israel camp. Reluctant to confront the administration on an appointment it could not block, AIPAC endorsed Hagel. Some of Israel's right-wing advocates assailed the organization for preserving bipartisanship rather than securing Israel's needs. Obama also named John Kerry, never meek in his opposition to Israeli policies in the territories, as his next secretary of state. Still taking flak for her remarks following the Benghazi incident, Susan Rice received the compensatory post of national security advisor.

As befitting a foreign ambassador, I kept silent on the confirmation process. I had never met Hagel, but I knew that every defense secretary learns to value the U.S.-Israel alliance and that this one would be no exception. Kerry and Rice, by contrast, were familiar to me and I thought they could establish good working relations with Israel. Obama's detractors, though, saw these appointments as a deliberate attempt to supplant friends of Israel—Clinton, Panetta, and

Tom Donilon—with outspoken critics. "Obama wants to hurt Israel," wrote the ultraconservative Israeli columnist Caroline Glick. "He is appointing . . . advisors and cabinet members not despite their anti-Israel positions, but because of them."

Imagine my relief, then, when the White House informed me that Obama's first trip abroad in his second term would not be to Turkey this time or to Cairo. I had long grappled with press and public questions of why Obama, as president, had never been to Israel. "He'll come when the time is right" was my standard answer, usually accompanied by reminders that Reagan had never once visited Israel and George W. Bush only at the very end of his presidency. Now I learned that Obama would spend three days, from Wednesday, March 20, to Friday, March 22, in my country. More than relieved, actually, I was ecstatic. Here, suddenly, was the opportunity to convey an image of American-Israeli strength and unity to a tired and riven region. Now, after more than four years of receiving mixed messages, the world would hear a single word: *ally*.

You Are Not Alone

I had, over the years, waited on many tarmacs, yet none as spectacular as this. Arrayed on either side of me stood Israel's civil, military, and religious leaders—ministers, generals, Supreme Court justices, rabbis, imams, and priests. IDF honor guards straightened their lines and a military band tuned its instruments. Behind us, the grandstands bristled with hundreds of cameras. And thousands of security personnel patrolled the grounds while, above, military helicopters circled. The sheer color of it all was stunning: the black cassocks and ivory turbans, gold braiding and silver scepters, a spectrum of uniforms from tan to navy and verdigris. But most eye-catching of all were the flags. In fluttering bouquets they lined the runway, sharing blues and whites and a profusion of stars, five-pointed and six. Only the reds of Old Glory stuck out against the bronzed background of the Judean Hills. Those reds reminded me of all the sacrifices required to reach this moment and of the many that might be prevented if this moment endured.

The midday sun, already scorching on this pre-spring day, pounded the crowd. Yet I barely broke a sweat. Worries about possible obstacles and faux pas preoccupied me. So, too, did the question of whether the visit would achieve the goals I originally held up. The first was to introduce Israelis to Obama—for them to see him up close, interacting with young people and communities from different backgrounds. In my conversations with Ben Rhodes, the president's unprepossessing but savvy advisor for strategic communications, I suggested that Obama conduct a town-hall meeting in a working-class Israeli neighborhood or play basketball with some disadvantaged teenagers. I hoped that, time and security precautions permitting, he could leave the Tel Aviv–Jerusalem corridor and reach out to Israelis north and south. But the second objective was even more pressing. The official visits and the president's remarks should broadcast the uniqueness of the U.S.-Israeli alliance and the indigenousness of the Jewish State.

Attaining the first goal, I quickly learned, would be difficult. The immensity of the president's entourage, including hundreds of advance team members and his personal staff, ruled out all but short-distance travel, and concerns for his safety understandably prevailed. "I have this fantasy that I can put on a disguise, wear a fake mustache, and I can wander through Tel Aviv and go to a bar," Obama told the talented Israeli news anchor Yonit Levi just before the trip. Going incognito, alas, was out of the question. So was visiting an outlying town or shooting hoops. At best, the president could interact with the members of a youth choir and speak before Israeli students.

By contrast, the second goal proved achievable and beyond my brightest hopes. Many of the tour's events were designed to vitiate the spurious claim that Israel existed solely because of the Holocaust rather than the Jews' millennia-long attachment to the Land. The message did not come cost-free; in addition to meeting Mahmoud Abbas in Ramallah, Obama agreed to visit Bethlehem. But the price seemed more than worth it. To the Palestinians and other Middle Eastern peoples who denied that a Jewish Temple once stood in Jerusalem, America's president would send a resounding "no!"

Now, as Air Force One glided into the skies over Ben-Gurion Airport, the schedule was immutably set and the throngs on the ground instinctively stiffened. The Boeing 747, similar in class and color to El Al's, touched down and taxied to the movable stairs. The main hatch swung open and, to a fanfare of "Hail to the Chief," President Obama emerged. He waved and descended in his trademark jog to the crimson carpet where President Peres and Prime Minister Netanyahu awaited. They viewed the honor guard and then mounted a podium.

"This is an historic moment," Netanyahu began, and proceeded to thank Obama for his support for Israel's defense and its right to exist as the Jewish State. Referring to the Yonit Levi interview, he added that arrangements had been made to enable the president to visit a few Tel Aviv bars. "We even prepared a fake mustache for you." The onlookers chuckled but then emotionally choked when Obama greeted them in Hebrew: "Tov L'hiyot shuv ba'aratez"—It's good to be back in the Land. He proceeded to describe Israel as "the historic homeland of the Jewish people" and to recall its three-thousand-year history. Then he extolled the alliance:

> We share a common story: patriots determined to be a free people in our own land, pioneers who forged a nation, heroes who sacrificed to preserve our freedom, and immigrants from every corner of the world. . . . We stand together because we are democracies, as noisy and messy as it can be. . . . It is in our fundamental national security interest to stand with Israel. That is why the Star of David and the Stars and Stripes fly together today. And that is why . . . our alliance is eternal.

He ended with another Hebrew word—*L'Netzah*—meaning "forever," which, despite the heat, left me shivering. Barack Obama had just articulated the vision that inspired most of my life decisions and still fortified me daily. Powerful emotions welled up within me, but not for long. After briskly shaking hands with the guests, the president hustled the hundred yards toward the Iron Dome.

Of course, the president had to visit the antiballistic system to which he contributed so generously. My original idea was to drive Obama to a hilltop overlooking Tel Aviv, and there, with the city it protected in the background, tour Iron Dome. But time constraints dictated that the hill come to Obama, and the battery was transferred to the airport. Striding briskly, the president took off his suit jacket and slung it over his shoulder. Netanyahu did likewise, exposing himself to Israeli media caricatures of a copycat. I followed closely behind them and, despite the heat quivering above the macadam, kept my jacket on.

Events moved quickly—almost too quickly—after that. The president surveyed the system's various components and shook the young soldiers' hands before his staff whisked him onto one of twelve U.S. military Black Hawks. A logistics foul-up left me jumping onto one of the American choppers for which I had no clearance, but there was no chance to change aircraft, and I flew with the U.S. Army crew to Jerusalem. At the landing site, I hitched a ride on one of the presidential limos for the meeting with Shimon Peres.

The four o'clock hour of the event was determined less by protocol than by Peres's need, at ninety, to take an afternoon nap. Even then, the motorcade arrived late as the president's eight-ton and heavily armored Cadillac—"the Beast"—broke down. We arrived, finally, at the President's House in Jerusalem. Shabby in comparison to Obama's stately Washington residence, the house nevertheless boasts classic Chagalls and handsome gardens where Obama planted his gift of a magnolia sapling. Journalists quickly learned that Israeli inspectors would have to uproot the tree and check it for disease, but the headline did not spoil Obama's meeting with the boys and girls who, waving miniature American flags, greeted him with peace songs. "The State of Israel will have no better friend than the United States," Obama pledged to Peres. The two presidents then left for their usual one-on-one to discuss the typical topics of peace, Iran, and Jonathan Pollard, before the motorcade moved on—literally, down the street—to the Prime Minister's Residence.

Stripped of pageantry, this was the substantive part of the trip. The standard face-to-face in Netanyahu's tiny private office went on, as usual, well beyond the allotted time. To the backdrop of somber Rubin paintings and ancient Roman lamps, the two teams sat bantering while our principals spoke discreetly and, hopefully, productively, about the future of the Middle East. Outside, in the courtyard, dozens of journalists waited impatiently for the Q&A. When Obama finally emerged—smiling, all noted—I warned him, "You think the Washington press corps is tough, these Israeli journalists can eat you for breakfast."

The bitterest portion, though, was served not by Israelis but by an American, NBC's political director, Chuck Todd. He posed four questions—"Hey, it's Passover time," he joked—relating to Obama's failure to reconcile with the Muslim world and to achieve an Israeli-Palestinian peace. Netanyahu rushed to the president's defense, telling Todd that "this is not a kosher question, but don't hog it." Obama stressed the lack of daylight between the United States and Israel on Iran and his continued opposition to containment. Netanyahu agreed, but clarified that, for Israel, the concern was not the estimated year in which Iran could assemble a bomb but rather its ability to break out toward that goal. The most memorable response of the night, though, related to Israeli intelligence reports of yet another chemical attack on Syrian civilians.

The State Department had already declared that the use of such weapons by the regime would constitute a "red line" that the president would strictly enforce. Now, presented with this latest report, Obama responded that, if Assad indeed "let that genie out of the bottle," then "the international community would have to act." While he did not actually repeat the words "red line," the president appeared to have redrawn one.

The press departed and the guests sat down for a working dinner. The setting was sui generis. Opposite Obama sat the prime minister and his wife, flanked by Foreign Minister Liberman, National Security Advisor Amidror, Strategic Affairs Minister Yuval Steinitz, and, for the first time in his new role as defense minister, Moshe "Bogie" Ya'alon. Both Steinitz and Ya'alon had been research fellows with me at the Shalem Center, and I knew that they would provide the president with hard-nosed and well-informed views. The American side also registered some firsts. This was Kerry's maiden visit to Israel as secretary of state and the first official trips of Senior Advisor Valerie Jarrett and Counselor Peter Rouse, who, though well-known in Washington, were unrecognizable to Israelis.

Over a fare of Jerusalem artichokes, roast beef, and an apple crumble dessert that the president, as usual, did not touch, the conversation toggled between the Israelis' military backgrounds—most had served in Sayeret Matkal or the paratroopers—and on the need for cyber cooperation. Sara Netanyahu presented the president with a silver Passover plate for his wife, David's harp medallions for his daughters, and even a rubber hamburger for his dog, Bo. Entertainment came in the form of internationally renowned Israel composer Idan Raichel, who, along with the Sudanese-born Ethiopian singer Cabra Casay, captivated Obama with a fusion of Hebrew, Arabic, and Amharic ballads. Then, after posing with the dreadlocked Raichel, the Americans said good night.

But the Israelis remained, working well past midnight to assess the day's events. Though still unwilling to specify a trigger for an American strike against Iran, Obama reinforced his position that Israel had the right to decide when and how to defend itself—perhaps a yellow light for Israeli action. "Yes, but at Israeli intersections, the yellow light precedes green," Ron Dermer reminded us. "In America, it precedes red."

I reported on my preparation talks with White House officials. Once again I inquired about the "diplomatic deliverable" the president would most appreciate receiving while in Israel, and the answer, again, was: an apology to Erdoğan for the 2010 flotilla incident. This sparked a knotty debate. The autocratic Turkish leader had never ceased denouncing Israel and, most recently, had called Zionism "a crime against humanity." Theologically close to Hamas, he supported the terrorist organization both diplomatically and militarily, and saw himself as the Sunni savior of the Middle East. Saying sorry to him would not alter his animus toward the Jewish State.

Yet here was an opportunity to give Obama a victory and the U.S.-Israel alliance a much-needed boost. Consequently, I came down on the conciliatory side, as did Dermer and Amidror. But Defense Minister Ya'alon pointed out that saying sorry meant admitting that our naval commandos had committed some offense when, in fact, they were merely protecting themselves. "We politicians would be off the hook," he said, "and our boys left holding the blame." Netanyahu, for his part, reserved judgment.

The question of whether Israel would grant Obama's wish remained open through the next day, which began, poignantly, with rocket fire from Gaza into southern Israel. The terrorists' attempt to disrupt the visit failed, though, as attention fixed on the president's tour of the Shrine of the Book. The alabaster, amphora-shaped structure housed the Dead Sea Scrolls, written by Judean Jews more than two thousand years ago. More than any other, this was the event I had pressed for, which unequivocally proclaimed Israel's rootedness in the Middle East.

Emerging from the shrine, visibly moved by the sacred texts he had viewed, Obama proceeded to the nearby Israel Museum. There the winners of a contest for Israel's most cutting-edge innovations waited to display their inventions. Robotic waiters invented by high school students delivered Passover *matzah* to the president and a mechanical worm, designed to locate earthquake victims trapped under rubble, nuzzled his arm. A female veteran of the Vietnam War, a paraplegic wearing a high-tech exoskeleton called ReWalk, stood and stepped toward Obama. The moment moved John Kerry, himself a Vietnam veteran, to tears.

Obama then left Jerusalem for Ramallah and meetings with Abbas and Prime Minister Fayyad. The president reiterated his commitment to ending the occupation and providing hope and dignity to the Palestinians. More contentiously, he drew a comparison between the opportunities once forbidden to young African-Americans such as his own daughters and those still denied to Palestinian youth.

The remark went largely unnoticed, though, and my energies remained concentrated on the proposed Erdoğan apology. Ensconced in the Prime Minister's Office with Ambassador Dan Shapiro, Ron Dermer, and the NSC's newly appointed Middle East expert, Phil Gordon, we pored over various drafts. Much of the language had already been worked out in previous talks with the Turks. Israel would apologize for possible tactical mistakes made by the IDF during the flotilla operation and offer to compensate the families of the Turkish nationals who were killed. In return, Erdoğan would return Turkey's ambassador to Tel Aviv and drop all present and future war crimes charges against Israeli commanders. This exchange would take place in Obama's presence, casting him as a peacemaker.

Contacts with Turkey continued that afternoon for what was billed as the trip's centerpiece. Visiting heads of state usually speak before the Knesset. Nearly twenty years earlier, I had listened to Bill Clinton render the rowdy Israeli parliamentarians spellbound with the story of his childhood pastor who made him promise never to abandon the Jewish State. But Obama's advisors recommended against a Knesset address, fearing that radical members might boo him. Instead they opted for a much grander appearance at Jerusalem's Convention Center, before an audience of more than two thousand Israeli college students.

Even this proved controversial. The U.S. embassy chose the attendees from essays they submitted on Obama and America-Israeli relations, but only from those enrolled at universities situated within the 1967 lines. Students from Ariel University, situated in a settlement bloc, demonstrated their exclusion outside the center, alongside protesters demanding Jonathan Pollard's release. The event nevertheless proceeded, and to wild applause and a flurry of American flags, Obama strode onto the stage.

I sat in the front row, awkwardly positioned between several right-wing ministers and a group of young Arab women with their heads traditionally covered. Obama began with an insider Israeli joke about how all the talk about tensions between Bibi and him were merely scripts written for *Eretz Nehederet,* a popular TV comedy show. But then he grew serious and almost poetic, comparing the ancient Jewish yearning for freedom to that of antebellum African-American slaves. He traced the "journey of . . . countless generations" that wound through "centuries of suffering and exile, prejudice, pogroms, and even genocide" before culminating in the State of Israel. And those who denied Israel's right to exist, Obama warned, "might as well reject the earth beneath them and the sky above, because Israel is not going anywhere." He praised Israeli democracy and innovation, and, of course, mentioned *Tikkun Olam.* But the most moving passage was one that, I, too, might have proclaimed. "The dream of true freedom finally found its full expression in the Zionist idea," Obama maintained. "To be a free people in your homeland."

Again and again, the students rose in applause—all except the Arab women, who continued to sit impassively. But Obama also praised the Palestinians for preserving their vision of statehood, and denounced the humiliation and the violence bred, he said, by the occupation. For the first time, a U.S. president called not only for self-determination for the Palestinians, but for "justice." The word, laden with historical associations, was no doubt deliberately picked; whereas Israelis traditionally want peace, the Palestinians always demand justice. Then Obama went further, urging the students to go out and protest against the policies of their democratically elected government. "Political leaders will not take risks if the people do not demand that they do," he asserted. "You must create the change that you want to see." Yet even these provocative lines spurred standing ovations from all those present—apart, paradoxically, from both the Israeli rightists and the Israeli Arabs. Obama concluded on an exalted note, in Hebrew assuring these young Israelis who had known only war, "Atem lo levad," you are not alone.

Could this be a transformative moment? I wondered. Could Obama see that, three years after the Cairo speech, Israel was the only place in the Middle East where he could still give a speech and be cheered? Did he appreciate how eagerly these students embraced his loving message, even when its love was tough?

The crowd swarmed toward the stage, still applauding. Only the Arab women remained in their seats, hands folded in their laps, silent. "Why didn't you clap?" I asked them. "The president of the United States just called for justice for Palestine." The women merely glared at me and one of them said, "That was a terrible speech. Totally Zionist."

Israelis, too, overlooked the pro-Palestinian segments of the speech and seized on its Zionism. Their feting of Obama continued that night at a gala state dinner hosted by Shimon Peres. The entire presidential entourage arrived, including prominent Jewish Congress members. I was trading political insights with New York's Eliot Engel and Debbie Wasserman Schultz when my cellphone rang. From Washington, my vigilant chief of staff, Lee Moser, called to warn me that microphones lined the area and everything we said was heard on international TV. Fortunately, I made no indiscretions and, more cautiously, went back to chatting.

Peres reciprocated the Presidential Medal of Freedom award he received from Obama by bestowing on him Israel's own Presidential Medal. More speeches followed, with boisterous musical interludes that had one White House aide complaining to me, "Don't you guys believe in quiet songs?" There were more speeches, more toasts, and photographs with Yityish Titi Aynaw, a tall and dazzlingly beautiful immigrant from Ethiopia who was recently crowned Miss Israel. I applauded the performances, posed with Yityish, all the while thinking: one more day to go.

This was to be the climactic day. It opened in Jerusalem with Obama ascending to Mount Herzl—Israel's equivalent of Arlington—to lay a wreath on its namesake's grave. No less than his viewing of the Dead Sea Scrolls, the gesture was dense with meaning. Theodor Herzl, Zionism's founding father, authored the book *The Jewish State,* published half a century before the Holocaust. By paying homage to Herzl, Obama again reminded the world that the United States regarded Israel as the Jewish State with origins predating the Final Solution. Watching the two of them—the president and Netanyahu—standing over the dark gray tomb again gave me hope that this trip might be a game changer.

My optimism rose further when the two leaders joined the Rabin family beside the resting place of the great general and statesman who so inspired me as a teenager. Then, after placing another wreath on the stone of Yitzhak Rabin, Obama allowed the prime minister to take him to another section of Israel's national cemetery. This time they stood alone, just the two of them, at the grave site of Yoni Netanyahu.

No state visit can be concluded without a visit to the Holocaust memorial at Yad Vashem. Obama toured the haunting galleries and then, after the standard prayer at the Eternal Flame, spoke words I never thought he would utter. "The State of Israel does not exist because of the Holocaust, but with the survival of the State of Israel there will never be a Holocaust again." I recognized the phrase from an article written by Yossi Klein Halevi, and excitedly tried to phone him.

The excitement of hearing my best friend's words in the president's mouth was quickly quelled, though, by an astonishing speech by Yad Vashem's chairman, Rabbi Yisrael Meir Lau. He and his diplomat brother, Naftali—who once hosted me for Shabbat dinners when I was a "lone soldier"—were the only members of their family to survive Buchenwald. Lau later became a chief rabbi of Israel and a champion of interfaith understanding. Now, with his untrimmed white beard and all-black attire, he cast a prophetic aura as he turned to Obama and recalled the non-Jewish GI who liberated him in 1945. Many years later, Lau said, that same veteran approached him and begged for forgiveness. "We were too late," the American cried. "And I say to you, Mr. President," Lau proclaimed, "do not be too late."

An audible gulp rose from the spectators, all of whom understood that Lau's warning related to Iran. The president also looked startled. But no one was more surprised—and incensed—than Netanyahu. "Who does Lau think we are?" he fumed back in his office, "Concentration camp inmates waiting for the Americans to save us?" A press statement went out asserting that Israel, a sovereign state, could defend itself, by itself, if necessary. The incident quickly passed, though, and attention returned to the closing hours of Obama's visit. The question remained: would Netanyahu apologize to Erdoğan?

The main stumbling block remained the issue of war crimes charges against Israelis that Turkey refused to relinquish. "Erdoğan will never concede that," Ambassador Dan Shapiro cautioned me. Still, Phil Gordon, a Turkey specialist whose mind seemed to work as fast as the pen he incessantly twirled in his fingers, refused to give up, and kept calling high-ranking figures in Ankara. While Obama left for the Church of the Nativity in Bethlehem—by car, after a violent sandstorm grounded his chopper—we continued refining the draft. Then, finally, at two o'clock on Friday afternoon, it was time to leave for the airport.

There, a prefab trailer was set up a short span from where Air Force One awaited its principal passenger. We crowded inside— Amidror, Gordon, Secretary Kerry, and others—elbowing to make room for Obama and Netanyahu. The phone calls continued, but still brought no closure. The time was well past three, with darkness approaching fast. Very soon, Israeli officials would have to return home in order to avoid violating the Sabbath. The chance to give Obama his diplomatic achievement would be lost. Not until the motorcade pulled up to the trailer, with only a few minutes to spare, did Dan Shapiro practically shout, "We got it! It's a deal!"

They sat across from each other with a small table and a telephone between them. Obama spoke extemporaneously through a translator and greeted Erdoğan as "my friend, Recep." Netanyahu, by contrast, read from a script of which we all had copies and followed closely. The necessary ingredients were all there—the apology for tactical mistakes perhaps made by the IDF, the compensation offer, the restoration of full diplomatic ties, and the removal of all war crimes charges. Netanyahu spoke slowly, purposefully, and, I felt, sincerely. The interpreter conveyed Erdoğan's words: his comments on Zionism were taken out of context and he bore no animosity toward Israel. The apology was accepted.

Obama and Netanyahu hung up the phone and everyone present sprang to their feet and started cheering. There were high-fives and even hugs. Outwardly, I was jubilant, but inside, torn. The leader of the Jewish State so recently lionized by the president of the United States had just conceded to the Islamist patron of IHH radicals who beat and stabbed our soldiers aboard the *Mavi Marmara,* the strongman who imprisoned journalists and activists for civil rights. Yet, at the same time, here was a prime minister who made a tough decision to place our bonds with America above just about all other considerations.

"We may have made a mistake," he admitted to me that evening as we sat, just the two of us, in his office. We watched a television newsman report that the mothers of the Shayetet 13 commandos were accusing Netanyahu of abandoning their sons, and that even some members of his cabinet were criticizing him. A triumphant Erdoğan was bragging about how he had humiliated the Israelis and would humble them further by forcing them to lift the Gaza blockade. The war crimes charges would not be dropped, he vowed. Wearily, Netanyahu repeated, "I think we made a mistake."

Perhaps I was too sleep-deprived or was still elevated by the president's final sendoff to share in his dismay. Protocol chief Capricia Marshall had shoved a pair of official Obama cuff links into my pocket—her way of saying thanks—and John Kerry had clasped my hands in his. "Thank you, Mr. President, for my children" were my parting words to Obama. Operation Unbreakable Alliance, as the Americans called it, succeeded beyond all expectations. Through the fog and deliriousness, I believed that Netanyahu had acted responsibly. Like our common hero, Levi Eshkol, Israel's prime minister in 1967, he had exhausted all possible diplomatic options—not only toward Erdoğan, but also with Obama.

"No, you made no mistake," I assured him. "You did the right thing. The statesmanlike thing."

Remaining to be seen, though, was whether the messaging of the president's trip, and the impressions it left, were permanent. Did Obama make the trip, as some jaded journalists insinuated, just to "check the box," or was he sincerely seeking to allay his first term's tensions with Israel? Would he value Netanyahu's attempted reconciliation with Turkey and the public's overflowing goodwill? And could Israelis build on Obama's warmth and willingness to honor some of their most symbolic national sites and place greater faith in him?

The answers to all of those questions could still be negative, I realized, and the mistrust and backbiting would resume. I recalled how, on the eve of the Six-Day War, when Arab armies assembled on Israel's borders, President Johnson warned Eshkol, "Israel will not be alone unless it decides to act alone." Similarly, Obama declared, *Atem lo levad*—"You are not alone"—but would he, too, qualify that statement? I wondered. Was it up to Israel to decide?

Kerry Ex Machina

The secretary of state set out to answer that question the very next day as his plane once again landed at Ben-Gurion Airport. After a stopover with Obama in Jordan, John Kerry returned to Israel to jump-start the long-stalled peace talks. I greeted him as a friend who had dined at my Residence and who treated me to wine and cheese at his summer home in Nantucket. I knew him in his former capacity as chairman of the Foreign Relations Committee, when he frequently visited Israel or invited me into his office for talks on Middle East issues. Back then he was eager to achieve a breakthrough between Israel and Syria and made some fitful starts at mediating between Damascus and Jerusalem. I encouraged him, even though I doubted Assad's sincerity or his willingness to defy his Iranian patrons. The ayatollahs were unlikely to watch passively while their best Middle Eastern friend made peace with their worst enemy, us.

Kerry's initiative died, along with more than two hundred thousand Syrians, most of them killed by the same regime that he and others judged moderate. Later, I often asked myself, What would have happened if Israel had concluded a deal that brought Syria back to the pre-1967 lines? The answer made me tremble. Black jihadist flags would be fluttering on the Sea of Galilee's shores.

Now, as secretary of state, Kerry switched his attention to reanimating the peace process with the Palestinians. "We have to keep working at this," he said, and inexhaustibly went to work. At age seventy, Kerry was devoid of body fat, capable of bicycling dozens of miles each day, and blessed with that helmetlike hair and Rushmore jaw so admired by Americans. Once, while greeting him at Ben-Gurion Airport, I was shocked to see him with two black eyes and stitches across his nose. "What happened?" I gasped. Kerry explained that he was playing hockey and stumbled over his teammate, actor Tom Hanks. His wounds looked excruciating, but the secretary never dwelt on them or let them interfere with his conversations. He remained, rather, like the godlike figure who, in classical Greek theater, swoops down to save the endangered heroes. So, too, did John Kerry descend onto the Middle Eastern stage to rescue Israel from tragedy.

Many Israelis, though, no longer wanted to be saved. While some 70 percent of the public still supported the two-state solution, a greater portion had lost faith in Abbas's ability to implement it. A majority wanted to see the Palestinians enjoy the right to self-determination, but not at the cost of denying Israelis the most fundamental right: to life. They looked around the Middle East and saw the overthrow of corrupt, nonelected Arab rulers and their replacement by Islamist radicals. Israelis saw the unraveling of the Arab states created by Westerners and wondered why the West would want to make another artificial state run by a corrupt, nonelected regime. They watched Mahmoud Abbas name public squares after suicide bombers and extol the murderers of innocent Israelis. Americans traumatized by the jihadist bombers who killed four and wounded more than 250 Bostonians during the April 15 marathon might understand why Israelis feared coming within rifle range of a state that praised terrorism and was likely to mount it.

Surprisingly, then, Kerry's first meeting with the top Israeli leadership was upbeat. Netanyahu and his senior ministers presented a compelling plan for moving forward incrementally but swiftly with Abbas. Each phase in the process required both sides to make difficult concessions while also garnering benefits. The prime minister's sticking point was, as always, security. Hezbollah smuggled missiles over the Syrian, not the Israeli, border, and rockets reached Hamas via Egypt, not Israel. Accordingly, Israeli forces would have to guard the eastern frontier of any future Palestinian state to prevent it from becoming another South Lebanon or Gaza. Israel could not rely on other troops to do the job—not Palestinian, not Jordanian, and not even American—only the IDF. "You are our ally," Netanyahu passionately reminded Kerry. "We look to you to back us in safeguarding our future."

Kerry was impressed and agreed to send U.S. military experts to assess Israel's security needs in detail. But the Palestinians again set preconditions for resuming talks: a complete construction freeze in the territories and East Jerusalem, Israeli acceptance of the principle of the 1967 lines with swaps, and the freeing of Palestinian prisoners from Israeli jails. Kerry succeeded in convincing Abbas to settle for just one of these demands, and to let Netanyahu choose which of the three to meet. I would have preferred another moratorium, which at least would have removed West Bank construction as a constant irritant in the process. But Netanyahu saw both the freeze and the 1967 lines as predetermining the outcome of the negotiations, and selected the prisoner release. The decision proved agonizingly controversial. The murderers of hundreds of Israelis—among them a Holocaust survivor hacked to death with an ax—would once again be greeted as heroes by the Palestinians.

Kerry also laid down rules that restricted the talks to a small number of negotiators—Yitzik Molcho and Tzipi Livni on Israel's side—who would pledge never to leak to the press. This left me with little role other than onlooker, and for the first time I was grateful. The axiom, widely attributed to Albert Einstein, defining insanity as "doing the same thing over and over again and expecting different results," sounded apt. The Oslo formula that I described as outdated to Senator Obama's advisors in 2008, five years and repeated failed peace attempts later, looked even more antiquated. The belief that somehow a more intensified initiative, even when launched by an energetic secretary of state, could somehow triumph where generations of mediators had stumbled, seemed unfounded at best.

Perhaps I had become jaded by the stop-and-go mediation efforts since 2009. Though still confident in the depth of Israel's yearning for peace and its readiness to make the requisite sacrifices, I could not perceive a Palestinian leader who was yet able and willing to sign. The necessary trust—not only between Israelis and Palestinians, but between both parties and the U.S. administration—was absent. As such, Abbas was likely to pocket any concessions that Kerry pried from Israel, declare a Palestinian state unilaterally in the UN, and then sue Israel in the International Criminal Court for illegally occupying that state. Israel would continue to announce new building projects in the areas considered occupied by most of the world, and each time be censored by Washington.

"Our problem is not that the Palestinians are not a people," I told Kerry's advisors. "It's that they're not a people ready to sustain statehood. Help them follow Israel's model of creating viable institutions first and then erecting the state on top of them." But my counsel remained unheeded. Kerry wanted results, and rapidly. He embarked on a shuttle mission that, at least in terms of its physical demands, was impressive, but it soon encountered familiar snags. Israel's announcement of its intention to legalize four unauthorized West Bank settlements sparked a harsh State Department response and even a caviling phone call to me from Kerry. On the Palestinian side, Salam Fayyad, the farsighted prime minister, the Texas-trained economist who pursued a nonviolent, corruption-free path to transparent institution building, was forced out of office by Abbas.

The administration, meanwhile, kept warning Israel about the dangers of international isolation and delegitimization campaigns—"on steroids," Kerry added—if it missed this diplomatic opportunity. Again, I tried telling Kerry's team that these statements made Israelis feel less secure and more resistant to risk-taking. The warnings about

Israel's deteriorating situation in the world nevertheless continued, along with other messages that the administration misguidedly believed would advance the talks. "People in Israel aren't waking up every day and wondering if tomorrow there'll be peace," the secretary said in Jerusalem on May 23, "because there is a sense of security . . . accomplishment and . . . prosperity." This was the same insulting "Israelis have it too good to make peace" argument that I once helped convince Hillary Clinton to drop. Regrettably, Kerry revived it.

In time, Kerry would caution Israelis about the outbreak of a Third Intifada if they failed to make peace, of facing economic boycotts and of becoming an apartheid state. Perceived as threats, these messages reinforced, rather than weakened, those most opposed to his initiative. Then, as his special Middle East envoy, the secretary named the veteran peace negotiator Martin Indyk. This, too, was counterproductive. British-born, raised in Australia, and naturalized as a citizen of the United States, where he initially worked for AIPAC, Martin later served twice as America's ambassador to Israel. There, and later, as the Brookings Institution's policy director, he had a frosty relationship with Netanyahu. I respected Martin's diplomatic experience and tried to advise him on ways of earning Netanyahu's trust. Still, the question hounded me: if Kerry was serious about the process, why did he seem intent on shaking Israelis' faith in it?

Kerry nevertheless kept shuttling throughout July, and, by pure persistence, managed to register some early gains. He convinced the Arab League to endorse possible land swaps between Israel and some future Palestinian state. In 2009, when Netanyahu called for an "economic peace" fueled by foreign investment in the West Bank, the Obama administration reacted coolly. Kerry now resuscitated the policy and tried to raise $4 billion for Palestinian economic development. When, in 2011, the White House looked askance at Netanyahu's decision to trade Corporal Gilad Shalit for more than a thousand Palestinian prisoners, claiming it strengthened Hamas, it now nudged him to release more than one hundred Palestinian prisoners to Abbas. The prime minister also accepted a nine-month timetable for talks, reflecting his concern that the longer the process, the broader its exposure to violent opposition.

Finally, on July 29, in the presence of Palestinian and Israeli negotiators on the State Department's mock-colonial eighth floor, the secretary announced the start of negotiations. "Reasonable principled compromise in the name of peace means that everybody stands to gain," he said. "A viable two-state solution is the only way this conflict can end, and there is not much time to achieve it."

Listening as Kerry spoke, I still questioned whether the American notion of win-win could apply to the Middle East, with its preference for zero-sums, and whether a century of conflict could be resolved in three-quarters of a year. My doubts about the Palestinians' willingness to give up their dream of repatriating to Jaffa and Haifa, and their demands to resettle millions of refugees in Israel proper, persisted. Israelis, too, would be asked to make immense sacrifices and take risks that increasing numbers of them regarded as futile or worse—suicidal. As I listened to Kerry, I was unconvinced, yet also hoping against my own inner conviction that he would nevertheless prevail. If, in this one dramatic swoop, Kerry could lift Israelis and Palestinians out of our impasse, I would more than welcome him onstage.

Behind the curtain, meanwhile, America was interacting with Iran. Despite the administration's repeated denials that it was negotiating directly with Tehran, Israeli officials feared that such talks were indeed taking place. Israel, in fact, had the greatest interest in exhausting all possible diplomatic options—and the most to lose if those options failed. Our fear was that Washington could forge an agreement with Iran that left the latter with the ability to make a bomb quickly and quietly behind the world's back. Israel could be permanently endangered.

One of the best safeguards against that outcome was Mahmoud Ahmadinejad. The Holocaust denier, hater of homosexuals, and self-proclaimed nemesis of the West, Iran's president helped strengthen global opinion that the Islamic Republic could not be trusted with military nuclear capabilities. Though the supreme leader and not the president made all the real decisions in Iran, Ahmadinejad happily collaborated in rejecting all diplomatic options—and exhausting America's patience. Consequently, the P5+1 would ramp up the sanctions and maintain the credible military threat necessary, in Israel's view, to convince Iran to dismantle its nuclear program entirely.

Accordingly, Israelis were anxious rather than relieved when Ahmadinejad concluded his term on June 15 and turned over the presidency to the newly elected Hassan Rouhani. Unlike his coarse, shabbily dressed predecessor, Rouhani was charismatic and refined, a Scottish-educated jurist who boasted a cleric's distinguished turban and robe. He was also an avowed moderate committed to reducing his nation's chronic inflation and unemployment. "Our goal is the shared interest between the two nations," he said of Iran's future relations with the United States. "Our goal is step-by-step creating trust between the governments and peoples." In his interviews and articles in the American media, Rouhani specifically renounced any Iranian intention of developing nuclear weapons. He called for a new compromise with the United States based on awareness of "the interests of others and . . . mutual respect."

These were almost the exact words Obama used in his first inaugural address in reaching out to the Muslim world, and that he used again in hailing the supreme leader's fatwa—Islamic decree—issued against nuclear weaponry and the "unique opportunity to make progress with the new leadership in Tehran." Perhaps more than any Muslim leader, Rouhani embodied the vision laid out in the Cairo speech: the authentic, democratically chosen leader ready to reconcile with the West. No wonder Obama spoke to Rouhani by phone on September 27, a day after Kerry met with his Iranian counterpart. The conversation between the two presidents represented the highest level of U.S.-Iranian contacts in more than thirty years.

And it was little mystery that Israelis were distressed. Rouhani, they reminded their American counterparts, was a product of the Islamic Revolution, one of five candidates carefully selected by the supreme leader, who still made all the real decisions in Iran. As the Iranian official responsible for negotiating with the West over the nuclear issue between 2003 and 2005, Rouhani boasted of exploiting the talks to "buy time to advance Iran's program." On Israel, too, he seemed to be playing a double game. After he had referred to the Jewish State as a "miserable country" and "a wound on the body of the Islamic world for years [that] should be removed," Iranian state television claimed he was misquoted. After tweeting Rosh Hashanah greetings to Iran's Jewish community, the president's office denied that he even had a Twitter account.

"Ahmadinejad was a wolf in wolf's clothing and Rouhani is a wolf in sheep's clothing," a clearly irritated Netanyahu told the UN General Assembly, "a wolf who thinks he can pull the wool over the eyes of the international community." The prime minister's insistence in branding Rouhani a fraud—and, by implication—Obama a dupe, put him again at odds with the administration. While in Washington the conventional assessment was that Rouhani represented a genuinely moderate wing of the regime and should therefore be strengthened, in Israel he was merely Iran's latest and most sophisticated feint.

Back in graduate school, I learned about *taqqiya,* the Shiite concept that permits believers to dissimulate their true ideas in order to advance the interests of faith. Iran had often practiced *taqqiya* in pursuing its nuclear program—lying about facilities, quoting antiproliferation fatwas that never existed—and so, too, might Rouhani. In time, the Iranian president would reinstitute the Holocaust denial conference started by his predecessor and authorize more executions, per capita, than in any other country.

Administration sources meanwhile continued leaking reports of IDF air strikes in Syria. One of these, a May 3 bombing of a Damascus warehouse purportedly containing yet another shipment of advanced missiles for Hezbollah, was said to have killed forty-two Syrian soldiers. Israel again withheld comment on the action, but the American leak spurred Assad to threaten counterattacks. At the embassy, I asked my staff what would impel some U.S. official to risk triggering bloodshed between Israel and Syria. Perhaps, one diplomat suggested, the White House wanted to distract Israel's attention from efforts to negotiate a nuclear deal with Iran.

The divergent views on Rouhani and the concern over the reported IDF air strikes were already chipping at the goodwill established during Obama's visit to Israel. The erosion was accelerated by a senior Israeli intelligence officer who revealed that Assad's forces had conducted multiple chemical attacks. The media promptly pounced on Jay Carney, the White House press secretary, with questions about whether Obama would now enforce his red line. "We know the Syrian government has the capacity to carry out chemical weapons attacks," Carney said, struggling to equivocate. "We remain skeptical of any claim that the opposition used chemical weapons."

Obama's red line nevertheless resurfaced. Irrespective of their attitudes toward Israel, Americans overwhelmingly esteemed its information-gathering capability and greeted Carney's response incredulously. When, they wanted to know, would the president stand by his mark in the sand?

At the September 2012 UN General Assembly.
By drawing a red line across the bomb, Netanyahu gave Obama "space and time"
for negotiating with Iran. The unusual gesture evoked comparisons with Wile E. Coyote.
The White House repaid Netanyahu by branding him a coward.

AP Photo/Seth Wenig

At the Pentagon with Defense Secretary Chuck Hagel, situated between Joint Chiefs of Staff Chairman General Martin Dempsey and Under Secretary (later Secretary) of Defense Ashton Carter. Across the table sits Defense Minister Ehud Barak, a wunderkind only Israel could have produced—concert pianist, former IDF chief of staff and prime minister, master commando, and tinkerer of clocks and locks.

Embassy of Israel to the U.S.

Touring an Iron Dome battery during Obama's March 2013 visit to Israel. This was the opportunity to convey an image of American-Israeli strength and unity to a tired and riven region. After more than four years of receiving mixed messages, the world would hear a single word: "ally."

Foreign Ministry of Israel

March 22, 2013: Netanyahu's "apology" to Turkish Prime Minister
Recep Tayyip Erdoğan. I had no illusions that the gesture would appease
the anti-Israel ruler. It was made to honor Obama.

Developed and deployed by Israel in a record four years, Iron Dome
became the first antiballistic system in history to work in battle.
As Hamas fired thousands of rockets at Israeli towns, Iron Dome
gave negotiators time to work out cease-fires, and saved the lives
of thousands of civilians who would have fallen victim to
an all-out ground war.
Missile Defense Advocacy Alliance

Devoid of body fat, capable of
bicycling dozens of miles each day,
Secretary of State John Kerry
tirelessly sought peace for Israel—
first with Syria, next with the
Palestinians. Both attempts failed.
"Help the Palestinians to build
viable institutions and only then
try to create a state," I advised his
staff. But my counsel went unheard.
The peace process, Kerry said,
"went poof."
Embassy of Israel to the U.S.

As the son of a former U.S. Army officer, I felt a special attachment to the military.
I tried to visit as many bases as possible and to interact with those
who defended our common values.

Embassy of Israel to the U.S.

In one of the perks of the job, I got to spend time with Israel's president Shimon Peres.
A founding father of the State, the architect of Israel's nuclear program, and a visionary
of peace, Peres was also a politician whose views often clashed with the prime minister's.
Here, at the White House, he receives America's highest civilian honor,
the Presidential Medal of Freedom.

Embassy of Israel to the U.S.

September 30, 2013: My last day on the job was typical.
In the Oval Office with Prime Minister Netanyahu and President Obama are (clockwise)
Vice President Biden, Secretary of State Kerry, National Security Advisor Susan Rice,
Ambassador Dan Shapiro, NSC Middle East expert Phil Gordon, and Middle East Envoy
Martin Indyk. To my left are Yitzik Molcho, Israel's peace negotiator,
and National Security Advisor Ya'akov Amidror.

White House

With Kulanu Party head Moshe Kahlon in January 2015, announcing my candidacy for Knesset. "Jumping into the mud"—as they say in Hebrew—of politics meant undergoing another radical transformation, but another opportunity to serve the State.

Dror Einev

"Behind the Iron Dome," I once said, "stands a marble dome—of the Capitol." Israel enjoys immense support in both houses of Congress. To help maintain that backing, I doubled the time I spent on the Hill. Among our greatest champions was the late Dan Inouye, the Democratic senator from Hawaii, seen here with Israel's dedicated congressional liaison, Aviv Ezra (right).

Shmuel Almany/Embassy of Israel to the U.S.

Israeli-designed and American-financed Iron Dome interceptors destroying a Hamas rocket, July 2014. The explosion was so close I took this photograph with my cellphone.

• • •

The question would be deferred for several months while America's attention once again swerved southwest, to Egypt. In spite of his USC degree and Obama's earnest efforts to bolster him as Egypt's first democratically elected president, Mohamad Morsi became indistinguishable from his predecessor, Mubarak. "The president can issue any decision or measure to protect the Revolution," the Muslim Brotherhood government decreed. "The constitutional declaration, decisions and laws issued by the president are final and not subject to appeal." In reaction to these draconian edicts, the deteriorating economy, and continued police brutality, protests broke out across the country.

Back in 2011, when a million demonstrators gathered in Tahrir Square, the American press covered the event round-the-clock. Just over two years later, in June 2013, when an estimated 14 million people protested in Cairo and 22 million signed a petition demanding Morsi's ouster, that same media all but ignored Egypt. The sole focus, rather, was on the trial of George Zimmerman, an armed neighborhood watchman in Florida who shot African-American teenager Trayvon Martin. Back in 2011, Obama determined that Mubarak had to step down immediately. Now the president called for restraint and personally phoned Morsi. He urged the Egyptian leader to be responsive to the demonstrators' wishes. "Democracy is about more than elections," the U.S. president said; "it is also about ensuring that the voices of all Egyptians are heard."

Morsi's reaction was to clamp down on his opponents. Hundreds of people were killed in clashes between opposing factions, and innumerable women were raped. The Egyptian Army, which had stood aside while Mubarak fell and the Brotherhood purged the military's senior ranks, now stepped in and called for immediate elections. Morsi stood fast, proclaiming, "We do not declare jihad against each other. We only wage jihad on our enemies." The army's response, delivered on July 3 by its commander, General Abdul Fattah al-Sisi, was to arrest Morsi and three hundred of his followers

The United States nevertheless continued to back Morsi. Obama said, "I now call on the Egyptian military to move quickly . . . to return full authority back to a democratically elected civilian government . . . and to avoid any arbitrary arrests of President Morsy [*sic*]

and his supporters." The result was an unprecedented wave of anti-Americanism throughout Egypt. Anne Patterson, the U.S. ambassador who so bravely helped rescue Israel's diplomatic staff in Cairo, was branded an "ogre." Posters of her smeared in bloodred paint bobbled over Tahrir Square, along with images of America's president with a Brotherhood beard and the label "Obama bin Laden."

Still, America's position remained unchanged. The reason was democracy. In a rare show of bipartisanship reminiscent of the early days of the Arab Spring, both Republicans and Democrats, Tea Partiers and Progressives opposed what all agreed was a military coup. The same president who, four years earlier in Cairo, declared, "No system of government can or should be imposed on one nation by any other," now championed Bush's "democracy agenda." No matter how autocratic and oppressive Morsi's rule, the mere fact that it arose from elections, and was ended by force, made it legitimate in American eyes.

And Israeli eyes once again rolled. Again I received calls from Defense Ministry advisor Amos Gilad questioning the Americans' reasoning. Again I had to explain that, for the United States, protecting democracy was similar to Israel's commitment to saving endangered Jewish communities abroad. To administration officials, I described Israel's inability to understand why they would support an antiliberal, antiwomen, antigay movement approved by a negligible majority in what was clearly a one-man-one-vote-one-time election. True, Morsi had cooperated in arranging the latest Gaza cease-fire, but he remained a radical opposed to virtually all of America's and Israel's fundamental ideals. Their reply was "Democracy means respecting the people's will, even if it's not to your liking." I thought—but did not say—"I wish you applied that same principle more often to Israel."

Coincidentally, just as I had been in the White House at the moment of Mubarak's demise, I was there again just as Morsi fell. The atmosphere was totally different. In place of the high-fives and exhilaration came distraught faces and silence. Al-Sisi's success in suppressing al-Qaeda cells in Sinai and clamping down on Hamas in Gaza—both deeply appreciated by Israel—went unheralded in Washington. Instead, the United States suspended the $1.55 billion in military assistance given to Egypt each year since it signed the peace accord with Israel. For the first time since Henry Kissinger extracted Egypt from Russia's orbit in the early 1970s, Cairo's leaders went arms shopping in Moscow.

By the summer of 2013, Obama's visit to Israel the previous March began to look like medieval history. The pace of events, especially in the Middle East, outstripped the ability of most decision makers—and much less the general public—to process. The resumed and accelerated peace process, the new Iranian leadership, chemical attacks in Syria, and political upheaval in Egypt—each posed immense regional challenges. And each threatened to strain the U.S.-Israel alliance in yet incalculable ways.

Surprises

My term in office, initially for two years and then twice extended by the prime minister for an additional year, was one of the longest of any Israeli ambassador to Washington. Throughout that period, I was often frustrated, exasperated, and stressed, but not for a second did I feel anything less than fulfilled. And I was never bored.

My day could begin at 7 A.M. with an interview on *Morning Joe* and proceed to a breakfast briefing with *The Washington Post*'s incomparable commentator Jackson Diehl. From there I might rush to Congress and meet with the heads of the Armed Services, Foreign Affairs, and Appropriations committees, and then hurry over to the White House for an update on the latest Middle East crisis. Lunch could be a snack with the eminent justice Stephen Breyer, followed by a Supreme Court hearing on the legality of terrorist fund-raising in the United States, or a quick bite with Jarrod Bernstein, President Obama's superresourceful liaison with the Jewish community. After I plunged into the Aquarium, Chief of Staff Lee Moser would seek my decision on always-urgent embassy issues, while Major General Ya'akov Aysh, our first-class defense attaché, furnished the latest news on military events in Iraq and Syria. Afternoons were spent giving speeches to evangelical or progressive groups or meeting with disabled U.S. veterans.

One daily schedule brought me to the Treasury to witness the signing of billions of dollars of U.S. loan guarantees for Israel; another shows me slipping in a moment to issue a statement supporting the appointment of my friend Samantha Power as America's ambassador to the UN. In the car between functions, I telephoned my kids or tapped out an op-ed on my laptop. Washington's social calendar filled my evenings with formal balls or costumed Purim bashes or soirées with the radiant arts patron Adrienne Arsht, who alone could get me to sing "I Get a Kick Out of You," in front of her guests. Starting at midnight, the calls could come in from morning-time Jerusalem.

Yet, somehow, I was not tired. Lighter by twenty pounds, I was in better shape than at any time in years. Much of that fitness was due to my quiet morning row, which could also contain surprises. Once, while sculling past a small fishing boat, I called out "Good morning" to the captain, who responded less amiably. "You went over my line," he screamed, "you fat, liberal, gay fuck!" Americans are nice until they aren't, I remembered. But I merely shrugged at him and pouted, "Fat?"

At a different dawn, however, the river fog parted to reveal an American bald eagle. Perched on a half-submerged stump, it eyed me, and I eyed back, for several moments without flinching. Finally, I smiled at the magnificent bird and said the first thing that came to my mind. "Morning, ally."

Such stimulation, for an ADHD person, was gratifying. So, too, was the realization—remarkably still astonishing—that I was Israel's representative to the United States. Whenever exiting the Eisenhower Executive Office Building I would pause and gaze at the First Division Memorial and the Washington Monument beyond, backlit by a sunset worthy of the Hudson River School. Amazed, I would wonder, "Am I really here?"

But I also missed Israel. With an almost aching frequency, memories recurred of Shabbat morning brunches with my family, hikes in the Jerusalem hills, and praying quietly in my neighborhood synagogue, where nobody questioned me about policy. I had done my best, I believed, and made a difference in far from uncomplicated circumstances. The time had come to return home.

Ron Dermer had expressed an interest in becoming the next ambassador, and we set a date for his arrival in the fall. My hope was that the intervening months would pass in relative tranquility. Yes, there would still be natural disasters, such as the tornados that ripped through Kansas and Oklahoma that spring, and the periodic shooting sprees that required immediate condolence notes from the prime minister. Israel, too, would have its crisis points, especially as the Palestinian prisoners—divided into four "tranches," each timed to keep Abbas at the negotiating table—were released. Still, over the years, my skin had thickened and my resilience steeled. Never again could I be surprised.

Or almost never. Like that time that Jeffrey Goldberg—whose life read like an excerpt from *Ripley's Believe It or Not*—was sunning on Martha's Vineyard and received a phone call from Fidel Castro inviting him to Cuba. "Sure," Jeff replied, and flew off to Havana. The visit, uproariously recalled in *The Atlantic,* had one serious side: the aging communist strongman and longtime supporter of Palestinian terror assured Jeff that he rejected Iranian attempts to deny the Holocaust and recognized Israel's right to exist. This remark, intended probably to shore up anti-embargo sentiment in Congress, reached the Prime Minister's Office. Someone there saw Castro's statement as an opportunity to drive a wedge between the European left, which idealized him, and their Islamist allies. Netanyahu merely had to write Castro a personal note welcoming his words and a threatening anti-Israel front would be splintered.

"Are you kidding?" I practically shouted at Ron Dermer on the phone. "The Cuban caucus in Congress is among our best friends. That letter will infuriate them."

"Gotcha," Ron replied. "I'll tell them to tear the letter up right away."

I hung up the phone only to be dumbstruck again. Moments later, Ron learned that his father-in-law had passed away, and he rushed home to join his wife. The letter from Netanyahu to Castro went out.

The result arrived within days. While riding with Sally to a black-tie event, my cellphone rang with a call from Congresswoman Ileana Ros-Lehtinen of Florida. The daughter of Cuban refugees, Ileana was passionate in her hatred of Castro. On the wall of her House office hangs a black-and-white photo of a disheveled man framed by stone-faced police. When I asked her why that, of all photographs, was on display, she said flatly, "That's Che Guevara being taken out for execution. The happiest day of my life."

Though short of stature, Ileana, when provoked, can instill fear. We befriended each other more than a decade earlier when, as a reserve officer accompanying Congress members on a visit to the Golan Heights, I watched her tell a brawny IDF general that he talked too much. Now the distinguished representative from South Florida lambasted Israel's perfidy. "For years, our community has done nothing but support you," she roared, "and you repay us by stabbing us in the back!" The tongue-lashing lasted roughly thirty minutes, until another Cuban caucus member called to complain.

My duty was to deliver the bad news to Netanyahu, who immediately understood and allowed me to arrange a reconciling conversation with Ileana. The incident was fortunately forgotten and the lesson learned. Several years later, when Obama lifted America's fifty-four-year-long embargo of Cuba, Netanyahu conspicuously refrained from praising the move.

If caught off guard by the Castro episode, I was utterly unprepared to be sued for libel by the Knesset's most prominent Arab member, Ahmad Tibi. In a *Foreign Policy* article on the robustness of Israeli democracy, I had cited Tibi's praise for Palestinian "martyrs"—a well-known Arabic synonym for suicide bombers—and suggested that such support for the terrorist murderers of one's fellow citizens would, in most open societies, result in disbarment or worse. Committed to free speech, though, Israelis kept Tibi in office. But Tibi, a former advisor to Yasser Arafat, denied he had made the statement and demanded restitution in court. Lamentably for him, a transcript of his homage to the families of "martyrs" in Ramallah was available. I would have welcomed the chance to ask Tibi, on the stand, whether or not he regarded a Palestinian who blew himself up on a bus and murdered dozens of civilians—my sister-in-law, for example—as a martyr. Fearing precisely that question, perhaps, the Knesset member dropped the case.

Dodging one sting did not mean I could evade them all, as I soon learned while addressing the Marines. As the son of a U.S. Army veteran, I made a special effort to visit military bases across the United States. From the Naval War College in Newport, Rhode Island, to the Command and General Staff College in Fort Leavenworth, Kansas, I met with officers and troops and spoke about Israel, America's ultimate ally. At the U.S. Military Academy at West Point, New York, an honor guard of cadets stood in line to greet me. Glancing at their name tags, I asked, "You guys are all Jewish, aren't you?" The young soldiers beamed at me and snapped, "Yes, sir!" Yet the one military facility I always wanted to see, the Marine Corps Training Base at Quantico, Virginia, though located near Washington, repeatedly eluded my schedule. Toward the end of my service, then, I made a point of visiting Quantico.

I went to the base—a sprawling, wooded campus the size of most cities—but in fact saw very little. A second before entering the main headquarters, I paused to take a phone call in my car. The last thing I remembered was a rectangular black object fixing toward my eyes. I woke up sometime later on the lawn, an ice pack numbing half of my face, and my entire head throbbing in pain. A Marine corpsman explained that I had been stung by a wasp—my cheeks were still smeared with venomous goo—and that I should nevertheless consider myself lucky. The stinger just missed my right eye. Sally was with me and asked if I wanted to go the hospital, but I said no. Eight hundred officers were waiting inside, and I was damned if some bug would prevent me from meeting them.

I vaguely remember speaking about the alliance again—dismayingly, someone told me it was my best lecture yet—and answering questions. Later, I chatted with the base commander and toured the Marine Museum, where I received a vial of volcanic sand from Iwo Jima. My skull, my teeth, my brain, it seemed, pounded, and my vision was blinkered by swollen cheeks. Yet I managed to thank and salute my hosts, and even to squeeze off a few shots on a rifle range, before departing for my doctor.

There was trauma, true, but also serendipity. A chance reunion with Elan Blutinger, a friend I had not seen since the eighth grade, now a successful Washington businessman, led to a fourteen-hour round-trip drive to Woodstock, New York, where we made a sick call to another middle school friend. There was the gala where Plácido Domingo, the famed Spanish tenor and conductor, greeted me in Hebrew, explaining that he began his career with the Tel Aviv opera, and the screen idol of my youth, Bo Derek, told me that she was my biggest fan.

The most rewarding surprise, though, occurred in my last month in Washington, when my schedule took me to a three-star hotel. Descending to the basement, I pushed through double doors into a fluorescent-lit hall and strode ahead of my security guards to a makeshift stage. Turning, I faced the crowd of fifteen-year-olds, members of an American Zionist youth movement on its annual visit to the capital. "On behalf of the State of Israel, thank you for your commitment and support," I started to say, but the words were lost in song.

"Heveinu Shalom Aleichem"—we welcome you in peace—the activists sang. They clapped and stomped their feet, and, forgetting my speech, I dropped off the stage and approached them. Many hands thrust toward me, and recalling that single shake that changed my life, I gratefully grasped them all.

Of all the surprises, none was more startling than the White House's response to the use of chemical weapons by Syria. Reports of unconventional attacks—and the administration's reluctance to confirm them—continued throughout the summer. Until August 21, that is, when sarin gas–exuding shells crashed into a rebel-held suburb of Damascus. As many as 1,500 civilians, almost a quarter of them children, choked to death.

"What happened in Syria is both a terrible tragedy and an awful crime," Netanyahu declared at the opening of his August 25 cabinet meeting. He expressed sadness for the innocent casualties of the attack but also warned Assad that Israel was watching him closely and was prepared to defend itself. "Our finger must always be on the pulse," he said. "Ours is a responsible finger and, if necessary, it will also be on the trigger." Contrastingly, Obama's reaction remained noncommittal. "This is clearly a big event of grave concern . . . this is going to require America's attention," he told CNN. "But that does not mean that we have to get involved with everything immediately." The president still questioned whether a chemical attack had indeed taken place and whether the United States could retaliate. "Without a UN mandate and without clear evidence, there are questions . . . whether international law supports it."

The evidence nevertheless mounted and quickly became irrefutable. The UN inspectors that the White House insisted investigate the site calculated that the chemical rockets had been fired from government positions. All eyes turned back to Obama and his red line, which could no longer be shifted or ignored. "Anyone who can claim that an attack of this staggering scale could be contrived or fabricated needs to check their conscience and their own moral compass," Secretary Kerry finally conceded on August 26. The president would hold Assad accountable, he pledged, and punish "those who would use the world's most heinous weapons against the world's most vulnerable people."

Over the next few days, as further details of the Damascus attack surfaced, Kerry remained the administration's point man. His message was that of a country on the cusp of war, a country concerned about maintaining its global credibility and showing its enemies resolve. At the same time, though, the secretary signaled that the U.S. response would be "limited and tailored," would not involve "boots on the ground" or incur "responsibility for a civil war already well under way." The image emerged of an administration determined to act forcibly, but not overly so.

I watched these mixed signals from the sidelines, following instructions to avoid being perceived as a player. Israelis, historically, had lived with the fear of Syria's unconventional arsenal, and many lined up for state-issued gas masks. For us there seemed no downside to an American military intervention aimed at deterring chemical weapons' use and weakening a dictator allied with Iran and Hezbollah. Yet Israel had no interest in becoming entangled in an internal American debate between a war-weary public and a president compelled to stand by his word. I watched and remained mute, all the while worrying that a failure to act would be seen as weakness on the part of the United States, a signal of its ally's vulnerability.

The Labor Day weekend approached and I assumed it would be a hot one. I canceled all my plans and instructed my staff to do the same. Both the British government and the Arab League had come out against the proposed U.S. strike, and yet the administration's own statements committed it to action. I went to bed on the night of August 30, fully prepared to be awakened at 3 A.M. with the news that American Tomahawk missiles were blasting the Syrian capital.

But the phone remained silent, and the only sound in the Residence the next afternoon was the TV news, which I habitually left on while shaving. The president was speaking in the Rose Garden, reminding the world that the mass gassing of Syrians represented "an assault on human dignity" and "a serious danger to our national security." The United States, Obama decided, should attack regime targets. Yet that was not his only decision. As "president of the world's oldest constitutional democracy," he added, "I will seek authorization for the use of force from . . . Congress."

The razor froze in mid-shave. Wiping the foam from my face, I rushed to the embassy. The once-sacred principle of "no surprises" in the U.S.-Israel alliance had fallen into desuetude during the Obama period, but never to this depth and on an issue so vital to our immedi-

ate security. The anxiety was audible in the hushed voices of Netanyahu and his national security advisor when I updated them by phone.
Even if Congress gave Obama a green light, Assad would have days
now to prepare his defenses. And while the president had received congressional cover for his action, Israel was left exposed. The entire Middle East, and especially the Iranians, now knew that America would
dither before enforcing an ultimatum.

Still, my orders were to keep clear of the imminent congressional
debate. No one wanted to revisit the experience of the Iraq War, which
Israel's critics in the United States blamed—unjustly—on Israel and
its supporters. The Senate, it seemed, was poised to authorize the
bombing, and so, too, the House, albeit reluctantly. Even so, if Americans balked at chastising Assad, it would be their business. Israel
would grapple with the consequences.

Staying out of the debate nevertheless proved tricky. National Security Advisor Susan Rice personally asked AIPAC to weigh in on the
side of action, leaving the organization little leeway but to accede.
Congress members meanwhile phoned the embassy inquiring about
Israel's position and obliging me to draw on all my hedging skills. "It's
the ghosts of [the wars] in Afghanistan and Iraq against the ghosts of
[the massacres] in Kosovo and Rwanda," I told them, "and Israel can't
get between your ghosts." Others just called to express their dismay.
"This is the most fucked-up thing I've seen in my entire political career," fumed John McCain.

Through these conversations, I learned that constituent calls were
running one hundred to one against military intervention, and in some
cases hundreds to one. Congress kept delaying the vote while senior
administration officials struggled to make their case. Defense Secretary Hagel warned that the missile strike would "not be a pinprick,"
but Kerry maintained that it would be "unbelievably small." Henry
Kissinger warned of a "humiliating outcome" for the United States
and of irreparable damage to Obama's international reputation.

Disgrace if not also danger loomed as I spent some of my last days
in office rushing around Washington in an attempt to ascertain the
possible impact of the Syria situation on Iran and other regional challenges. In the course of this frenzy, though, I heard of a proposal to
peacefully remove Syria's chemical arsenal. The idea originated with
an Israeli minister, Yuval Steinitz, who first pitched it to the Russians,

who were eager to avoid an American intercession that they could not stop. Netanyahu next brought it to Obama and received a green light. The "Framework for the Elimination of Syrian Chemical Weapons," provided for the export and destruction of Syrian's sarin, mustard gas, VX, and assorted nerve agents by the summer of 2014.

In subsequent interviews, Obama rarely missed the chance to cite the neutralization of Syria's chemical capabilities as an historic diplomatic achievement. Russian president Vladimir Putin also took credit for the initiative and praised this "vivid example of how the international community can solve the most complex disarmament and nonproliferation task." Israel's role remained unmentioned, but its citizens were relieved not to have to sign up for more gas masks. Happiest, perhaps, were the Syrians, and rightly so. Assad's massively destructive weapons succeeded in realizing their primary goal of preserving his regime. Part of the problem while possessing chemical arms, by removing them Assad became key to the solution. Henceforth, he would enjoy utter immunity while butchering his own people with barrel bombs and other conventional ordnance. The phrase "Assad must go" vanished from Obama's vocabulary.

These turns of events stunned me in unprecedented ways. Starting in 2009, I had made it my goal never to be surprised by Obama. Like a sound historian, I returned to the sources—the books the president wrote about himself and the speeches he made to the world. These revealed a leader who remained ambivalent about America's military might but unequivocal in his affinity for the Middle East, an advocate of engagement who, when crossed, could nevertheless resort to lethal force. They showed a president who preferred to pass many international initiatives on to others, such as the French and the UN, but who was also capable of making tough decisions—eliminating bin Laden, for example. This was a politician, I concluded, acutely sensitive to shifts in the press and an ideologue whose *kishke* issues included nonproliferation. All that should have translated into a one-time lightning strike against vital Syrian facilities.

It did not. But there was no time to ponder my unpreparedness. The president was set to give a major White House address on Syria, and Israel needed a categorical statement of its right to defend itself, even by massive means, if attacked. Summoning all the relationships I had cultivated over the years, the precise wording was finally settled.

But not until Obama actually declared, "Our ally Israel can defend itself with overwhelming force," and had "the unshakable support of the United States of America," did I finally feel relieved. And no longer surprised.

The Things I Carried Home

Inextricably caught in downtown Manhattan traffic, late for an address to the heads of American Jewish organizations, I turned to Lee Moser and said, "Let's get out of the car and run." So we ran as, suddenly, thunder rumbled down Madison Avenue and the sidewalks darkened with rain. We ran, totally drenched, with my chief of staff's ankles bleeding from her high heel shoes and water squirting from my socks. Yet all I could do was laugh. "Just remember, Lee," I shouted at her over the deafening peals, "these are the best days of our lives!"

And so they were. For all the trials, the crises, those moments when I thought my capacity for composure and cogent thinking were long surpassed, nothing could replicate the profound privilege—and, yes, the joy—of representing Israel in America. There were times when I imagined that, through sheer force of will, I was holding the alliance together, and other times when I realized that those bonds were far stronger than any individual's ability to fray or fortify them. Either way, serving as the emissary to the land of my father from the land of my forefathers, to the America of my birth from my birthright, Israel, remained an inestimably rewarding experience.

Now it was concluding. The end of an ambassador's term can be as event-jammed as its outset. There were numerous dinners held in honor of Sally and me. The Senate held a farewell reception for us, as did the State Department, hosted by Wendy Sherman. There were many toasts and even several tears. In between, we packed. Decades ago, I had made *aliya* with merely a backpack, but now I stared at a cardboard ziggurat composed of some two hundred boxes—books, mostly, but also a single crate especially reserved for memorabilia.

Filling it, I was reminded of Tim O'Brien's immortal short story, "The Things They Carried," about American soldiers fighting in Vietnam. Into battle they bore with them not only necessities such as bandages and bug spray, but also the mementos that signified their lives. Now I had to choose those few items that encapsulated the past four years. According to Israeli law, an ambassador must hand over to the

State all the gifts received while in office. Exceptions could be made for certain items, upon special request. The things I carried home were intensely special.

The first articles packed were quirky, such as a laminated copy of a *Los Angeles Times* crossword puzzle in which question 12 Down was "Israel's Envoy in Washington." Next came the Tiffany apple, a present from New York mayor Michael Bloomberg, with a glossy heft that recalled my heady student days in the Big Apple. Into the box went the "In Google We Trust" magnet I received while visiting the Internet giant's California headquarters. The tour of the amusement park–like campus included a chat with Executive Chairman Eric Schmidt. I shared with him Israel's concerns about Google Earth, the global mapping program, which terrorists had used as a targeting device. Google Earth, Schmidt explained, was designed to bring people closer together. "Yes," I acknowledged, "but does it have to bring Hezbollah closer to my children?"

Following the apple and the magnet into the box went my souvenirs from the reenactments of the battles of Manassas and Gettysburg. Watching thousands of blue- and gray-uniformed "living historians" firing muskets and cannons was pure fun for the Civil War fanatic in me, even though dozens of the participants fainted from the heat. And as the only Israeli ambassador—and perhaps the only foreign diplomat—ever to attend these extravaganzas, I was hosted with the deference due to a Union or Confederate general. But beyond enjoyment, the replica kepi and minié balls I saved reminded me that liberty was often wrought at an excruciating price. They, too, were crated.

The oddest entry of all was a bottle of Poland's finest vodka. This was presented to me by Maryland's Barbara Mikulski, the longest-serving woman senator. I had first met Barbara in the 1990s, at a special Senate ceremony honoring my father. On December 16, 1944—the first day of the Battle of the Bulge—when many GIs retreated in the face of the advancing German army, my father and his friend Jimmy Hill dug in with a bazooka and knocked out the lead Panzer tank. Bureaucracy delayed the medals due to my dad and Jimmy, but when they finally arrived, Barbara bestowed them. I was always grateful to her for that honor as well as for her unswerving support for Israel, which began when she, the granddaughter of Polish immigrants, first visited Auschwitz. Barbara succeeded the great Dan Inouye as the chair of the Senate Appropriations Committee, proving to me, once again, the power of providence.

"I thought about what I could get you, cuff links or something," she told me on my last visit to the Hill. "But then I decided on this."

The vodka bottle, which I would cherish but never open, was inscribed "To Ambassador Oren—a leader for Justice and Freedom."

More conventional but no less touching was the formal letter inviting me, the Jewish State's representative, to address one of Washington's largest iftars. Another invitation welcomed me to New York's Cathedral of St. John the Divine on 110th Street, where, before the altar with bishops and Harlem community leaders, I danced an ecstatic hora to the Middle Eastern rock music of Idan Raichel. Especially valued was the note naming me the keynote speaker at the annual Equality Forum, America's oldest gay rights organization. I spoke about the achievements of Israel's LGBT community, about the successful fight for equal status in the IDF and the foreign service, about the Palestinian homosexuals who found shelter in Israel, and about Tel Aviv, now listed as the world's most gay-friendly city and host to Asia's largest gay pride parade. But I also admitted that the struggle against prejudice in Israel continued. "We are a work in progress," I said, "but we are also a work of progress."

There were plaques—almost as many as boxes. A plaque from Columbia University's John Jay Fellows, presented by some of my college classmates, and a plaque signed by hundreds of student body presidents who, in the wake of the Irvine protest incident, urged me to speak on their campuses. The plaque from my security guards featured a spy camera that I could hang behind my desk, just over my shoulder, and never feel alone.

Into the box went the elongated, amber shofar I received from American Jewish leaders. As a chubby child presumably with a surfeit of wind, I was given a baritone—essentially a small tuba—to play in the school band. Oompahing on that horn invariably led to blowing the shofar in my family's synagogue on the High Holidays. One Rosh Hashanah, as a guest of Gary Ginsberg's Town and Village Synagogue in Manhattan, I was asked to sound that ram's horn. Unpracticed for many years, my initial notes fizzled. But suddenly the purest tone emerged. It reverberated over the pews and seemed to lift my soul with it. That shofar was coming home with me.

An ambassador accrues no end of ashtrays, paperweights, and

medals, but there were several items that meant more to me than all those keepsakes combined. Two Stars and Stripes, gifts of Senators Ed Markey and Roy Blunt—a Democrat and a Republican—both flown over the Capital and folded into neat triangles, took pride of place in the box. So, too, did a simple glass monolith emblazoned with my name and the words "Outstanding Learning Disabled Achiever Award." I never knew how it happened, but someone in Washington heard about my childhood struggles with dyslexia and other disabilities. The result was a call from the Washington Lab School, an inspiring institution dedicated to teaching young people with similar challenges, offering to honor me. Previous recipients included Vice President Biden, the school said. But I needed no prodding. Here was the opportunity, at last, to confront a painful past.

Before a black-tie, august audience, for the first time publicly, I confessed what it was like to be deemed the dumbest kid in the class, to be lumped together with other "underachievers," given the worst teachers, and automatically the lowest grades. "There were no tutors, no allowances for disabilities—there weren't even terms for the handicaps I had." I admitted the humiliation I felt coming from the Jewish community, where students were expected to excel. Then I retraced the agonizing ascent from that darkness—the poetry I began to write and publish, the high school English teacher who let me into his honors class on the condition that I teach myself how to spell, and my battle with standardized testing, which ended in the Ivy League. Finally, I talked about Yoav, Lia, and Noam—my kids—who grappled with tougher learning obstacles than I ever faced and overcame them even more courageously. "These children, not the degrees, not the books, not the ambassadorial titles," I concluded, "are my greatest success in life."

The box was nearly full. There remained a little space for some tokens from where I grew up. I often told audiences that "I spend more time defending the state of New Jersey than I do the State of Israel," and invariably got a laugh. Yet, even if it did not allow me to be a cowboy guiding herds around Golan minefields, New Jersey was a perfectly good place for an American upbringing. And to honor it, I packed the pin of crossed Garden State and Jewish State flags given to me by Governor Chris Christie, who attended a rival high school, and the poster labeled, "From Asbury Park to the Promised Land," inscribed with the words, "With warm wishes to another Jersey guy," and signed by Bruce Springsteen. I kept the leaf of official White House stationery on which President Obama wrote, "Michael, your life of service embodies the bonds between our nations—not bad for a kid from New Jersey."

I closed and sealed the box, aware that some of the most precious tokens could not be shipped. Among these were the moments spent with my parents. Now in their late eighties, they still lived in the same house where they raised me. After so many years of being separated by thousands of miles, suddenly a mere five-hour drive united us. Joined by my sisters, Karen and Aura and their families, a visit from my mother and father transformed our run-down Residence into a palace of familial joy. But it also served as a shelter. In October 2012, when Hurricane Sandy smashed into the East Coast and devastated large swaths of New Jersey, my parents' phone went dead. I did manage to reach their rabbi, though, who found them shivering in bed. I told my folks to get into their car and drive south as far as possible—Delaware's gas stations were open—and come to us. Through the storm, these members of the Greatest Generation drove and arrived, frightfully chilled, at our doorstep. More frozen still were the many pounds of meat my mother had loaded into the trunk. Her brisket, too, had escaped from New Jersey.

Yet part of me, I knew, needed to go back, just once. "No way," Lee Moser scolded me. "There's simply no time." Nevertheless, I insisted on making that time and so, one afternoon, escorted by the West Orange police and Board of Education, I visited my high school. I took a photo in front of my old locker and embraced my former principal, Jerry Tarnoff, who had come out of retirement to greet me. In the main auditorium, several hundred students gathered to hear me speak. The faces had changed since my day. In place of the Jews and Italians who once made up 90 percent of the school, now were mostly African-Americans and Asians. But their aspirations, I assumed, remained the same.

"Forty years ago," I began, "I stood on this very stage and played the role of Don Quixote in the musical *Man of La Mancha*. It's the story about a man who refuses to give up on his principles. People called him outdated. People called him insane. Yet he kept wearing his rusty armor. He continued to fight."

The assembly was silent, uncertain, perhaps, of what to make of me. But I went on, recalling how I sang the song, "To Dream the Impossible Dream," and even attempted a few bars. The students finally laughed and applauded and I laughed with them. But then I grew serious. "I, too, had a dream. It was to move to Israel and then come back as Israel's ambassador to the United States. Each of you has your dreams as well. And just know . . ." I paused, once again growing sentimental. "That no dream is impossible."

My last day as ambassador, September 30, began before dawn, typically, on a tarmac. Prior to addressing the UN General Assembly in New York, Netanyahu planned a one-day visit to Washington. The musky smell of autumn mixed with the tang of jet fuel as the El Al airliner touched down. Three U.S. Air Force colonels saluted, Chief of Protocol Capricia Marshall smiled, and I, for the last time, shouted above the engines, "Baruch Habah"—welcome—"Mr. Prime Minister."

The day, too, was characteristic enough, starting at the State Department and a conversation on the peace process with Secretary of State Kerry. From there we motorcaded to the White House to meet with Vice President Biden and Susan Rice. Locked in a seemingly irresolvable budget debate with Congress that threatened to shut down the federal government, President Obama was not expected to devote much time to Netanyahu. But the one-on-one meeting between them lasted more than twice the allotted time. When the American and Israeli teams finally entered the Oval Office, we found the two leaders— once again routinely—smiling as if in total conformity.

The president indeed affirmed that the United States would not be deceived by Rouhani's "charm offensive," would enter "clear-eyed" into any future talks with Iran, and would judge it by actions, not words. Obama even thanked Netanyahu for his cooperation with Kerry's initiative. Though unnerved by the recent conversations between the U.S. and Iranian presidents, the prime minister similarly expressed gratitude for America's commitment to preventing Iran from acquiring nuclear weapons. And while not opposed to negotiations with Tehran, these, Netanyahu stressed, should only be conducted under heightened sanctions and a credible military threat.

In spite of this seeming harmony, I knew, disagreements over the Palestinian issue and Iran would likely persist and sharpen. These two leaders, despite their four-year familiarity, would continue to clash.

Obama was no longer the inexperienced president of 2009, and yet time and events had not altered his outlook. He still referred to a "Muslim world"—a world that contained the Iranian regime but excluded Sunni jihadists and al-Qaeda—and refused to utter the words "Islamic terror." Committed to Israel's defense, he also remained invested in the Palestinian cause and in efforts to achieve a nuclear deal with Tehran. Netanyahu, meanwhile, was no less determined to safeguard Israel's security and to fulfill the role that history reserved for him.

Obama and Netanyahu chatted and I went on nodding approvingly. My face wore the upbeat expression I had long perfected. My thoughts, though, kept wandering elsewhere.

Starting tomorrow, I would once again be a civilian, no longer bound by protocol or government positions, but a free person in possession of ideas. The realization was at once liberating and scary. I would get up in the morning, but then, I fretted, do what? Rahm Emanuel supplied one answer. "Take a five-week vacation," the mayor advised me during a recent farewell visit to Chicago. "You're more tired than you know. Sometime during the second week you'll admit to yourself, 'Holy shit, was I tired.'" Though I still felt energized, right there on the blue-striped Oval Office sofa, images of alabaster beaches beckoned.

But David Rothkopf had different plans for me and they did not involve taking a break. "Of course, you're going into politics," he said matter-of-factly during the course of our farewell lunch. My jaw froze in mid-chew. "I have zero political experience," I managed to gulp while David merely laughed. "Don't be silly. For years now you've been doing nothing but politics and at the highest level."

The thought of running for public office had never occurred to me, but David planted a seed. I knew that I wanted to keep serving Israel and believed that I could bring all that I had learned and experienced to bear. And at a time when Israel faced fateful challenges, how could I stand aside? But, then again, I questioned whether I could handle the rough-and-tumble of Israeli politics, the constant press scrutiny, and the chaos of the Knesset, where speakers are routinely shouted down. If, in America, candidates throw their hats into the ring, in Israel they "leap into the mud." Could I, at this age, begin a new and more onerous quest?

The conversation between Obama and Netanyahu meanwhile moved on to Syria, which, the prime minister predicted, might soon break apart, and then to America's policy on Egypt, where, the president averred, "we cannot act as if it's business as usual."

Within my mind, meanwhile, another dialogue took place. "If you will it, it is no dream," I imagined Theodor Herzl saying. William Butler Yeats agreed but reminded him that, "In dreams begin responsibility."

Snapping out of this reverie, I heard Obama assure Netanyahu, "If war comes, we're with you, because that's what the American people want." The remark recalled the conclusion I reached back in 2009, that Obama's position on Israel reflected his understanding of its place in American affections. Still, I found myself wishing that the president would say, just once, "We're with you because it's the right thing to do." Or, "We're with you, because that's in America's interest. We're with you, because, both strategically and morally, Israel is our ally."

With that wistful thought, I left the Oval Office for the final time and boarded the prime minister's limousine for our last stop of the day. More than 125 Congress members—a quarter of the House—waited to say goodbye to me. This, in itself, represented an immense honor, but I was unprepared for what was said.

Majority Leader Eric Cantor thanked me for "making it so much easier for us in Congress to step up and defend democracy," and his Democratic counterpart, Nancy Pelosi, lauded the "eye of an historian, the skill of a diplomat" that deepened America's appreciation of Israel, "the greatest single achievement of the twentieth century." Majority Whip Kevin McCarthy praised the "knowledge, passion, and persuasiveness" that ensured continued bipartisan support for Israel. Steny Hoyer, the great Democratic whip, described me as holding "fast to the Zionist dream of a peaceful Israel—strong in arms and equally strong in its democratic principles, while recognizing the difficult road to realizing all of our dreams, America's as well." On an exalted note, Steny concluded, "Two countries, one dream."

If left blushing by these encomiums, the prime minister's remarks stirred me. After portraying me as a "human bridge" between the United States and Israel and citing my *Power, Faith, and Fantasy* book about America in the Middle East, Netanyahu revealed as much about his own worldview as mine:

History is not just a flat chronicle of events. History is an understanding of the forces that work, the values that shape present action and direct the future. If you have that knowledge, you are empowered in ways that you can't get by watching the nightly news or reading the morning editorials. We live in an ahistorical age when many people's memories go back to breakfast, but if you're armed with that insight you have immense power for good.

More superlatives were offered, many of them directed at Sally, who had hosted so many of the members present and impressed with her sincerity and warmth. The speakers sat down, the list exhausted except for one.

No time was available to prepare a text, so I thanked the members for the confidence they had showed in me, for helping to defend Israel, and for assuring our people that "above the Iron Dome, stands the marble dome" of the Capitol. Recalling my years of research, I admitted how "immensely humbling this job had been, for the alliance was far deeper and multidimensional than anything I could have read in a library." And I evoked my youth, my love for the United States, "its values, its principles," and how "the fulfillment of the Zionist idea became, for me, the fulfillment of the American idea." I was getting choked up, and admitted it. So, before embarrassing myself, I cut to the end. "For the last time, in the name of the Government, the State, and the People of Israel, I say to each and every one of you, *todah rabah*. Thank you."

Early the next morning, the movers carted our boxes to the truck. Ron Dermer and his family would enter a newly built house. The Residence, the former home of Yitzhak Rabin and so many other worthy ambassadors, would be shuttered. Reluctant to watch that process and confident that Sally had everything under control, I allowed myself to slip away.

Security precautions limited the ambassador's maneuverability, but I was no longer Extraordinary and Plenipotentiary, nor even Your Excellency. I was just a private Israeli citizen who, for the first time, strode out of his front door and onto the street, unescorted by guards. I descended the hill toward Rock Creek Park, dressed in jeans and sneakers. Nobody saw me and, even if they had, few would have recognized me out of customary diplomatic garb.

Cloaked in that anonymity, I stood on a wooden bridge just as the early October sun pierced the trees. Leaves were already falling, see-sawing down to the water, where they melted into a golden flow. Autumn was always my favorite season, a time for reflection and taking stock. Thinking back on the past four years evoked many emotions—frustration and fulfillment, exhilaration and fear. Overwhelmingly, though, the deepest feeling was gratitude.

A NIGHT AT
KIBBUTZ NA'AN

THE BAR MITZVAH PARTY HAD JUST STARTED ON THE LAWN OF Kibbutz Na'an, near central Israel. In a truly collective celebration, all of the community's thirteen-year-olds and their families had gathered on a lawn illuminated by decorative lanterns. Sally and I, along with Lee Moser and her husband, Dar, were the guests of my former spokesman from Washington, Aaron Sagui, whose son, Gal, was among those being honored.

The scene appeared festive, yet the mood felt subdued. The date was July 7, 2014, just days after Hamas terrorists abducted and murdered three Israeli teenagers not much older than Gal. Israel retaliated with aerial strikes against Hamas targets in Gaza. And Hamas was certain to fire back. As we drove into the kibbutz, I turned to Sally and said, "You know we're in range."

Suddenly a siren wailed and hundreds of guests frantically ran for cover. Only there was no cover. The rockets would take less than a minute to reach the kibbutz, and we were caught in the open.

Nine months had passed since moving back to Israel. Renting an apartment in Tel Aviv, Sally and I reunited with our children and reveled in Ariel and Romi, our first two Israeli grandchildren. Mornings, I rowed on the Yarkon River—a creek compared to the Potomac, but calmer—and then thrilled to the city's nonstop effervescence. When trekking to Jaffa along the beachfront, passing classical string quartets, Hare Krishna proselytizers, triathlon trainers, senior citizen group dancers, and a profusion of frolicking kids, I was reminded of how youthful and creative Israel remained, and how cool. Landing here, any American would at once feel at home. And I sometimes wondered why any Amer-

ican would want to weaken this familiar patch of freedom that flourishes only a few hours' drive from the killing fields of Iraq and Syria.

But Israel was not only Tel Aviv promenades. The nation I returned to grappled with staggering challenges, from mind-numbing
bureaucracy to rising poverty rates and a declining quality of education. It faced growing Ultra-Orthodox and Arab communities that
rejected the state's raison d'être, and settler violence that darkened its
reputation. It wrestled with the West Bank Palestinians who, if given
independence, could mortally threaten Israel's existence but who, if
granted citizenship, could undermine its Jewish and democratic character. Sovereignty is messy, I recalled, and, yes, that mess was our responsibility to repair.

Meanwhile, I went back to work. Holding the Abba Eban Chair in
International Diplomacy at the Inter-Disciplinary Center—IDC—in
Herzliya, and a fellow of Washington's Atlantic Council, I engaged in
"track two" diplomacy on Middle East issues with U.S. and European
officials. On the pages of *Foreign Policy,* David Rothkopf and I published our visceral exchange on the relationship between Israel and
American Jews.

David wrote:

There are many Americans who support Israel. . . . But
the . . . construction of settlements . . . has undercut its moral
high ground. Israel has almost systematically made it harder
for those who would be supportive to follow through on that
impulse.

And I replied:

It's time that American Jews see Israel not as a Hollywood or
Hebrew school fantasy but . . . as a real country made . . . of
humans caught in inhuman circumstances. . . . Tired after
two wars in which the vast majority [of Americans] didn't
fight? Try dealing with eight . . . together with thousands of
rockets raining on your cities, countless bombs blowing up
buses. . . .

David asserted:

Today there are other safe places for Jews in the world, nota-
bly America. Today there are other ways for Jews to live and

be true to their traditions that don't involve the harsher realities of a garrison state.

And I retorted:

Israel, in spite of unspeakable pressures, managed to stay democratic, open, creative, self-correcting (frequently to a fault), self-defending, ultra-literate (in Hebrew), and Jewish.

"Israel cannot be the Jewish state," David argued. "It can be a Jewish state. But . . . to be a moral state, it must guarantee the rights . . . of every citizen. . . . It is hard to say Israel does that now."
And I maintained:

Israel is the Jewish State because it, alone, is situated in our ancestral homeland, provided refuge to Jews from more than seventy countries, revived the ancient Jewish language, and observes a national Jewish calendar. It is the Jewish State because it will aid you and your family . . . because you are Jews. When I relinquished my U.S. citizenship, an American consul punched a hole in my passport. But no one can punch a hole in the passport linking you to Israel because your passport is your membership in the Jewish people.

While writing for American readers, I also became a frequent guest on Israeli TV. Here was another trying transition. Who was I now? A spokesman for the government still or a private citizen? An ambassador whose job it was to preserve bridges and not shake them? It took many stilted interviews before I regained my sense of self and commented freely on the alliance.

In the interim, I searched for the right way to contribute all that I had learned and experienced to strengthening Israel's foreign policy, and to take responsibility. I did not heed Rahm Emanuel's advice to lie on some beach for five weeks, but neither did I have the chance. Events moved entirely too swiftly.

Less than two months after I left Washington, the administration finally admitted that it had been secretly negotiating with the Islamic regime for the previous seven months. Israel had long feared such bilateral talks, in part because Washington's position on Iran was the most flexible of the Western members of the P5+1. France, for example, demanded that Iran disclose its previous work on nuclear weaponization, while the United States apparently did not. Though Obama's spokespeople insisted that "no deal with Iran is better than a bad deal," some senior Israeli analysts began to question whether, for this White House, a bad deal was better than none.

Israeli anxieties appeared to be validated on November 24, when the P5+1 signed an interim agreement—the Joint Plan of Action—with Iran. This removed the Iranian store of 20 percent–enriched uranium and intensified international monitoring. But the nineteen thousand centrifuges remained intact, as did the vastly larger stockpile of 3.5 percent–enriched uranium, and no limits were placed on Iran's nuclear research or missile development. Sanctions for the first time would not be ramped up, but eased by some $7 billion.

"There is no daylight between . . . Israel and the United States," Secretary Kerry told American television. "Israel is, in fact, safer than it was yesterday." This was news to Netanyahu. "This is an historic mistake," he fumed. "Today the world has become a much more dangerous place because the most dangerous regime in the world has taken a significant step toward attaining the most dangerous weapon in the world." Former secretaries of state Henry Kissinger and George Shultz agreed, telling Congress that Iran had "outmaneuvered" the United States and set the stage for a Middle East nuclear arms race.

Common to Netanyahu, Kissinger, and Shultz was the realization that the Security Council's original goal of eliminating Iran's nuclear program had been supplanted by an arrangement that actually preserved it. In place of denying the ayatollahs the ability to break out and produce a weapon before the world could react, the deal threatened to cement that ability. Rather than demand that Iran cease supporting terror and threatening America's allies, the arrangement implicitly recognized Iran's regional aspirations and its right to enrich uranium. The sanctions built up over more than a decade would, for the first time, be lessened. "The cracks in the sanctions began last night," Rouhani trumpeted, "and in the future those gaps will grow."

Though originally slated to last six months, the interim agreement was extended for an additional half year while negotiations with Iran dragged on. The window for diplomacy that the administration consistently warned would not remain indefinitely open so far proved to be precisely that. Israel supported a congressional initiative to increase pressure on the Iranians—"They're on the ropes," Netanyahu urged; "Don't let them off the mat"—only to encounter unflinching resistance. Ben Rhodes, Obama's strategic communications advisor, urged liberal lobbyists to ask Congress members, "Are you for solving this diplomatically or being forced . . . to war?" That binary view— negotiations or conflict—discounted the third option of heightened pressure on Iran. Nevertheless, it worked. The new sanctions bill, which Israel insisted would keep the Iranians at the table but Obama warned would drive them away, was deferred.

Most disturbing for me personally was the realization that our closest ally had entreated with our deadliest enemy on an existential issue without so much as informing us. Instead, Obama kept signaling his eagerness for a final treaty with Iran. In a personal letter to the supreme leader—his fourth—the president purportedly suggested that, in return for scaling back its nuclear program, Iran could cooperate with the United States in combating radical Sunnis in Syria and Iraq.

Huge swaths of both countries were being conquered by the Islamic State (IS), which aimed to replace them with a jihadist caliphate. In the second half of 2014, as IS's black flags neared Baghdad, an English-speaking masked murderer beheaded two American journalists. Theatrically filmed, the executions were designed to go viral in the media and goad the press-sensitive administration to intervene militarily. This posed little threat to IS, which had witnessed America's retreat from Afghanistan and Iraq. Yet a de facto alliance between the United States and the Shiite and Iranian forces battling IS was seen as an effective Sunni recruiting tool.

And Obama obliged. Acting to "degrade and ultimately destroy" the Islamic State, U.S. jets joined with a coalition of Western and Arab forces in fighting the terrorists. The decision nevertheless represented a setback for the president, who styled himself as the ender, rather than the reviver, of Middle Eastern wars. As in his earlier response to Syria's use of chemical weapons, he sought congressional approval for action against IS.

The movement nevertheless metastasized throughout the region and especially in Libya, where the terrorists beheaded twenty-one Egyptian Christian workers. But in contrast to its criticism of President al-Sisi and Egypt's air campaign against IS in Libya, the administration downplayed Iran's ground action against IS in Iraq. The supreme leader repeatedly denounced IS as an American plot, but, just as consistently, the administration signaled its interest in finding a common ground with Iran. The major hurdle, Obama intimated, was the nuclear program.

"[I]f we were able to get Iran to operate in a responsible fashion," he told *The New Yorker*, "you could see an equilibrium developing between [it and] Sunni . . . Gulf states." Once restored to the international community, Iran could become a "very successful regional power," the president said in subsequent interviews, and indicated that, once relieved of sanctions, the regime might devote its wealth to peaceful purposes. And just as Nixon-era America's opening to China and Russia favorably altered their behavior—proponents of an agreement claimed—so, too, might the current engagement policy change Tehran. "Iran is a complicated country just like we're a complicated country," Obama observed. A strategic threat with a nuclear weapon, Iran with a contained ability to make an atomic bomb was the gateway to stability—the White House seemed to suggest.

From a position of "I don't bluff" about his willingness to use armed force against nuclear sites, Obama appeared to rule out any military option. Instead, a final agreement with Iran represented "the biggest thing President Obama will do in his second term on foreign policy," according to Strategic Communications Advisor Ben Rhodes. The treaty-making process, Rhodes noted, would be shielded from Congress members who were "very attentive to what Israel says on its security issues."

Congress's attentiveness to Israel intensified after the November 2014 elections, when the Republicans regained the Senate. To those Israelis who regarded this turnover as a godsend, I recalled that a president blocked by both houses from pursuing his domestic agenda would naturally turn to foreign affairs. I reminded them that a second-term president concerned with leaving a legacy could ignore congressional objections much as Obama did the following month by lifting America's fifty-four-year embargo of Cuba. Finally, I sensed that the same commander in chief who sought congressional authorization for warlike actions against Syria and the Islamic State would try to sidestep the Senate in signing what he portrayed as a peace arrangement with Iran.

• • •

Far less prophecy was required to foretell the failure of Kerry's peace initiative. The Israeli government released three large groups of Palestinian prisoners and reportedly agreed to an American "framework agreement" setting out the territorial parameters of a two-state solution. The country braced for the fourth release, which, for the first time, included Israeli Arabs jailed for murdering Israeli Jews. As a purported quid pro quo for these concessions, Kerry offered the release of Jonathan Pollard. But when Israeli leaders insisted that Abbas commit to remaining at the table, he bolted. Instead, on April 24, the Palestinian president announced his Authority's adherence to fifteen international treaties. Once again, Abbas attempted to create a Palestinian state, without making peace, unilaterally through the UN. And once again, Abbas made a reconciliation pact with Hamas.

A solid majority of Israelis were convinced that their leaders had surpassed the extra mile, and reports later revealed that Netanyahu was willing to make major concessions. Yet Kerry indicated differently. Settlements remained the contention point, specifically Israeli building in the blocs and the Jewish areas of Jerusalem. "Israel announced it would build seven hundred settlement units," the secretary told the Senate Foreign Relations Committee, and the peace process went "poof." The units were slated for Gilo, the Jerusalem neighborhood that in any future agreement with the Palestinians would certainly remain within Israel's borders.

I spent the next day on Israeli TV trying to find the Hebrew equivalent for *poof.* I labored to explain the administration's refusal to condemn Abbas's reconciliation with Hamas, even after the organization took credit for murdering the three Israeli teenagers. I tried, unsuccessfully, to analyze why Special Envoy Martin Indyk, in a flimsily disguised Israeli press interview with a "senior U.S. diplomat," placed the bulk of the blame on Israel's settlement policy. Netanyahu purportedly swore that he would never deal with Indyk again.

Stoking these tensions, Israeli ministers were quoted calling Kerry obsessive, detached from Middle East realities, and even "messianic." In a closed session leaked to the press, right-wing Knesset members took Ambassador Dan Shapiro to task for the administration's alleged attempts to undermine Israeli democracy and its "anti-Semitic" policy toward Pollard. Anonymous Israeli sources also asserted that Netanyahu had given up trying to work with Obama and would wait out the end of his presidency. Along with "no surprises" and "no daylight," the long-held principle of not airing soiled U.S.-Israeli laundry for the world to see was dangerously discarded.

We ran. As the siren droned on that July 7 night, I gripped Sally's hand and sprinted across the abandoned lawn of Kibbutz Na'an. I headed for the nearest house, which was made of concrete and might provide partial shelter. But its front door was locked. So we huddled on the porch, together with Lee, Dar, and several other Bar Mitzvah guests, beneath a corrugated awning. A couple shielded their infant son with their bodies. Sufficiently experienced in shellfire, I kept my composure, though others shook and even whimpered. Any second, the rockets would hit.

No one that night imagined that Israel was on the brink of a desperate war with Hamas that would last for fifty days. The terrorists fired some 4,500 rockets and mortar shells at Israel and staged attacks through more than thirty tunnels dug deep under Israel's border. Seventy-two Israelis, soldiers, and civilians were killed—an agonizing cost for our small Jewish State. Responding with Operation Protective Edge, Israel managed to inflict massive damage on its enemy. But Hamas's tactic of shooting at Israeli civilians from behind innocent Palestinians again served its media and diplomatic strategy of producing pictures of Palestinian suffering. Though roughly half of the 2,100 Palestinian dead were combatants, the images of the civilian casualties again sparked outcries from abroad.

Some of the most strident protests emanated from Washington. Obama reiterated his support for Israel's right to defend itself from the rockets and rejected charges of Israeli war crimes. But he also criticized Israel for allegedly failing to live up to its own moral standards by harming Palestinian civilians. The president described these losses as "appalling," an adjective so strong it had no Hebrew equivalent, and which he had last employed to characterize Gaddafi's massacre of Libyans. Hamas, by contrast, had acted "extraordinarily irresponsibly," Obama said, by firing indiscriminately at Israeli homes. "Gee," a young friend of mine quipped, "one might expect Hamas to act more responsibly."

Each day of the operation subjected the alliance to seemingly insuperable strains. The brutal murder of a Palestinian teenager by deranged Israelis, and the beating of a Palestinian-American youth by Israeli police, sparked unprecedentedly harsh condemnations from the White House—despite Israel's repeated apologies. Kerry, meanwhile, caught by an open microphone, cast doubt on Israel's seriousness about limiting civilian casualties and revealed that neither Israel nor Egypt had asked him to mediate a cease-fire. The reason was that the secretary had tried to enlist Turkey and Qatar, both backers of Hamas, in the diplomacy. For the first time since 1967, the United States was uninvolved in an effort to end fighting between Arabs and Israelis.

And the administration reacted heatedly. Marking another first in recent memory, it delayed the delivery of munitions needed by the IDF, and then, after a Hamas rocket landed just under one mile from Ben-Gurion Airport, declared the facility off-limits to all U.S. planes. Though Ambassador Shapiro assured me that the decision was required by federal regulations, most Israelis believed that it was punitive. Irrespective of the motive, the suspension of American flights to Ben-Gurion spurred mass cancellations from other airlines. Hamas won its greatest-ever strategic victory.

I followed these events with a conflicting sense of angst and detachment. While sickened by the depth to which the alliance had sunk, I was too focused on defending Israel publicly to despair. Having earlier signed on as CNN's exclusive Middle East analyst, I canceled my contract in order to make Israel's case in the international media. Entire nights were spent speaking before foreign cameras before staggering into Israeli studios at dawn to comment on our international plight. In between, I published op-eds in the American press, including a front-page *Wall Street Journal Review* piece, "In Defense of Zionism," composed on my laptop between my 2 and 4 A.M. interviews. "In a region reeling with ethnic strife and religious bloodshed, Zionism has engendered a multi-ethnic, multi-racial, and religiously diverse society," I wrote. "Deriving its energy from a people which has doggedly refused to disappear—that insists, instead, on thriving—and its ethos from history-tried ideas, Zionism cannot be cowered."

In my few free hours, I visited wounded "lone soldiers" in the hospital and delivered the eulogy for one of them, Max Steinberg, who had moved to Israel from Los Angeles and fell in the Gaza fighting. "We thank Max, who gave his life so that we can live as a free people in our own land," I consoled his parents at the grave site on Mount Herzl. To get there, I had to thread through thirty thousand Israeli mourners who, though they never met Max, also came to say "thank you."

Operation Protective Edge left parts of Gaza in ruins and aspects of the U.S.-Israeli alliance in tatters. Several American Jewish leaders told me that, in closed briefings, administration officials had cited Israel's actions in Gaza as the reason for sharply rising anti-Semitism in Europe. Those leaders reminded the officials that Europeans had hated Jews for centuries before Israel's creation and that anti-Semitism now often disguised itself as anti-Zionism. The Israeli press, meanwhile, reported that Ambassador Dermer was now effectively barred from the White House. Finally, in a new nadir, Obama gave yet another interview with Jeffrey Goldberg.

My razor-witted friend continued to serve as Obama's conduit on all things Israel-related. In a controversial talk with Jeff the previous March—conspicuously made when Netanyahu was in flight to Washington—the president again warned Israel of its growing isolation in the world and vulnerability to boycotts. "I took it to be a little bit of a veiled threat," Goldberg later told Charlie Rose, interpreting Obama's remark as "nice little Jewish state you got there, I'd hate to see something happen to it."

The threats turned ad hominem, though, on October 28, 2014, in Jeff's talk with senior White House officials—including, some readers speculated, Obama himself. They assigned every possible invective to Netanyahu, including the politically incorrect "Aspergery," and labeled him a coward. Coming from individuals who probably never wore a uniform, the insult was sufficiently offensive, though not as stinging as their exultation over having deterred Netanyahu from attacking Iran. "Two, three years ago, this was a possibility," one of them boasted. "But ultimately he couldn't bring himself to pull the trigger. Now it's too late." The prime minister whom Obama once thanked for granting him the time and space to negotiate with Tehran was now branded "chickenshit" for showing restraint.

As with the "poof" precedent, I again spent the next day on Israeli television trying to translate *chickenshit* into Hebrew. Interviewers asked me to explain how America's president could show more respect to Putin and Khamenei than he did to Netanyahu. Would the United States veto a Palestinian attempt to declare statehood in the Security

Council, they wanted to know, or merely abstain? I replied as soberly as possible, emphazing that the alliance was about much more than the Netanyahu-Obama rapport, but what I really wanted was to shout "Stop!" An America that slanders the democratically elected leader of its ally is one that is respected neither by its friends nor its enemies. And an Israel whose primary military supporters openly mock its deterrence power is a target. I could not imagine that relations between American and Israeli leaders could have sunk lower, but then, as 2015 began, they plummeted.

Benjamin Netanyahu was invited to address another joint meeting of Congress. House Speaker John Boehner announced the event on January 20, the day of the State of the Union speech, after Obama vowed to veto any bipartisan effort to strengthen the sanctions. After sealing the invitation with Ambassador Dermer, the Speaker refrained from informing the president. "There's no secret about the animosity that this White House has for Prime Minister Netanyahu," he explained, "I frankly didn't want that getting in the way." Asserting Congress's rights as a "co-equal branch of government," Boehner stressed the need to hear Netanyahu's views on "the grave threats radical Islam and Iran pose to our security and way of life."

Netanyahu's gambit followed indications that the United States and other members of the P5+1 might meet the late March deadline for an agreement with Iran, which, for Israel, would indeed be a "bad deal." Retaining thousands of centrifuges and a sizeable stockpile of 3.5 percent–enriched uranium, Iran could break out and make a bomb in a matter of months, Israelis feared. Reports also suggested that all restrictions on the Iranian program, international monitoring included, would be lifted after ten years. "Anyone . . . jumping to say we don't like the deal, doesn't know what the deal is," Kerry complained to Congress, to which Netanyahu responded, "If there are those who think this is a good agreement, why must it be hidden?"

Now, with Republican backing, Netanyahu would assail Obama's Iran policy in the president's congressional backyard. And the White House, predictably, was enraged. It warned that the United States would no longer share intelligence on Iran with Israel and that no one—not the president, the vice president, or even the secretary of state—would receive the prime minister. "The protocol would suggest that the leader of one country would contact the leader of another country when he's traveling there," Press secretary Josh Earnest said. Yet the president offered a different reason for the snub—not Netanyahu's discourtesy but rather his candidacy for reelection. The United States, Obama explained, did not interfere in its allies' internal politics.

Successive coalition crises had brought down Israel's government and elections were indeed set for March 17. Scheduled for two weeks earlier, Netanyahu's speech could look less like an attempt to preempt a bad deal with Iran than like a vote-catching stunt. Controversy between pro- and anti-speech advocates mounted in both Israel and the United States, snaring me in the middle, for I had finally "leapt into the mud" of Israeli politics.

While still in Washington, I met a visiting Knesset member named Moshe Kahlon, a former Likud minister credited with breaking the cellphone monopolies and radically reducing the cost of calls. Soft-spoken and empathetic, Kahlon, who had risen from poverty to national prominence, left the Likud to establish a social and economic reform party. Kulanu (All of Us) inspired me with its commitment to closing the income gaps that deeply divided Israelis and drove thousands of them to emigrate. It gave me the opportunity to continue serving my State. Kahlon also empowered me to forge Kulanu's diplomatic platform in which I invested nearly forty years' experience studying and practicing Middle Eastern diplomacy.

Set out in a *Wall Street Journal* article titled "The Two-State Situation," the plan called for "building peace the Middle Eastern way, not with treaties but through understandings," and laying the groundwork for a final agreement, even in the absence of a Palestinian negotiating partner. Israel would only build in the settlement blocs and in the Jewish neighborhoods of Jerusalem—in accordance with the 2004 Bush-Sharon letter—and proactively improve the lives of the 90 perecent of West Bank Palestinians already enjoying de facto independence. "Instead of demanding what each side cannot do, we must ask what each side can," I concluded. "The window remains open to realistic horizons, even over an uncertain Middle East."

From the start, I relished taking part in Israel's raucous democracy. In parlor meetings, public debates, and visits to open markets where each vendor plied me with the "best-ever" hummus, I promoted my party's ideas. Having transformed myself from citizen to diplomat and back again over the course of several months, I plunged into an even profounder change—from citizen to politician—in a matter of days. Yet no challenge proved more daunting, even agonizing, than responding to Netanyahu's speech.

While I fully supported the prime minister's position on Iran, I disagreed with his decision to present it in Congress. This would insinuate himself—and Israel—between Republicans and Democrats and exacerbate our differences with the White House. I felt the confusion and hurt of those American Jews torn between their devotion to Israel and their allegiance to the president. The same speech could have been given at that week's AIPAC conference, I suggested, or postponed until after the Israeli elections, removing the impression of grandstanding. "It's incumbent on every Israeli leader to do the utmost to prevent Iran from getting the bomb," I told the media. "But it's just as vital to preserve bipartisan support for Israel in America. The first goal should not be attained at the latter's expense." I reminded Israelis that Americans salute the rank, not the person, and that even Obama's critics—Fox News, for example—would resent what they perceived as affront to the presidency.

These positions brought me rebuke from Netanyahu's backers as well as from his detractors who demanded an unconditional condemnation of the speech. Tom Friedman, so rarely right on Middle Eastern issues, urging Netanyahu to take the "intelligent advice . . . of his previous ambassador in Washington," brought me no solace. Nor, certainly, did the administration's increasingly vehement remarks. National Security Advisor Susan Rice called the speech "destructive of the fabric of the [U.S.-Israel] relationship," and John Kerry recalled Netanyahu's support for the U.S. invasion of Iraq. "We all know what happened with that decision," he told the House Foreign Affairs Committee, forgetting his own endorsement of that war. The subtext was clear: with a single speech, Netanyahu was dragging America into another ill-conceived conflict and, in the process, undermining the alliance.

Such invective guaranteed that the address would achieve massive media coverage. Focused on the upcoming speech, journalists downplayed Obama's description of the jihadists who deliberately murdered four French Jews in a kosher supermarket as "vicious zealots who . . . randomly shoot a bunch of folks in a deli." Similarly under-reported were Ayatollah Khamenei's demands for 190,000 centrifuges, his chants of "death to America," and the blowing up of a model U.S. aircraft carrier by Iranian missile boats. Even the imprisonment on false espionage charges of *The Washington Post*'s bureau chief in Tehran failed to impress most journalists.

Rather, the headlines focused on the fifty-five Democratic representatives who intended to boycott Netanyahu's speech. Among these were many members of the Congressional Black Caucus, among them the legendary John Lewis, offended by what they saw as the prime minister's disrespect for the first African-American president. The decision by Lewis, long my personal hero, was especially painful. Sally also seemed depressed. "Everything we worked for, all we built," she lamented. "It's gone."

The speech, delivered on March 3, galvanized world attention. In place of the absentee Democrats were Republican philanthropist Sheldon Adelson, New England Patriots owner Robert Kraft, and, most movingly, Elie Wiesel, who felt compelled to speak out against yet another possible genocide. Netanyahu opened by denying that his motivations were political and by praising "all that Obama has done for Israel." But then he assailed the president's tendency to view Iran as potential ally against IS by asserting that, in the Middle East, "the enemy of my enemy is my enemy."

Tying Churchill's record for the most joint meeting appearances, Netanyahu reveled in Churchillian locutions. "This deal doesn't block Iran's path to the bomb, it paves Iran's path to the bomb," he declared, and, "This deal won't be a farewell to arms. It would be a farewell to arms control." But then, substantively, the prime minister attacked the purported ten-year limit to the Iranian deal—"a decade is a blink of an eye in the life of a nation . . . [and of] our children," he said. He rejected the administration's binary claim of either diplomacy or war, asserting, "The alternative to this bad deal is a much better deal." Such an agreement, Netanyahu specified, must be conditioned on ending Iranian support for terrorism, aggression against neighboring countries, and threats to destroy Israel. Pointing at the image of Moses painted on one of the chamber's walls, Netanyahu quoted him in Hebrew and then translated: "Be strong and resolute, neither fear nor dread them."

The address spurred a spate of ovations and relentless controversy.

A visibly downcast president told interviewers that he had not watched the speech but nevertheless dismissed it as "politics" and "theater," and denied that it contained anything new. Once distant from Obama, indignant Democrats rallied now around him. "I was near to tears," Nancy Pelosi bemoaned, "saddened by [Netanyahu's] insult to the intelligence of the United States and the condescension toward our knowledge of the threat posed by Iran." Forty-seven Republican senators, by contrast, were emboldened to dispatch a letter to the supreme leader warning him that any deal signed by Obama without congressional approval could be rescinded by future presidents. Bipartisan bills challenged the White House's ability to relieve sanctions on Iran without congressional approval. Beyond becoming a wedge issue, Israel, I feared, might be dragged into one of the bitterest-ever constitutional battles between the executive and legislative branches.

Israelis, meanwhile, were caught up in their own democratic struggle as their election day approached. A candidate for a poor party, I traversed the country in my own car, footing my own expenses, to canvas votes. As in earlier elections, these were to an extraordinary degree about Netanyahu—"It's Us or Him," warned the opposition's posters—and the prime minister lagged behind. In a move widely interpreted as desperate, Netanyahu backed away from his earlier support for a two-state solution. "Anyone who moves to establish a Palestinian state . . . gives territory away to radical Islamist attacks against Israel," he proclaimed. And then, as reports showed steep gains for the newly founded joint list of all of Israel's Arab parties, Netanyahu warned that "the right-wing government is in danger. Arab voters are going en masse to the polls. Left-wing NGOs are bringing them on buses."

For the first time, an Israeli prime minister issued a statement that many Israelis and their supporters worldwide regarded as racist. "What if a U.S. president had warned voters that too many blacks were voting?" an incensed American Jewish leader asked me. As someone who had worked with Netanyahu and never heard a prejudicial word from him, his action astonished me, but, having experienced discrimination in my youth, it wounded me as well. Proudly, my party—Kulanu—denounced the remark as "rash and inappropriate." "Israel's government," I told CNN, "is elected not by Jews and Arabs, but by Israelis."

Yet Netanyahu won. The retreat from the two-state plan and the fear of a left-wing success ignited his right-wing base and propelled him to victory. Likudniks rejoiced, but so, too, did we in Kulanu. With virtually no budget and a list of political underdogs, the party's platform of social reform nevertheless garnered us ten seats, mine included.

On March 31, I stood as my name was called out in the Knesset and committed to uphold the laws of the State. Looking down on me from the gallery were Sally and my children as well as my eighty-six-year-old mother and ninety-year-old father, who had just arrived in Israel. Having attended the presentation of my credentials at the White House, they were not going to miss my swearing-in ceremony at the Knesset. They watched as I cast my first vote reelecting the Speaker to a second term, and then as I left my seat to embrace that Speaker, Yuli Yoel Edelstein, whom I first met in Moscow in 1982.

Throughout, I could not help reflecting on my own journey, beginning with the day I descended from the bus to Kibbutz Gan Shmuel. How could I have seen, squinting through the dust, that someday I would be elected to the first sovereign Jewish parliament in two thousand years? Who could have imagined the tortuous route ahead and the divides—American and Israeli—yet to be crossed?

And who could have halted the acute decline of the U.S.-Israeli alliance? Though Netanyahu later reiterated his support for the two-state solution—conditions were just not ripe for one, he clarified—and apologized to Israeli Arabs for his offensive statement, the administration rejected the gestures. Instead, Obama said that the prime minister's words "erode the name of democracy" in Israel, and necessitated a "reevaluation" of America's policy toward the Jewish State—that lone pocket of Middle East stability—"to make sure that we don't see a chaotic situation in the region." The same White House that once refused to refute charges of Israeli spying against the United States began making them, evoking harsh Israeli denials. Israeli papers meanwhile leaked—or perhaps disleaked—Netanyahu's advisors claiming that his congressional speech was worth provoking Obama and accusing the president of interfering in Israel's elections.

Against this irascible background, on April 2, the P5+1 unveiled its Framework Agreement with Iran. This limited Iran's ability to break out and make a nuclear bomb to one year, but only for a ten-year period. It reduced the number of centrifuges by two-thirds, and froze those remaining underground in Fordow. Enrichment would be capped at 3.75 percent and the stockpile cut down from ten thousand to three hundred kilograms. The Arak facility would be reconfigured to prevent production of plutonium bombs. International inspectors would aggressively monitor all aspects of Iran's nuclear program, including uranium mines and the importation of parts, for as long as twenty-five years. Fulfilling these terms would relieve Iran of the sanctions, all of which could "snap back" if it failed to comply. Praising this "historic" agreement, President Obama warned Congress that killing it could trigger another Middle East war for which America would be blamed. "International unity will collapse and the path to conflict will widen."

Numerous Congress members, commentators, and, of course, Benjamin Netanyahu read the treaty differently. In addition to activating one-third of its centrifuges and dismantling none, Iran would keep its entire nuclear infrastructure. Obama cited Iran's good faith in upholding the interim agreement—in spite of the IAEA's claim that Iran violated that treaty by increasing its nuclear stockpile by 20 percent—and insisted that sanctions would not be lifted unless Iran complied with the Final Framework. Critics, though, pointed to Tehran's opposition to shipping its enriched uranium abroad and to truly intrusive inspections of its facilities. Iran insisted on instantly removing all sanctions that, having taken many years to impose, could never be "snapped back," the agreement's detractors claimed. Most deplored was the treaty's failure to tie acceptance of Iran's status as a nuclear threshold state to the slightest change in its behavior. Ceasing all attempts to destroy Israel, much less recognize it, was never an American demand.

"The United States appears to have lost the courage of its convictions," Natan Sharansky, the former Prisoner of Zion, bemoaned in *The Washington Post*. "Democratic governments made a critical mistake before World War II and they are making a grave mistake now," Netanyahu declared at Yad Vashem on Holocaust Remembrance Day, 2015. "The bad deal with Iran—a country that clearly states its plans to exterminate six million Jews—demonstrates that this lesson has not been internalized." The man who would be Churchill, who once likened Obama's policies to Roosevelt's refusal to bomb Auschwitz, was now identifying new Neville Chamberlains seeking to appease, rather than defeat, evil.

Whether for or against the framework, all observers agreed that the document remained unsigned. Recalling how the Palestinians always pocketed American and Israeli concessions and then left the table, I wondered whether the Iranians would do the same. After all, they had already secured recognition of their nuclear rights and their Middle East preeminence without paying any real price. The sanctions might already break down, as evidenced by Russia's willingness to sell sophisticated weaponry to Tehran. Like Syria's Assad, who built chemical arms to ensure his regime's survival, the ayatollahs created a nuclear program to preserve their rule and extend their Middle East hegemony. And just as Assad's willingness to forfeit his arsenal restored his international legitimacy, so, too, did Iran's openness to nuclear negotiations facilitate its regional expansion. Assad, international investigators later charged, continued to kill his people with chemical weapons, but the world was no longer interested. Once part of the problem, Iran, like Syria before it, was now seen as the solution. Few countries would be concerned about evidence to the contrary.

"I'm an historian," I routinely say in response to anybody asking me about the future. "I have enough difficulty predicting the past." Many decades from now scholars will still be debating whether Netanyahu's effort to stop the Iranian bomb presciently succeeded or tragically failed. Was an Israeli-Palestinian accord really possible in these years, they will ask, and, if so, which party bore the greatest responsibility for undermining it? Did Obama achieve his goal of bringing Arabs and Israelis together not through peace but—paradoxically—through their common fear of his policies? Chroniclers will quote Obama's affirmation of his "deep and abiding friendship and concern and understanding for Israel," made in an interview with Tom Friedman, and weigh it against the facts. Similarly, they will judge if Netanyahu's repeated pledges "to act alone, if necessary" against a nuclear-empowered Iran were serious or simply bluster. Later generations will recall the duel between Obama's quest for legacy and Netanyahu's claim to destiny, and determine which of them prevailed.

History has this humbling habit of diminishing the events we see as monumental and of reducing our roles in them to footnotes. And yet, what choice do we have? Our responsibility is to strive for the objectives we see as fateful for our time. Entering government, my primary task would be to uphold Israel's historic alliance with America. Despite the policy disagreements of the previous years, the personality

clashes and periodic crises, I remain convinced that the U.S.-Israel relationship is essential to both countries' interests. It assures a modi-
cum of Middle East stability and sends a message of American
dependability to the world. The time had arrived for U.S. and Israel
leaders to cease sparring and reaffirm the vitality, and the centrality, of
their ties.

Israel needs America. Though cobbled from disparate cultures, situated in an epicenter of strife, the Jewish State is remarkably resilient.
Nothing history throws at us—wars, economic upheavals, an entire
region unraveling—dulls our determination to thrive. Deprive of us
water, we will build the desalination plants that make us water export-
ers. Give us a land without oil or natural riches, and we will resource-
fully plumb our minds. "It's what we Jews are best at," the revered
Bank of Israel governor Stanley Fischer, later vice chairman of the
Federal Reserve Board, once assured me. "Dealing with uncertainty."

But our plight arises not from what we cannot know, but rather
from what we do. Hamas and Hezbollah aim more than a hundred
thousand rockets at our homes. Instability surges on all of our borders
and radical Islamists—Sunni and Shiite—dream of our demise. Europeans, claiming they care about the Palestinians but also revealing
their deep-seated difficulty with Jews, threaten to cut off commerce
with Israel, and even Turkey has turned hostile. Resilient, rooted, and
innovative, Israel is nevertheless vulnerable. National Security Advisor
Tom Donilon once asked me to describe Israel's geopolitical situation
in historical terms. "At best we're in May 1967," I replied. "At worst,
it's May 1948."

At both those times, Israel appeared on the verge of destruction,
surrounded by belligerent forces and shorn of international friends.
So, too, today, Israeli decision makers awake—when they manage to
sleep—to a spectrum of dangers rarely confronted by their predecessors. And yet, one immense distinction separates contemporary Israel
from that of the eve of the 1967 and 1948 wars: Israel is no longer
alone.

The deep, multifaceted alliance with America that emerged after
the Six-Day War enabled Israel to make peace with two of its bitterest
foes, Egypt and Jordan. It assisted us in absorbing more than a million
refugees from the former Soviet Bloc and Ethiopia, and reinforced

global confidence in our economy. In international forums, the United States consistently resisted an almost unbroken procession of anti-Israel resolutions. Above all, the alliance fortified our ability to defend ourselves. Israel's enemies saw not only the Made in the U.S.A. weaponry, the jet aircraft, and the joint maneuvers, but also the solidarity underlying them.

Preserving and strengthening that unity is a supreme Israeli interest. In making strategic choices, Israeli leaders must always take into account the impact of those choices on the United States. They must reaffirm the democratic principles so cherished by America, and their seriousness in the search for peace. They must contribute to the vitality of the American Jewish community and fulfill Israel's promise as the nation-state of all the Jewish people. And if those leaders occasionally have to act in ways unpopular among some Americans, they must do so with the utmost reluctance, and always with an earnest "Thank you, but . . ." While the perspective of a minuscule Middle Eastern state can never dovetail entirely with that of a distant superpower, Israeli decision makers must never lose sight of how the Middle East—indeed, the world—looks from Washington. Israel needs to acknowledge that view and, whenever possible, adapt to it.

During my time in Washington, support for Israel among Americans rose steadily to some 74 percent. Even during the last Gaza war, despite the critical press, that backing climbed. But we can never take that affection for granted nor cease courting it. The outreach is one-way and imperative. More Israeli resources must be allocated to enable Americans from multiple backgrounds to visit the Jewish State and see us as we are, a normal nation grappling with abnormal circumstances. And as American society continues to change, Israelis must chart those transformations and navigate them. Burgeoning communities—Hispanic, African-American, Asian—must be introduced to Israel and helped to understand why it is in their interests, as Americans, to support a sliver of a country located thousands of miles away. They should know how that state, scientifically and technologically, enriches their families' lives, and how its security forces help protect them.

For America needs Israel as well. Though the dependence is not, of course, symmetrical, the presence of an American ally at the world's most strategically crucial crossroads, deploying an army more than twice the size of Britain's and France's combined, cannot be undervalued. Neither can the willingness of its citizens to fight. During the Protective Edge operation, the IDF called up ninety thousand reservists, all of whom—women and men—unhesitatingly left their jobs and homes to defend their country. All knew that some would never return. In how many democratic countries today would this happen?

That asset must not be squandered. Just as Israel benefits from a strong America—an America viewed as strong from Ukraine to the South China Sea—so, too, does the United States gain from a secure and powerful Israel. For all of the talk about "pivoting to Asia," the United States will remain inextricably linked to the Middle East, bound to the region both by the profits and the threats it generates. Americans cannot detach from the Middle East, for it will follow them home. A robust Israel helps to keep that Middle East at bay and assists in safeguarding that home.

The world, meanwhile, watches us. Friends and adversaries alike— the French and the Iranians, the Japanese and jihadists—all look at the alliance as a litmus of America's willingness to stand up for its fellow democracy and even to stand up for itself. The alliance is vital not only for its two partners, but also for the security of all nations.

Which is why, after a half decade of tensions, we must begin the process of repair. The greatest single quality in a leader, I have long observed, is clearsightedness. The foreign relations field is dense with fog, and the ability to see through it is essential. American and Israeli leaders must discern their confluent interests and work to realize them. They must restore those three "no's"—no surprises, no daylight, no public altercations—in their relations. They must revisit the meaning of *ally*.

Being an ally, for example, means not insisting that Israel, a sovereign country with a globally renowned judicial system, conduct "swift and transparent investigations" of security incidents. Americans would surely be offended if such demands were leveled at them by a foreign government, yet the United States routinely makes them of Israel. But being an ally also means that Israel should not repay America for supporting it in the Security Council by building in isolated settlements. Being an ally, on the one hand, means releasing Jonathan Pollard and recognizing Israel's capital in Jerusalem, and on the other, respecting American Jewish pluralism and the prerogatives of the world's mightiest power. Allies respect the decisions of one another's democratically chosen leaders, even when they disagree. They back one another on principle and not merely to placate domestic constituents. Their bonds are elemental, meaningful, and mutually, enduringly beneficial.

Unusually but understandably, thoughts about the U.S.-Israel alliance were absent from my mind that night on Kibbutz Na'an as the siren continued to blare. Together with Lee, Dar, and the Bar Mitzvah guests, Sally and I squeezed under the corrugated awning. The young parents shielded their sleeping child. Where would the rockets land, I worried, and how many people would be hit? Even while racing, my heart hurt for those thirteen-year-olds whose happiest day had become a lifelong trauma.

I held Sally's hand and glanced over my shoulder just as two Hamas rockets roared in. Then, with twin booms that rattled the tin overhang and shook the ground below, the missiles exploded. Iron Dome interceptors, developed by Israel and funded by the United States, scored perfect hits. For moments afterward, as we emerged into that uncertain night, the glow of those bursts hovered over us, beaming like kindred stars.

ACKNOWLEDGMENTS

This book crossed multiple divides—creative, political, strategic, moral, and emotional—and writing it required many allies.

Foremost among these were the benefactors of the Abba Eban Chair in International Diplomacy at Herzliya's Inter-Disciplinary Center (IDC). My deepest thanks go to Ronald Lauder, Seth and Beth Klarman, Shmuel and Eleanor Katz, Lief Rosenblatt, Robert and Arlene Kogod, Marc Rowan, Ted and Annette Lerner, Suzie and Michael Gelman, Larry and Judy Tanenbaum, Elan and Eva Blutinger, Linda Frum and Howard Sokolovski, Lawrence and Fran Bloomberg, Harry Gross, Robin Neustein, Alan and Amy Meltzer, Ronnen Harrary, Stuart Kurlander, Alma and Joe Gildenhorn, Sheldon Inwentash and Lynn Factor, Michael Bregman and Kate Osborne, Gary and Tamara Fine, Ricardo and Raquel Di Capua, and the many others whose generosity made this book a reality. My special gratitude goes to Gerry Schwartz and Heather Reisman for their sage guidance, their unflagging commitment to Israel, and their invaluable friendship.

The book was also made possible by the Atlantic Council, through the vision of the incomparable Adrienne Arsht and under the inspired leadership of Fred Kempe. I also owe an immense debt to my brilliant assistant at the Council, Sarah Trager.

Arnon Milchan, a friend and font of expert advice, and his tireless representative in Israel, Hadas Klein, were instrumental in seeing this book through to publication. So, too, was my brother-in-law, Fred Kuperberg.

The IDC and its president, Prof. Uriel Reichman, provided a supportive and stimulating environment for writing *Ally*. I was blessed with a supremely motivated staff. To Arielle Heffez, Danny Brown-Wolf, Na'ama Moskovitz, and Tamar Katzir—thank you all. Ariel

Steinberg, my former student from Yale who made *aliya* to Israel, served in the IDF, and later joined me at the IDC, lent me his wisdom, his keen editorial insights, and loyalty. While not formally a staff member, Netta Koren, a cherished friend and an "advisor for all seasons," deserves many thanks as well, as do Roy Elman and Chen Lev, who graciously volunteered their time and skills.

A number of extraordinary individuals who assisted me in fulfilling my ambassador role were not mentioned in book. Most of them, I know, would not even want to be thanked, but I will do so anyway. My deepest appreciation goes to Gil Shefer, Paul Berger, Haim Saban, Stuart Eizenstat, Ruth and Leonard Wisse, Yaakov Ne'eman, Ed and Debra Cohen, Stuart and Wilma Bernstein, Michael and Anne Mandelbaum, Michael and Amanda Alter, John and JoAnn Mason, Dan Poneman, Morad Zamir, Sharon Shalom, Edna Halabani, Orit Moshe, Jane Harmon, Yifat Sharon, Josh Block of the Israel Project, Jordana Kotler, Pamela Reeves, Heather Klein, Arnold Angrist, Stefanie Pearson Argamon, Phil and Laura Vallerand, Bob and Sally Burkett, Ken Weinstein, Amy Kauffman, Bill Knapp, Jeannie Milbauer, Karen Yianopolos, Danny Klionsky, Nechama Shemtov, Ann Moline, Simcha Weinblatt, and Rabbis Levi Shemtov, Gil and Batya Steinlauf, Julie Schonfeld, Rick Jacobs, Eric Joffe, and Steven Weil.

This is also the opportunity to salute the hundreds of dedicated staff members of Israel's Embassy in Washington, its Mission to the United Nations, and its Consulates throughout the United States. Though I cannot cite all of these colleagues, I want to recognize Ambassador Ron Prosor, David Siegel, Roey Gilad, Daniel Meron, Ofer Babli, Ofer Aviram, Aviv and Einat Ezra, Dana Oren, Miri Katz, Anat Beck, Deydra Cavazos, Alexa Wertman, Kerry Brodie, Eran Levy, Sarit Arbell, Liat Weintraub, Shai Shkargy, Mali Gal, Booni Cohavi, Na'ama Brenner, Ohad and Monika Lev-Cohen, Jed Stein, Shmulik Almany, Valentine Silverio, Carmen Vicencio, and Ivy Samar.

A vital, if often painful, part of writing any book is receiving criticism from discerning readers. These included my sisters-in-law Nancy Ayalon and Amy Malale, John and Marion Krivine, the esteemed Gary Ginsberg, and my soul-friend, Yossi Klein-Halevy. According to Israeli law, books written by senior state employees must be approved by the Military Censor as well as by a review committee composed of representatives of the Defense, Justice, and Foreign Ministries. The devoted professionals who saw *Ally* through this process earned my highest respect.

No writer could want for a finer, more supportive, and inspiring agent than Jennifer Joel, my longtime representative at ICM, or for a more attentive and talented editor than Will Murphy. Indeed, the entire team at Random House—Susan Kamil, Thomas Perry, Mika Kasuga, London King, and so many others—was, for me, a dream team.

My previous books opened with a dedication to my beloved family and this book will end with one. To Sally, Yoav, Lia, and Noam, who never stopped believing, caring, and loving, *todah rabah*. Thank you.

PROMINENT
FIGURES IN *ALLY*

Abbas, Mahmoud   Chairman, Palestine Liberation Organization (2004–present); President, Palestinian Authority (2005–present).

Abrams, Elliott   Deputy National Security Advisor for Global Democracy Strategy (2005–2009); Senior Fellow for Middle Eastern Studies, Council on Foreign Relations (2009–present).

Ackerman, Gary   Democratic congressman from New York (1983–2013).

Ahmadinejad, Mahmoud   President of the Islamic Republic of Iran (2005–2013).

Amidror, Maj. General (res.) Yaakov   National Security Advisor of Israel (2011–2013).

Anderson, Brooke   Chief of Staff and Counselor, White House National Security Staff (2011–2012).

Arad, Uzi   National Security Advisor of Israel (2009–2011).

Arbell, Dan   Deputy Chief of Mission, Embassy of Israel (2009–2011).

Assad, Bashar al   President of Syria (2000–present).

Axelrod, David   Senior Advisor to President Obama (2009–2011).

Barak, Ehud   Israel's Minister of Defense (2007–2013); Prime Minister (1999–2001).

Barkat, Nir   Mayor of Jerusalem (2008–present).

Ben-Ami, Jeremy   Executive Director, J Street (2008–present).

Bennett, Naftali   Israel's Minister of Economy, Leader of Jewish Home Party (2013–present).

Berman, Howard   Democratic congressman for California (1983–2013); Chairman, House Committee on Foreign Relations (2008–2011).

Blair, Tony   British Prime Minister (1997–2007); Quartet envoy (2007–present).

Boehner, John   Republican congressman from Ohio (1991–present); Speaker of the House of Representatives (2011–present).

Bolton, John   U.S. Ambassador to the United Nations (2005–2006).

Boxer, Barbara   Democratic senator from California (1993–present).

Brazile, Donna Vice Chairwoman, Democratic National Committee (2001–present); CNN political commentator.

Burns, William J. U.S. Deputy Secretary of State (2011–2014).

Cantor, Eric Republican congressman from Virginia (2001–2014); House Majority Leader (2011–2014).

Carney, Jay White House Press Secretary (2011–2014).

Carville, James Political commentator and strategist.

Castro, Julian Mayor of San Antonio (2009–2014); Secretary of Housing and Urban Development (2015–present).

Cohen, David Under Secretary of the Treasury for Terrorism and Financial Intelligence (2011–2014); Deputy Director, CIA (2015–present).

Clinton, Hillary First Lady of the United States (1993–2001); Democratic senator from New York (2001–2009); Secretary of State (2009–2013).

Crowley, Philip J. "P.J." Assistant Secretary of State for Public Affairs (2009–2011).

Crown, Lester American Jewish leader and philanthropist; Director, General Dynamics Corporation (1974–2006).

Dagan, Major General Meir Director of the Mossad (2002–2011).

Daley, William White House Chief of Staff (2011–2012).

Dayan, Moshe Chief of Staff, Israel Defense Forces (1953–1958), Defense Minister (1967–1974); Foreign Minister of Israel (1977–1979).

Dempsey, General Martin Chairman of the Joint Chiefs of Staff (2011–2015).

Dermer, Ron Economic attaché, Israeli Embassy in Washington (2005–2008); Senior Advisor to Prime Minister Benjamin Netanyahu (2009–2013); Israel's Ambassador to the United States (2013–present).

Deutch, Ted Democratic congressman from Florida (2010–present).

Diskin, Yuval Director of Shin Bet, Israel's internal security service (2005–2011).

Donilon, Thomas Deputy National Security Advisor (2009–2010); National Security Advisor (2010–2013).

Eban, Abba Israel's Ambassador to the United Nations and the United States (1948–1959); Deputy Prime Minister (1963–1966); Foreign Minister of Israel (1966–1974).

Edelstein, Yuli Knesset member from the Israel Home Party and Likud (1996–2013); Speaker of the Knesset (2013–present).

Ellison, Keith Democratic congressman from Minnesota (2007–present).

El–Sisi, Field Marshal Abdel Fattah Egyptian Minister of Defense and Commander of the Armed Forces (2012–2014); President of Egypt (2014–present).

Emanuel, Rahm Democratic congressman from Illinois (2002–2008); White House Chief of Staff (2009–2010); Mayor of Chicago (2011–present).

Engel, Eliot   Democratic congressman from New York (1989–present).

Erdoğan, Recep Tayyip   Prime Minister of Turkey (2003–2014); President of Turkey (2014–present).

Erekat, Saeb   Chief Palestinian negotiator for peace talks with Israel (1993–present).

Eshel, Major General Amir   Chief, Israel Defense Forces Planning Directorate (2008–2012); Commander, Israeli Air Force (2012–present).

Fayyad, Salam   Prime Minister, Palestinian Authority (2007–2013).

Feinstein, Dianne   Democratic senator from California (1992–present); Chair, Senate Intelligence Committee (2009–2015).

Firouzabadi, Major General Hassan   Chief of Staff, Iranian Armed Forces (2002–present).

Flournoy, Michèle   Under Secretary of Defense for Policy (2009–2012).

Ford, Robert   Ambassador to Syria (2010–2014).

Foxman, Abraham   National Director, Anti-Defamation League (1987–2015).

Friedman, Thomas L.   *New York Times* reporter (1981–1994); columnist (1994–present); author, *From Beirut to Jerusalem* (1988), *The Lexus and the Olive Tree* (1999), *The World Is Flat* (2005), and *That Used to Be Us*, with Michael Mandelbaum (2011).

Funnye, Capers   Rabbi, Beth Shalom B'nai Zaken Ethiopian Hebrew Congregation of Chicago (1985–present).

Gaddafi, Colonel Muammar   Libyan dictator (1969–2011).

Gantz, Lieuteneant General Benjamin   Defense attaché in Washington (2007–2009); Chief of Staff, Israel Defense Forces (2011–2015).

Gates, Robert   U.S. Secretary of Defense (2006–2011).

Gibbs, Robert   White House Press Secretary (2009–2011).

Giffords, Gabrielle   Democratic congresswoman from Arizona (2007–2012).

Gilad, Major General (res.) Amos   Director of the Political-Military Affairs Bureau, Israel Defense Forces (2003–present).

Ginsberg, Gary   Executive Vice President, Corporate Marketing and Communications, Time Warner Inc. (2010–present).

Gold, Dore   Israel's Ambassador to the United Nations (1997–1999); advisor to Prime Ministers Ariel Sharon and Benjamin Netanyahu (2001–2006, 2009–present); author, *Hatred's Kingdom: How Saudi Arabia Supports the New Global Terrorism* (2003), *Tower of Babble: How the United Nations Has Fueled Global Chaos* (2004), *The Fight for Jerusalem: Radical Islam, the West, and the Future of the Holy City* (2007), and *The Rise of Nuclear Iran: How Tehran Defies the West* (2009).

Goldberg, Jeffrey   Author, *Prisoners: A Muslim and a Jew across the Middle East Divide* (2006); national correspondent, *The Atlantic* (2007–present); columnist, *Bloomberg View* (2011–present).

Goldstone, Richard Appellate Division, Supreme Court of South Africa (1989–1994); Committee Chairman, United Nations Fact Finding Mission on the Gaza Conflict (2009).

Gordon, Philip Assistant Secretary of State for European and Eurasian Affairs (2009–2013); Special Assistant to the President and White House Coordinator for the Middle East, North Africa, and the Gulf Region, National Security Council (2013–present).

Graham, Lindsey Republican senator from North Carolina (2003–present).

Hagel, Chuck Democratic senator from Nebraska (1997–2009); Secretary of Defense (2013–2015).

Halevi, Yossi Klein Senior Fellow, Shalom Hartman Institute; author, *Memoirs of a Jewish Extremist: The Story of a Transformation* (1995), *At the Entrance to the Garden of Eden: A Jew's Search for God with Christians and Muslims in the Holy Land* (2001), and *Like Dreamers: The Story of the Israeli Paratroopers Who Reunited Jerusalem and Divided a Nation* (2013).

Hauser, Zvi "Zvika" Cabinet Secretary of the State of Israel (2009–2013).

Hoenlein, Malcolm Executive Vice Chairman, Conference of Presidents of Major American Jewish Organizations (1986–present).

Hoyer, Steny Democratic congressman from Maryland (1981–present); Majority Whip (2007–2011).

Ignatius, David Associate Editor and columnist, *The Washington Post* (2002–present).

Indyk, Martin Founder, Washington Institute for Near East Policy (1985); Senior Director of Near East and South Asian Affairs, NSC (1992–1994); Ambassador to Israel (1995–1997, 2000–2001); Special Envoy for Middle East Peace (2013–2014); author, *Innocent Abroad: An Intimate Account of American Peace Diplomacy in the Middle East* (2009).

Inhofe, Jim Republican senator from Oklahoma (1994–present).

Inouye, Daniel Democratic senator from Hawaii (1963–2012).

Israel, Steven Democratic congressman from New York (2001–present).

Jabari, Ahmed Chief of Staff, Hamas's military wing (2002–2012).

Jarrett, Valerie Senior Advisor to the President (2009–present).

Jones, General James L. National Security Advisor (2009–2010).

Jordan, Vernon Civil rights lawyer and Democratic political advisor (1960s–present).

Kagan, Elena Supreme Court Justice (2010–present).

Kahl, Colin Deputy Assistant Secretary of Defense for the Middle East (2009–2011); National Security Advisor to the Vice President (2014–present).

Kaine, Timothy Governor, State of Virginia (2006–2010); Democratic senator from Virginia (2013–present).

Kerry, John   Democratic senator from Massachusetts (1985–2013); Chairman, Senate Foreign Relations Committee (2009–2013); Secretary of State (2013–present).

Khamenei, Ali   Supreme Leader of the Islamic Republic of Iran (1989–present).

Kirk, Mark   Republican senator from Illinois (2010–present).

Kohr, Howard   Executive Director, AIPAC (1996–present).

Kristol, William (Bill)   Founder and editor, *The Weekly Standard* (1995–present).

Lapid, Yair   Israel's Minister of Finance (2013–2014); Chairman of the Yesh Atid Party (2013–present).

Lauder, Ronald   U.S. Ambassador to Austria (1986–1987); President, World Jewish Congress (2007–present).

Levi, Yonit   News anchor, Israel's Channel 2 (2002–present).

Levey, Stuart   Under Secretary of the Treasury for Terrorism and Financial Intelligence (2004–2013).

Lew, Jack   Deputy Secretary of State (2009–2011); White House Chief of Staff (2012–2013); Secretary of the Treasury (2013–present).

Liberman, Avigdor "Evet"   Chairman, Israel Home Party (1999–present); Foreign Minister of Israel (2009–2014).

Lieberman, Joseph   Democratic (later, Independent) senator from Connecticut (1989–2013).

Livni, Tzipi   Likud minister (2001–2005); Kadima Party Minister of Justice (2006–2007); Foreign Minister of Israel (2006–2009); Opposition Leader (2009–2012); Minister of Justice and co–chief negotiator for peace talks with the Palestinians (2013–2014).

Love, Reggie   Personal aide to President Barack Obama (2009–2011).

Maher, Bill   American political satirist; host of *Real Time with Bill Maher* (2003–present).

Marcus, Ruth   columnist, *The Washington Post* (1984–present).

Marshall, Capricia   U.S. Chief of Protocol (2009–2013).

McCain, John   Republican senator from Arizona (1987–present); Chairman of the Senate Armed Services Committee (2015–present).

McCarthy, Kevin   Republican congressman from California (2007–present); House Majority Whip (2011–2014); House Majority Leader (2014–present).

McConnell, Mitch   Republican senator from Kentucky (1985–present); Senate Minority Leader (2007–2014); Senate Majority Leader (2015–present).

McDonough, Denis   Deputy National Security Advisor (2010–2013); White House Chief of Staff (2013–present).

McKeon, Howard "Buck"   Republican congressman from California

2010); Commander of the International Security Assistance Force (2010–2011); Director of the CIA (2011–2012).

Posner, Michael   Assistant Secretary of State for Democracy, Human Rights, and Labor (2009–2013).

Rabin, Yitzhak   IDF Chief of Staff (1964–1968); Israel's Ambassador to the U.S. (1968–1973); Prime Minister of the State of Israel (1974–1977, 1992–1995).

Reid, Harry   Democratic senator from Nevada (1987–present); Senate Majority Leader (2007–2015); Senate Minority Leader (2015–present).

Rhodes, Benjamin   Deputy National Security Advisor for Strategic Communications and Speechwriting (2009–present).

Rice, Condoleezza   National Security Advisor (2001–2005); Secretary of State (2005–2009).

Rice, Susan   Ambassador to the United Nations (2009–2013); National Security Advisor (2013–present).

Rogers, Michael   Republican congressman from Michigan (2001–2015); Chairman of the House Intelligence Committee (2011–2015).

Romney, Mitt   Governor of Massachusetts (2003–2007); Republican presidential candidate (2012).

Rosenberg, Lee   President, American Israel Public Affairs Committee (AIPAC) (2010–2012); AIPAC Board Chairman (2012–2013).

Rosenthal, Hannah   Special Envoy to Monitor and Combat Anti-Semitism (2009–2012).

Ros-Lehtinen, Ileana   Republican congresswoman from Florida (1989–present); Chair of the House Committee on Foreign Affairs (2011–2013).

Ross, Dennis   U.S. Special Envoy to the Middle East (1993–2000); Special Advisor to the Secretary of State for the Gulf and Southwest Asia (2009); Special Assistant to the President and Senior Director for the Central Region, National Security Council (2009–2011).

Rothkopf, David   CEO and editor, FP Group (2012–present); author, *Running the World: The Inside Story of the National Security Council and the Architects of American Power* (2006), *Superclass: The Global Power Elite and the World They Are Making* (2008), *Power, Inc.: The Epic Rivalry Between Big Business and Government—and the Reckoning That Lies Ahead* (2012), and *National Insecurity: Making U.S. Foreign Policy in an Age of Fear* (2014).

Rouhani, Hassan   President of the Islamic Republic of Iran (2013–present).

Rouse, Peter   Senior Advisor to the President (2009–2010); White House Chief of Staff (2010–2011); White House Counsel (2011–2014).

Ryan, Paul   Republican congressman from Wisconsin (1999–present); vice presidential candidate (2012).

Saban, Haim   Cofounder, Saban Entertainment (1983–2002); Founding Chairman and CEO, Saban Capital Group (2001–present).

Satloff, Robert   Executive Director, Washington Institute for Near East Policy (1993–present).

Schumer, Chuck   Democratic senator from New York (1999–present).

Shalit, Gilad   Israel Defense Forces soldier captured by Hamas during a cross-border raid in June 2006. Released in October 2011 in exchange for 1,027 Palestinian prisoners.

Shapiro, Daniel   Senior Director for the Middle East and North Africa, National Security Council (2009–2011); U.S. Ambassador to Israel (2011–present).

Sharansky, Natan   Soviet human rights activist and prisoner of Zion (1973–1986); Israeli minister (1996–2005); Chairman of the Executive, Jewish Agency for Israel (2009–present).

Sharon, Ariel   Major General in the IDF (1948–1973); Minister of Defense (1981–1983); Minister of Industry (1984–90); Foreign Minister (1998–1999); Prime Minister (2001–2006).

Shavit, Ari   Columnist, *Haaretz* (1995–present); author, *My Promised Land* (2013).

Sher, Susan   Chief of Staff for First Lady Michelle Obama and Special Assistant to the President and Associate White House Counsel (2009–2011).

Sherman, Wendy   Under Secretary of State for Political Affairs (2011–present).

Simon, Steven   Senior Director for the Middle East and North Africa, National Security Council (2011–2012).

Solow, Alan   Chairman, Conference of Presidents of Major American Jewish Organizations (2009–2011).

Steinberg, Jim   Deputy Secretary of State (2009–2011).

Steinitz, Yuval   Israeli Minister of Finance (2009–2013).

Stephens, Bret   Editor in Chief, *The Jerusalem Post* (2002–2004); Deputy Editor, *The Wall Street Journal* (2004–present).

Stevens, J. Christopher   U.S. Ambassador to Libya, killed in 2012 attack on Benghazi (2012).

Todd, Chuck   Political Director, NBC News (2007–present); Chief White House Correspondent, NBC News (2008–2014); host, *Meet the Press* (2014–present).

Vietor, Thomas   Spokesperson, National Security Council (2011–2013).

Villaraigosa, Antonio   Mayor of Los Angeles (2005–2013).

Walters, Barbara   American broadcast journalist, host of *The View* (1997–2014).

Weintraub, Lior   Chief of Staff, Israeli Embassy in Washington (2009–2011); Embassy Spokesman (2011–2012).

Wexler, Robert Democratic congressman from Florida (1997–2010); President, S. Daniel Abraham Center for Middle East Peace (2010–present).

Wiesel, Elie Holocaust survivor and author of the *Night* trilogy (1960–1962); Nobel Peace Prize laureate (1986).

Wieseltier, Leon Literary Editor, *The New Republic* (1983–2014).

Will, George Political commentator and *Washington Post* columnist.

Ya'alon, Moshe "Bogie" Israel's Minister of Strategic Affairs (2009–2013); Defense Minister (2013–present).

Yishai, Eli Leader of Israel's Shas Party (2000–2013); Minister of Internal Affairs (2009–2013).

INDEX

ABOUT THE AUTHOR

MICHAEL B. OREN is an American-born Israeli historian and author, and was Israel's ambassador to the United States from 2009 to 2013. He has written two *New York Times* bestsellers—*Power, Faith, and Fantasy: America in the Middle East, 1776 to the Present* and *Six Days of War: June 1967 and the Making of the Modern Middle East,* which won the *Los Angeles Times* Book Prize for history and the National Jewish Book Award. Throughout his illustrious career as a Middle East scholar, Dr. Oren has been a distinguished fellow at the Shalem Center in Jerusalem, a contributing editor to *The New Republic,* and a visiting professor at Harvard, Yale, and George-town. *The Forward* named Oren one of the five most influential American Jews, and *The Jerusalem Post* listed him as one of the world's ten most influential Jews. He currently lives with his family in Tel Aviv. He is a member of the Knesset and serves on its Foreign Affairs and Defense Committee.